REVISITING THE YOM KIPPUR WAR

Israeli History, Politics and Society
Series Editor: Efraim Karsh, King's College London
ISSN 1368-4795

Providing a multidisciplinary examination in all aspects, this series serves as a means of communication between the various communities interested in Israel: academics, policy-makers, practitioners, journalists and the informed public.

Other books in the series:

Peace in the Middle East: The Challenge for Israel
edited by Efraim Karsh

The Shaping of Israeli Identity: Myth, Memory and Trauma
edited by Robert Wistrich and David Ohana

Between War and Peace: Dilemmas of Israeli Security
edited by Efraim Karsh

U.S.–Israeli Relations at the Crossroads
edited by Gabriel Sheffer

From Rabin to Netanyahu: Israel's Troubled Agenda
edited by Efraim Karsh

Israel at the Polls 1996
edited by Daniel J. Elazar and Shmuel Sandler

In Search of Identity: Jewish Aspects in Israeli Culture
edited by Dan Urian and Efraim Karsh

Israel: The Dynamics of Change and Continuity
edited by David Levi-Faur, Gabriel Sheffer and David Vogel

Israel: The First Hundred Years (5 volumes)
edited by Efraim Karsh

Revisiting the Yom Kippur War

Editor

P. R. Kumaraswamy

Harry S. Truman Research Institute for the Advancement of Peace,
The Hebrew University of Jerusalem

FRANK CASS
LONDON • PORTLAND, OR

First published in 2000 in Great Britain by
FRANK CASS PUBLISHERS
Newbury House, 900 Eastern Avenue
London IG2 7HH

and in the United States of America by
FRANK CASS PUBLISHERS
c/o ISBS
5804 N.E. Hassalo Street
Portland, Oregon 97213-3644

Website: www.frankcass.com

British Library Cataloguing in Publication Data

Revisiting the Yom Kippur War. – (Israeli History, politics
and society)
1. Israel–Arab War, 1973
I. Kumaraswamy, P. R.
956'.048

ISBN 0 7146 5007 2 (cloth)
ISBN 0 7146 8067 2 (paper)
ISSN 1368-4795

Library of Congress Cataloging-in-Publication Data

A catalog record for this book is available from the Library of Congress

This group of studies first appeared in a Special Issue on
'Revisiting the Yom Kippur War' of *Israel Affairs* 6/1 (Autumn 1999)
ISSN 1353-7121 published by Frank Cass.

Printed in Great Britain by
Antony Rowe Ltd., Chippenham, Wilts.

Contents

DEDICATION

To Amnon and thousands of others who survived the war.

Preface

EFRAIM KARSH

The 1973 Yom Kippur War (in Arab parlance, the Ramadan War) was a watershed in the history of the Arab–Israeli conflict, on a par with its two formidable precursors: the 1948 and the 1967 wars. If the former war confronted the Arabs with the reality of Jewish statehood in their midst, and the latter underscored their inability to eradicate this perceived artificial entity, the 1973 war redeemed Arab dignity and self-esteem, allowing Egyptian President Anwar Sadat to use his newly-gained pre-eminence to extricate his country and, as a consequence, much of the Arab World, from its fateful encounter with the Jewish State.

No less importantly, Israel was profoundly humbled. The complacency that had gained hold of the Israeli psyche following the astounding 1967 victory was irrevocably shattered. For the first time since the establishment of their state, Israelis felt that its existence lay in the balance. The Bar-Lev line along the Suez Canal, the embodiment of military prowess in the minds of many Israelis, collapsed like a house of cards. The Golan Heights, the presumed shield of the northern Galilee, proved no barrier to a surprise Syrian attack. As the Arabs were consolidating their early gains, the mood in Jerusalem was grim. Defence Minister Moshe Dayan was talking about the impending collapse of the 'Third Temple'. A nuclear alert was reportedly called.

Consequently, the Israel that emerged from the 1973 trauma was a different nation: sober, mellowed, scarred in many lasting ways. It was still wary of its neighbours, yet better tuned to signs of regional moderation; highly apprehensive of the security risks attending territorial concessions, yet aware that land could not buy absolute security. Indeed, successive opinion polls in the wake of the October War showed a steady growth in public support for the 'territory for peace' formula. Even at the time of the 1977 elections, when Labour lost power to Menachem Begin's right-wing Likud Party, three out of four Israelis were ready to trade part of the occupied territories, or all of them, in return for peace. The idea of withdrawal from the Golan, inconceivable until 1973, was no longer anathema to one third of Israelis.

Efraim Karsh is Professor and Head of the Mediterranean Studies Programme, King's College, University of London.

This means that the 1977 elections were less of a victory for Likud, let alone for its territorial maximalism, than a vote of no confidence in Labour's incompetence and corruption by a young and angry generation of Israelis. This would be vividly illustrated in future years by the fact that only 100,000–150,000 Israelis (2.5–3 per cent of Israel's Jewish population) would make their home in the occupied territories, thus allowing the Israeli leadership to trade the entire Sinai Peninsula for a peace treaty with Egypt, and to engage, 14 years later, in the most far-reaching peace process with the Palestinians and the neighbouring Arab states.

P.R. Kumaraswamy is to be congratulated for assembling such an impressive collection of essays on the various aspects of the Yom Kippur War: from the sources of Israel's 1973 intelligence failure, to the military lessons of the war, to its impact on Israeli society and politics; from the Egyptian–Syrian war aims and gain-distribution, to Soviet–American intervention. In the electronic media age of immediate gratification and short collective memory, the importance of considered reflection on key past events cannot be overstated.

Nor can the timing of this volume be more opportune: not merely because a quarter of a century is as good a time as any for stocktaking, but because of the demise of Jordan's King Hussein – the war's absent protagonist. In June 1967, the then young King made the greatest blunder of his political career by joining Egypt in its war against Israel, a move which led to the loss of the Hashemite Kingdom's West Bank. Six years later, he decided to remain largely aloof in a war which he did not want (going so far as to warn Israel's Prime Minister Golda Meir of its imminent outbreak), and whose destabilizing consequences he dreaded. Had he ventured into the West Bank, he would have been able to establish a foothold, which would have possibly made him a partner to any future settlement over this territory. As he failed to do this, the Palestine Liberation Organization (PLO) was to succeed Jordan as the spokesman for the inhabitants of the West Bank. Either way, the King's two decisions exerted a profound effect on the evolution of Palestinian national identity, though not in a way he envisaged or would have approved, which was to irrevocably change the course of the Arab–Israeli conflict.

Revisiting the Yom Kippur War: Introduction

P.R. KUMARASWAMY

> The preparations for a War usually occupy several months.... It therefore rarely happens that one State surprises another by a War, or by the direction which it gives the masses of its forces.
>
> *Carl von Clausewitz, 1882*

* * *

On 24 October 1973, when Israel had finally implemented the cease-fire agreement, nothing stood between its advancing troops and the Egyptian capital, and the forces led by Ariel Sharon were about 'sixty miles from Cairo and at the gates of the Ismailia'.[1] Israel had gained complete control over the entire front. Even though it did not expel the Egyptian forces from Sinai, bypassing these positions, it had established a firm presence and control on the western banks of the Suez Canal. Facing an imminent threat to Cairo and hence to the regime itself, President Anwar al-Sadat was desperately seeking heightened Soviet intervention and even direct military involvement to secure an early cease-fire. But for the intense American pressure preceded by a US–Soviet nuclear alert, Israel would have annihilated the stranded and encircled Egyptian Third Army. The story was more or less the same in the north where the Syrian advances on the Golan Heights were stopped and reversed, and the outskirts of Damascus were brought within the range of Israeli artillery.

After initial surprises and setbacks Israel had bounced back, stopped the Arab offensive, repulsed some enemy advances and reversed the course of the battle. If the Arab military offensive was motivated by a desire to change the status quo in Sinai or on the Golan Heights, Israel had throttled them. The October 1973 cease-fire lines significantly

P.R. Kumaraswamy is a Research Fellow at the Harry S. Truman Research Institute for the Advancement of Peace, The Hebrew University of Jerusalem.

improved Israel's position and witnessed a large Israeli enclave West of the Suez canal. Above all unlike the previous wars, there were no civilian Israeli casualties.

In the long run, the Yom Kippur War substantially enhanced Israel's strategic interests. It planted the seeds of Egyptian–Israeli peace and ironically provided the Arab states, especially Egypt, a much needed 'ladder' to climb down from their refusal to accept and recognize the presence of the Jewish state in the Middle East. It signalled the end of Arab unity against Israel and ushered in the process of direct and separate peace between Israel and the neighbouring Arab countries. Absolutist rhetoric of the past began to give way to a more pragmatic approach to the Arab–Israeli conflict. While the conflict exposed Israel's political and diplomatic isolation, it also highlighted and strengthened Israel's strategic relationship with the US. The Arab oil boycott and the reluctance of the NATO allies to provide landing or refuelling facilities did not inhibit the US from launching a massive airlift of military supplies to Israel. Controversies over the reasons for the initial delay could not diminish the military value and political significance of the American airlift.

There are thus sufficient reasons to recall the war with 'satisfaction and pride'. As Charles Liebman observed, portraying the Yom Kippur War 'as a defeat is not only a myth but a distortion of reality because the successful conclusion of the War and the subsequent outcome were significant achievements'.[2]

This, however, did not happen. Even a quarter of a century later the Yom Kippur war remains the most traumatic phase in Israel's history. The co-ordinated Arab effort in initiating the hostilities and breaching the 1967 cease-fire line still haunts many. Such an event occurring on Yom Kippur, the holiest day in the Jewish calendar, had heightened the sense of loss associated with the war. It is remembered and discussed primarily for the initial Israeli 'unpreparedness' and far less for the subsequent military successes and peace dividends. With fewer than 3,000 killed, 15,000 wounded and about 1,000 POWs, the Israeli casualties were the highest since the Arab–Israeli conflict of 1948.[3] The death and destruction were physical as well as psychological. For many the war extracted a heavy personal price. It shattered many dreams, ruined numerous careers, slaughtered holy cows and disproved popular myths. Erstwhile euphoria following the June war of 1967 suddenly transformed into worse nightmares. For the first time since its establishment, Israel was seen to be on the brink of collapse. When the initial counter-offensive against Egypt failed on 8 October, some feared the fall of the Third Temple. Driven by apprehensions and even panic, Defence Minister Moshe Dayan apparently sought nuclear options to reverse the military trends.

The June war of 1967, which some Israelis viewed as the last of the Arab–Israeli conflict, ironically sowed the seeds of the Yom Kippur war.

The loss of Sinai provided a strong incentive to Sadat to regain the Egyptian territory by all available means, including a military confrontation with Israel. At the same time, intoxicated by the spectacular military successes, the political-military echelon in Israel was overconfident of its military powers and intelligence capabilities.

On 6 October barely a couple of hours before the hostilities started the Israeli cabinet unanimously decided against pre-emptive strikes, apparently to underscore and identify the aggressor. The reasons were political rather than military. For months neither the political nor the military leadership was anticipating a war in 1973. This situation was quite different from the pre-war period in 1967 when Israel assessed that the crisis created by President Gamal Abdul Nasser's expulsion of the United Nations Emergence Force (UNEF) from Sinai could be remedied only by military action. Even before the induction of Moshe Dayan as Defence Minister, Israel was contemplating a pre-emptive option.

Accordingly the head of the Mossad Meir Amit flew to Washington to assess the American position and possible reaction. He met Defence Secretary Robert McNamara and informed him, 'I'm personally going to recommend that we take action, because there's no way out, and please don't react'. During that meeting, informing Amit of Dayan's appointment, McNamara asked

> two questions, only two questions. He said 'How long will it take?' And I said 'Seven days'. That was our assessment. And then, 'How many casualties?' Here I became a diplomat. I said less than in 1948, when we had 6,000. That's all; I think the whole meeting lasted forty minutes or so.[4]

Israel was prepared for military action and sought American understanding if not a 'green light'. It thus had 'three weeks' time to prepare, to dig in and when the thing started it was like a striking fist'.[5]

This was not the case in 1973. The intelligence establishment repeatedly assured the political leadership that the chances of the Arab countries initiating a war were minimal and low, if not negligible. Under this circumstance, Israel was unable to pre-empt a non-existing threat let alone seek American guarantees and understanding before the commencement of the hostilities.

Furthermore, the next war was supposed to be a repeat performance of 1967 when Israel simultaneously fought in three fronts, inflicted massive damages to the enemy air and ground forces within the first 48 hours and was able to capture a territory four times its pre-1967 size. The security establishment was convinced that the Arab powers, especially Egypt, were incapable of launching war and would definitely not initiate a conflict until certain conditions were met. These included: the political and military support of the Soviet Union, improved quality of the Arab armies especially the air force, the formation of an Arab war coalition to initiate and pursue a military confrontation under a joint

command and well-defined military objectives. The victory in 1967 and
Israel's presence and fortifications along the Eastern banks of the Canal
were seen as sufficient deterrence against Arab miscalculations and
misadventures.

The prevailing military doctrine sought to deter wars through Israel's
qualitative superiority. Even the prolongation of the costly War of
Attrition did not alter this fundamental approach to security. If a
confrontation became inevitable, the military was confident that it would
have sufficient early warning to initiate a pre-emptive strike and inflict a
surprise blow on the enemy. The possibility of Israel being taken by
surprise was not considered seriously. In the words of one former
intelligence official: 'You cannot suspect a stupid enemy of deceiving you
who are smarter, because the mere fact that he can deceive you makes
him smarter than you, an idea that was completely unacceptable in
1973'.[6]

Firmly entrenched in this concept, the security establishment,
especially the higher echelons of the Military Intelligence, AMAN, were
unable as well as unwilling to read any information and assessment that
suggested a different Arab approach. They were taken by surprise both
by the Arab initiative itself and by the scale of the Egyptian war
machines. The failure to forecast the war had more to do with incorrect
assessments than with inadequate data. As Uri Bar-Joseph elaborates
advance warnings went unheeded and lower echelons of AMAN who
dared to offer different interpretations were sidelined or silenced. In
short, 'contradictory data, both in April-May and September-October,
regardless of its reliability and relevance, was filtered out. Some were not
analyzed; some was analyzed but not understood; and some was just
filed.'[7]

All the information that did not fit in with the *concept* was summarily
dismissed as unimportant and irrelevant. Even when convincing
explanations were not available, AMAN and its head, Major-General Eli
Zeira, chose to ignore crucial pieces of information. Inter-agency cooperation was abysmal. The unprecedented personal warnings of King
Hussein to Prime Minister Golda Meir in late September 1973 were not
followed up adequately. Likewise the sudden evacuation of family
members of the Soviet advisers from Egypt as well as Syria barely 48
hours before the commencement of the hostilities was not interpreted
correctly. Confident of the deterrence and the *concept*, the AMAN
leadership even shied from elementary co-ordination among its various
desks. The concept was all-pervasive and blinding. Such a powerful
concept could only be destroyed and not disproved.

Israeli presence in the sovereign Egyptian territory, especially along
the Suez Canal, was politically unacceptable for Nasser as well as Sadat.
Egyptian hopes of the US repeating its 1956 performance and ensuring
Israeli withdrawal were quickly dashed. On the contrary, the June war
saw the emergence and consolidation of an alliance between Israel and

the US. Before long Egypt realized that what was lost in a war cannot be recovered peacefully, especially when it was reluctant to embark on direct negotiations with Israel.[8] Sadat also recognized that the Super Powers would not abandon the Arab–Israeli status quo unless their interests were affected by a military confrontation with Israel. Having pronounced 1971 as a decisive year, the absence of follow up actions even two years later could only undermine his domestic authority and regional influence.

If he were to pursue a military option, Sadat understood that his preparations would elicit only limited external support. The Soviets were not willing to endorse his strategy, let alone provide the necessary offensive capabilities that he demanded. His regional options were also limited. While the participation of Syria was essential for military as well as political reasons, the usefulness of Jordan was rather marginal. His limited trust in King Hussein proved accurate as the Jordanian monarch personally cautioned Prime Minister Meir of an impending joint Egyptian–Syrian attack against Israel. The failure of Meir to act on this prior warning significantly enhanced Sadat's strategic surprise. As Avraham Sela argues, the establishment of a formal Arab coalition would have significantly compromised his intentions and sabotaged his principal arsenal: strategic surprise. Hence even though he significantly moderated Egypt's policy towards conservative monarchs such as Saudi Arabia, other than Syrian President Hafiz al-Asad, he did not take any Arab leader into confidence about his war plans and objectives.

For its part the army was confident of repeating and improving its June 1967 accomplishments. Any military confrontation would be quickly carried into the enemy territory and away from Israel's population centres. Even the possession of a vast area following the 1967 war and the need to defend so many strategic points and geographical areas did not basically dilute this desire and confidence. The economic and social cost of full mobilization seemed to outweigh the military advantages. The joint Egyptian–Syrian offensive exposed the fundamental weaknesses of the prevailing strategic doctrine. Even if deterrence failed, the security establishment, especially the intelligence authorities, were confident of advance warning. Largely to ensure Israeli presence and control of the waterline along the Suez and partly to provide advance warning, Israel opted for the establishment of a series of observation posts and fortifications. Completed in March 1969, this defensive arrangement, known as the Bar-Lev line, was expected to hold any Egyptian attempts to cross the Canal until the mobilization of the reserves.

When the war broke out, the isolated fortifications were unable to hold on to their positions against the massive Egyptian invasions. In so doing, they failed to perform their primary role: to hold and defend the 1967 cease-fire lines until the complete mobilization of the reservists. As a result the Bar-Lev line witnessed some of the heavy casualties suffered by Israel in the southern front.[9] As Stuart Cohen argues, the absence of sufficient advance warning proved to be costlier and, as a result, the mobilized reservists were directly sent to the battlefield with little co-ordination and limited logistical support.

When the Yom Kippur War broke out, the US was in the midst of domestic turmoil over the Watergate scandal. President Richard Nixon's apprehensions over possible impeachment and removal from office, however, did not inhibit him from taking decisive actions in support of Israel. Even a quarter of a century later, speculation about the person responsible for the initial delays in an American airlift remains inconclusive. Secretary of State Henry Kissinger was often seen as the prime culprit.[10] In this volume Simcha Dinitz, Golda Meir's close confidant and Israel's ambassador in Washington during the Yom Kippur War, rests the blame on the shoulders of Secretary of Defence James Schlesinger. Prime Minister Golda Meir's eagerness to secretly visit Washington amidst the hostilities for expediting the arms supply underscored the acute military situation on the ground. During the month-long operation, Israel received nearly 24,000 tons of arms, ammunition, tanks, missiles, howitzers, and a host of other non-combatant logistics. Continuing even after cease-fire came to force, the airlift underscored the American resolve, determination and ability both to replenish the military losses and to underscore a strong political message to Israel's neighbours.

Sadat's desire to abandon Nasser's pro-Soviet policies and his dramatic expulsion of Soviet advisers in July 1972 did not win him expected favours in Washington. Even when he returned to Moscow the following year for arms supplies the results were minimal. The Soviets were neither willing to abandon the newly established détente with Washington nor willing to endorse his war military option. As Galia Golan argues the Soviets, however, were reluctant to abandon their Arab allies and once the hostilities started they not only initiated critical arms supplies to Egypt and Syria but also were instrumental in the preservation of the Egyptian Third Army from being annihilated or humiliated by Israel.

Even if the prime failure rests on the shoulders of AMAN, one cannot ignore that Prime Minister Meir's cabinet had as many as four former generals and chiefs of staff and none of them differed with AMAN's assessment of low probabilities of a war.[11] As Gabriel Sheffer analyses, the Mapai/Labour dominated political and military elite which shaped and governed Israel since 1948 bore the brunt of the Yom Kippur War. Their prolonged exclusion from power and hence their involvement in the 'earthquake' partly contributed to the electoral success of the Right in 1977. The position of the national religious bloc was somewhat different. As members of the ruling coalition, they were responsible for the 'earthquake' but their defection to the Right in 1977 and their desire to view the war as a success against heavy odds and initial reversals, had partly diluted any adverse response to their role and involvement in the Yom Kippur War.

The war also extracted a high political price in Israel. The commission of inquiry led by the President of the Supreme Court Shimon Agranat examined the question of intelligence failure and submitted its preliminary report on 2 April 1974. On the same day Chief of Staff Lieutenant-General David (Dado) Elazar submitted his resignation and a week later Prime Minister Golda Meir and her entire cabinet, including Defence Minister Dayan, bowed out. This was followed by Zeira's premature departure. Dayan did make a comeback to national politics when he joined Prime Minister Menachem Begin's cabinet in 1977 as Foreign Minister, and by playing a critical role in the Egyptian–Israeli peace agreements at Camp David he partly restored and rehabilitated his reputation. For the rest, however, the Yom Kippur War proved to be their political Waterloo. Besides these visible leadership changes, as Susan Hattis Rolef suggests, the war had accelerated various social changes that were taking place since the 1967 war.

The Agranat Commission, nonetheless, had its limitations. It did not look into the role of political leadership and its overall responsibility in the 'unpreparedness'. In other words, the Commission 'did not consider it to be our task to express an opinion as to the implications of their parliamentary responsibilities'. Some of its findings have since been questioned in the light of new information. Some of the crucial data that challenge its findings were apparently not available to the Commission. The 'intelligence failure' was systematic and widespread.

As outlined by the Agranat Commission Report, 'the Conception' was based on one basic premise: Egypt would not initiate a war against Israel before it had acquired sufficient air power to conduct a deep strike into Israel, particularly its principal airfields, so as to paralyze the Israeli air force. With hindsight it is obvious that this assumption was based on Israel's operational successes in the June war and on the Arab strategic calculations and postures. While Egypt would not be able to attack Israel proper without air power, this capability was not a pre-condition for any operations within Sinai. A limited operation along the Canal as envisaged by Sadat instead required an effective air defence system to prevent Israel from repeating its pre-emptive strikes against Egyptian positions. The SAM batteries along the Western banks of the Suez Canal would provide the necessary air cover to cross the Canal. Since the Bar-Lev line was a cluster of isolated, defensive and poorly manned positions, an effective air defence system could minimize if not neutralize Israel's air superiority. In short, 'the conception' did not consider the possibility of a limited and even symbolic Arab objective aimed at political rather than military victory over Israel.

The domination of the political concept, coupled with AMAN's inability to read the April-May noises, camouflaged the Egyptian intentions and planning. Following a few false alarms in early 1973, the

Egyptian military build up in September was dismissed as part of a planned military exercise. Egyptian President Anwar al-Sadat's repeated pledges of 'year of decision' had become 'noises' for domestic and inter-Arab consumption. As Gabriella Heichal suggests, as the only centre for the evaluation of military intelligence, AMAN enjoyed the complete monopoly over the flow of information and assessments. This monopoly coupled with the attitude of some senior officials in stamping out and silencing dissenting assessments clearly led to an incorrect assessment about the Arab objectives and plans.

Its success in warding off an offensive in May 1973 further consolidated AMAN's position. Following reports of a combined Egyptian–Syrian military build up, Chief of Staff Elazar ordered a total mobilization of forces that cost about $35 million, a huge sum in 1973. Since the war did not materialize, the military leadership came under criticism from a number of Cabinet ministers, especially Finance Minister Pinhas Shapir, for 'needlessly' wasting so much money when the earlier mobilization passed off without any hostilities. Since the events proved AMAN right, its assessment in September became credible. AMAN 'was "right" (in May) for the wrong reasons and this was the root of the problem (in October)'.[12] The Egyptian war plans were cancelled because of the Soviet pressures on Egypt and since this was not read correctly by AMAN it proved to be a false alarm. An internal study conducted in 1985 concluded that the real mistake was made in May and not September.

> If (*AMAN*) had assessed the situation in May, as did the Chief of Staff and Minister of Defence, and as it should have, given the available information, concluding that war was imminent, then when it (AMAN) discovered that it was 'mistaken' and there was no war by June or September, it would have sought the reasons for its error. And it would have undoubtedly discovered the reason, because the information that was available from May through August made it clear why war had not broken out.

Things went tragically wrong. 'When you decide that there would be no war in May because enemy does not have the capability or the intent to go to war, then you do not look for the reason why there was no war.'[13]

Even the military performance was not always optimal, and there were unnecessary and avoidable delays, deaths and destruction. The failure of the counter-offensive on 8 October has been regarded as the most critical phase of the war, especially as it led to Dayan's reported option to nuclearize the conflict. Shmuel Gordon suggests that the previous day was critical for the air force. Having been surprised by the Arab offensive, on 7 October the air force was asked to operate against the advancing enemy forces first in the Egyptian front and later in the Syrian front. However, because of inefficient and insufficient operational planning, the air force was unable to neutralize the enemy missile batteries. Most of the air force losses during the war happened within the first 48 hours when they were employed in uncoordinated operations.

The War also brought the nuclear genie out in the open and ushered in an intense debate over Israel's nuclear capabilities and strategy. There is no convincing evidence to suggest that Sadat's limited war objectives were influenced by his assessments and apprehensions over Israel's perceived nuclear capabilities.[14] At the same time, it is widely suggested that faced with military reversals Israel seriously contemplated exercising the nuclear option to turn the tide of the battle. On 8 October after the first Israeli counter offensive was routed, Prime Minister Meir called a meeting of her inner cabinet which reportedly issued an order to nuclearize the war and to deploy missiles with nuclear warheads. This meeting, first reported by *Time* magazine in April 1976, has since been picked up and commented upon by various authorities. In the absence of primary sources, any assessment can only be a conjecture. Yair Evron suggested that, deeply disturbed by the failure of Israeli counter-offensive, Dayan

> did indeed raise in a rather *tentative* manner some ideas connected with Israel's nuclear capability. However, both Israel Galili and Yigal Allon strongly and vehemently opposed Dayan's idea. ... Golda Meir, who usually relied heavily on Galili's views, accepted their advice and ruled against Dayan's *tentative* proposals.[15]

Others have challenged that Dayan had ever issued such orders.[16]

The 'decision' of the kitchen cabinet apparently was not motivated only by the reversals in Sinai but also by Israel's frustrations with Washington. Israel was desperate for emergency supplies of arms and ammunition from the US to sustain the all-out war. Even though the initial request was made shortly after the outbreak of hostilities, the request was not approved, let alone implemented. Faced with military reversals, the cabinet 'decision' was seen as a pressure tactic, if not blackmail, to expedite the US airlift.[17] Implementation of the 'decision' of the kitchen cabinet would not only have nuclearized the conflict but also undermined the non-proliferation policies of the US.

Furthermore, angered by Israel's attempt to expand its gains after both the superpowers had agreed to a cease-fire and its desire to encircle and annihilate the Egyptian Third Army, Moscow sought direct military intervention. This unexpected twist led to the US declaring a state of nuclear alert which was subsequently cancelled following the Israeli acceptance and implementation of the cease-fire. In short, the Yom Kippur War nearly brought the region to the nuclear threshold, thereby underscoring the stakes involved.

Unlike other Arab–Israeli conflicts and hostilities, this war has many names: Ramadan war, October war or the more neutral 1973 war. This volume is primarily an introspection of the war and its impact upon

Israeli society; hence it opts for the more specific expression, the Yom Kippur War. In presenting a comprehensive understanding of the war and its impact upon Israeli society, the editor is grateful to all the contributors for their co-operation and participation. Recognizing the import and delicate nature of the subject, they worked amidst extremely tight schedules and commitments. I have enjoyed the support and hospitality of the Harry S. Truman Research Institute for the Advancement of Peace, and its library staff Ben-Arieh, Greenhause and Schwed have been exceptionally helpful. For long Professors Irene Eber and Avraham Altman have functioned as my intellectual springboards and I remain indebted. Above all I am grateful to Efraim Karsh for his trust, confidence and encouragement. Any omissions and commissions are mine alone.

NOTES

1. Ariel Sharon with David Chanoff, *Warrior: The Autobiography of Ariel Sharon*, London: MacDonald, 1989, p.333.
2. Charles S. Liebman, 'The Myth of Defeat: The Memory of the Yom Kippur War in Israeli Society', *Middle Eastern Studies* 29/3, July 1993, p.409.
3. Edgar O'Ballance, *No Victor, No Vanquished: The Arab–Israeli War, 1973*, Novato, CA: Presidio Press, 1997, p.182.
4. Amit's first person account in Richard B. Parker (ed.), *The Six-Day War: A Retrospective*, Gainesville, FL: University Press of Florida, 1996, p.140.
5. Ibid., p.152.
6. Yoel Ben-Porat, 'The Yom Kippur War: A Mistake in May Leads to a Surprise in October', *IDF Journal* 3/3 (Summer 1986) p.61.
7. Ibid., pp.60–61.
8. For a recent discussion on the possibility of a peace settlement prior to the Yom Kippur war, see Mordechai Gazit, 'Egypt and Israel: Was there a Peace Opportunity Missed in 1971?', *Journal of Contemporary History* 32/1 (1997) pp.97–115.
9. For a detailed discussion, see Yaacov Bar-Siman-Tov, 'The Bar-Lev Line Revisited', *Journal of Strategic Studies* 11/2 (June 1988) pp.149–76.
10. For example, see Matti Golan, *The Secret Conversations of Henry Kissinger: Step-by-Step Diplomacy in the Middle East*, New York: Quadrangle/The New York Times Books, 1976, pp.45–62.
11. They were Yigal Allon (Deputy Prime Minister); Moshe Dayan (Defence Minister); Haim Bar-Lev (Commerce and Industry); and Israel Galili (Minister without Portfolio). Moreover, Transport Minister Shimon Peres had a long association with the defence establishment and from 1953 to 1965 had run the ministry first as Director-General and then as deputy minister of defence.
12. Ben-Porat, 'The Yom Kippur War', p.53.
13. Ibid., p.60.
14. However, based on his conversations with Egyptian writer Mohammed Heikel, Seymour Hersh claimed that the Soviet reports about the Israeli nuclear arming 'were taken very seriously (but they) had no impact on the overall Egyptian military operations'. Seymour M. Hersh, *The Samson Option: Israel's Nuclear Arsenal and American Foreign Policy*, New York: Random House, 1991, p.235n. For a sceptical view of this argument see Yair Evron, *Israel's Nuclear Dilemma*, London: Routledge, 1994, p.286n.
15. Evron, *Israel's Nuclear Dilemma*, p.72, emphasis added.
16. Shlomo Aronson, *The Politics of Nuclear Weapons in the Middle East: Opacity, Theory and Reality, 1960–1991 – An Israeli Perspective*, New York: SUNY Press, 1992, p.147.
17. Hersh, *The Samson Option*, pp.225–40. It is in this context that one would view Meir's suggestion to undertake a secret visit to the US right in the middle of the hostilities.

Israel's 1973 Intelligence Failure

URI BAR-JOSEPH

> As long as logic, in Arab limitations, will remain dominant. ... I
> think that in coming years the Arabs do not estimate that they
> can win a war against Israel.
>
> *Director of Military Intelligence Major-General Eli Zeira,*
> *in a cabinet meeting, 24 April 1973*[1]

After the end of the War of Attrition in August 1970, Egypt conducted
three emergency deployments along the Suez Canal: at the end of 1971
and 1972, and in April 1973. On 18 April 1973, against the background
of such deployment, the Director of Military Intelligence (DMI), Major-
General Eli Zeira, described to Prime Minister Golda Meir his agency's
ability to provide a strategic warning against a surprise attack. He said:
'I am sure [that if Egypt would launch a massive crossing of the Suez
Canal] we will know about it ahead, and we will be able to give a
warning, not only a tactical one but also an operational one, that is, a
number of days in advance'.[2]

About four months later, on 23 August 1973, following a two-day
secret discussion between Syrian and Egyptian military delegations in
Alexandria, the Egyptian Chief of Staff, Lieutenant-General Saad el
Shazly, and his Syrian Colleague, Yusuf Shakkur, formally agreed on two
possible dates for the war: 7–11 September and 5–10 October. Less than
a week later, Egyptian President Anwar al-Sadat and his Syrian
counterpart, Hafez al-Asad, decided to launch the war on 6 October.[3]
On 22 September Sadat informed his War Minister and the Chief of Staff
that war would start in 14 days.[4] In the following two weeks Egypt and
Syria accelerated their war preparations.

Uri Bar-Joseph lectures in the Department of Political Science at the University of Haifa,
Israel.

Israel's intelligence agencies, primarily Military Intelligence (AMAN), closely followed these developments and provided their consumers with precise reports on Arab growing *capability* to attack. In addition, Israel obtained at least 11 strategic warnings, informing that the increasing military preparations near its borders were not geared to defensive needs (Syria) or exercise (Egypt), but were *intended* for war. Nevertheless, on the day before the war started DMI Zeira told Meir: 'We still see as highly probable the possibility that the Egyptian and the Syrian state of alert derives from fear from us, and as slightly probable that the real intention of Egypt and Syria is to carry out hostile acts on a limited scale. ... [We estimate the option of] crossing the Canal at the lowest probability. ... Neither Egypt nor Syria are optimistic with regard to their possible military success, if they make a large-scale attempt, especially because of their air inferiority.'[5]

Even in the singular history of intelligence fiasco, AMAN's failure to provide the warning it was committed to provide is unique, principally because of the immense number of warnings it received prior to the outbreak of hostilities. This article will first describe – primarily on the basis of evidence made accessible in recent years – the intelligence information which was available to Israel on the eve of the war about Arab preparations, the way it was processed, and the way it was presented to policy makers. It will then explain why, despite the wealth of intelligence information available, Israel was taken by surprise on 6 October.

THE INFORMATION

Egyptian military plans to cross the Suez Canal were formulated in 1971–72. The principal decision to go to war without waiting for additional arms was made by President Sadat at a meeting with his top military echelon on 24 October 1972.[6] His cabinet discussed this decision and approved it on 5 April 1973.[7] Given its vulnerability to Israel Air Force (IAF) deep penetration raids, special emphasis was given by Egypt's war planners to overcoming this weakness, primarily by gaining the ability to attack Israel's hinterland. In part this goal was reached when attack fighters – Hawker Hunters and Mirage Vs – started to arrive in Egypt from Iraq and Libya in early 1973. On the eve of the war the order of battle of the Egyptian Air Force already included 30 Mirage Vs from Libya as well 20 Hunters from Iraq, and Egyptian pilots gained experience in flying Libyan planes.[8] In addition, in March 1973 the USSR agreed to sell Egypt a brigade of surface-to-surface Scud missiles. These arrived in Egypt in late July 1973, and early in August Soviet instructors started training the newly established brigade.[9]

Israel had no concrete information about Sadat's principal decisions to go to war. It nevertheless gained some information on the basis of which 'it could be concluded that already in early 1973 a change took place in the position of the Egyptian government which reached the conclusion that in its fight against Israel Egypt would have to fight with the available military means'.[10] AMAN's analysts, however, were not sensitive enough to assess that such a change had occurred. They were more familiar with Egypt's and Syria's war plans. In mid-April 1972 AMAN provided its consumers with a 40-page detailed report with maps of the Egyptian war plan, including the goals of the Egyptian offensive, the planned array of the seven divisions scheduled to take part in the invasion, the crossing zones of each of the five infantry divisions projected to cross first, and the location of the ten crossing bridges (two for each division) that were to be thrown over the Suez Canal. According to Zeira, the only significant operational change in October 1973 was that one brigade crossed the Canal a few miles from where it was predicted to cross according to AMAN's 1972 report.[11] In addition to providing Egypt's war plan, AMAN obtained and distributed the Syrian war plan as well about six months before the war.[12]

Israel was well aware of Egypt's need to be able to counter IAF deep penetration raids. This stemmed not only from the logic of the situation but from information from a Mossad human source with a good accessibility to Egyptian decision-makers. The information provided by him, years before the war started, served as the basis for AMAN's estimation that Egypt and Syria would not be ready for war before 1975. According to this source Sadat believed that politically Egypt and Syria should initiate a war if the diplomatic efforts to move Israel back to the 1967 borders according to UN resolution 242 failed. Militarily, the necessary condition was that Egypt receive advanced fighter squadrons capable of attacking Israel's hinterland, and Scud missiles, which would enable Egypt to deter Israel from attacking Arab strategic targets. Thus was born, in 1971, the first component of what would later become known as the 'conception'.[13] Its second component was the estimate that Syria saw itself as being unable to launch a war against Israel alone. On this basis, AMAN's analysts assessed in January 1973 that war was unlikely at least until 1975.[14]

In April 1973 the agency reported that 18 Libyan Mirage and 16 Iraqi Hunter attack-fighters had arrived in Egypt, and that others, from Saudi Arabia and Kuwait, were scheduled to arrive.[15] But DMI Zeira estimated that objectively this made no significant change in the Egyptian-Israeli balance of military capabilities though, as he put it, the Egyptians might have viewed it differently.[16] Shortly after the establishment of the Egyptian Scud brigade, AMAN reported on this development, and that its commanding officers were, for the time being, Soviet.[17]

In mid-September Israel received its first concrete warning about a coming war. It came from a good source, probably human intelligence (Humint), informing that Sadat had decided to initiate a war at the end of 1973 and that Asad was informed of this decision and promised to attack Israel simultaneously on the Golan Heights. According to this piece of information, the Syrian president made his decision after Soviet advisers promised him that if Egypt and Syria attacked Israel simultaneously, the Syrian army would completely occupy the Golan Heights in 36 hours.[18] As far as is known, the warning did not turn any red light in AMAN's corridors.

Thus, months before the war started Israel had much of the relevant information about Egypt's and Syria's war preparations and at least one warning about their intention to launch the war soon; from September 1973, as war preparations accelerated, concrete information about them started to flow. It nevertheless failed to seed doubts in AMAN's conception, which, at this stage, had become almost dogmatic. This was clearly evident in the way its analysts interpreted the available information with regard to both Syria and Egypt.

Syria

Syrian war preparations began even before Presidents Sadat and Asad made their decision to launch the war on 6 October. AMAN gained first early warning (EW) indicators for these moves in early September. On 7–8 September it reported that the Syrian front line had been reinforced with elements of an infantry brigade and that the state of readiness of its air force has been raised. Three days later air photographs revealed that 130–140 tanks and 35 artillery batteries had been added to the regular deployment of the Syrian front line. Unaware of the decision to go to war, AMAN interpreted these moves as motivated either by President Asad's planned visit to Algeria or in preparation for an Israeli operation in retaliation against Syrian-sponsored terror acts.[19]

After 13 September, when 13 Syrian MiG-21s were shot down in a large-scale air battle, AMAN's prime explanation for the increase in war readiness was Syrian need to take revenge for its air losses, or fear of greater escalation. In the weeks that followed the Syrian war preparation continued. Air photographs taken on a sortie on 23 September showed that the Syrian army was fully deployed in its first line of defence and that its tank reserves, artillery, and infantry divisions had been advanced to the rear of this line. AMAN reported these findings a day later. This led the Chief of Northern Command, Major-General Yitzhak Hofi, to conclude that the present Syrian array already left no room for additional EW indicators.[20]

In the following days Israel received four warnings that Syria's preparations were for a war. The first came on 25 September. King Hussein of Jordan, accompanied by Prime Minister Zayd al-Rifai, arrived in Israel in his helicopter and met with Prime Minister Golda Meir upon his urgent request. According to the protocol of the talk, Hussein told Meir: 'From a very sensitive source in Syria, from which we received information in the past and passed it on … all the [Syrian] units which were scheduled to be in training have now, for more or less the last two days, been in positions for a pre-attack. ... This includes their aircraft, their missiles, and everything else. ... The Syrians are in pre-jump positions.' Meir asked: 'Is it possible that the Syrians will start something without complete cooperation with the Egyptians?' The king answered: 'I don't think so. I think they are cooperating.'[21] Following the meeting Meir immediately called Minister of Defence Moshe Dayan, who asked Chief of Staff Lieutenant-General David Elazar and DMI Zeira to evaluate this warning. He came back with a calming response, and Meir left for a trip abroad the morning after.

This calming response did not reflect, however, a consensus in AMAN's Research Branch. The head of the Jordanian section, Lieutenant-Colonel Zusia Kaniazer, who *ex officio* was aware of the Hussein–Meir meeting, reported its content through unofficial channels to the head of the Syrian section, Lieutenant-Colonel Aviezer Ya'ari. In comparison to other officers in their branch, these two officers estimated the warning to be of a more alarming nature. Ya'ari, who had already a reputation of being an 'alarmist' about Syrian military preparations, discovered that significant information, directly relevant to his ability to provide an effective warning, was not delivered to him in official channels. When he complained about it to the head of the Research Branch, Brigadier-General Aryeh Shalev, the latter admitted that regarding certain sensitive information this was and would remain the case. Shalev also rebuked Kaniazer for passing on, without authority, sensitive information to Ya'ari.[22]

The second warning came on 28 September from a 'good source' which reported that Syrian ground forces were on a fifty per cent alert and their air force and ground forces had taken up combat positions. The source quoted many Syrian officers who believed 'that this time it will be a war and not just a clash'. Nevertheless, the source also gave indications that Syria was not yet ready for war.[23] A third warning came on the night of 29–30 September from very reliable US intelligence sources, which warned Israel that as of the end of September a Syrian offensive aimed at occupying the Golan Heights could be expected. According to the sources, which also described the essence of the Syrian attack plan, the Syrian army had already started its battle procedure.[24] Finally, at the end of September the CIA warned Prime Minister Meir and Defence Minister Dayan of a coming war. The American warning, which was delivered through the Mossad, was based on information similar to the information Meir received in her meeting with King Hussein. It seems that the king gave the same warning to the CIA, which delivered it to Israel.[25]

Additional EW indicators which arrived on 30 September indicated that further reinforcement, including tanks and surface-to-air missile (SAM) batteries, had taken place on the Syrian front, that war deployment was complete in the second line of defence also and that all leave had been cancelled. On 2 October AMAN reported that during the previous 24 hours the Syrian army moved bridging equipment and additional forces to the front; fighters had been advanced to a forward air base; and some of the medium-range artillery batteries in the central front section had removed their camouflage nets.[26] Summarizing the state of Syrian military readiness, AMAN reported on 3 October that in contrast to the earlier emergency deployments (September 1972 and March–April 1973), this time the Syrians

- had advanced two squadrons of SU-7 attack fighters from their rear base in T4 to forward airfields;
- had advanced a bridge-laying tank regiment to the front;
- had deployed 31 SAM batteries, 15 of which were of the advanced SA-6 type, south of Damascus; and
- had taken emergency measures, including the preparation of shelters and of hospitals and inspection of fuel reserves, to prepare their rear for war.[27]

On Friday morning, about 30 hours before the war began, DMI Zeira summed up the information available on Syrian military preparations. 'Since 5 September', he said, 'the Syrians have gradually built their deployments. Today they are poised in full emergency array at the Israeli border.'[28]

For a number of intelligence and military officers, some EW indicators sufficed to conclude that Syria had prepared a military initiative. Thus, the IDF's Deputy Chief of Staff, Major-General Yisrael Tal, regarded the forward deployment of the bridging tanks units and the surface-to-air batteries as clear indicators of Syrian offensive intentions. Similarly Lieutenant-Colonel Shabtai Brill, who in 1973 served in AMAN's main signal intelligence (Sigint) unit, concluded that the advancement of the SU-7 aircraft to a front airbase meant that the Syrian and the Egyptian military preparations were for war.[29] But the most significant incident in which warning signals were translated into a concrete alert took place on the night between 30 September and 1 October, following a telephone call Lieutenant-Colonel Ya'ari received from the head of the Egyptian section in the Research Department, Lieutenant-Colonel Yona Bandman. Bandman informed Ya'ari that according to a warning received earlier that night, war would start on 1 October. He added that the information was analyzed and found to be false (see below). Nevertheless, coming on the background of earlier warnings and being the first to link Syrian war preparations to Egyptian intention to launch war, Ya'ari decided to take this warning more seriously. He called the Intelligence Officer of Northern Command, Lieutenant-Colonel Hagai Mann, and suggested that the Command's state of alert be raised. This was done. In the morning, after his initiative became known to his commanders and war did not break out, Ya'ari was rebuked by Shalev for expressing outside the Research Branch an estimate that contradicted the Branch's official assessment.

The same day, on the background of calming estimates of AMAN's high echelons, the increased state of alert of the Northern Command was called off.[30]

Indeed, the dominant view among AMAN's top analysts was not alarmist. Due to the agency's fundamental belief that Syria did not perceive itself capable of fighting Israel alone, and that Egypt did not regard itself as ready for war, the air battle of 13 September served as its main explanation for the unusual Syrian moves. Thus at a General Staff meeting on 1 October, DMI Zeira expressed the belief that 'the Syrians are deterred by the IDF's ability to defeat their army in one day'. During the first days of October, when Syrian war preparations reached their height, AMAN assessed that 'the Syrians are far from believing that they can launch, by themselves, a successful offensive in the Golan Heights, because of their basic weakness, especially in the air'.[31] Consequently, a day before war broke out Zeira told Golda Meir and her cabinet ministers that according to his estimation the unusual Syrian deployment was geared by fear of Israeli hostile action. Asking what could have caused such fear, he gave a number of answers:

- They are always afraid.
- They perceive the air battle as a trap we set them. This is on account of our difficult situation. The world isolates us. An eastern front is being established and we want to destroy it.
- Our actions: (a) a paratrooper exercise; (b) a mobilization exercise in the [Golan] Heights ...; (c) we have reinforced extensively in the Syrian front; (d) the Minister of Defence visited the Golan Heights on New Year's eve; (e) the Chief of Staff gave a warning at a paratroops gathering [which was held a few days earlier].[32]

Consequently, then, AMAN's final report, which was distributed on Friday noon, described in detail the many indications of Syrian war preparations. But at the end of this long list it nevertheless said that, 'there is no change in our evaluation that Syrian moves derive from apprehension, which has increased during the last day, of an Israeli action. The probability of an independent Syrian action (without Egypt) *remains low*.'[33]

Egypt

The five infantry divisions which, according to the Egyptian plan, were to storm the Bar-Lev line, had been deployed along the Suez Canal since the end of the War of Attrition. Hence, preparations for war in the Egyptian front were kept to a minimum. Consequently the first significant indicators of Egyptian military preparations could have been the mobilization, on 27 and 30 September, of some reserve forces. But since more than 20 such mobilizations had taken place since the beginning of 1973 as part of Egypt's deception plan, these acts lost much of their alarm value.[34]

First information on Egyptian military movements to the front reached Israel on 25 September, and on 28 September AMAN reported that the state of readiness in the Egyptian air force, navy, anti-aircraft units, and part of the ground forces had been raised. Its analysts had various explanations for these moves: fear of Israeli aggression following the Syrian–Israeli air battle of 13 September; standard operational procedure (SOP) linked to the third anniversary of Nasser's death and the feast of Ramadan; fear of domestic upheaval in light of economic problems; and preparations for the large scale 'Tahrir ('Liberation') 41' manoeuvres which were scheduled to start on 1 October.[35]

On the night of 30 September – 1 October, Israel received the first of a series of concrete warnings of Egypt's intention to go to war. A good Mossad Humint source reported that the large-scale Egyptian crossing exercise that started on 30 September would on 1 October become a real crossing of the Canal with the Syrians joining in.[36] As recalled, the warning triggered a temporal raise in the state of alert of the Northern Command. Similarly, it brought Major-General Shmuel Gonen, the head of Southern Command, who received this warning through unofficial channels, to call off leave in his command. Colonel Yoel Ben-Porat, the commander of AMAN's Sigint unit, also decided to put his unit on a war readiness state of alert.[37]

But AMAN's dominant interpretation of the situation was very different. DMI Zeira delayed relaying the warning to Chief of Staff Elazar and Minister of Defence Dayan. He told Elazar on the morning of 1 October that after a night discussion with his analysts it was concluded that war would not break on 1 October and that in order to let the Chief of Staff have a night's sleep he did not convey his conclusions to him. Elazar immediately told Dayan about this message. While Dayan seemed to have been disturbed by Zeira's conduct he avoided taking concrete measures against him.[38] AMAN's interpretation of the situation was expressed in a report of 30 September which stated that:

> A large-scale combined arms headquarters exercise for the occupation of Sinai [*Tahrir* 41] is to be held between 1 and 7 October. It appears that the headquarters of the air, air-defence, and naval arms, as well as the field armies, divisions, and special forces, will participate. Because of the exercise the level of readiness will rise (as of 1 October) to the highest in the air force and all participating units, and leaves are cancelled. ... From the information about the expected exercise and the call up of reserve soldiers for a limited time, it becomes apparent that the advancement of forces and other preparations which are taking place or are expected in the coming days, such as completion of fortifications, mobilization of civilian fishing boats, and checking of operational readiness of the units, which could be seen as alarmist, are connected only to the exercise.[39]

AMAN continued to track and report the massive build-up of the Egyptian front line during the following days. On 2 October it reported that about 120 trucks carrying water-crossing equipment, bridging gear, and boats had moved from west of Cairo towards the eastern desert during the night of 1–2 October. On the same day it also reported that 40 out of 85 crossing spots in the Egyptian Third Army's sector had been prepared for crossing in recent days and that an Egyptian naval commando unit had been deployed near Sharm el Sheikh. Two days later AMAN reported – which *post factum* was to become known as highly indicative – that Egyptian soldiers were ordered to break the Ramadan fast. Air photography interpretation of a sortie of 4 October enabled the agency to report, merely 30 hours before the outbreak of the war, that a dramatic increase in Egyptian military concentrations along the Suez Canal was taking place, and that 'the whole Egyptian army was in an unprecedented emergency deployment'. In comparison to the earlier sortie, taken on 25 September, the number of artillery pieces had increased by 308 and was now 1,100. Most positions for water-crossing equipment now contained this equipment. In places where single tanks were positioned at regular times, tank platoons were now identified. Some more tank regiments were advanced forward.[40]

The fast accumulation of EW indicators in early October was accompanied by two more warnings of Egypt's intention to go to war. The first came from an unidentified source on 1 October. It reported that Egypt had decided to cross the Canal and take over the Mitla and the Gidi Passes, hoping that superpower intervention would permit the reopening of the Suez Canal and the beginning of negotiations of a permanent Egyptian–Israeli political settlement. The source also reported that all forces of the Egyptian Army, including its bridging units, were moving from Cairo to staging areas near the Suez, and that breaches which would facilitate the laying of bridges had already been opened in the embankment along the western bank of the Canal. Nevertheless, the source maintained that no decision on the exact D-Day had yet been made.[41] A day later, a Mossad source warned, probably in continuation of his report of two days earlier, that (a) there was an intention to attack Israel; (b) the Egyptian army was in full state of alert; and (c) the operation would start as an exercise, but according to all indications would transform into a real attack.[42]

But the warnings fell on deaf ears. Estimating Egypt as being incapable for the time being of overcoming its vulnerability to Israeli deep penetration raids, '*Tahrir* 41' served as AMAN's explanation for the war preparations along the Suez Canal. Thus, Brigadier-General Aryeh Shalev, head of AMAN's Research Department, told Prime Minister Meir on 3 October:

> According ... to the best of my knowledge and opinion ... on the
> basis of a lot of material we have from recent days – Egypt still

believes that it cannot go to war. ... This [Shalev's estimate] derives
from the possibility of knowing, and impressions of things they
themselves think, that the possibility of a joint Egyptian-Syrian war
does not seem to me as probable. Since there is no change in their
estimate of the [IDF] forces in Sinai, that [these forces] can go on
fighting in Egypt, I reach the conclusion that this is merely an
exercise. On the 10th of the month they are already releasing their
reserve forces.[43]

Similarly, even after the interpretation of the air photographs, which
showed a dramatic increase in Egyptian war preparedness along the
Canal, AMAN's estimation did not change. Paragraph 40 in the agency's
summary of the situation some 24 hours before war started said:
'Though the mere emergency setting along the Canal front implies,
allegedly, indicators for aggressive action, to the best of our knowledge
there is no change in the Egyptians' evaluation of their balance of forces
with the IDF. Hence, the probability that the Egyptians intend to renew
fire is low.'[44]

The Collapse of the Concept

Considering the fact that alarming information failed to change AMAN's
solid conception of Arab war intentions, not surprisingly the most
important EW indicators Israel received prior to the war were neither
Syrian nor Egyptian but Soviet, namely the decision to start an
unprecedented emergency evacuation of families of Soviet advisers from
Syria and Egypt and of Soviet warships from Egyptian ports. The
decision, as Soviet Foreign Minister Andrei Gromyko told his close
advisors, was motivated by fear for the lives of some 7,000 Soviet
citizens in Egypt and Syria, and it was taken despite the fact that it could
serve as a clear signal to the USA and Israel of Arab war intentions.[45]

First indications of the civilian evacuation arrived in Israel on 4
October at 4pm (and not, as was described in earlier accounts, on the
night between 4 and 5 October).[46] AMAN's experts, who followed the
confusion among Soviet families in Syria and Egypt throughout the
evening, learned that while the advisers were ordered to stay, their
families were instructed to arrive at special concentration areas by 12pm.
At 10pm AMAN identified a Soviet airlift of 11 cargo planes – of which
six were of the giant Antonov 22 type – on the way to the region. The
agency distributed its first written report on this intriguing development
after a lag of almost 11 hours, on 5 October at 2:40am. On Friday
morning, it reported that two cargo planes had left Cairo for the USSR.[47]
At the same time it learned that the USSR was taking action to reduce its
naval presence in Egypt. AMAN's report of 5 October at 10am said that
'7 out of 12 Soviet warships, which are positioned in [the Egyptian ports
of] Alexandria and Marsa Matruch, were scheduled to leave this
morning'.[48]

The Soviet move planted, for the first time, a seed of doubt in the validity of the conception. DMI Zeira suggested three possible explanations for it:

- the Soviets knew that Egypt and Syria were going to attack Israel and wanted to protect their citizens, or hint to their clients that they did not support the war initiative;
- Moscow feared that Israel was going to attack;
- or a sudden crisis had erupted in Soviet relations with Syria and Egypt.[49]

The evacuation of Soviet ships was considered in AMAN's reports of 5 October as 'certainly an extraordinary move'.[50] Similarly Zeira told Golda Meir and her cabinet ministers 'such a move took place only once, when there was a fear that the Egyptians might implement what they defined as "the year of subduing". It was in 1971: an act that signifies the USSR's reservations about an Egyptian attack.'[51] In a discussion earlier that day he expressed, for the first time, doubts with regard to the conception's validity. He told Dayan: 'Though in the fundamental assessment I do not see a change, I do not see either Egypt or Syria attacking, despite the Russian action, but this gives me doubt.'[52] Perhaps in light of this doubt, Zeira added during Friday morning's discussions that he was waiting for additional information, which might shed some light on the Soviet decision.[53] Against this background, Zeira's behaviour in the hours that followed is puzzling.

On 5 October at about 5:00pm, about 21 hours before 'H' hour, AMAN's Sigint unit obtained information, from a good source, which said: 'We have learned that Syria has decided to evacuate the Soviet experts and that Soviet planes have started flying them from Damascus to Moscow'. This, according to the message, was the outcome of a 'Syrian and Egyptian intention to launch war against Israel'. The message triggered Ben-Porat, the commander of the Sigint unit, to urgently call the head of AMAN's Research Department, and to read him the top-secret information on an unsecured telephone line. It was telexed to the department at 5:15pm.

According to the standard operational procedure the duty officer of the Research Branch drafted an emergency report to be immediately disseminated to political and military consumers according to a dissemination list. Before sending it, however, he consulted his direct superior who advised him to consult the department's head. Shalev directed him to consult DMI Zeira, who decided to delay the distribution of this report. It was finally disseminated on Saturday only a few hours before hostilities broke out, when it had already lost its warning value.[54] Zeira's instructions delayed by a number of hours the final collapse of the conception. This collapse took place only at 4:30am of 6 October, less than ten hours before the breakout of hostilities.

The chain of events that brought about the sudden realization that Egypt and Syria were on the verge of attack started more than 24 hours earlier. On 4 October, at about 2:00am, the Mossad's best Humint source[55] gave his case officer in Europe the code word for a possibility of war. In answer to questions the source added that war was very near. He informed his case officer that he was flying to meet him in Europe and suggested that the highest Mossad authority should participate at the meeting. Zvi Zamir, the director of the Mossad, was informed about it immediately.[56] Zamir took the opportunity of a call from his colleague in AMAN, Zeira (about the Soviet emergency evacuation that had taken place during that night), to inform him of the message he had just received. He also instructed his aide-de-camp to communicate the warning to the military secretary of Prime Minister Meir. Somewhere along the line the message halted. Later, Zamir would be criticized by the Agranat Commission for failing to call Meir personally.

The head of the Mossad left for Europe less than three hours after receiving the warning. On Friday night he met the source and heard from him that war would probably break out on the evening of the next day. This warning arrived in Israel at about 4:00am (H hour minus 10) and was immediately delivered to the Prime Minister, Minister of Defence, and the Chief of Staff, who now took it as clearly meaning that war would break out in a few hours. According to additional information which arrived in Israel at about 7:00am, the Arab attack was to start before sunset and there was a possibility of preventing it by publicly warning Egypt that Israel knew of its plan and was ready to meet it.[57]

The warning also succeeded in breaking AMAN's conception that war was unlikely. On the morning of 6 October, at around 7:00am, it distributed a report on the Soviet evacuation which, for the first time, said: 'This evacuation may be linked to Arab preparations for war'.[58]

THE INTELLIGENCE BLUNDER: HOW DID IT HAPPEN?

The volume of research and professional literature on the Yom Kippur intelligence debacle is very small compared with the body of literature on similar events such as Barbarossa and, especially, Pearl Harbour. AMAN, the main organ responsible for Israel's dramatic intelligence failure, has never investigated its performance on the eve of the war. The same, as far as is known, is also true with regard to the Mossad, though its responsibility for the failure was far smaller. The Agranat Commission, Israel's official commission of inquiry which was established under public pressure to look into the intelligence and the military blunders of the war, was the sole body to conduct a relatively comprehensive investigation of this case. But lack of preliminary investigations in the intelligence community, limited means and time, and (perhaps) political pressures, prevented it from gaining access to all relevant material and to key witnesses such as senior officers in AMAN's

Research Department. Moreover, memoirs in recent years about the subject are coloured by personal biases, and although they shed some new light on this case they do not provide a solid enough basis for a comprehensive and authoritative explanation.

In light of these difficulties the following explanations are of a limited value as well. They are grouped into four categories: academic accounts, mostly of the 1970s, which attempted to explain the blunder on the basis of the limited empirical evidence that was available then; explanations which focus on Arab deception plans; the explanations suggested by the Agranat Commission; and explanations which focus on DMI Zeira's actions on the eve of the war.

Early Academic Explanations

Most academic students of the 1973 case accepted the Agranat Commission's prime conclusion that adherence to a conception which (*post factum*) proved to be outdated was the main cause of Israel's intelligence failure. Hence, the main question most of them attempted to answer was what made Israel's intelligence experts, military officers, and policy makers so unreceptive to the many signals which indicated that this preconception was wrong.

Some answers are wider than others. Michael Handel, for example, identified three interrelated 'noise barriers' which distorted the signals which had to pass through them. The first barrier involved different sources of threat in the international system as well as a too quiet international environment (e.g., the détente of the early 1970s), which directed the victim from the real threat and distracted its ability to correctly assimilate the signals of the coming attack. The second barrier was created by the initiator's attempts to conceal its plans and mislead the victim with regard to its real intentions. The last barrier was the noise generated unintentionally by the victim, and which furthermore hampered the proper assimilation of the signals of the impending threat. Not surprisingly, the interaction between the three barriers had led Handel to conclude that 'surprise can rarely be prevented'.[59]

Other studies focused on what Handel termed the 'third barrier'. Abraham Ben-Zvi compared the case of Yom Kippur to some other surprise attacks. He concluded that to a large extent this failure was the outcome of an Israeli tendency to give priority to strategic assumptions (that war was still too risky for the Arabs) over tactical information (which reflected actual preparations for war).[60] Avi Shlaim explained Israel's intelligence failure by identifying certain psychological and institutional obstacles which were rooted in its domestic, intelligence, military, and political environments.[61] Janice Gross Stein suggested that elements of group-thinking dominated intelligence and decision-making processes on the eve of the war, adding another cause for Israel's misperception of reality.[62]

Other students of the subject, more familiar with AMAN's performance than with general academic theories, suggested explanations closely related to their personal experience. Alouph Hareven, an experienced intelligence officer, who compared this case to Israel's intelligence failure of 1954, known as the 'Unfortunate Business', concluded that institutional pathologies within AMAN and between intelligence producers and consumers were a major explanation.[63] Another practitioner, Zvi Lanir, focused his study on the distinction between fundamental and situational surprises. His conclusion was that the fundamental surprise of Yom Kippur was not merely the product of Israel's misperception of Arab intentions and capabilities, but also the outcome of misconceived beliefs regarding Israel's own capabilities which led its military and political elite to overestimate its military might *vis-à-vis* the Arab armies.[64] A closely related cause for the Israeli failure was offered by the commander of AMAN's Sigint unit during the war, Yoel Ben-Porat. According to him, pretension as well as arrogance on the part of Israeli intelligence officers, who believed that they could correctly grasp the complex strategic calculus of Arab leaders such as Sadat and Asad, accounted for much of the 1973 debacle.[65]

Given that the Yom Kippur failure to provide warning despite available information is such a complicated puzzle involving numerous variables, none of the above explanations are mutually exclusive and, to a large extent, they complement each other. They suffer, however, from two weaknesses: first, they fail to provide a comprehensive explanation of the Israeli failure; second, their empirical basis is weak. Hence the need to look for additional explanations.

Deception

Deception is '[t]he process of influencing the enemy to make decisions disadvantageous to himself by supplying or denying information.'[66] It stands at the foundation of every surprise attack. Egypt's war planners were well aware of the need to deceive Israeli intelligence as a means to obtain strategic surprise. They based their plans on the Soviet doctrine, at the centre of which lies the conception that a primary way to conceal real preparations for war is to disguise them as an exercise.[67] The principal measure taken to achieve this goal was hiding the true nature of the war preparations. Thus, the commanders of Egypt's two armies that were to storm the Bar-Lev line learned about the plan to go to war on 1 October; their divisional commanders learned about it on 3 October; and the brigade commanders a day later. Platoon commanders heard that they were to start a real war only six hours before the attack.[68] A high level of secrecy was also maintained in the Syrian army.[69]

In addition, various active means were taken on the Egyptian front to convince the Israelis that the intensive military preparations were for the *Tahrir* 41 exercise, one in a series of exercises for the occupation of Sinai, which the Egyptian military had conducted since 1968. Among these measures were: the selection of the sacred month of Ramadan to start the war; extensive mobilization and demobilization of reserve forces prior to the war; the issue of false orders to military units to return to routine activity on 7 October, at the end of *Tahrir* 41; the issue of orders to officers who were on military courses but participated in the exercise to return to routine training activity on 9 October; the distribution of information about registration of soldiers for the pilgrimage to Mecca in late October; and the creation of 'a business as usual atmosphere' along the front in the days before the outbreak of war.[70]

Successful deception is tailored to suit the dominant (but wrong) conception of the opponent. As we have already seen, on the eve of Egypt's final preparations for war AMAN foresaw that these acts would be performed in the framework of an exercise.[71] Similarly, on 3 October, the head of the Research Branch told Golda Meir about the increased Egyptian readiness: 'There are indicators that this is an exercise. There is clear information on exercise. One example: it is their Ramadan now. We checked if there were large-scale exercises in Ramadan. We found out that there was one, two years ago. In addition, the War Minister issued internal instruction that officers who want to go to Mecca will be able to do so in the third part of the month of Ramadan.'[72]

Zeira told the Agranat Commission after the war: 'I had no piece of information prior to the war that I could present as evidence. I could present the information as information which suits an exercise. I could bring proofs of the date when the exercise is to be over, about arrangements to demobilize the reserve forces, and preparations to send the officers to Mecca.'[73] *Post factum,* Zeira had to give credit to Egyptian strict compartmentalization: 'If the Egyptian President and the High Command had not managed matters so that no one in the army, or almost nobody in the Egyptian army, knew whether it was an exercise or war, we would have known.'[74] Egyptian active and passive deception and Syrian concealment of war preparations contributed significantly to their success. Much of its effectiveness derived, however, from Israel's persistent belief in the validity of the existing conception. More interesting questions, then, are what made this conception so rigid, and what was its impact on action taken in Israel on the eve of the war.

The Agranat Commission's Explanations

The official inquiry into the intelligence blunder of October 1973 explained it by a number of factors, e.g., technical difficulties in getting earlier information in order to compare it with new information, the need to avoid false alarms, the need to protect sources, or the difficulties involved in separating, in real time, signals from noise – which hampered AMAN's ability to properly understand the available information.[75] But the main obstacle to understanding the true nature of Egypt's and Syria's war preparations was the conception. The Agranat Commission concluded that:

- The conception ... had become AMAN's conclusion in advance, in estimating the danger of war.
- As in the period of April–May 1973, so also in September (after the shooting down of the 13 Syrian planes) and – mainly – in the critical days of the first week of October until and including the fifth, the above-mentioned conclusion of AMAN served as the fundamental basis of its evaluation, which it expressed on various occasions to the highest military and civilian echelons in the country, that the possibility that Egypt and Syria would start a general war against Israel, on two fronts, was of low probability, which, in actuality, was the same as estimating that such a danger was almost non-existent.
- The doubt that was raised in the mind of the head of AMAN on 5 October, because of the news about the emergency evacuation of the families of the Soviet experts from Syria and Egypt, was insufficient to uproot the critical influence of the conception on the above-mentioned evaluation.[76]

Defining the dogmatic adherence to the conception as the main cause of AMAN's failure was, as the Commission itself noted, an insufficient explanation. Consequently it looked into the causes which made the conception so rigid, and came up with three complementary explanations.

The first was *over-confidence* in the IDF's ability to defeat the Arab armies even without a strategic warning. This feeling was shared by policy makers as well as military generals, but its impact was especially grave when it came to intelligence officers. DMI Zeira expressed vividly this type of arrogance when explaining why he did not disseminate to the Chief of Staff and the Minister of Defence the message which arrived on the afternoon of 5 October and which explained the Soviet emergency evacuation by Arab decision to go to war:

> I did not find it necessary to alert the Chief of Staff at 11:00pm [in fact Zeira had received the information a few hours earlier] and to tell him: there is such information, and to add what we wrote later, that the source was not so reliable and there are mistakes and we think the same. And it should be remembered that the whole IDF is in its highest state of readiness ... and we all stand with a finger on the trigger. This was, I presume, the feeling of the Chief of Staff, and mine also during that night. This was not a situation of 'out of the blue' that everyone went home, and we have to alert. So the Chief of Staff would have seen it, [and] I assume he would have said: OK, but [head of Southern Command Shmuel Gonen] Gorodish has ... [Air Force Commander] Benny Peled has all the pilots in the bases, [head of the Northern Command Yitzhak Hofi] Haka has ... Everyone stands with his finger on the trigger? Fine.[77]

A second devastating factor was AMAN's *working method*, which led consumers to misperceive the true nature of the agency's assessment. In general, an intelligence assessment can be presented to policy makers in two ways: (a) as a balanced document which integrates contradicting interpretations of the situation into a coherent single report, and (b) as multiple interpretations which reflect contradicting estimates about a specific issue within the agency. As became known after the war, AMAN's analysts did not speak in one voice and some of them assessed that Arab military preparations were for war. But since AMAN's *modus operandi* was to provide consumers with a single 'research opinion', the estimation that policy makers received included no reference to debates within the Research Department and portrayed a wrong impression that all AMAN's analysts shared the same conception.[78]

The third factor that contributed to the rigidity of the conception was the monopoly held by the Research Branch in making national assessments. Within AMAN, the Research Branch dominated alternative centres of intelligence evaluation such as naval and air intelligence, the intelligence bodies of the three commands, or combat intelligence. Senior army officers, such as the heads of northern, central, and southern commands, or the deputy Chief of Staff, were dependent on AMAN's estimates, at least in part because of the monopoly AMAN held on raw intelligence. Within the intelligence community, AMAN held a monopoly over intelligence analysis. Neither the Mossad, nor the Foreign Office had any analytical apparatus. And while the political echelon, primarily the Defence Minister and the Prime Minister, could produce autonomous assessments, they were nevertheless dependent on AMAN's expertise and monopoly on information, especially in military affairs. As a result, no organ or single person in Israel's security establishment could challenge AMAN's dominant estimation of the situation during the days before war broke out.[79]

The explanations suggested by the Agranat Commission are sound and are based on a solid body of empirical evidence. It seems, however, that for certain reasons the Commission avoided focusing on one aspect of the puzzle that could provide additional useful explanations. This involves certain intentional actions taken by DMI Zeira on the eve of the war – actions which caused military and civilian policy makers to misperceive the reality when such misperceptions had become most critical.

DMI ZEIRA'S PERSONAL ROLE

AMAN's monopoly on intelligence analysis, the high ranking status of its heads as senior estimators in the eyes of policy makers, and Zeira's persistent belief in the validity of the conception, created in early October 1973 a unique decision-making environment which assigned the Director of Military Intelligence a critical role in determining the outcome of the political and military discussions on the eve of the war.

As had become evident in recent years, believing that war was highly unlikely, Zeira consciously used his unique standing in a way that significantly eroded incoming warnings. He did this in three different ways: first, by creating an atmosphere that suppressed beliefs in AMAN that war was imminent; second, by preventing the dissemination of critical pieces of information, which indicated that war was imminent; and third, by refusing on the eve of the war to activate special means of collection which could produce high quality warning signals, and by reporting to his superiors, who asked about the operational status of these means, that they had been activated.

Many details regarding the way in which suppression of analysts who believed that war was likely despite Arab military weaknesses are still unavailable. It seems that the tendency towards such unofficial policy started after the 'Blue-White' state of readiness, which Chief of Staff Elazar and Defence Minister Dayan decided to initiate in spring 1973, despite AMAN's persistent assessment that war was not expected. The fact that DMI Zeira, head of the Research Branch Brigadier-General Aryeh Shalev, and head of the Egyptian section Lieutenant-Colonel Yona Bandman proved to be right in this case increased their confidence in the conception's validity. Zeira, characterized by a dominant personality and tendency towards 'a commander's indisputability which resulted from enormous self-confidence',[80] seems to have created an atmosphere in which an open discussion about the probability of war had become more and more difficult. Though of a different personality, Shalev contributed to this ambience when rebuking senior officers for taking action which did not correspond with the dominant conception. For example, following the incident in which Shalev rebuked Ya'ari, for alerting the Northern Command (October 1), the latter had become more prudent when expressing his estimation that Syria prepared for war.[81] In some cases, senior analysts who believed that war was possible were kept unaware of relevant information which indicated that they could be right. The most important case of this kind is probably the attempt to compartmentalize Ya'ari from Hussein's warning that Syria was ready for war following Meir–Hussein meeting on 25 September.[82]

Such actions led to the creation of an artificial consensus in the Research Department that war was unlikely. Combined with the agency's *modus operandi* of presenting consumers with a single 'research opinion' document, it made disagreements among analysts about the probability of war unknown to outsiders. It can be assumed that had consumers known that a group within the agency estimated that war was likely, this would have had an impact on their belief in the validity of the conception, which was presented so persistently by the heads of AMAN in the days before the war.

Failing to disseminate critical information relates to three important warnings. The first was the message which arrived from a reliable Mossad source on 30 September – 1 October saying that 'today starts a large-scale Egyptian crossing exercise which will end in a real crossing and the Syrians will join the war'. As recalled, the warning triggered an increased state of alert in various IDF units, but Zeira informed Chief of Staff Elazar and Minister of Defence Dayan about it only on the morning of 1 October. The Agranat Commission concluded that the director of the Mossad, the agency that collected the information, was also responsible for this mishap.

The second case involves the warning, which arrived in the Mossad on 4 October, at about 2:00am. As recalled, the director of the Mossad, Zvi Zamir, took the opportunity of a phone call from Zeira that night to inform him of this warning, describing it as a 'war alert'. The Agranat Commission criticized Zamir for failing to call the Prime Minister personally about this warning, but it is clear that Zeira shares much of the blame as well. Unlike Zamir, who was not in Israel on the Friday morning, when three critical meetings were held, Zeira participated in all three. Although he reported, at least once, that Zamir was called urgently during the night 'in connection with a strategic warning', there is no indication that he ever made it clear to his consumers who the source of the information was, or the nature of the warning. Golda Meir, Dayan, and Elazar knew who this source was. They knew he was considered the best Humint asset of Israel's intelligence community; they regularly received his reports in raw form, and they were aware that AMAN's preconception (that is, that war was unlikely before 1975) was based, first and foremost, on information provided by him. Hence, it is likely that if Zeira had told them about the source of the warning and its exact content they would have taken it far more seriously.[83] By not providing them with complete information about this warning Zeira erred professionally, contributing significantly to the decision not to mobilize the reserve army on Friday at noon.

Finally, Zeira's decision to delay the distribution of the emergency report which was drafted in AMAN on Friday, about 21 hours before war broke out, and which linked the Soviet emergency evacuation to Arab intentions to launch a war, delayed the collapse of the conception in additional hours. Zeira probably wanted to know what Zamir's source in Europe had to say about the likelihood of war, but under the special circumstances of that day he was clearly wrong. As Chief of Staff David Elazar said three months after the war:

> (On Friday the 5 October) I was in my office until 9:00pm and the whole GHQ staff was in the office until about 7:00pm We could do everything. I went home at 9:00pm thinking to myself that everything that had to be done according to the intelligence information was done, not knowing that four hours earlier, war information arrived in the floor above me [in AMAN's Research Department] and nobody showed it to me. ... Had I seen the information at 5:00, 5:30, 6:00pm – I would have issued a

mobilization order for the reserve army. Because we were already under grade C state of alert since the morning, the mobilization offices were opened. Everything could have been done fast. The cabinet ended its Friday meeting deciding that if mobilization of the reserve army was required, I and the Minister of Defence had the authority to do it – without additional cabinet approval. Had we done so on Friday at 6:00pm, the reserve units of the Northern Command would have reached the front line before the beginning of the war, and the Syrians could not have broken through the front. The reserve forces of the Southern Command would not have arrived [on time], but at least they could have moved to the front in an orderly fashion and not a tank here and there, like crazy, unequipped and not on tank transporters. Moreover, I would have had a whole night for the regular army. ... According to the 'Dovecote' plan [the defence of the Canal line by the regular army] that was exercised a few times, I would have flown a paratroop brigade to the [Bar-Lev] strongholds and we would have taken them all, including the empty ones. Thirteen artillery batteries could have been deployed on the Canal. The regular division of Sinai would have been deployed at the front. The Egyptians would not have crossed the Canal. Perhaps they could have succeeded in the gaps, between the strongholds, but not along the whole line, without casualties and as if they were on parade.[84]

Disuse of special means of collection and lying to superiors about it must have had a similarly devastating effect. As is known today, as part of AMAN's war preparations, over the years the agency had built up certain means of intelligence collection to be used only in emergency situations. Israeli policy makers, who knew of the existence of these special means, tended to view them as a sort of a national insurance policy.[85] As tension before the war grew high, Zeira's superiors questioned him about the operational status of these means and Zeira always told them that AMAN was using *all* its means of intelligence collection.[86]

Zeira, however, did not tell his bosses the truth. Lieutenant-General Ehud Barak, the IDF Chief of Staff between 1991 and 1995, confirmed in 1993 that 'until 5 or 6 October the intelligence community did not use all the sources it could have used in order to ask whether there would or there would not be war'. The commander of AMAN's Collection Department in 1973, Colonel Menahem Digli, and the commander of the agency's Sigint Unit, Colonel Yoel Ben-Porat, testified similarly. Furthermore, each of them asked Zeira, on several occasions since 1 October, to activate these special means. Each time he refused, and on Friday, 5 October at 5:00pm such means had still not been activated.[87]

Zeira's decision to avoid using these means of collection, while telling his superiors that they had been activated, had a devastating effect on

Dayan's and Elazar's calculations with regard to the likelihood of war. The Agranat Commission concluded that Dayan's 'confidence in AMAN's evaluation [that war was unlikely] increased after the chief of AMAN answered on 5 October that he was using all available means to collect all possible information and warnings'.[88] The Chief of Staff said after the war: 'Before the war, when I asked Eli [Zeira] whether, when he said "low probability", he was relying also on these [special] means, his answer was positive. ... This, of course, confused me even more – since I knew the capability [of these means]; and if they did not provide information on war, it was a sign that everything was all right. Now I understand that I was not told the truth.'[89]

To analyze why Zeira, an intelligent and experienced officer, behaved the way he did is beyond the scope of this study. But summarizing his actions on the eve of the war leads to the conclusion that altogether he reduced, in three ways, the number of signals which could have been available to Israeli decision-makers. First, by creating an artificial consensus within the Research Branch that war was unlikely, he presented a biased 'research opinion' to policy makers. Second, his decision not to disseminate certain warnings to the appropriate parties made the most critical information, which indicated that war was imminent, unavailable to Defence Minister Dayan and Chief of Staff Elazar, precisely when they had to decide whether or not to mobilize the reserve army. And third, by banning the use of AMAN's special means of collection, Zeira actually prevented Israel's intelligence insurance policy from providing benefits, precisely when they were most needed. By hiding these unauthorized actions from his superiors, moreover, he presented them with a distorted intelligence picture in which, because the number of signals had been artificially reduced, the signal-to-noise ratio did not properly reflect the quality and the quantity of the information available to Israel's intelligence community on the eve of the war.

SUMMARY

During the first 18 hours of the war the Egyptian army occupied most of the Bar-Lev line and transferred to the eastern bank of the Suez Canal 90,000 soldiers, 850 tanks, and 11,000 vehicles. The cost was 20 tanks and 5 planes destroyed and 280 soldiers killed.[90] The IDF was left after the first 18 hours of the war with 103 tanks out of the 290 with which it started its fighting in the south. Israeli air losses (including the Syrian front) during the first 27 hours of the war were 30 planes.[91] Eight days later, on 14 October, Egypt launched its second offensive. This time the intelligence community provided a high quality warning of the coming attack and the IDF was prepared accordingly. The Egyptian army lost in this offensive about 260 tanks, 200 other armoured vehicles, and about 1,000 casualties and gained no new territorial gains. Israel lost less than

40 tanks.[92] These numbers demonstrate, in a very vivid way, the impact of AMAN's failure to produce a strategic warning prior to the outbreak of the war, on Israel's ability to achieve its war targets and the price it paid for this.

Given the magnitude of the intelligence failure on the eve of the war and its traumatic impact on Israeli history, it could be expected that a thorough investigation into this episode would be made. This, however, has never happened. The investigation conducted by the Agranat Commission was the only inquiry into the intelligence blunder. The Commission was unaware of some of the intelligence information that was available to Israel before the war, it did not question some key witnesses, especially in AMAN's Research Branch, and it worked under time pressure, and possibly under political pressure as well. Under these circumstances the validity of many of its conclusions is still questionable.

NOTES

1. *The Commission of Inquiry – The Yom Kippur War, An Additional Partial Report: Reasoning and Complement to the Partial Report of April 1, 1974*, 7 volumes, Jerusalem: 1974, Vol. 1 (hereafter Agranat, Vol.1) p.71 (Hebrew).
2. 'A stenographic protocol of a consultation at the house of the Prime Minister on 18 April 1973', Ibid., p.69; Aryeh Braun, *Moshe Dayan and the Yom Kippur War*, Tel Aviv: Edanim, 1992, pp.21–2 (Hebrew); Eli Zeira, *The October 73 War: Myth Against Reality*, Tel Aviv: Yedi'ot Ahronot, 1993, p.80 (Hebrew).
3. Lt. General Saad el Shazly, *The Crossing of Suez*, Tel Aviv: Ma'arachot, 1987, pp.146–7 (Hebrew); Mohamed Abdel Ghani El-Gamasy, *The October War: Memoirs of Field Marshal El-Gamasy of Egypt*, Cairo: The American University of Cairo Press, 1993, pp.182–3.
4. Shazly, *The Crossing of Suez*, p.149.
5. Braun, *Moshe Dayan*, p.63; *Agranat*, Vol. I, p.28.
6. Gamasy, *The October War*, pp.149–52; Shazly, *The Crossing of Suez*, pp.126–34.
7. Gamasy, *The October War*, pp.176–8.
8. Ibid., pp.108; 143; Lon Nordeen and David Nicolle, *Phoenix Over the Nile: The History of the Egyptian Air Power, 1932–1994*, Washington, DC: Smithsonian Institution Press, 1996, pp.269–73.
9. Ibid., pp.144–5.
10. Zeira's evidence, *Agranat*, Vol.1, p.85.
11. Zeira, *The October War*, pp.68–9.
12. Ibid., p.210.
13. Ibid., pp.85–7; *Agranat*, Vol.1, pp.61, 64, 84–5.
14. Ibid., Vol.1, pp.87–8.
15. Braun, *Moshe Dayan*, p.23.
16. 'A stenographic protocol of a consultation at the house of the Prime Minister on 18 April 1973', *Agranat*, Vol.1, pp.69–70.
17. Zeira, *The October War*, p.92.
18. Braun, *Moshe Dayan*, p.35.
19. Ibid., p.34.
20. Ibid., pp.38–9; *Agranat*, Vol.1, p.166.
21. Aharon (Roni) Bergman, 'Hussein warned Golda', Letter to Editor, *Ha'aretz*, 9 June 1998, p.5b.
22. Braun, *Moshe Dayan*, pp.39–40; Zeira, p.96; Shlomo Nakdimon, 'Hussein Told Golda: The Syrian Army Took Offensive Positions', *Yedi'ot Ahronot*, 29 Sept. 1993; Ze'ev Schiff, 'Was There a Warning?' *Ha'aretz*, 12 June 1998; an interview with Lieutenant-Colonel (retd.) Aviezer Ya'ari, 10 August 1998. According to Zeira (p.95), this was the first time the king gave concrete warning of a coming war. Braun (p.24)

notes that a senior person, implying the king, warned Israel in late April 1973 of military movements from various Arab states to Egypt. According to this warning, this concentration of forces in Egypt made a military confrontation in the near future unavoidable.

23. Braun, *Moshe Dayan*, p.56.
24. Ibid., p.44.
25. Zeira, *The October War*, p.143. King Hussein had been on the CIA's payroll since the 1950s. See, e.g., John Ranelagh, *The Agency: The Rise and the Decline of the CIA*, New York: Touchstone, 1987, p.580; and Bob Woodward, *Veil: The Secret Wars of the CIA 1981–1987*, New York: Simon & Schuster, 1987, p.218.
26. Braun, *Moshe Dayan*, pp. 45, 49.
27. Zeira, *The October War*, pp. 128, 134–5, 152, 199; Braun, *Moshe Dayan*, p.33.
28. Zeira, *The October War*, p.152.
29. *Agranat*, Vol.1, pp.171–2; Yair Sheleg, 'The Lieutenant-Colonel Who Believed in the Concept of High Probability', *Kol Ha'ir,* 24 Sept. 1993; Yossi Melman, 'A Story that Remained Unlocked', *Ha'aretz,* 21 Aug. 1996.
30. *Agranat*, Vol.1, pp.159–60; and personal interview with Ya'ari.
31. Braun, *Moshe Dayan*, pp.47, 49.
32. *Agranat*, Vol.1, pp.76–7.
33. Ibid., p.79.
34. Shazly, *The Crossing of Suez*, p.150.
35. Braun, *Moshe Dayan*, pp.39, 42.
36. Ibid., p.45; Zeira, *The October War*, p.128; Yoel Ben-Porat, *Neila: Locked-On*, Tel Aviv: Edanim, 1991 (Hebrew), pp.23, 49–50.
37. *Agranat*, Vol.2, p.309; and Ben-Porat, *Neila*, pp.48–50.
38. Braun, *Moshe Dayan*, pp.44–6; and *Agranat*, Vol.1, pp.159, 174.
39. *Agranat*, Vol.1, p.12.
40. Braun, *Moshe Dayan*, pp.42, 49, 57; Zeira, *The October War*, p.152; and *Agranat*, Vol.1, pp.21, 310.
41. Braun, *Moshe Dayan*, p.48.
42. Ibid., p.49. The Agranat Commission concluded that the Mossad's director, Zvi Zamir, should have informed Moshe Dayan and Golda Meir of this warning, which he did not (ibid., p.54).
43. *Agranat*, Vol.1, p.16.
44. Ibid., p.79.
45. Victor Israelyan, *Inside the Kremlin During the Yom Kippur War*, University Park, Penn State Press, 1995, pp.3–4.
46. Hanoch Bartov, *Dado: 48 Years and 20 Days*, Tel Aviv: Ma'ariv, 1978 (Hebrew), p.314.
47. *Nakdimon*, 29 Sept. 1993; Ben-Porat, *Neila*, pp.58–60, 61; Braun, *Moshe Dayan*, p.57; and Zeira, *The October War*, p.152.
48. Braun, *Moshe Dayan*, p.62; and Zeira, *The October War*, p.152.
49. *Agranat*, Vol.1, p.75.
50. Braun, *Moshe Dayan*, p.62.
51. Ibid., p.78.
52. Ibid., p.76.
53. Ibid., pp.75–6.
54. Ran Edelist, 'This Was the Head of the Mossad?' *Hadashot*, 24 Sept. 1993, p.20; Nakdimon, 'Hussein told Golda', and Ben- Porat, *Neila*, p.115.
55. The identity of this source remains secret even today. In his memoirs Dayan defined it merely as 'reliable'. Moshe Dayan, *Story of My Life*, London: Sphere Books, 1976, p.463. But in actuality this source was the jewel in the crown of Israel's intelligence community. Recruited by Mossad after the 1967 war he proved to be extremely reliable and with good accessibility to the 'political and military intentions of a number of Arab countries'. Some of the verbal and documented information he provided, which arrived at close to real time, was considered as 'hard information, which is the dream of every intelligence agency'. Given his quality, the Mossad distributed his reports in their raw form to a select few: Golda Meir, Israel Galili (Minister without Portfolio and Meir's closest adviser), Moshe Dayan, David Elazar, and Eli Zeira.
    In addition to providing the information which was the foundation of the conception, the source also provided Israel with strategic warnings prior to the war. In December 1972 he warned that war was possible within a few weeks and he repeated

this warning in April 1973. This warning played a critical role in Israel's decision to increase the state of military readiness – the 'Blue-White' alert – during the spring and early summer. Zeira, *The October War*, pp.85–7, 92–3, 119, 123.

56. Edelist, 'This Was the Head of the Mossad?', p.20.
57. Zvi Zamir, 'The Mossad's Information on the Breakout of the War Did Not Reach the Chief of Staff because of a Standing Order of the Head of AMAN', *Yedi'ot Ahronot*, 24 Nov. 1989, pp.16–18; Shlomo Nakdimon, 'The Agranat Commission Reached Its Verdict: Zamir Made a Mistake', *Yedi'ot Ahronot*, 24 Nov. 1989, p.17; Eitan Haber, *Today War Will Break Out: The Reminiscences of Brig.-Gen. Israel Lior, aide-de-camp to Prime Minister Levi Eshkol and Golda Meir*, Tel Aviv: Edanim, 1987 (Hebrew), p.11; *Nakdimon*, 29 Sept. 1993; Edelist, 'This Was the Head of the Mossad?', pp.22–3; Braun, *Moshe Dayan*, pp.71–2.
58. *Agranat*, Vol.1, p.136.
59. Michael I. Handel, *Perception, Deception and Surprise: The Case of the Yom Kippur War*, Jerusalem Papers on Peace Problems, Hebrew University of Jerusalem, The Leonard Davis Institute for International Relations, 1976, no.19, pp.7–8.
60. Abraham Ben-Zvi, 'Hindsight and Foresight: A Conceptual Framework for the Analysis of Surprise Attacks', *World Politics* 28/3 (April 1976) pp.381–95.
61. Avi Shlaim, 'Failures in National Intelligence Estimates: The Case of the Yom Kippur War', *World Politics* 28/3 (April 1976) pp.348–80.
62. Janice Gross Stein, 'The 1973 Intelligence Failure: A Reconsideration', *The Jerusalem Quarterly* 24 (Summer 1982) pp.41–54.
63. Alouph Hareven, 'Disturbed Hierarchies: Israeli Intelligence in 1954 and 1973', *The Jerusalem Quarterly* 9 (Fall 1978) pp.3–19. The 'unfortunate business' (*Esek Habish*) is the name given to an unauthorized operation conducted by AMAN in 1954 in order to sabotage Anglo-Egyptian negotiations for the evacuation of the British military presence from the Suez Canal Zone. For a description and analysis of this case see Uri Bar-Joseph, *Intelligence Intervention in the Politics of Democratic States: The United States, Israel and Britain*, University Park, PA: The Pennsylvania State University Press, 1995, pp.149–254.
64. Zvi Lanir, *Fundamental Surprise: The National Intelligence Crisis*, Tel Aviv: Ha'kibbutz Hameuchad (Hebrew 1983), pp.54–7.
65. Yoel Ben-Porat, 'Intelligence Estimates – Why Do They Collapse?' in Zvi Offer and Avi Kober, eds, *Intelligence and National Security*, Tel Aviv: Ma'arachot, 1987 (Hebrew), pp.223–50.
66. Michael I. Handel, 'Introduction: Strategic and operational Deception in Historical Perspective', in Michael I. Handel, ed., *Strategic and Operational Deception in the Second World War*, London: Frank Cass, 1987, p.1.
67. Aharon Zeevi, 'The Egyptian Deception Plan', ibid., pp.431–8.
68. Shazly, *The Crossing of Suez*, p.153.
69. Gamasy, *The October War*, pp.197–8.
70. Zeevi, pp.432–5; Gamasy, *The October War*, pp.181, 194–7; Shazly, *The Crossing of Suez*, pp.150–1.
71. *Agranat*, Vol.1, p.12.
72. Ibid., p.15.
73. Ibid., p.147.
74. Ibid., p.152.
75. Ibid., Vol.1, pp.142–5.
76. Ibid., p.80.
77. Ibid., p.157.
78. Ibid., pp.157–60.
79. Ibid., pp.160–75.
80. Agranat Commission, *The Agranat Commission Report*, Tel Aviv: Am Oved, 1975 (Hebrew), p.34.
81. *Agranat*, Vol.1, p.159.
82. *Ha'aretz*, 12 June 1998.
83. Zvi Zamir, *Yedi'ot Ahronot*, 24 November, 1989, pp.16–18; Shlomo Nakdimon, *Yedi'ot Ahronot*, 24 November, 1989, p.17; Nakdimon, *Yedi'ot Ahronot*, 29 September, 1993; Edelist, 'This Was the Head of the Mossad?', pp.22–3; Zeira, *The October War*, pp.85–7, 92–3, 119, 123; Braun, *Moshe Dayan*, p.59.
84. Ben-Porat, *Neila*, p.103.

85. Alex Fishman, 'Even Today He Does Not Believe that War Broke Out', *Hadashot*, 24 September 1993, p.32.
86. Ben-Porat, *Neila*, p.103; and Braun, *Moshe Dayan*, pp.58, 71.
87. *Israel's Television*, 19 September 1993; Ben-Porat, *Neila*, pp.53, 55, 66; *Fishman*, 'Even Today He Does Not Believe that War Broke Out'.
88. Agranat Commission, *The Agranat Commission Report*, p.46.
89. This is a conflation of Elazar's words as published in: Moshe Zonder, 'Yoel did Not Tell Me This Is War', *The Tel Aviv Magazine*, 4 October 1991; *Fishman*, 'Even Today He Does Not Believe that War Broke Out'; and Ben-Porat, *Neila*, p.103.
90. Shazly, p.168.
91. Bartov, *Dado*, pp.52, 70. According to an Egyptian source during the first day of the fighting against Egypt the IAF lost 27 jets (Nordeen and Nicolle, p.281).
92. Trevor N. Dupuy, *Elusive Victory: The Arab-Israeli Wars, 1947-1974*, New York: Harper & Row, 1978, p.487.

The 1973 Arab War Coalition: Aims, Coherence, and Gain-Distribution

AVRAHAM SELA

International military coalitions constitute a deliberate action of several partners designated to get specific political goals, either directly through military means or indirectly through diplomatic means affected by the military gains.[1] As such, coalitions intrinsically involve a measure of interdependence among the partners, as well as an unequal distribution of duties, risks and gains. Within this context the theoretical literature addresses questions regarding the extent of symmetry and mutuality in the context of interdependence, namely, how integration affects the gaps among the allies/partners.

The liberal approach that adheres to economic integration and free international trade maintains that such cooperation leads to greater benefits for all partners. However, the question is how these benefits are distributed among the partners and whether such interdependence widens or reduces the discrepancies of power between them, because partners tend to evaluate their situation in relation to other partners, not necessarily in absolute terms compared to their previous position. Hence, uneven distribution of pay-offs among partners to a coalition might affect the existing balance of power, instigate tension and suspicion, and destabilize relations among them. Paradoxically then, even though cooperation is said to result in common benefits, in fact it appears to confirm the pessimistic concept of political realism in international relations. Indeed, alliances tend to be complex, a form of competition, with mixed motives rather than 'zero sum game'.[2]

The question of 'who gets what' is closely related to the definition of victory, of 'winners' and 'losers'. Yet although military victory has been the classic criterion for winning a war,[3] taken as an instrument of national policy, victory, or rather, success in war should be measured by

Avraham Sela is Senior Lecturer at the Department of International Relations, The Hebrew University of Jerusalem, Israel.

the extent of achievement of the objectives for which the war was waged.[4]

Regimes of developing countries generally tend to be reluctant about building sustainable economic or military cooperation with one another, as a means to preserve maximum sovereignty and secure their domestic political position.[5] Military cooperation among regimes in Third World countries might be particularly inhibited due to its direct implications on national security, which is often identified with regime security.[6] The Arab states, although in agreement on the principle of Israel's illegitimacy and commitment to redeem the territory of historic Palestine, seemed to represent no exception to this pattern. Indeed, the possibility of an all-Arab military alliance had always been taken as a working assumption by Israeli national security planners and decision-makers, representing the 'worst-case scenario' which Israel, should deterrence fail, must be able to defeat.

Yet, one of the most striking phenomena of the Arab–Israel conflict from its outset was the absence of a joint Arab strategy, peaceful or military, designated to bring the conflict to an end. Between 1948 and 1967, the single most important reason explaining that fact was the lack of direct interest in war with Israel, because it was the Palestinian land, not the national territories of the Arab sovereign states, that had been taken by Israel. This had apparently reduced the Arab states' interest in the confrontation with Israel to the context of domestic and inter-Arab rhetorical competition and involvement in short-of-war activities, such as economic boycott, strategic blockade, and guerrilla warfare.[7]

Indeed, Arab states proved rarely capable of maintaining durable military cooperation due to historical rivalries and mutual suspicions, but mainly due to different, sometimes contradictory, state interests, anchored in regional and foreign powers' considerations. One of the obstacles to regional Arab cooperation in a successful offensive against Israel is the vast geographic space over which Arab military potential is distributed which entails difficult choice to the Arab military planner, especially if a surprise offensive is intended. Moreover, there is no territorial contiguity between the western (Egypt) and the northern and eastern one (divided between Jordan, Syria, Lebanon), the two major components of any Arab military coalition against Israel. The eastern front itself was traditionally affected by political fragmentation among its members – including Iraq, traditionally considered a potential participant in war against Israel through expeditionary forces – due to regime rivalries, incompatible military capabilities, and different interests. This division of the Arab front is further aggravated by Israel's perception of the threats originating from each front, and the priorities it may set in confronting each of them.

This article investigates the political behaviour of the 1973 Arab war coalition by identifying its shared assumptions and aims, as viewed by each of the main partners, especially Egypt and Syria; how each attempted to influence its allies' action in a favourable course;[8] and finally, how the spoils of war were distributed among the Arab partners. The Arab coalition's success will be measured by three major interrelated criteria: the initial war aims and outcomes in terms of gains and losses; and their contribution to the strategic objectives that produced the war.

This article aims to explain the causes that shaped the Arab war coalition and especially its level of coherence along the course of hostilities and their short-term aftermath, when the military gains secured during the war were to be translated to political values. The most relevant issues in this context seem to be the partners' mutual coordination and adherence to the agreed initial war, especially against the backdrop of their asymmetrical military gains or losses, geographic separation of their respective fronts, and Israel's ability to manoeuvre forces and priorities between the two fronts and aggravate their cleavages due to gains and losses discrepancies.

The reasons of the 1973 war ('The Fourth Round') were obviously rooted in the loss of Arab territories to Israel in June 1967 and failure of all the diplomatic efforts to bring the conflict to a peaceful settlement. However, it was not until early 1973 that actual coordination between Egypt and Syria had begun, aimed at launching a joint offensive against Israel. The Egypt–Syria collaboration later proved to be the ultimate nucleus of a larger Arab coalition, combining military, economic and political resources that came to full-blown demonstration during the last week of the war. A host of reasons might explain the unprecedented effectiveness of the inter-Arab military alliance of October 1973, but they were primarily rooted in domestic and regional causes. The single most important explanation to the emergence of the Arab war coalition was Egypt's regional behaviour and policies toward other Arab regional actors concerning the war effort. Hence, much of the following discussion focuses on Egypt, and more specifically, on Sadat's strategic perception and practical conduct of war and diplomacy.

ARAB COALITIONS PRIOR TO 1973

From the first Arab–Israeli war of 1948, inter-Arab military cooperation against Israel proved to be impracticable, despite ideological consensus toward Israel and formal existence of institutional frameworks for political and military cooperation. The Arab coalition of the 1948 war was consolidated during the two weeks that preceded the Arab invasion of Palestine – though finally established only three days before the D-Day when the Egyptian Senate approved the government's decision to interfere with the Palestine war. Egypt, Iraq, Syria and Jordan[9] held intensive political and military consultations which resulted in a vaguely phrased announcement as to the aims of their military intervention in the civil war in Palestine, as well as in an invasion plan, including its exact date and hour. But as the war began, this early coordination turned out to be about all they could agree upon. King Abdullah unilaterally altering the plan a few hours before the invasion to suit his particular aims further decreased its chances of success. The conduct of war operations by the Arab armies was marked by lack of coordination and divisiveness due to inter-Arab competition over tangible and perceived gains – land and prestige, respectively – and independent policies.

The main result of the inter-Arab cleavages during the war was Israel's freedom of manoeuvre and flexibility in moving forces from one front to another and in concentrating maximum capability for decisive offensives on each front. Nonetheless, the Arab governments collectively tackled the process of decision-making regarding the UN-imposed truce regime, reflecting their attempt to share responsibility and protect their domestic power from the people's rage over the poor military performance on the battlefield. The end of the war with separate armistice agreements between Israel and its immediate neighbours ('the confrontation states') was the culmination of the inter-Arab rivalries, which had been deepened by the unequal distribution of payoffs and losses in the war.

Between the end of the 1948 war and the Suez campaign, two Arab military pacts were signed, ostensibly to enhance the level of collective Arab security *vis-à-vis* Israel.[10] In reality, however, these pacts reflected the continued struggle between Iraq and Egypt for regional leadership, and attempts at balancing each other's regional influence rather than any sincere intention to bring the Arab states into practical cooperation against Israel. Thus, when in late October 1956 Egypt faced a joint British–French–Israeli offensive, the Arab signatories of both pacts remained idle. Two weeks later, a summit conference, which was convened in Beirut to discuss a collective Arab response, merely expressed support for the United Nations' decision on the matter and denounced the tripartite aggression against Egypt.[11]

The second significant Arab war coalition emerged in 1967. It was short-lived and marked by formal, rather than actual, attributes of political and military cooperation in every respect, such as common planning, central command, and practical military coordination during the war, and entire absence of defined common strategy and war aims. Similar to the 1948 war, the Arab coalition that emerged in late May 1967, consisting of Egypt, Syria, Jordan and Iraq (Lebanon remained passive), was the product of domestic and regional pressures rather than of early consultations and mutual understanding among the partners. These pressures derived from growing enthusiasm among the Arab masses in general and in Jordan, in particular, at Egypt's escalatory measures beginning 15 May, accompanied by Gamal Abdul Nasser's provocative declarations that brought the crisis with Israel to the brink of war. During these three weeks of crisis Egypt's pivotal role in the region towered, looming greater and more revitalized than ever since the painful break-up of unity with Syria in 1961. And it was Egypt that

Jordanian and Iraqi rulers joined, while Syria, though officially allied with Egypt by a mutual defence treaty since November 1966, refused to accept 'reactionary' Jordan as an ally and indeed refused cooperation with it during the war.

The swift Arab response to Nasser's moves after 15 May revealed a syndrome that was to recur in the 1973 war, namely, the powerful combination of core Arab leadership combining military power, charisma and militancy towards Israel. Above all, it underlined Egypt's decisive role in rallying the Arab world behind its leadership. From a militant Arab viewpoint it was the first time since 1956 that Nasser seemed determined to embark on a military venture against Israel. In fact, such venture was the official goal of the Arab summit conferences and common Arab action that Nasser himself had championed since 1964, namely, to prepare and mobilize Arab military capabilities under Egypt's leadership toward a future war with Israel, whose schedule would remain indefinite.[12] Indeed, Egypt's escalatory measures as of 15 May 1967 represented a clear shift from its previous reluctance to take any military action against Israel. Egypt's refusal to be entangled in untimely war with Israel had been repeatedly announced by Nasser himself since the early 1960s, and strictly demonstrated in response to Israel's military actions against Syria over the latter's efforts to implement the collective Arab plan to divert the tributaries of the Jordan River and over cultivation of the disputed demilitarized areas between the two states, or after Israel's retaliations against Jordan and Syria following Palestinian sabotage activities.

If any coordination took place during the war, it was between Egypt and Jordan, based on a defence pact signed by King Hussein and Nasser on 31 May 1967, which brought the Jordanian front under Egyptian command. Conversely, Syria ignored all Egyptian requests for action on its front, despite their mutual defence pact of 1966 and consequent military coordination efforts, and though false information about Israeli military concentrations at the Syrian border was the immediate trigger for Egypt's decision to mass forces into Sinai.[13] Iraq, which joined the Egypt–Jordan pact two days after it had been signed, deployed in east Jordan just before the war broke out an air force unit and a division-size force which remained practically idle. Sudan and Kuwait also sent token forces to Egypt.

In spite of the swift defeat sustained by Egypt, it by no means brought to an end collective Arab action or gestures of solidarity with Egypt. Algeria transferred arms from its own arsenal to Egypt and Kuwait volunteered financial aid (even before such aid was institutionalized in the Khartoum summit conference of September 1967). The Arab oil producers announced a boycott of oil supplies to the United States and Britain, but it proved to be short-lived and left little impact on the world oil market. Nasser and King Hussein reconfirmed their alignment and coordination, this time regarding diplomacy as an option for retrieving the occupied Arab lands, though with strict prohibition on separate settlement with Israel.[14] These manifestations of solidarity with Egypt, however, faded out shortly after the war, once Nasser seemed willing to adopt the option of internationally-mediated political settlement, even though he reportedly perceived it as a tactic to obtain the needed time for completing the preparations for a 'liberation war'.[15]

NASSER'S LEGACY: WAR AND DIPLOMACY

Given Nasser's announcement even before the war came to its end that 'what was taken by force will be returned by force', and the deep agony suffered by the Arab states, the question arises: what is the explanation for the six-year span until the envisioned war could be initiated by the Arabs? Reflecting his desperate effort to survive politically despite the defeat and the unbearable presence of Israel on the other bank of the blocked Suez Canal, Nasser was neither able to accept Israel's demands for peaceful settlement nor reject the international diplomatic initiatives altogether, especially with his armed forces practically decimated. Hence, Nasser adopted a dual policy of power and diplomacy that would provide him time and manoeuvrability. In any event, the renewal of Egypt's military capability (thanks to massive arms supplies by Soviet air and sea-lift) and preparations for war to liberate Sinai became a top national priority, taking precedence over the Palestine cause. This priority was clearly defined in the war's strategic aim, elaborated by the Egyptian General Command and approved by the government in November 1967. It was phrased as the 'liberation of the occupied land of Sinai ... till the Egypt-Palestine border, and *political use* [emphasis added] of the success for restoration of the Palestinian people's rights'.[16]

Egypt's military plan to 'eliminate the traces of [Israel's] aggression', shaped in the late 1960s ('Plan 200'), maintained a three-year long incremental development of activities of the armed forces, parallel to the process of revitalization of their moral and operational competence, from passive to active defence, including crossing commando raids into Sinai. A specific plan had been prepared for crossing the Canal and capturing bridgeheads that would secure control of the main roads leading into Sinai ('Granite 1'), which was later developed to include the conquest of the Gidi and Mitla passes deeper in Sinai ('Granite 2').[17]

Nasser maintained that a comprehensive mobilization of Arab military and financial resources would be required for war against Israel capable of liberating the Arab occupied territories, but his efforts in this regard were to no avail. The Arab summit conference held in Rabat in 1969 failed to meet Egypt's overwhelming requests for financial and military aid. Egypt, however, continued its military preparations for war independent of the rest of the Arab states. In March 1969 Egypt began a War of Attrition, which was meant to be an interim stage toward an all out war that would liberate Sinai. Yet, Egypt remained essentially alone

on the war front with Israel, repeatedly frustrated by its Arab allies –
Syria, Jordan and Iraq – who failed to meet Egypt's expectation for
parallel military effort on their part under the umbrella of the 'Eastern
Command'.[18]

Jordan refused to risk another war with Israel and, while seeking a
diplomatic solution, it fought to prevent the Palestinian guerrilla groups
from waging attacks against Israel from its territory. Syria, led by an
antagonistic regime and immersed in internal power struggles between
rival military factions, encouraged Palestinian guerrilla activity against
Israel from Jordan and Lebanon, but could hardly ally with any other
state over a common agenda. And Iraq, which had undergone a coup
which brought the Ba'th Party to power in 1968, became a bitter rival to
Syria's Ba'th regime. The September 1970 Jordan–PLO showdown,
which dragged Syria into a direct military conflict with the Jordanian
army, was a faithful reflection of the unavailing plans for Arab military
coalition in the Fertile Crescent states. In summer 1971, the elimination
of Palestinian guerrillas' presence in Jordan, the withdrawal of the Iraqi
expeditionary force from that country, and most of all, Jordan's
determination to prevent the use of its territory for further military
activity against Israel, all but inflicted a death blow on the Eastern
Command.

Before the end of 1970 the regional Arab setting had undergone
significant changes that were to bring in another era in inter-Arab relations
and in the Arab strategy toward Israel. The defeat of the Palestinian
guerrilla groups in Jordan in September, Nasser's death in the course of
dramatic efforts to mediate a settlement between King Hussein and Yasir
Arafat that month, and the ascendancy of Hafiz al-Asad to power in Syria
in November symbolized the collapse of the Arab revolutionary tide and
the decisive weight of state-like thinking and behaviour. Although Nasser
himself adopted a conciliatory line toward other Arab regimes following
the 1967 defeat, he still adhered to a pan-Arab line regarding the envisaged
war with Israel in which Egypt set the pace and distribution of duties.
Moreover, Egypt's War of Attrition with simultaneous cooperation with
the international mediation efforts with Israel based on Security Council
Resolution 242 was viewed with suspicion by conservative and
revolutionary regimes alike.[19] This was strongly demonstrated by the
Palestinian revolt against Nasser's decision to accept the American
initiative for a three-month cease-fire along the Canal and renewal of UN
envoy Gunnar Jarring's mission to the Middle East.

Egyptian historiography explains Nasser's consent to the American
government's peace initiative as a means to advance the ground-to-air
missile batteries to the Canal, as part of the preparations for war that
would provide the Egyptian army with air defence umbrella while
crossing the canal into Sinai. According to this line of argument, with this
action the Egyptian army had effectively completed its preparations for
war.[20] Whether or not this was the genuine reason for Egypt's acceptance

of the American proposal, by deploying missile batteries along the canal Egypt violated the cease-fire conditions, which resulted in Israel's refusal to renew the contacts with Jarring.

Apart from a staggering economic burden, Sadat inherited from Nasser a huge body of armed forces which had remained mobilized since 1967, a strategic plan for the liberation of Sinai that the army had been ostensibly ready to implement, and a strictly limited cease-fire, which had come into force in August, at the peak of the War of Attrition. Sadat's early months in power heralded a change in Egypt's policy regarding the balance between war and diplomacy. Although the diplomatic option had been adopted before, it assumed different perceptions by Nasser and Sadat. Nasser apparently viewed the political settlement as a recurrence of Israel's withdrawal from Sinai in 1957 under joint American–Soviet pressure, without involving political concessions on Egypt's part. Sadat, for his part, was willing to conduct indirect negotiations with Israel and spell the term 'peace agreement' as the final Arab concession in return for Israel's full withdrawal from the territories occupied in June 1967, in accordance with Resolution 242. Unlike 'peace treaty', which he interpreted as normal relations, Sadat perceived the 'peace agreement' as equally qualitative with the armistice agreement of 1949, namely, end of the state of war.[21]

SADAT'S FUTILE DIPLOMACY AND DECISION ON WAR

During his first three years in power Sadat's strategy in the conflict with Israel seemed ambiguous enough to generate some bewilderment regarding his real intentions: Was Egypt bent on breaking the cease-fire along the Canal, or on resorting to a political settlement? The on-going de-facto prolongation of the cease-fire along the Canal, on the one hand, and Sadat's statement that 1971 would be 'the year of decision' – followed by a similar statement about the year 1972 – on the other hand, accounted for a wait-and-see attitude in the Arab world as a whole, a stance most Arab leaders found convenient. Sadat's lingering decision on war initiative obviously reflected his strong wish to avoid that venture in favour of diplomacy.

Although he conceived the chances of a political settlement to be very low, Sadat was aware of Israel's military eminence and was doubtful concerning the military option as a realistic means to retrieve Sinai, thus viewing war as a last resort.[22] In the best case, Sadat conceived the war in terms of limited strategic aims, to be complemented therefrom by diplomacy. Minister of War Muhammad Sadiq (May 1971 – October 1972) and other Egyptian generals maintained that Egypt must acquire further capabilities, such as a balance of 2:1 in Egypt's favour, long-distance bombers to threaten Israel's rare and mobile ground-to-air missiles, all of which would elevate the prospects of success of the offensive in Sinai to 60–70 per cent.[23]

Conversely, Sadat's approach, combining sophistication and realism, reflected his growing sense of urgency as time passed by without action. The military action in Sadat's view was to be part of a radical strategic shift in Egypt's social and political orientation, some components of which he had begun to shape before October 1973, namely, liberalizing Egypt's political and economic systems, freeing himself from dependence on the Soviet Union and fostering closer relations with the United States as the ultimate power that might be able to force Israel to implement Resolution 242.[24] Sadat's war thus aimed at breaking the state of 'no war no peace' in the conflict with Israel, a stalemate affected by the superpowers' détente, and catalyzing a diplomatic process by forcing the Superpowers to take action and resume the diplomatic process under more favourable conditions to the Arabs as a result of a war.

Sadat's review of the previous two years with the Egyptian high command in October 1972 underlines his approach to the essence and timing of the military option: to have the greatest effect on catalyzing an American diplomatic effort in the conflict with Israel. Sadat wished to be ready for a large-scale military operation when the American President would have enough time in office and be least exposed to domestic pressures.[25] Hence, his initial order to the Minister of War was to ensure the preparation of the armed forces by the time of elections to the Congress (November 1972). This directive, however, was not implemented due to differences of approach between the President and General Sadiq regarding the prerequisites for war, which led to the latter's dismissal in late October 1972.

The timing and context of Sadat's final decision on war were shaped by four major factors, which underlined his independent strategy. First, his frustrated diplomatic efforts and contacts with Washington revealed the low priority the United States administration had been giving to peacemaking in the Middle East due to perceived Israeli military eminence and unbridgeable gap between Arab and Israeli positions. Second, the Soviet Union was reluctant to provide Egypt with the offensive weaponry it deemed necessary for a major war against Israel. Cairo related this to the Soviet commitment to détente with the United States.[26] Third, on the domestic arena an almost full military mobilization since 1967 and yet inaction raised doubts about Sadat's credibility, which were expressed by student riots and public debate regarding Egypt's policy in the conflict triggered by leading intellectuals. Fourth, the fear of losing the good will manifested by Arab regimes to support Egypt as well as the favourable international attitude toward Egypt's case in the conflict with Israel, especially among the non-aligned countries influenced Egypt's decision to go to war.[27]

On 4 February 1973, against the backdrop of near expiration of the prolonged cease-fire along the Canal, pressures of the Nasserist ruling elite and the military command to go to war, and internal struggle within the inner circle of power, caused Sadat to prolong the cease-fire by another month. During this time a partial withdrawal of Israeli forces from the canal – to the al-'Arish–Ras Muhammad line, as specified later – would be realized and works to reopening the Suez Canal for navigation begun. Sadat explained that this should be a first step in a comprehensive implementation of all the provisions of Resolution 242 according to an agreed upon timetable. Yet in spite of public welcome to Sadat's approach by Israel's Prime Minister Golda Meir and secret communication through American channels to this effect, the Egyptian initiative never took off the ground. On 7 February, Jarring, launching his last mediation effort, submitted to Israel and Egypt an aide-memoir suggesting full Israeli withdrawal to the international border, security arrangements and Egyptian acceptance of peace with Israel. Jarring's proposals, which ignored Sadat's initiative, effectively confirmed Egypt's interpretation of Resolution 242. No wonder Israel responded in the negative while Cairo welcomed the new proposals concerning conditions regarding withdrawal from Gaza Strip and settlement of the Palestinian refugee problem.[28] In March Sadat announced his refusal to prolong the cease-fire, declaring 1971 as 'the year of decision', either for war or peace. Practically, the cease-fire was preserved and diplomatic effort continued.

In the absence of an American willingness to exert pressure on Israel, the gap between Cairo and Washington remained unbridgeable, though the latter repeated its commitment to bring about a comprehensive settlement of the Middle East conflict. This became evident at Sadat's meeting in Cairo with US Secretary of State William Rogers in May to discuss a new American proposal for an interim agreement along the Canal, based on Sadat's February initiative.[29] Sadat's adherence to 'step-by-step' diplomacy reflected his intention to win the good will of western Europe by reopening the Suez Canal, and bring about an Egyptian presence – even a token one – on the eastern bank of the Canal, which in the future could become a springboard for a large-scale military operation if peace efforts failed.[30]

Israel conceived the interim settlement as an indefinite cease-fire, securing its free passage in the canal in return for partial withdrawal of its forces and strict demilitarization of the evacuated territory. Apart from demanding direct negotiations with the Arabs, Israel refused to return to the pre-June 1967 border even in return for peace with Egypt, adhering to Resolution 242's formula of the right of all states in the region for 'secure and recognized borders'. Conversely, Egypt was willing to end the state of war with Israel and allow it free navigation in the canal in return for full implementation of Resolution 242. Sadat objected to a separate settlement, insisting that any interim agreement should be part of a comprehensive one based on full Israeli withdrawal to the pre-1967 borders and solution to the Palestinian problem. Any interim settlement, including a military disengagement, was to be temporary and linked to a comprehensive settlement.[31]

By June 1971, the interim agreement diplomacy came to its futile end. Further talks between Foreign Minister Mahmud Riyad and Secretary of State Rogers in September that year proved no more fruitful. The end of the Vietnam War led to increasing Arab pressure on the US President to undertake active involvement in Middle East peacemaking. In April 1972, Sadat started communicating with the White House through secret intelligence and Saudi channels. Sadat reportedly assumed that the US had the ability to pressure – in his meeting with Rogers in May 1971 he used the term 'squeeze' – Israel to accept a political settlement which Egypt would approve.[32]

With the failure of the efforts to reach an interim settlement in early 1971, international peacemaking diplomacy effectively came to a standstill. This was a reflection of a *de facto* cease-fire along the Suez canal and the Jordan River, as well as of the growing intimacy in the relations between Washington and Jerusalem, which resulted in unprecedented levels of military aid to Israel. Israel and the US seemed to share the conviction that regional stability could be secured by Israel's military edge over any Arab coalition, and that Sadat had no real military option.[33]

Sadat's relations with the Soviets were particularly rocky following the removal of the Nasserist 'centres of power' in mid-May 1971, which secured his authoritarian rule in Egypt. It was against this Soviet sense of insecurity about Egypt's new ruler that Sadat was willing to sign that same month a Treaty of Friendship for 15 years to calm their concerns and to ensure smooth arms supplies to Egypt.[34] Yet while the Treaty deepened American and Israeli reservations as to an interim agreement, it failed to meet Egypt's expectations for adequate arms supplies. Sadat was indeed trapped in an alliance with the Soviet Union that could do very little to help him advance a peaceful settlement with Israel, and whose growing interest in a détente with the United States dictated an avoidance of confrontation in the Middle East and the continued 'no war no peace' mode. This interest, represented by the two summit meetings held by Nixon and Brezhnev in May 1972 and May 1973, seemed to Cairo to be closely linked to Moscow's policy of procrastination and restriction on supplying Egypt the specific offensive weaponry required by Egypt, both in quality and pace, a policy that turned into a source of bitterness at the highest Egyptian political and military echelons.[35] On the other hand, his contacts with the US administration on a settlement with Israel aggravated his uneasy relations with the Soviets and fell short of producing benefits to Egypt.

Although secret contacts for a dialogue with Washington continued, a breakthrough in the latter's Middle East diplomacy – even after Sadat's 'bombshell' of expelling, on 8 July 1972, some 8,000 Soviet combat personnel and military advisers – still proved unrealistic. The idea of ending the mission of the Soviet combat units and military experts had been advocated – aside of Saudi Arabia – by the high military command as well as by the Egyptian public, and was discussed with the Kremlin as early as April of that year during Sadat's visit. Apart from scoring domestic and worldwide prestige, Sadat viewed this step mainly as a significant advancement of his independent strategic decision-making. Moreover, by ridding himself from the Soviet experts and military units Sadat effectively signalled to the western world and the international community that Egypt was not a Soviet vassal and thus deserved their support in accordance with Egypt's pivotal status in the Middle East. Sadat allegedly meant to indicate to Washington that he was willing to rid himself of Soviet influence altogether if he could secure more active US diplomatic support in the peacemaking effort. Yet although the decision indeed led to an immediate invitation from Henry Kissinger to open a secret dialogue on a Middle East settlement, it turned out to be fruitless.[36]

These contacts with the White House, including two secret meetings (February and May 1973) between the national security advisers of both countries, Hafiz Isma'il and Kissinger, made it clear to Cairo that Washington had perceived the gap between Egypt and Israel as too wide for the US administration to bridge. Washington was willing to play an active role in the peacemaking process if Egypt had moved further toward Israel's position. Meanwhile, Kissinger advised Sadat to refrain from a military move that could lead to another Arab defeat. The first meeting confirmed that a military initiative was inevitable. On 5 April, Sadat established a war cabinet under his presidency in which a specific decision on war had been made though, as the second Kissinger–Isma'il meeting showed, it was not irreversible.[37]

Despite the ensuing freeze of Egypt–Soviet relations, in October 1972 Sadat dismissed General Sadiq and appointed Ahmad Isma'il 'Ali as the new Minister of War, whom he instructed to prepare the armed forces for war within the existing means at Egypt's disposal. The new appointment and decision to prepare for war were necessary to stabilize the domestic arena and bring the Egyptian General Staff in line with the President's concept of a limited war aimed at securing a foothold on the east bank of the canal. The depth was immaterial and in his directions to the military, Sadat emphasized – with some exaggeration – that what was needed for breaking the political stalemate was the 'canal crossing and occupation of ten centimetres' of Sinai.[38]

The growing Soviet–Egyptian tension that culminated in the expulsion of the Soviet advisers in July 1972 prompted Moscow to reinforce its relations with other Arab clients. In April, the Soviet Union concluded a Treaty of Friendship with Iraq, followed by substantial arms supplies. In July, Moscow concluded with Syria a $700 million arms deal, following which the number of Soviet military advisers soared dramatically. This set the motion for a continued process of warming up of Syrian–Soviet relations even without a formal treaty. Moreover, in March 1973, a new arms deal, unprecedented in its financial volume, was reached between Egypt and the USSR, the cost of which was to be covered mostly by oil-rich Arab states. Although the main part of this deal was to be implemented only during the October war, its very conclusion – enabling the return of 1,500–2,000 Soviet military advisers to Egypt – and early supply of Scud missiles enhanced Egyptian confidence in their military capability. Hence, the USSR did play a central role in Arab preparations for war, which, by April–May 1973 gathered a discernible momentum. Indeed, despite Moscow's adherence to diplomatic resolution of the conflict, and interest in détente with the US, supply of advanced weapons to Arab clients was necessary to preserve its influence in the area, especially in the face of Egypt's determination to go to war. In the case of Syria, this could be justified by the repeated manifestations of Israel's air-force preponderance in clashes with Syria triggered by Israel's retaliations to Palestinian guerrilla operations.[39]

EMERGENCE OF THE ARAB WAR COALITION

With Nasser's demise the Egypt–Jordan coalition came to an end and was replaced by Egyptian resentment toward the Jordanian king. Held responsible for massacring the Palestinian guerrillas and preventing them from resuming activity on his soil, King Hussein was resented and isolated by his Arab counterparts. In an attempt to control his losses both in the Israeli-occupied West Bank and the Arab world as a whole, in March 1972 King Hussein announced the United Arab Kingdom plan.[40] This further aggravated Jordan's position, leading to Cairo severing its diplomatic relations with Amman. The hostility demonstrated by Egypt, Syria, Libya and other non-traditional Arab regimes toward Jordan derived from their eagerness to gain legitimacy through declarative support for the PLO as the authentic representative of the Palestinian people and in compensating their military inaction toward Israel. This was particularly the case with regard to Sadat's enhanced diplomatic efforts in the conflict with Israel.

The early 1970s witnessed a low-keyed collective Arab policy-making through institutionalized inter-Arab forums. Nasser's humiliating failure at the Rabat summit (December 1969) indicated the futility of convening this forum without an agreement over basic assumptions and principles of common action. Such agreement was unrealistic as long as Egypt's policy seemed ambiguous and indecisive, swinging between diplomacy and unfulfilled promises about the use of force. Neither the Arab League's forums, nor a full-fledged summit – which failed to convene in the four years before the October war – played an essential role in forging Arab political or military cooperation. At the same time far-reaching changes occurred on the bilateral level without which neither the war coalition nor its political aftermath would have been possible, underlining a remarkable structural change in post-1967 – and especially post-Nasser – inter-Arab politics. Particularly the newly emerged regimes in Egypt and Syria turned to revise previous ideological and strategic concepts against the backdrop of strict constraints, changing regional balance of power and global atmosphere. Paradoxically, it was the decline of Egypt's dominating posture in the Arab world and shift of power to Sadat that enabled Cairo to assume a central role in forging a new pattern of inter-Arab alignment, serving as an axis for a trilateral core coalition with Syria and Saudi Arabia.

Sadat's concept of inter-Arab relations played a major role in shaping the new inter-Arab alignment, away from Nasser's legacy of being the ultimate interpreter of Arab nationalism and vehement intrusion in other Arab states' affairs. Once his position as an authoritative president had been secured, Sadat turned to building equitable relations with other Arab states, particularly those relevant to advancement of Egypt's strategic goals in both diplomacy and war. At the same time, Sadat was sceptical about Arab states' willingness to share with Egypt the burden of a future war with Israel without entangling him in undesirable commitments and public bickering. Therefore, he opted for relying on the emotional rallying force of war against Israel rather than forging a formal inter-Arab war coalition. By enlisting the support of other Arab countries Sadat would be committing Egypt to sharing the spoils of the war even before the first shot was fired. Furthermore, by taking more people into confidence, he would be compromising the element of surprise, his principal edge over Israel.

Sadat perceived cooperation, including reception of material aid, with any Arab partner conditional on mutual respect of each other's sovereignty and independent decision, which represented a new approach in Egyptian regional policy. Sadat strongly held the view that there was no meaningful Arab front without Egypt, and that Egypt's willingness to fight for the return of Sinai was fateful for the whole Arab nation. Yet, he repeatedly emphasized that Egypt must take action on its own and break the image of passivity ('a dead corpus') related to it. He viewed with scepticism the possibility of collective Arab thrust against Israel and was reserved about an early mobilization of Arab military resources toward a future war while Egypt itself was not ready.[41] Sadat maintained that once Egypt embarked on war other Arab states would not be able to linger on joining the battle along with Egypt.[42]

Another significant contribution to the ensuing tripartite coalition was Hafiz al-Asad's final ascendancy to power in Damascus in November 1970. Unlike his predecessor he adopted a pragmatic approach to cooperation with other Arab regimes, regardless of their ideology. At the same time, Asad was well aware of his shaky position as a member of the Alawi community, a religious minority whose Islamic nature was always doubtful to the majority of Sunni Muslims. His personal link to the loss of the Golan Heights (he was the Defence Minister in 1967) and the military threat posed by Israel to Damascus by its military presence on the Syrian plateau might have been another factor in his eagerness to redeem the Syrian occupied territory.

Although Sadat and Asad shared an urgent need for legitimacy and fresh pragmatic approach to inter-Arab cooperation, they differed in their political philosophy and type of leadership. The main difference between the two figures hinged on the strategy in the conflict with Israel, which was to surface in the aftermath of the October war. Sadat was a master tactician to whom strategy served mainly as a source of legitimacy, a proclamation of intentions under which practical policy making was to be shaped according to opportunities and constraints rather than be rigidly determined by the ideological principles. Sadat strove to resolve the conflict with Israel through a comprehensive settlement based on Resolution 242, and the establishment of a Palestinian state in the West Bank and Gaza Strip. This strategic goal would not preclude interim settlements, even if they meant political concessions to Israel to the extent of ending the state of war in return for its withdrawal to its pre-1967 war borders. In contrast, Asad represented a strong commitment to militant Arab nationalism and quest for continued struggle against Israel until its final elimination, though without precluding the use of diplomacy as long as it was not to compromise the strategic goal. Thus, his tactic was rigidly linked to the strategic aim, stemming from an overall perception of the struggle against Israel as a 'zero-sum' conflict, which determined its resolution primarily by military means.[43]

Induced by Syrian military inferiority Asad was determined to forge a coalition with Egypt – and other Arab states, if possible – to avoid isolation and perhaps to prevent a potential separate Egyptian–Israeli settlement. Since the paramount goal was the struggle with Israel, military coordination among the confrontation states, primarily with Egypt, was a *sine qua non* irrespective of ideological and political differences. Moreover, failure to join Egypt in war against Israel could expose Syria to a formidable danger in case Egypt was defeated.[44] Asad could hardly count on his immediate neighbours for effective military cooperation against Israel. Iraq would be a natural ally for such purpose had the two Ba'thist regimes not been immersed in ideological and political hostility. Jordan was anathema to the ultra-nationalist regime in Syria, especially after September 1970. Lebanon was militarily weak and traditionally uninterested in military actions against Israel, though its border had been most active due to the Palestinian guerrilla raids and artillery shelling from its soil and Israeli retaliations thereupon.

Syria's new inter-Arab approach was clearly indicated by its joining the federation of Egypt, Sudan and Libya under the Tripoli Charter only two weeks after the coup that consolidated Qadhafi's power. The Charter paved the way to the foundation in April 1971 of the Federation of Arab Republics (FAR) comprising Libya, Egypt and Syria (Sudan withdrew its participation for domestic reasons). The FAR stipulated full political, military and economic union, in accordance with Egypt's needs for regional support in the post-1967 years. For Syria, however, given its geographic separation, the union's main purpose was to enhance the new regime's inter-Arab legitimacy. The FAR could have served as a nucleus for an Arab war coalition, but it proved totally ineffective as far as the Egypt–Libya relations were concerned, due to growing mistrust and contempt between Sadat and Qadhafi.[45]

Egypt's quest for tangible inter-Arab military cooperation was thus limited to Syria, with whom high-ranking military contacts had been maintained since early 1971. A rapid rapprochement between the two leaders took place despite Egypt's initial acceptance of Resolution 242 and Sadat's diplomatic efforts to advance a settlement based on that resolution, which Syria still rejected. Asad's assent to Egypt's proposal for a military initiative was preceded by an apparent moderation of the Syrian position on a political settlement. In March 1972, while emphasizing the need for combined military and political action, Asad stated that Resolution 242 would be acceptable if it was understood as a framework for total Israeli withdrawal to the 1967 lines and the restoration of the Palestinian people's rights. Whatever the two countries' divergent views on a political settlement, Asad could hardly turn down the opportunity for a joint military initiative with Egypt which would serve his regime's needs and follow what Damascus had been advocating for years.[46]

The Egyptian–Syrian rapprochement coincided with a basic change in Egypt–Saudi relations. Egypt's declining standing in the Arab world following its defeat in 1967 and growing economic dependence on the Arab oil states were already evident at the Rabat summit, when Saudi Arabia and Kuwait spurned Cairo's appeals for increased aid. Nasser's death and Sadat's ascendancy paved the way for rapprochement between Riyadh and Cairo, which from then became firmly based on mutual interests and respect of sovereignty. An impoverished, enfeebled Egypt, without Nasser and his ambition for regional hegemony, no longer threatened the Saudi dynasty, which became increasingly active in spreading its own brand of Islamic revivalism in the Middle East and beyond. Saudi Arabia's growing regional and international influence could indeed be of great value to Egypt, through direct financial aid as well as by lobbying for American support for Sadat's diplomatic overtures and political claims in the conflict with Israel.

A paramount objective of King Faisal was to distance Egypt from Qadhafi's radicalism and Soviet influence. Faisal deplored Egypt's heavy reliance on the USSR, although the Saudis could discern that Sadat was far less committed to Moscow than his predecessor and that his affinity for them was grounded in practical military needs: given the proper inducements, they were told, Cairo would terminate its alliance with Moscow. For his part, Sadat was amenable to opening a new chapter in relations with King Faisal, based on equality between their countries and recognition of Riyadh's leading position in the Arabian Peninsula. Improved relations between the two regimes were both spurred and reinforced by personal understanding and secret contacts between the two leaders.

Ever since his ascendancy, Sadat, a devout Muslim, had been battling against Nasser's ideological and institutional legacy which was anathema to the Saudi monarch. Faisal was instrumental in bringing about an understanding between Sadat and the Muslim Brotherhood whose renewed activity was expected to enhance Sadat's domestic stature.[47] Following the Soviets' expulsion, Sadat's relations with the Saudis and other Gulf monarchies were strengthened, leading to the latter's growing financial aid for Egypt's arms procurement from the Soviets as well as from Britain. The Arab financial aid to Egypt for military purposes, primarily from Kuwait, Qatar and Abu Dhabi, reached $1,250 million; out of this $700 million paid directly to Moscow for Egypt's arms deal of March 1973, most of which was to be delivered during the war.[48]

The early 1970s witnessed a dramatic rise in the role and influence of Arab oil-producing countries in the international energy market and politics. The change was a result of rapidly surging demand for oil throughout the world, which could be supplied only from Middle East sources. It was particularly the case of the US where a declined oil-production and reserves, compounded by a monetary crisis, intensified its dependency on Middle East – mostly Arab – oil. Against this favourable backdrop, a revolutionary change occurred in the old pattern of relations between Middle East oil-producing countries and the concessionaire companies. The former consolidated their national control over their oil resources and, while jacking up oil prices, saw to secure for themselves a growing share of the revenues.[49]

Initially pushed by radical states such as Libya and Algeria, the Arab oil-producers' bloc, led by Saudi Arabia, played a pivotal role in this trend, amidst intensified threat to cease oil supplies to the western world due to its pro-Israel stance in the Middle East conflict. Particularly Qadhafi, and from late 1972 King Faisal as well, were active in pressuring Black African states to sever diplomatic relations with Israel. Under these circumstances the Saudis were ready to play their part in coordination with Egypt's war plans for their own benefit. During Sadat's visit to Saudi Arabia in late August 1973, Faisal informed Egypt that he would be willing to use oil as a weapon in the campaign against Israel provided that the war would be sufficiently prolonged so as to enable Saudi Arabia to enlist other oil producers' support, and force the West to experience the full impact of the oil shortage.[50]

As preparations for war ripened, at the initiative of Sadat and Asad on 10 September a mini-summit meeting was held in Cairo with the participation of King Hussein, apparently to induce the Hashemite monarch to take part in the war by opening a third front against Israel. When the King declined, mainly on grounds of Jordan's lack of air defence, his counterparts insisted that he undertake to defend his territory against a possible Israeli attempt to outflank the Syrian defences and threaten Damascus. The gesture toward King Hussein represented Sadat's and Asad's wish to maximize the prospects of success in their joint military venture, despite their acrimonious relations with King Hussein and his well-known refusal to use his long border with Israel for waging war against it. By mending their fences with the king, Asad and Sadat sought to oblige him to take an active role in the war, while for King Hussein it was an opportunity to gain Syria's and Egypt's renewed recognition.

It is doubtful, however, that Asad and Sadat would have realistically expected the king to be ready for war at that late stage (less than a month from its defined D-Day) or that he had been fully informed about its details and timetable. Such information had not been revealed to the king even during the visit of General Nawfal of Egypt to Jordan on 3 October aimed at examining the level of preparedness of the Arab Army.[51] In any event, Egypt's and Syria's reluctance to share fully their military plans with the king was vindicated by his reported secret visit to Israel on 25 September when he warned Prime Minister Golda Meir of the imminent war that Syria and Egypt had been planning, though without defining its date or substance.[52]

Indeed, Jordan's vulnerability to Israeli air strikes apparently played a role in the king's calculations. But even if the king had been entirely reassured about Israel's defeat, the prospects that active participation in the war would secure Arab backing for his claim to the West Bank were deemed uncertain at best, especially in view of Sadat's official support for the PLO as the legitimate representative of the Palestinian people and call on it to accept a transitory stage of establishing a mini-Palestinian state in the West Bank and Gaza. Hussein's standing as a legitimate claimant of the West Bank had been eroded significantly and at his first meeting with Kissinger in February 1973, Sadat's national security advisor Hafiz Isma'il spoke of Hussein as the possible party to a settlement on the West Bank, even though he might not ultimately govern this area.[53]

Sadat's approach to building an effective war coalition and insistence on refraining from routine inter-Arab bickering (*muzayada*) over marginal issues was manifested in his sour relations with Qadhafi. Sadat was interested in Libya's financial and material aid but showed little patience with Qadhafi's pressures to realize unity with Egypt amidst encroaching on Egypt's sovereign decisions on foreign policy. Qadhafi's drive to be involved in the Palestine issue and, as of early 1972, to establish unity with Egypt, represented his own security needs in the face of both domestic and external threats. Qadhafi had apparently sought to establish Egyptian economic dependence on Libya and was uncomfortable about Sadat's rapprochement with Asad and Faisal because it seemed to diminish his own standing *vis-à-vis* Egypt. As a revolutionary, Qadhafi rejected Resolution 242 and saved no abuse from the oil monarchies of the Arabian Peninsula. As a devout Muslim, who considered Communism heretical, he missed no chance to discredit the Soviets and their arms, though it did not prevent him from underwriting a large part of Egypt's purchases from them.[54] Sadat's strained relations with Qadhafi explain why the latter was not informed of the secret war plan until the last minute, despite his considerable material contribution to Egypt's war effort in the form of weapons, oil deliveries and financial aid. Sadat's troubled relations with Qadhafi culminated in a crisis during the 1973 war and set the tone for their mutual hostility for the rest of Sadat's presidency.[55]

The concept of war as a political instrument held by Sadat was fully manifested in the Arab efforts to consolidate the Third World's support against Israel before and during the October war. Israel's political posture in world politics had undergone serious erosion, especially since 1970, due to the rising impact of Arab oil in the international arena, growing international sympathy with the Palestinian national cause and Sadat's peace diplomacy. Geared to isolate Israel and weaken it in the international arena, these efforts culminated in the conference of the Organisation of the Non-Aligned States convened in Algiers on 5 September. With 78 countries taking part, the Arab leaders unanimously called for concrete political measures against Israel, in what was to become the main form of Arab political warfare in the conflict with Israel after October 1973.

The resolutions adopted at the conference called for support for the Arab confrontation states and readiness to assist them with all means to liberate their lands. The conference constituted a major Arab success, reflecting the growing influence of Arab oil and the concomitant fear of many African countries that they would lose their energy sources unless they acted to isolate Israel and express solidarity with the Arab cause. The conference also called for ending US military and other aid to Israel, and recognized the PLO as the sole legitimate representative of the Palestinian people. However, the Arabs' key achievement lay in engineering resolutions encouraging Black African states to cut diplomatic relations with Israel. Indeed, 22 African states did so either during or immediately after the war (eight states had severed relations before the war) when further prodded by Sadat following the crossing of the Suez Canal by Israeli forces, as an act of solidarity with an African sister state that became a victim of aggression.[56]

STRATEGIC AND MILITARY COORDINATION

Sadat had initially named December 1972 as the time for the Egyptian offensive, but was obliged to postpone it once it became clear that Syria was not ready and that military coordination needed more time and preparations. Even though Sadat had told his generals that Egypt must act, even if alone, he could not ignore the advantages of sharing the burden – and increasing the chances of success – by collaborating with Syria. In January 1973 Syria and Egypt appointed General Muhammad Isma'il Ali as Commander-in-Chief of their joint armed forces, starting intensive military planning and coordination between the two armies. Apart from exchange of information, 'Ali's efforts of coordination focused on preparing a surprise joint air strike, aimed at paralyzing the Israeli air force and its electronic warfare and control systems; communication and control procedures between the two GHQs; and the role of Arab expeditionary forces.[57]

Despite Sadat's scepticism regarding early mobilization of Arab military resources, once the decision of war had been made, Egyptian GHQ in conjunction with the new Secretary-general of the Arab League Mahmud Riyad embarked on a systematic effort to seek active participation of Arab forces in the anticipated battle. In meetings of the Arab League Defence Council since December 1971, pledges for unprecedented contributions of combat units had been underwritten by the Arab states, though some of them were to be implemented only after war had begun. By and large, those pledges were obtained through bilateral meetings with Arab heads of state – conducted by Riyad and Egypt's Chief-of-Staff Saad El-Shazly. They totalled 14 squadrons, one armoured division, and some armoured and infantry brigades.[58]

In April 1973, following the futile Kissinger–Isma'il talks, Sadat and Asad met secretly in the presidential resort of Burj al-'Arab in Egypt and agreed on a common platform and timetable for launching a coordinated attack on Israel. Despite the growing military coordination between the two states, it was only in late August, following the conclusion of new arms deals with the USSR, that the D-Day and zero hour of the joint offensive – code-named '*Badr*' – was confirmed in a meeting of Sadat and Asad in Damascus.[59]

Already at the initial stage of political coordination differences of interests surfaced. Egypt's military situation dictated a limited war goal, namely, crossing the canal and occupying a secure bridgehead along the east bank in the depth of 10–12 km. Syria insisted that Egypt commit itself to take over the strategic Gidi and Mitla passes – 30 km deeper in Sinai – which, if realized, would remove a strategic obstacle from Egypt's way to liberate Sinai as a whole. To ensure Syria's participation in the war, Sadat ostensibly accepted Asad's condition and instructed his military aides to prepare a plan for reaching the passes and re-define the war goal accordingly. In practice, however, it was only a facade meant to satisfy the Syrians. Recognizing that the idea of reaching the passes was militarily theoretical, the Egyptian GHQ's revised plan – later revealed by Chief-of-Staff Shazly to have been sheer deception – remained in fact unchanged in its limited goals.[60]

According to one source, new differences surfaced shortly before the beginning of hostilities due to opposition within the Syrian military Ba'th Party echelons over the timing and nature of collaboration with Egypt.

They argued against being dragged behind Egypt as a secondary and assistant actor, and thought the war should be postponed to spring 1974 to enable Syria to complete its armament with further Soviet deliveries. Another disagreement related to the D-Day and zero hour, originally set for 6pm to suit the Egyptian needs of crossing the Canal by night, while from a Syrian viewpoint the ideal time would be 6am with the sun in their back. The contention obliged Egyptian Minister of War to meet with Asad secretly in Damascus on 3 October to settle the differences, reportedly arguing that Egypt was determined to enter the war as had been decided, with or without Syria. Finally, the two parties reached a compromise on the zero hour, set for 2pm.[61]

The Egyptian and Syrian political leadership defined the strategic war aim as follows:[62]

> To inflict a comprehensive defeat to the Israeli enemy's forces in Sinai and the Golan Heights and take-over of strategically important areas, in order to prepare the appropriate conditions to complete the liberation of the occupied territories by the force of arms and enforce a just political solution to the problem.

The specific assignments to each state's armed forces were defined as follows:

> Egypt would plan a breakthrough of the Suez Canal, destroy the Bar-Lev Line and capture bridgeheads at a depth of 10–15 km on the east bank of the canal, amidst inflicting the heaviest possible casualties on the enemy. In addition, [Egypt] would contain and destroy every counter attack of the enemy and would be ready to execute any further combat mission assigned to it later.

As to Syria, it was assigned:

> ...to attack and break through the enemy's defence lines on the Golan, divide its concentrations and destroy its forces and reach the River Jordan's line and the eastern shore of Lake Tiberias.

The offensive was to be launched in surprise, covered by a deception plan, the core of which was pretending a strategic manoeuvre (*'Tahrir 41'*) – the kind of which had been repeatedly exercised by the Egyptian armed forces, the last of which took place in May and from which a real offensive could be swiftly developed. In April 1973, shortly after Sadat had assumed the premiership of new government, information concerning his intention to start hostilities began to reach the media. Just how real the possibility of war seemed to be, in April a Hawker Hunter squadron arrived in Egypt, followed within a few days by a Libyan Mirage squadron. Israel responded with a general military alert (April–August 1973), though without mobilization of reserve forces, assuming that Egypt might take a limited military action in order to break the stalemate and trigger a process of political settlement. In retrospect, although the alert turned out to be too early, it instigated military developments and generally elevated the level of preparedness of the Israeli forces.[63]

It has been argued by a former Israeli senior intelligence officer that the war was initially intended to take place in May but was postponed due to the Nixon–Brezhnev summit held the same month. Yet there has been no clear evidence, especially on the inter-Arab level, that war was indeed to begin in May, or that it had been cancelled due to the summit. The first week of May and October 1973 were the ideal times recommended by the Egyptian high military command for an offensive based on strict meteorological and marine study. The Egyptian armed forces indeed raised their alert in early May without any presidential instructions.[64]

The limited aims of the war shaped by Sadat became a matter of conflicting interpretations: had the limited goals of the war been affected by Israel's perceived nuclear capability,[65] or was it due to conventional balance of power, with no relevance of Israel's believed or real nuclear deterrence?[66] Even 25 years later the available source material provides no evidence to support the argument that Israel's nuclear deterrence shaped the Egyptian war aims or conduct. In the absence of documentary evidence the key issue to be considered in this context is the balance of perceived capabilities *vis-à-vis* defined goals to understand what, if any, limitations had been set for the Egyptian high command's strategic plan. The assumption that Israel's nuclear capability played any role in shaping the Egyptian strategic aims ignores the latter's acknowledged limited capability and its translation into limited strategic goals. In other words, the argument that the Egyptians waged a limited war in view of Israeli nuclear power would have been valid had the Egyptians – despite their perceived capability – deliberately employed less than their overall military potential, or could have operated more decisively in order to achieve further territorial or military gains, but refrained from so doing.

A scrutiny of the Egyptian self-perceived military capability during 1967 and 1973, as well as the process of planning and actual implementation of the war, shows that the war goals were strictly tailored to the perceived limited capability of the Egyptian armed forces and for realizing the goal of capturing and ensuring a safe bridgehead on the east bank of the Canal. Even this modest goal was viewed with pessimism by the Egyptian military elite due to estimated heavy losses. Sadat estimated that there was 30 per cent chance of total failure.[67] Such goal was indeed consistent with Sadat's concept that the war was meant to break the strategic stalemate and to initiate a diplomatic process with active American involvement.

Given the balance of power, the objectively complex operation of crossing the Canal and Israel's believed superiority in airforce and mobile armoured warfare, Egypt's options were limited. Hence, Sadat emphasized the need to offset them by meticulous planning and strict implementation of operations. More specifically, the Israeli advantages were to be balanced by the following means and procedures:[68]

- Forging a deception plan to attain full strategic surprise in the early stage of the war, exploiting the span of time Israel would need to mobilize its reserve forces.
- Attacking coordinately and simultaneously from two fronts.
- Attacking all along the 175-km front so as to prevent Israel concentrating its counter attack against a specific Egyptian thrust.
- Massive use of anti-tank missiles by infantry units.
- Maximum prolongation of the war in order to exhaust Israel's capabilities and allow other Arab states to join in, militarily and economically.

THE ARAB COALITION IN ACTION

The first achievement Egypt and Syria realized as allies in accordance with the original plan was their ability to implement the deception plan successfully. This success was partly facilitated by the rigid concept of the Israeli political and military elite, who firmly believed that Egypt would not enter an all-out war before certain conditions were met, and believed in the ability of its intelligence to provide early warning in case of 'real' war. Both these factors combined to blur the meaning of plentiful signals of the approaching war. The Israeli military intelligence maintained, up to the zero hour, that Egypt had not been prepared for war, hence the state of alert and large-scale concentrations of forces, armaments and equipment on the west bank of the Canal were believed to be part of a large-scale manoeuvre. Although the preparations on the Syrian front seemed to be more threatening, they seemed to be separate from what had been taking place on the Egyptian front, ostensibly linked to the air battle on 13 September, in which 13 Syrian fighter aircraft were shot down by Israel. Indeed, the main failure of the Israeli intelligence was its inability to identify the limited nature of Egypt's war aims and its close coordination with Syria.[69]

The breakout of war took most of the Arab leaders by surprise. Nonetheless, the Egyptian and Syrian offensives' initial success and the relative duration of hostilities generated immense enthusiasm and solidarity in the Arab world indicating the compelling force of hostility toward Israel. The immediate result was unprecedented military, economic and political assistance to the embattled Arab states. Nine Arab states (Iraq, Algeria, Jordan, Libya, Morocco, Tunisia, Kuwait, Sudan and Saudi Arabia) dispatched forces and weaponry – albeit mostly token – to the front. Furthermore, Pakistani and North Korean pilots operated on both the fronts. Saudi Arabia and Kuwait, as well as Morocco, failed to meet their pledges to send Lightning and F-5 squadrons respectively, but did send ground forces. Other Arab states lived up to their promises or even exceeded them. On the whole, the total magnitude of Arab expeditionary forces was significant: ten squadrons, one armoured and one mechanized division, five armoured and two infantry brigades, and two infantry battalions.[70]

This inter-Arab cooperation, however, also underlined the problematic employment of foreign military forces without early coordination and joint training, familiarity with the battlefield, or common strategic aims. This weakness was especially salient on the Syrian front, where the Iraqi, Jordanian and Moroccan forces operated. Even before a formal request from Syria on 6 October, Iraq decided to take part in the war. The decision reflected Baghdad's domestic and regional interest to take part in the confrontation with Israel, a constant issue on the Iraqi agenda. The participation was also intended to acquire political prestige and influence over any future attempt to translate the Egyptian and Syrian military gains into a diplomatic effort which was bound to marginalize Iraq.[71]

Thus despite the deep-seated hostility and mistrust between the two Ba'th regimes, Iraq sent the largest expeditionary force – arriving until 24 October – which totalled two armoured/mechanized divisions and four squadrons to the Syrian front in addition to the squadron that was sent to Egypt in April 1973. Syria was initially cautious, approving the Iraqi decision with little enthusiasm. However, once the Syrian assault was repulsed and Israel began its in-depth bombings and counterattack, Iraq came under growing pressures to expedite the arrival of no less than two divisions in the front. The transfer of the Iraqi forces to the Syrian front was marked by slow movement due to poor communications, insufficient tank-carriers, exposure to Israeli air raids and the need to be logistically self-sufficient. These characteristics led to incremental arrival of military formations in the front without being able to gather massive capability that would enable decisive military efforts in a narrow front.

Thus the first Iraqi battalion arrived in the front on 9 October while the first full armoured brigade arrived only two days later. Not only was there no strategic coordination concerning Iraq's participation in the war, but even on the operative and tactical levels there was little coordination with the Syrian command. These causes obviously affected the performance of Iraq's forces, which was markedly poor and mediocre. The Iraqis failed to employ any battle formations larger than brigade, even when such option was available. The appearance of the Iraqi forces in the battlefield was too late to affect the strategic results of the war, namely, the repulse of the Syrian offensive and Israeli penetration into Syria's territory beyond the 'purple line' (the cease-fire line of 10 June 1967), or the Israeli decision to shift its main effort from the Syrian to the Egyptian front. However, the arrival of Iraqi forces in the Syrian front constituted an operative and tactical success, preventing a total collapse of the Syrian defence system.[72]

King Hussein withstood heavy external and domestic pressure to open a third front, on grounds of fear that retaliatory Israeli air strikes would decimate his forces and bring disaster on Jordan. Hussein remained adamant on keeping his territory out of the war, overriding appeals by Sadat to permit Palestinian guerrilla raids from Jordan against

Israel, as well as Syrian appeals to enter the war and score sure success due to the poor Israeli deployment along the border. Similarly, Hussein refused to allow the passage of Iraqi ground forces through Jordan to Syria, even though Iraq offered to provide Jordan with air defence. Hence, despite some redeployment measures taken by the Jordanian army along the northern border with Israel, advancing armoured and artillery units, the Jordanian front remained entirely quiet and the bridges over the Jordan River open all along the war.[73] Jordan's aloofness and apologetic rhetoric could no longer be sustained in view of the Israeli successful counterattack on the Syrian front that started on 10 October. Yielding to the pressures both external and from the ranks of the Jordanian army, after confiding his decision to Israel, on 12 October, the King sent an armoured Jordanian brigade to Syria. As of 16 October, this brigade took part in containing the Israeli counterattack, together with the Iraqi forces, both sustaining heavy losses.

On the Egyptian front, the Libyan (manned by Egyptians), Algerian and Iraqi squadrons took part in bombing Israeli targets and providing air assistance to ground operations. Additional Arab forces operating on the Egyptian front were a Libyan armoured brigade and a Kuwaiti infantry battalion which had been deployed in Egypt before the war, and an Algerian armoured brigade which arrived on 17 October. Neither of these units took an active part in the war. After the cease-fire went into effect, a Sudanese infantry brigade also arrived in the front.

For the first time in the annals of the Arab–Israeli conflict the oil weapon was used effectively, even though no cohesive or comprehensive boycott plan existed before the war started. Sadat, anxious to avoid Nasser's mistakes, did not ask any Arab state to make a prior commitment to wield the oil weapon, believing they would follow the Saudi lead once the war began. Still, it was not until 10 October that Sadat approached the Saudis with a request to use the oil weapon, as a counter measure to the American airlifting of supplies to Israel. On 16 October, Arab oil ministers met in Kuwait and proclaimed an embargo on petroleum shipments to the US and Holland. Tagged on to the embargo was an ultimatum: it would be rescinded only after Israel withdrew from all Arab territories occupied in 1967 and the rights of the Palestinians were guaranteed. To pressure other countries, it was decided to cut their oil supplies by 5 per cent per month until the Arabs' terms were met. Beyond economic calculations, the oil-producers' decisions were to demonstrate their own contribution to the war effort and to ensure their immunity in the face of Arab radicalism.[74] Algeria, Saudi Arabia, the UAE and Qatar supported the war effort financially as well. The former offered Moscow $200 million to underwrite emergency military aid for both Egypt and Syria, while the Gulf monarchies gave Egypt the same amount as a grant.[75]

Yet even while the fighting still raged, it was apparent that the Arab military cooperation was far from solid. The initial spirit of Arab solidarity and euphoria faded shortly after Israel had retrieved the military initiative, but more so because of Sadat's war diplomacy, giving way to mutual recriminations and bitter inter-Arab differences over both operative and strategic goals of the war and its desired course. Qadhafi publicly assailed Sadat's conception of a limited war and called for total war. Saudi Arabia and Kuwait, the chief repositories of foreign currency reserves, were also the chief wielders of the oil weapon, while others used it sparingly, if at all. Libya and Iraq, their radical postures notwithstanding, did not join the boycott on grounds of disagreement with Sadat's war diplomacy. Their calculations were partly economic – a chance to increase their revenues as Iraq stepped up its oil output in this period – and partly political: to show their displeasure at Saudi hegemony in this domain.[76]

Most significantly, ruptures in the united Arab front appeared between Syria and Egypt, the two main protagonists and partners. By 9 October, the Syrians, who had scored impressive achievements in the Golan Heights during the first two days of the war, were turned back to the 'Purple Line' amidst fierce Israeli air-raids against in-depth strategic targets, while the Egyptian forces in Sinai continued to dig in, showing no intention of advancing their offensive further to the east. The Egyptian pause was perceived in Damascus as a breach of Sadat's commitment to advance the offensive to Sinai passes. The Syrian demand that Egypt launch an immediate charge toward the passes grew enraged and turned inescapable for Sadat following Israel's offensive as of 10–11 October, which brought the suburbs of Damascus within the striking distance of the armoured forces. However, Sadat's orders to his GHQ to wage the requested offensive faced strong objection from the Egyptian field commanders and when eventually executed on 14 October, it ended with disastrous results. The one-day Egyptian offensive – later presented as a political decision undertaken to shift Israel's pressure from the beleaguered Syrians – paved the way for the Israeli counter attack and the canal crossing to Egypt's territory on 16 October.[77]

The timing and conditions for cease-fire were also a cause for tension and suspicion between Sadat and Asad. On 8 October, the Soviet ambassador to Cairo informed Sadat that Asad had asked the Soviet Union to submit a draft resolution to the Security Council, suggesting cease-fire, as a result of heavy losses suffered that day by Syria. Obviously, such a decision would preserve the Syrian initial gains in the Golan, while Egypt had been still in the process of stabilizing its grip on the east bank of the Canal (the last Israeli stronghold along the Canal was conquered only on 13 October). Following Sadat's request for clarification, Asad dismissed the allegation that Syria had asked for a cease-fire, emphasizing that any such decision must be made in agreement between Syria and Egypt.[78] Later, it was Egypt's unilateral acceptance of the cease-fire that caused discord between Cairo and Damascus. Almost from the beginning of the war, Kissinger, by then

Secretary of State, maintained direct communications with Egypt and sought to obtain a cease-fire and return to the pre-5 October lines. Egypt responded by demanding an Israeli pledge for full withdrawal to the pre-1967 boundary at a specified time limit, repeating its willingness for ending the state of belligerency as soon as the withdrawal was completed, to be followed by a peace conference. Though neither the United States nor Israel would accept such conditions, the tone of the Egyptian message, pledging to refrain from expanding the fighting into Israel and threatening western interests, was interpreted by Kissinger as an invitation for continued dialogue.[79]

Egypt's conditions for a cease-fire, fully encouraged by Moscow, remained intact until the Israeli forces' growing penetration west of the canal forced Sadat to accept a cease-fire. On 19 October, Sadat notified Asad of his intention to accept a cease-fire along the current fronts. Perceived as a breach of faith, the Egyptian decision left Syria with little choice other than to follow suit, accusing Egypt of acting out unilaterally. By so doing, Damascus claimed, Egypt forced Syria to break off hostilities before having retrieved any of the territory Israel had captured in 1967. The Syrian dilemma was further aggravated by Iraq's rejection of the cease-fire ordered by the UN Security Council Resolution 338 as of 22 October. In addition to reaffirming the need to implement Resolution 242, it also called for immediate negotiations between the parties concerned to reach peace settlement 'under appropriate auspices'. Thus, a joint Syrian–Iraqi offensive planned for 23–24 October was called off by the Syrian command, without consulting the Iraqis. Baghdad threatened – and, when Syria accepted the cease-fire, stood up to its threat – to remove its troops from Syria in the name of 'the rights of the Palestine Arab people' and 'serious military and security matters'.[80]

The October war was marked by unprecedented American and Soviet involvement with their respective clients as well as between them in managing the crisis and preventing repercussions on their own relations. This took the form of efforts to bring about a cease-fire and, from 9–10 October, a Soviet air and sea lift of arms to Syria and Egypt, followed by an American air lift to Israel which prolonged the fighting and allowed Israel to turn over the military situation in its favour. Despite their crisis-management efforts, a point of declaring nuclear alert by the United States was reached when, on 24 October the Soviets threatened to intervene militarily to stop Israel's renewed offensive in spite of the initial cease-fire.[81]

The crucial moment between the superpowers reflected the critical situation of Egyptian decision-makers in the face of possible military defeat and loss of the strategic fruits of the October war. Israel's success in gaining a strategic advantage in the war was manifested by its success in bringing the Third Army on both banks of the Canal under entire siege and by its threat of annihilation of the Third Army following the latter's loss of its air-defence capabilities and means of communications over the

Canal.[82] Rescue of the Third Army could only be conducted by political means, closely linked to rescuing the anticipated fruits of war. This underlined Egypt's necessity and its swift shift toward the United States, to bring it into full commitment not only in managing the crisis but also in resolving the conflict.

CONCLUSION

The Arab war coalition of 1973 underlined the emergence of a core triangle of Arab power, comprising Egypt, Syria and Saudi Arabia. Despite ups and downs it was to shape the collective Arab strategy in the conflict with Israel until Sadat's visit to Jerusalem in November 1977. Its most important contribution was the definition of new Arab strategy in the conflict with Israel, namely, the 'strategy of phases', which in principle accepted coexistence with Israel in its pre-1967 borders and lay new ground rules for seeking that goal. The official approval of the diplomatic option by the Arab summit conference held in Algiers shortly after the cease-fire constituted a turning point in Arab–Israeli relations and paved the way to Arab participation at the Geneva Conference stipulated by Security Council Resolution 338.

Indeed, by virtue of its relative success and joint decisive political and moral resources, the Arab war coalition turned out to be no less significant in the post-war peace process than in the war itself. This was conspicuously manifested in the role this core coalition played in articulating and conducting a new and open concept of international relations, which was an antidote of the Nasserist anti-western 'third worldism' and antagonism on the regional level. Whether or not the 'strategy of phases' had originally meant to be an ongoing, piecemeal process of weakening Israel until its final collapse, it revealed the Arab world's limitations concerning Israel, even after a war initiated and conducted probably under the most favourable strategic and military conditions.

In principle, the war thus bore the fruits envisioned by its architect and leader, Anwar al-Sadat: a 'step-by-step' peace process mediated by the United States and backed by Arab and international pressure on isolated and weakened Israel. Indeed, from the outset, the war planners, particularly on the Egyptian part, set limited military goals, which by the end of the war turned out to be only partly achieved. However, the war succeeded in alerting the superpowers and demonstrating the dangers of the Middle East conflict to their own relationship. Moreover, although Israel managed to repulse the joint Arab offensive, the relatively long war claimed a high, painful number of casualties, and the first few days of being strategically surprised, exposed to a co-ordinated attack on two fronts, left an unforgettable impression on public morale in Israel.

Obviously, the closer the Arab military achievements in the war to the planned aims were, the better the prospects for a rewarding and smooth

political settlement. In this context even though the Israeli forces
reached the km 101 from Cairo and the Third Army faced the threat of
total destruction, Egypt managed to preserve its military presence on the
east bank of the Canal, while Syria ended the war with the loss of further
territory, with the Israeli forces at gun-range from the outskirts of
Damascus. Both parties, however, apparently gained from the Arab oil
boycott and other measures linked to the conflict with Israel no less than
from their military achievements.

Indeed, despite their poor military gains in the war, both Egypt and
Syria were politically rewarded though Egypt proved to have gained
much more in territorial and political terms. Egypt's desperate military
situation and potential defeat notwithstanding, it once again was able to
set the tone for the rest of its Arab partners in shaping post-war
diplomacy and extracting the lion's share of its revenues. In addition to
the more tangible military results on its part, Egypt was in a better
position to exploit the war results due to a number of reasons that
provided Sadat with wider margins of political manoeuvrability both
internationally and domestically:

- Sadat was ready for a strategic shift from the Soviet orbit to the
  United States which he perceived the key to recovering Sinai. His
  pragmatism and previously expressed interest in a 'step-by-step'
  process of settlement made him an easier partner to an American-led
  peace process.
- The geostrategic depth provided by the sizeable and scarcely
  inhabited Sinai to both Egypt and Israel offered better opportunities
  than other occupied Arab lands for the American peace strategy.
- Egypt's regional weight and leadership, coupled with centralized
  decision-making embodied by the president and a political-military
  establishment, encouraged both Israel and the United States to focus
  on peacemaking with Egypt in order to undermine a future Arab war
  coalition. Also, Egypt's status as a pivotal Arab state enabled Sadat to
  act semi-independently, in spite of the compelling collective force of
  the Arab regional system.

Sadat's conduct of the peace process was motivated by clear priority
of Egypt's interests and needs. Yet even though he could theoretically
gain more by taking a separate course from the rest of the Arab states and
the Palestinians, he had to adhere, with some margins of manoeuvres, to
a collective policy, seeking equal progress with Syria in retrieving the
occupied territories. Sadat also had to restrict his independent policy to
prevent damage to Egypt's pivotal status in the Arab world or risk a
cutback in the Arab economic aid which helped him to stabilize the
Egyptian domestic arena.

In contrast, Asad had to cope with an entirely different reality. The
peace process was by far less crucial for Syria economically or
strategically. Asad shared neither Sadat's diplomatic experience with the

United States nor his authoritative presidential decision-making potential. Representing the 'Alawi minority and the Ba'th ideology, Asad's regime was inherently challenged by radical opponents at home as well as by his radical neighbour Iraq, now more hostile than ever. Syria's politicized military elite and strong commitment to radical Pan-Arab ideology turned any settlement with Israel extremely complicated, slow, and conditional on advance understanding regarding the final objective. Syria's long-cultivated self-image as the standard bearer of Arab nationalism and carrier of the banner of uncompromising struggle against Israel had the paradoxical effect of fanning Syria's own fears of isolation in the Arab world in the face of the Israeli military threat. Unlike Sadat's reliance on diplomacy and tactical approach, Asad rigidly adhered to the strategic goal, insisting that Israel would give up territory only under military pressure produced by a unified Arab front.[83]

Ultimately, mainly due to Egyptian and Saudi commitments and pressures on the US, Syria too was rewarded in territorial terms for its war effort, despite its military inferiority and different approach to a settlement with Israel. It was also instigated by Syria's renewed hostilities in the form of 'war of attrition' along its borders with Israel, which threatened to prevent any other step toward further settlements unless a disengagement of forces was effected on the Syrian front as well.

The conduct of the post-war peace process underlined the significance of the adversary's perception and priorities in deciding the distribution of the war benefits, especially in such case as the 1973 war, whose main goal was to trigger political settlement with Israel. Israel's peacemaking policy and essential understanding with the United States on its strategic goals intensified inter-Arab differences. Jerusalem gave priority to a settlement with Egypt that would divide the Arab front and diminish considerably the threat of another Arab offensive, even if no further progress in the peace process was to be made. In contrast to Sinai, the limited size and strategic significance of the Golan Heights, the religious and national attachment to the West Bank, and the proximity of both to Israel's populated areas, rendered both these territories difficult objects for compromise and interim agreements.

Hence, Israel's intimate contacts and willingness to negotiate separately with Jordan on the future of the West Bank, remained theoretical, while the Hashemite attempts to effect a military disengagement along the Jordan River only aggravated Syria's and the PLO's anxiety lest they be left out of the settlement's circle.[84] To prevent such a scenario, Syria led the strategy of collective Arab action in the quest for peaceful settlement with Israel that would guarantee a comprehensive settlement. This policy accounted for Syrian radicalized regional policy in the face of Sadat's growing autonomy in seeking Egypt's interest in further territorial settlements with Israel embodied by the 1975 interim agreement over Sinai, and eventually by his historic visit to Jerusalem.

NOTES

1. Harvey Starr, *War Coalitions: The Distributions of Payoffs and Losses*, Lexington, MA: Lexington Books, 1972, pp. 8–9.
2. R. Keohane and J. Nye, *Power and Interdependence*, Boston: Little Brown, 1977. D.A. Baldwin, 'Power Analysis and World Politics: New Trends Versus Old Tendencies', *World Politics* 31 (1979) pp.186–7.
3. Karl von Clausewitz, *War, Politics and Power*, translated and edited by E.M. Collins, Chicago: Henry Regnery, 1962, pp.65, 233.
4. Berenice Carrol, 'How Wars End: An Analysis of Some Current Hypotheses', *Journal of Peace Research* 4, (1969) p.305; Clausewitz, *War, Politics and Power*, p.255.
5. Roger W. Cobb and Charles Elder, *International Community: A Regional and Global Study*, New York: Holt, Reinhardt & Winston, 1970, pp.134–6.
6. Mohammad Ayoob, 'The Security Problematic of the Third World', *World Politics* 43/2 (1991) pp.259–70, 278–81.
7. Malcolm Kerr, *Regional Arab Politics and the Conflict with Israel*, Santa Monica: Rand, 1969, pp.29–30; Ahmad Baha' al-Din, *Wa-Tahattamat al-'Ustura 'Ind al-Duhr: Qadiyyat Harb October 1973* [*And the Legend was Smashed by Noon: The Case of the 1973 War*], Cairo: Dar al-Shuruq, 1974, pp.54–5; Muhammad Fawzi, *Harb al-Thalath Sanawat 1967-1970: Mudhakkirat al-Fariq Awwal Muhammad Fawzi* [*The Three-Year War 1967-1970: The Memoirs of General Muhammad Fawzi*], Beirut: Dar al-Mustaqbal al-'Arabi, 1990, p.49.
8. Robert Rothstein, *Alliances and Small Powers*, New York: Columbia University Press, 1970, p.76ff.
9. Lebanon was also represented in the consultation but its military forces failed to fulfil their assigned role.
10. The Pact of Joint Defence and Economic Cooperation, known as The Arab Collective Security Pact (1949), and the Egypt–Syria–Saudi Arabia–Yemen pact (1955), which was joined by Jordan in the spring of 1956.
11. *Al-Hayat* (Beirut), 11–16 November 1956.
12. On the weaknesses of the Joint Arab Command and its difficulties to function effectively, see Avraham Sela, *The Decline of the Arab-Israeli Conflict: Middle East Politics and the Quest for Regional Order*, Albany: SUNY Press, 1998, chapters 4–5.
13. Fawzi, *Harb al-Thalath Sanawat*, pp.48, 144.
14. Ibid., p.192.
15. Ibid., p.188.
16. Ibid., p.199.
17. For some differences in defining the aims of those plans see ibid., pp.200–3; Musa Sabri, *Watha'iq Harb October* [*The Documents of the October War*], Cairo: al-Markaz al-Misri al-Hadith, 1975, p.18; and Mohamed H. Heikal, *October 73, al-Silah wal-Siyasa* [*October 1973, the Weapon and Politics*], Cairo: Markaz al-Ahram, 1993, p.275.
18. Sela, *The Decline of the Arab–Israeli Conflict*, pp.112–23.
19. Ibid., pp.119–25.
20. Fawzi, *Harb al-Thalath Sanawat*, pp.210–11.
21. Sabri, *Watha'iq Harb October*, p.41.
22. Anwar el-Sadat, *In Search of Identity: An Autobiography*, New York: Harper and Row, 1978, pp.221–2; Saad el Shazly, *The Crossing of the Suez*, San Francisco: American Mideast Research, 1980, pp.18, 31; Muhammad 'Abd al-Ghani al-Jamasi, *Harb October 1973* [*The October 1973 War*], Paris: al-Manshurat al-Sharqiyya, 1990, pp.214–15; Heikal, *October 73*, p.226.
23. Proceedings of two meetings of the Higher Council of the Armed Forces headed by Sadat on 2 January 1972 and 24 October 1972, quoted, respectively, by Heikal, *October 73*, pp.244–52; and Sabri, *Watha'iq Harb October*, pp.37–89.
24. Heikal, *October 73*, pp.241–3.
25. Sabri, *Watha'iq Harb October*, pp.45–7.
26. Mahmud Riyad, *Mudhakkirat 1948-1978* [*Memoirs 1948-1978*], Beirut: al-Mu'assassa al-Harbiyya lil-Dirasat Wal-Nashr, part II, 1987, pp.420–2, 427; William B. Quandt, *Decade of Decisions: American Policy Toward 1967-1976*, Berkeley: University of California Press, 1977, pp.128–9; Galia Golan, *Soviet Policies in the Middle East From World War Two to Gorbachev*, New York: Cambridge University Press, 1990, p.82.

27. Heikal, *October 73*, p.298.
28. Mordechai Gazit, *The Peace Process 1969-1973: Efforts and Contacts*, Jerusalem: The Magnes Press, 1983, pp.61–5; Sadat, *In Search of Identity*, pp.219, 279.
29. For the main points of the American proposal and its failure, see Heikal, *October 73*, pp.209–22.
30. Sadat in his meeting with the Egyptian high command, 24 October 1972, Sabri, *Watha'iq Harb October*, p.41.
31. Muhammad Hafiz Isma'il, *Amn Misr al-Qawmi fi 'Asr al-Tahaddiyat*, [*Egypt's National Security in the Era of Challenges*], Cairo: Markaz al-Ahram, 1987, pp.173–9; Sadat, *In Search of Identity*, pp.279, 299, 301; Moshe Dayan, *Avnei Derekh* [*Milestones*], Jerusalem: Idanim, 1976, pp.525–8.
32. Mohamed H. Heikal, *The Road to Ramadan*, London: Collins, 1975, pp.116, 140, 152–5; Henry Kissinger, *White House Years*, Boston: Little Brown, 1979, pp.1280–93; Quandt, *Decade of Decisions*, pp.133–43; Shimon Shamir, 'Nasser and Sadat', in I. Rabinovich and H. Shaked, eds, *From June to October: The Middle East Between 1967 and 1973*, New Brunswick: Transactions, 1978, pp.195–6; Riyad, *Mudhakkirat*, pp.343, 410; Muhammad Fawzi, *Harb October 'Aam 1973, Dirasa wa-Durus* [*The October War of 1973, Study and Lessons*], Cairo: Dar al-Mustaqbal al-'Arabi, 2nd edition, 1989, p.51.
33. Quandt, *Decade of Decisions*, pp. 122, 147; Mahmud Riyad, *The Struggle for Peace in the Middle East*, London: Quartet Books, 1981, p.223; Henry Kissinger, *Years of Upheaval*, Boston: Little Brown, 1982, pp.206, 221; Gazit, *The Peace Process 1969–1973*, p.11.
34. Heikal, *October 73*, pp.214–15, 224–5.
35. Isma'il, *Amn Misr al-Qawmi fi 'Asr al-Tahaddiyat* p.180; Heikal, *The Road to Ramadan*, pp.167–70; Sadat, *In Search of Identity*, p.225; Golan, *Soviet Policies in the Middle East From World War Two to Gorbachev*, p.77; Kissinger, *White House Years*, p.1284; Saad el Shazly, *The Crossing of the Suez*, pp.127–9, 173–4; Jamasi, *Harb October 1973*, pp.214–15.
36. Isma'il, *Amn Misr al-Qawmi fi 'Asr al-Tahaddiyat*, pp.206–8, 210–20; Sabri, *Watha'iq Harb October*, pp.53–4, 66; Riyad, *The Struggle*, p.232; Sadat, *In Search of Identity*, pp.228–30; Quandt, *Decade of Decisions*, pp.151–2.
37. Isma'il, *Amn Misr al-Qawmi fi 'Asr al-Tahaddiyat*, pp.256–81; Sadat in *al-Ahram*, 7 October 1977; Kissinger, *Years of Upheaval*, pp.215–16, 225; Quandt, *Decade of Decisions*, pp.154–5, 160–2.
38. Sadat, *In Search of Identity*, p.244; Sabri, *Watha'iq Harb October*, p.83; Isma'il, *Amn Misr al-Qawmi fi 'Asr al-Tahaddiyat*, p.233; Fawzi, *Harb October*, pp.5–6; Shazly, *The Crossing of the Suez*, p.106; Jamasi, *Harb October 1973*, pp.225–6.
39. Robert O. Freedman, 'The Soviet Union and Syria: A Case Study of Soviet Policy', in M. Efrat and J. Bercovich, *Superpowers and Client States in the Middle East: The Imbalance of Influence*, London: Routledge, 1991, pp.145–6.
40. Hussein's plan, *al-Dustur*, 16 March 1972, proposed the establishment of a federation between Jordan and Palestine namely, the two banks of river Jordan, that were to assume autonomous executive and legislative authorities, leaving open the possibility of including Gaza in the kingdom as well.
41. For a similar view, of Tunisia's president Bourguiba, regarding the severe inter-Arab divisions, see Sabri, *Watha'iq Harb October*, pp.119–21.
42. Ibid., pp.71–2, 75–6.
43. Moshe Ma'oz, *Asad: The Sphinx of Damascus*, London, Weidenfeld and Nicolson, 1988, pp.45–7, 86; Moshe Shemesh, *The Palestinian Entity 1959–1974: Arab Politics and the PLO*, London: Frank Cass, 1988, pp.187–8; Yehoshafat Harkabi, *Arab Strategies and Israel's Response*, New York: Free Press, 1979, pp.41–63.
44. See Sadat's report to the Higher Council of the Armed Forces on his recent meeting with Asad, Sabri, *Watha'iq Harb October*, p.71.
45. *Al-Thawra* (Damascus), 17 November 1970; Daniel Dishon, ed., *Middle East Record*, Vol. 5, 1969–1970, Jerusalem, 1977, pp.598–600; Ma'oz, *Asad*, p.39; Mary-Jane Deeb, *Libya's Foreign Policy in North Africa*, Boulder, CO: Westview, 1991, pp.72–5.
46. Patrick Seale, *Asad, The Struggle for the Middle East*, Berkeley: University of California Press, 1988, pp.190–1; Itamar Rabinovich, 'Continuity and Change in the Arab–Israeli Conflict', in Rabinovich and Shaked, *From June to October*, p.225. On the military coordination, see Jamasi, *Harb October 1973*, pp.216–17.

47. Heikal, *October 73*, pp.228–9, 241.
48. Mohamed H. Heikal, *Kharif al-Ghadab: Qissat Bidayat wa-Nihayat 'Asr al-Sadat* [*The Fall of Wrath: The Story of the Beginning and End of Sadat's Era*], Beirut: Sharikat al-Matbu'at, 1983, pp.124, 163, 269–70; Heikal, *The Road*, pp.119–20, 157, 184; Shazly, *The Crossing of the Suez*, pp.147–9; *al-Akhbar*, 23 May 1972; *al-Usbu' al-'Arabi*, 3 September 1973; *al-Ahram*, 2 July 1973; *al-Anwar*, 24 August 1972; 'Adil Hussein, *Al-Iqtisad al-Misri, Min al-Istiqlal Ila al-Taba'iyya, 1974–1979* [*The Egyptian Economy, From Independence to Dependency*], Cairo: Dar al-Mustaqbal al-'Arabi, 1986, pp.79–80.
49. Shwadran, *Middle East Oil, Issues and Problems*, Cambridge: Schenkman, 1977, pp.17–25; and his *Middle East Oil Crises Since 1973*, Boulder: Westview Press, 1986, pp.34–40.
50. Heikal, *The Road*, p.266; Anwar El-Sadat, *Those I Have Known*, New York: Continuum, 1984, p.69; and his interview, *Ruz al-Yusuf*, 3 February 1975; Arye Oded, *Africa and the Middle East Conflict*, Boulder: Lynne Rienner, 1987, p.5.
51. Jamal Hammad, *October* (Egypt), 25 November 1984. According to Heikal, *October 73*, pp.308–9, the Cairo summit was a cover for Sadat–Asad secret and final discussions of the joint military plan once again, setting the final D-Day and leaving open the zero hour.
52. *Al-Ahram*, 12–13 September 1973; Riyad, *Mudhakkirat*, pp.431–3, 440. On Hussein's visit to Israel, see *Yedi'ot Aharonot* and *Ha-aretz*, 15 September 1993.
53. Kissinger, *Years of Upheaval*, pp.215–16, 219.
54. Sadat, *In Search of Identity*, pp.233; Deeb, pp.78–81; Heikal, *The Road to Ramadan*, pp.190–1, 194, 196; Fouad Ajami, *Arab Predicament*, Cambridge: Cambridge University Press, 1992, pp.125–6; Ruth First, *Libya: The Elusive Revolution*, New York: Penguin African Library, 1974, pp.233–5; Shazly, *The Crossing of the Suez*, pp.74–95.
55. Heikal, *The Road to Ramadan*, p.196, estimated these contributions at $1 billion; Sadat in *Ruz al Yusuf*, 13 January 1975; Deeb, pp.74–5. Official Egyptian version minimized Libya's assistance to the war effort: Hassan al-Badri, Taha el Magdoub and Mohammed Dia' el Din Zohdi, *The Ramadan War 1973*, Virginia: Dunn Loring, 1978, pp.15–27; Sadat, *Those I Have Known*, p.46.
56. *Al-Ahram*, 4, 9–10 September 1973; Sadat, *In Search of Identity*, pp.239–40; V.T. Levine and T.W. Luke, *The Arab–African Connection, Political and Economic Realities*, Boulder: Westview Press, 1979, pp.7, 15–16.
57. Badri *et al.*, *The Ramadan War 1973*, pp.88–9, Heikal, *October 73*, pp.267–70.
58. Jamasi, *Harb October 1973*, pp.245–6; Fawzi, *Harb October*, pp.18–19; *al-Hawadith*, 29 March 1973; Riyad, *The Struggle*, pp.234–5; Shazly, *The Crossing of the Suez*, pp.195–7, 277.
59. Sadat, *In Search of Identity*, p.242; Badri *et al.*, pp.88–9; Shazly, *The Crossing of the Suez*, p.39. Jamasi, *Harb October 1973*, pp.267–8; Shamir, 'Nasser and Sadat', in Rabinovich and Shaked, *From June to October*, p.201.
60. Shazly, pp.37–9; Isma'il, *Amn Misr al-Qawmi fi 'Asr al-Tahaddiyat*, p.304; and Fawzi, *Harb October*, pp.7, 93. Jamasi, *Harb October 1973*, pp.387–91, strongly denies the allegation of deception, and maintains that occupying the passes area was a genuine Egyptian military aim.
61. 'Abdu Mubashir, *Yawmiyyat October fi Sina' wal-Julan* [*The October Diary in Sinai and the Golan*], Cairo: Dar al-Ma'arif bi-Misr, 1976, pp.24–5.
62. Hasan al-Badri, Taha al-Majdub and Dia' el Din Zohdi, *Harb Ramadan* [*The War of Ramadan*] (fourth edition), Jerusalem: Matba'at al-Sharq al-Ta'awuniyya, 1975, pp.50–1.
63. Hanokh Bartov, *Dado: Arba'im Shana Ve'od 'Esrim Yom* [*Dado: Forty Years and Twenty Days*], Tel Aviv: Ma'ariv, 1978, pp.245–51.
64. Yoel Ben-Porat, 'Milhemet Yom Hakippurim: Ta'ut Bemay Vehafta'a Beoctober' [The Yom Kippur War, Mistake in May and Surprise in October], *Ma'arachot* 299 (July–August 1985), pp.2–9; Sabri, *Watha'iq Harb October*, p.24. According to Heikal, *October 73*, pp.282, 301, the postponement was requested by King Faisal of Saudi Arabia.
65. Shlomo Aronson, 'The Nuclear Dimension of the Arab–Israeli Conflict: The Case of the Yom Kippur War', *The Jerusalem Journal of International Relations* 7/1-2 (1984), especially pp.116–20.

66. Yair Evron, 'The Relevance and Irrelevance of Nuclear Options in Conventional Wars: The 1973 October War', *The Jerusalem Journal of International Relations* 7/1-2 (1984), especially pp.158–63.
67. Sabri, *Watha'iq Harb October,* p.27. In January 1972, General Sadiq estimated the losses at the crossing by 17,500 and during the first four days (based on Soviet estimates) by 35,000; Heikal, *October 73,* p.251.
68. Sabri, *Watha'iq Harb October,* pp.69–70.
69. Bartov, *Dado,* pp.279–300.
70. Shazly, *The Crossing of the Suez,* pp.277–9; Fawzi, *Harb October,* p.14.
71. Tzvi Ofer, ed., *Tzva Iraq Bemilhemet Yom Hakippurim* [*Iraq's Army in the Yom Kippur War*], Tel Aviv: Ma'archot, 1986, p.67. The book is mostly a translation of a semi-official Iraqi book, published by al-Markaz al-'Arabi lil-Dirasat al-Istratijiyya, *Dawr al-Jaish al-'Iraqi fi Harb Tishrin 1973* [*The Role of the Iraqi Army in the October 1973 War*], Beirut: al-Mu'assassa al-'Arabiyya lil-Dirasat wal-Nashr, n.d.
72. 'Mavo' [Introduction], ibid., pp.20–1. For the Iraqi version regarding the lack of coordination, see ibid., pp.253–4.
73. David Inbar, 'Tzva Yarden Bemilhemet Yom Hakippurim' [The Jordanian Army in the Yom Kippur War], ibid., p.276.
74. Shwadran, *Middle East Oil,* p.72; Uzi B. Arad, 'The Short-Term Effectiveness of an Arab Oil Embargo', in H. Shaked and I. Rabinovich, eds, *The Middle East and the United States: Perceptions and Policies,* New Brunswick: Transaction Books, 1980, pp.244–5.
75. Ismail Fahmi, *Negotiating for Peace in the Middle East,* London: Croom Helm, 1983, p.109; Shazly, *The Crossing of the Suez,* p.278; Heikal, *The Road,* pp.267–70; Isma'il, *Amn Misr al-Qawmi fi 'Asr al-Tahaddiyat,* p.325.
76. Shwadran, *Middle East Oil,* pp.72–3. With the breakout of war Iraq nationalized the American share in the Basra Oil Company.
77. Isma'il, *Amn Misr al-Qawmi fi 'Asr al-Tahaddiyat,* p.315; Heikal, *The Road,* pp.214–16, 226–7; Sadat, *In Search of Identity,* pp.252–3; Seale, *Asad,* pp.210–11; Shazly, *The Crossing of the Suez,* pp.245–51; Fawzi, *Harb October,* pp.93–6. For another argument, suggesting that the offensive was an integral part of Egypt's strategic plan, see Jamasi, *Harb October 1973,* p.385.
78. For the texts of Sadat's and Asad's messages, see Heikal, *October 73,* pp.388–90.
79. Kissinger, *Years of Upheaval,* pp.499–500; Isma'il, *Amn Misr al-Qawmi fi 'Asr al-Tahaddiyat,* p.317.
80. Heikal, *The Road,* p.230; Sadat, *In Search of Identity,* pp.259–65; Riyad, *Mudhakkirat,* pp.466–8; *Baghdad Radio,* 29 October 1973, FBIS/DR, 30 October 1973; Ofer, *Tzva Iraq Bemilhemet Yom Hakippurim,* pp.255–7.
81. Golan, *Soviet Policies in the Middle East From World War Two to Gorbachev,* pp.88–94; Kissinger, *Years of Upheaval,* pp.545–99.
82. Shazly, *The Crossing of the Suez,* p.196.
83. Asad's interview, *Newsweek,* 25 February 1975; Ma'oz, *Asad,* pp.49, 105–6.
84. Kissinger, *Years of Upheaval,* pp.779–81, 783–4, 936–7; Seale, *Asad,* pp.227–49.

Operational Limitations of Reserve Forces: The Lessons of the 1973 War

STUART A. COHEN

Analyses of the performance of the Israel Defence Forces (IDF) in the Yom Kippur War of 1973 conventionally focus on two aspects of that episode. One is the cluster of circumstances responsible for the fact that the outbreak of war occurred under conditions which caught Israel totally by surprise. The other is the chronology of the military operations which eventually turned the tide of battle in Israel's favour, initially on the northern (Golan) front and subsequently in the south (Sinai) too.

These two phases of the Yom Kippur War have produced very different historiographical offspring. Retrospective accounts of the initial stage of surprise still generate heated debate: specifically, controversy continues to rage over whether responsibility for the failure to anticipate the outbreak of war lay more with Israel's military leaders than with its politicians.[1] By comparison, analyses of the subsequent battles seem to be suffused with an aura of general consensus. All accounts agree that – considering the disadvantageous conditions under which the IDF entered the war – its ultimate performance in each of the various theatres of fighting was outstanding. All also note that, of the several factors which turned the tide of the war, undoubtedly the most obtrusive was the heroic performance of the IDF's reservists. Plucked from their homes and synagogues with brutal suddenness, and pitched into the thick of battle at what was literally just a moment's notice, Israel's citizen-soldiers entirely fulfilled whatever expectations were held of them. Indeed, only their performance in the field saved Israel from military humiliation.[2]

Besides generating considerable national pride, the accomplishments of Israel's reservists also produced more practical results. Their performance was regarded as a vindication of the IDF's force structure as a whole. Whereas several other dimensions of Israeli strategic thinking were, as a result of the Yom Kippur War, subjected to critical scrutiny

Stuart A. Cohen is Professor of Political Studies at Bar-Ilan University, Ramat Gan, Israel.

(and in some cases overhauled[3]), the IDF's commitment to the retention of its traditional frameworks of military service was not affected at all. If anything, one of the lessons which the IDF High Command derived from the events of October 1973 was the need to reinforce the existing force structure, not least by expanding the reserve complement still further. During the course of 1974 and 1975, accordingly, draft registers were entirely overhauled; numerous categories of persons previously excused from reserve duty were recalled to the ranks; and regulations with respect to exemptions from service considerably tightened up.[4]

Under those conditions, the insistence on the need to maintain reserve strength, always paramount, became dogma. Indeed, such is still the case. Despite all the changes which have occurred in Israel's overall strategic environment in the quarter of a century since the Yom Kippur War,[5] and notwithstanding too the revolution currently affecting the composition of the IDF overall,[6] reliance on the reserves continues to dominate much of Israeli military thinking. Largely as a result of the lessons supposedly imparted by the course of the Yom Kippur War, it is still widely assumed that should the IDF ever again be committed to large-scale fighting the brunt of the burden will similarly have to fall on the reserve formations. As recently as 1996, one authoritative military account could still claim that 'The reserve army must be counted amongst the most important of the people of Israel's collective national creations'.[7]

The present article will not comment on the merits of that particular analysis. Instead, it aims to re-examine the extent to which it might be supported by the course of the Yom Kippur War. As far as the reservists are concerned, we shall argue, the lessons of 1973 in fact seem to be less straightforward than was once thought. True, IDF reservists did play a vital role in bringing about the ultimate battlefield outcome. What also has to be recognized, however, is the possibility that Israel's decision to rely so heavily on reserve forces might itself have contributed to the situation which made their heroic accomplishments so necessary. To put matters another way, the present article will suggest that one of the principal conclusions to be drawn from the events of 1973 is the span of operational *constraints* inherent in the maintenance of what is essentially a militia force structure. Israel's failure to recognize those constraints, and to integrate them into the IDF's military doctrine, constituted as much a part of its 'misconception' in 1973 as did its refusal to acknowledge the possibility that Egypt and Syria might go to war. Thus, whereas most studies of Israel's surprise on Yom Kippur indicate a conceptual failure most manifest at the level of intelligence 'anticipation',[8] the present article will point to similar faults at the planning level. Not the least of the IDF's shortcomings in the run-up to October 1973, we shall attempt to show, was its lack of attention to the highly complex infrastructure which a reserve army mandates and to the limited flexibility which it permits.

The article is divided into three consecutive parts. The first outlines Israel's pre-1973 military-strategic concepts as far as they affected the mobilization and deployment of reserve forces. The second analyzes the degree to which those concepts rose to the challenge of war. Finally, the article will posit some of the conclusions which might be drawn from this particular case study.

A word on sources: To the best of my knowledge, there exists no publicly available analysis of the mobilization of IDF reservists on 6 October 1973. Consequently, this article largely relies on memoirs and secondary accounts, many of which are more concerned with other aspects of the Yom Kippur War. Its main source, however, is the final version of the *Agranat Commission Report* [hereafter *ACR*], which although originally compiled in 1974, was not made available to the general public until over 20 years later (and even then with some deletions and in a limited form).[9] Even so, the Report remains the fullest available account of what transpired in Israel before the Yom Kippur War and during its initial stages. Indeed, the first-hand material which it contains, based primarily on interviews and cross-examination of key witnesses, is hardly ever likely to be bettered. Even if the IDF's archives are one day opened to public scrutiny, it is doubtful whether in relation to this particular subject they will be able to shed much more substantive light on events – if only because in the atmosphere of panic which suffused all levels of the IDF command on 6 October, very few precise records were kept.

RESERVES IN ISRAEL'S SECURITY DOCTRINE, 1949–1973

Recognition of the chronic demographic disparity between Israel and its potential enemies has always constituted one of the three basic parameters of the IDF's operational environment (the other two are (a) the absence of territorial 'strategic depth'; and (b) the imbalance in material means). True, the country has occasionally managed to benefit from the supplements to its indigenous pool of human resources provided by intermittent waves of large-scale Jewish immigration, such as occurred during the 1950s, with the arrival of large numbers of Jews from both the Orient and eastern Europe, and again during the early 1990s, with the influx of Jews from Ethiopia and the former USSR. Nevertheless, although obviously helpful, even these injections of manpower have amounted to only minor palliatives. Notwithstanding its comparatively high 'military participation ratio', Israel has never been able to place under arms anything more than a fraction of the human resources at the disposal of even its immediate neighbours, let alone the inhabitants of more distant Arab and/or Muslim lands.

Ever since 1949, the IDF's response to the strategic dilemmas posed by its inherent numerical disadvantage has taken two principal forms. One has been to offset quantitative demographic inferiority with qualitative human superiority, principally by exploiting to the utmost the edge provided by the comparatively high standards of Israeli high-school education and military training. The IDF's other response has been to maximize whatever resources are available for military purposes. Amongst other things, this has always meant treating reservists as an integral – and in some cases essential – component of Israel's overall order of battle. Neither in theory nor in practice has the IDF High Command ever regarded its reservists as 'supplementary' forces, who could only be entrusted with secondary duties and would not be called upon to fulfil serious fighting roles. Rather, Israel's reservists were always considered to be core combat troops – the most numerous, and indeed the most important, component of the IDF's total complement. In the words of David Ben-Gurion (1886–1973), Israel's first Prime Minister and Minister of Defence (he held both positions between 1948 and 1953 and from 1955 until 1963) and the man principally responsible for creating the IDF and defining Israel's formative security doctrines: 'Our security is based first and foremost on the reserve army ... on a fighting people which will be mobilized rapidly when the need arises.'[10]

The credo thus articulated explains why, from the very first, reserve units were fully integrated into the overall structure of IDF commands and formations. By law obliged to perform military duty of about one month every year until middle age, IDF reservists were trained (from battalion level and above) to operate alongside conscript forces. Hence, not only did reserve units share the burden of 'current security' missions, such as border patrols and guard duty. More to the point, their participation in battle was judged essential to victory in large-scale warfare, which has traditionally been categorized as a 'basic security' task.[11] By themselves, the IDF's standing forces (consisting of both professionals and compulsory conscripts) could only check and delay an enemy attack. Reservists would have to be fed into battle if the Force were ever to realize its aim of carrying the fight to the enemy's territory and attaining a military 'decision' in a series of deep, swift and preferably pre-emptive thrusts.[12]

Like virtually every other aspect of Israel's original military and strategic doctrine, the IDF's concept of the mobilization and utilization of reservists seemed to have been fully vindicated by the course of events during the Six Day War of 1967. In the euphoria of victory, little attention was paid to possible shortcomings in the IDF's force structure.[13] Instead, and perhaps inevitably, attention was focused on its benefits. First amongst the latter, of course, was the very high standard of battlefield dedication and tactical competence displayed in all the campaigns of June 1967 by the reserve troops themselves, whose experience and enthusiasm had made such large contributions to the ultimate results. But to this was added, in retrospect, a second and broader set of institutional and logistic benefits. Long-practised, the IDF's method of reserve mobilization had seemed to work efficiently, thereby allowing the High Command to deploy the maximum number of personnel and equipment at precisely the right locations, and to feed them into battle at exactly the right times.[14] In short, the IDF's victory in 1967 seemed to be as much a triumph of method as of will. It could be said to have owed almost as much to the reserve *system* as to the men (and women) responsible for its implementation.

This hypothesis was always misleading. After all, the Six Day War of 1967 had broken out in very special circumstances – of which the most relevant (certainly as far as any comparison with the Yom Kippur War is concerned) is that it was preceded by an extended 'waiting period'. This had lasted from 15 May 1967, when Egyptian forces first crossed into the Sinai in strength, until 6 June, when the IDF finally struck back. Although undoubtedly a psychologically stressful time, from an operational viewpoint those three weeks had constituted an immense military asset, since they allowed the IDF to iron out whatever faults in the reserve mobilization may have become apparent after the initial call-ups.[15] The situation was to be very different in 1973, when the vast majority of reservists did not receive a summons to duty until after fighting had commenced and hence possessed no leisure to rectify whatever faults in mobilization were bound to arise.

Altogether, in fact, the initial enthusiasm which characterized post-1967 analyses of the virtues of the IDF reserve structure seem to have been somewhat misplaced. They certainly provided no grounds for an assumption that the measures adopted in the past constituted an automatic recipe for success in the future. If anything, quite the opposite was the case. In several respects, the very extent of the IDF's martial success in 1967 necessitated a revision of the structures and frameworks which had helped to bring it about. Confronted with an entirely new geo-strategic situation, Israel's military planners should altogether have re-structured their operational doctrines and capabilities in order to meet novel demands.[16] Not least was this true where the reserve forces were concerned. In this particular area, the need for re-consideration was mandated by the fact that the very extent of the IDF's victory in 1967 had itself eroded some of the foundations upon which faith in the reserve structure had once rested. Changes were apparent in three major areas: societal, political and operational.

Although broadest in scope, the shift in the *societal* environment relative to the reserve forces in the period between 1967 and 1973 is the easiest to summarize. Given the post-1967 mood of disdain towards Arab military capabilities prevalent both in the IDF in particular and in Israeli society at large, it was now becoming doubtful whether all reservists could be relied upon to invest as much effort as before in attaining and maintaining the standards required in order to continue to offset the continuing Arab numerical advantage. (Combat reservists certainly evinced high motivation to service during the War of Attrition [1968–70]. Nevertheless, this situation did not necessarily apply to rear echelon troops. As we shall see below, by 1973 standards of maintenance at several IDF depots had become staggeringly negligent – a state of affairs for which only a hefty dose of hubris can possibly account.)

The intrusion of new *strategic* considerations, secondly, directed events in a similar direction. Once they had themselves recovered from the shock of victory, Israel's leaders had been emphatic in their insistence that the lines now occupied by the IDF were the most defensible, and hence 'the best' which the country could ever hope for. Basically, this was because they provided precisely the kind of territorial 'strategic depth' whose absence had thereto been one of Israel's primary weaknesses. But the claim that the country's security had never been more assured could hardly be sustained were the IDF to institute 'emergency' reserve mobilizations as regularly as had been the case when the frontiers had run much closer to centres of Israeli population.[17] This background explains much of the criticism which senior members of Israel's political echelon directed towards David Elazar, the Chief of Staff (COS), in April and May 1973, when he had announced that war might be imminent and had insisted on taking some limited precautions.[18] By some accounts, the same consideration, this time buttressed by the fact that elections were only a few weeks away, also explains much of Dayan's resistance to Elazar's demand for a large-scale mobilization of reserves early in the morning of 6 October 1973.[19]

Necessarily, however, the most important considerations relative to the reserves to have altered in the wake of the Six Day War were more narrowly *operational*. More specifically, they focused on the element of time. Prior to 1967, the shortness of distances between Israel's borders and the IDF's forward bases had virtually ensured that, once mobilized, reserves would be able to arrive on the scene of fighting almost immediately. Hence, even if surprised by a sudden movement of enemy forces, the close geographical proximity of Israeli bases and stores to the front-line had enabled the establishment of a reserve-based 'buffer' force with reasonable speed. That, for instance, is precisely what occurred in February 1960, when the IDF mobilized a limited number of reservists ('Operation Rotem') in response to an unexpected concentration of Egyptian troops in the Sinai.[20] After 1967, however, there existed no guarantee whatsoever that such exercises could be repeated. On the contrary, the IDF now seemed more vulnerable to operational surprise than at any previous stage in its history. So extensive had been Israel's conquests in the Six Day War that the distances from forward bases to all the front lines had been lengthened – and in the case of the most important front (i.e. southern command) as much as tripled. Equally extended, therefore, were the travelling times now required by the reserve troops themselves. As Elazar himself pointed out to the IDF General Staff on 8 May 1973:

> There is another problem, and it is the duration of the preparations which we need in order to be ready for war. ... We need a sum total

of 'X' hours ... in order to deploy the force without stress.... The entire purpose of all this argumentation is to emphasize one thing: the concentration of forces [known in IDF jargon as '*kuf*'-hour] has to start before the shooting begins ['*shin*'-hour].[21]

How to earn the extra time now required in order to bring the full weight of the IDF's reserve strength to bear on the battlefield thus became a cardinal operational question. Indeed, according to one retrospective account, searches for an answer lay at the very heart of much of the Israeli General Staff's post-1967 contingency planning.[22] One possible solution was to re-locate a larger number of emergency depots closer to the front lines, and thereby cut down on the distances to be covered by much of the reservists' cumbersome and relatively slow-moving transports and equipment. Another was to strengthen fortifications along the new frontiers themselves, and thereby increase their value as delaying devices in the event of an enemy attack. Both ideas generated considerable discussion. In practice, however, very little was accomplished prior to the outbreak of war in October 1973. True, several steps were taken to improve matters in the north – both by constructing a new set of forward depots in the eastern Galilee (considerably closer to the Golan Heights than were the old bases in the Haifa area) and by laying mine-fields along the anti-tank ditch on the Golan itself. But nothing similar was accomplished on the Sinai front. There, if anything, some regression seems to have occurred. Not only did southern command fail to implement various suggestions for improving its reserve assembly and dispatch abilities. It also permitted the string of strongholds and fortified points along the Canal (the *ma'ozim* and *ta'ozim* which made up the so-called 'Bar-Lev line', constructed between 1968 and 1970) to fall into considerable disrepair. By October 1973, many of the posts were – deliberately – not manned at all. Of the remainder, several were barely adequate even as 'observation posts'. As 'delaying devices' they were useless.[23]

Instead of implementing many of the concrete measures which might have given Israel's reserves the extra time which they now needed, between 1967 and 1973 the IDF General Staff seems to have resorted to a completely different option. It preferred to rely on AMAN, the IDF Intelligence Branch, to provide adequate warning of any impending attack.[24] On the assumption that sufficient warning would indeed be forthcoming, it was simply taken for granted that the reserves would have enough leisure to mobilize, equip themselves and deploy prior to their services being required. In the prevailing atmosphere of almost mystic confidence in AMAN's ability to receive and interpret the necessary warning signals, most senior officers in the IDF regarded as much as a week's notice of an impending attack to be a 'reasonable' expectation, and five to six days a 'realistic' prospect; 48 hours' notice was considered virtually the barest minimum.[25] Anything less was simply relegated to the level of a 'catastrophe' – and in that case (according to the Vice-Chief of Staff) 'there's no point in making any plan at all'(!)[26] As a somewhat hapless Elazar later attempted to explain to the understandably incredulous Agranat commissioners:

> We really never did plan [for a contingency] in which '*kuf*' coincided with '*shin*'.... That is to say, from the very start we never planned that '*kuf*' and '*shin*' would be simultaneous and that we would have no warning.... So we always had this assumption that there would have to be some advance warning, and we never planned that '*kuf*' equals '*shin*'.[27]

Thus to indicate the weaknesses underlying senior IDF thinking prior to 1973 is not to suggest that Israel's senior military commanders did not expect ever to need to confront an enemy attack on one or more of their borders. On the contrary, they drew up very detailed plans in order to meet precisely such an eventuality. What the evidence does show, however, is that they expected an enemy attack to occur under a very specific set of (favourable) circumstances. To put matters another way, their shortcoming did not consist of their failure to anticipate *any* attack. Rather, theirs was a failure to anticipate the sort of attack which might nullify the entire cluster of preconceptions upon which their battle plans ultimately rested. As much becomes evident once attention is focused on the IDF's operational plans themselves.

Basic to all IDF operational planning, certainly under the aegis of Elazar, were two fundamental concepts: one relating to the character of the fighting; the other more specifically concentrated on its locus. As to the character, there was general agreement that the next war – unlike the War of Attrition of 1969–1970, but in keeping with the operational style adopted by the IDF in all its other previous campaigns – would have to end with a decisive and smashing military victory. Only thus could Israel be granted another lengthy 'breathing space' from future conflict.[28] Victory on that scale was not to be achieved, however, by allowing the invading Arab armies to penetrate Israeli-held territory and then trapping them in a massive armoured vice from which they could not possibly escape. Attractive though such a prospect might initially appear (Elazar once bragged: 'that would be a new chapter for Clausewitz'[29]), it was ruled out by the need to prevent the enemy making any initial local gains on the ground, which he might thereafter be able to convert into political capital. Instead, Israeli forces were to move as quickly as possible on to the offensive, and to carry the battle – with all forces at their disposal (that is, including the reserves) – to enemy territory. In the COS's own directives, issued to his staff at the conclusion of a planning session held on 2 May 1973:

> ...I want us all to be absolutely aware of the fact that our problem – should war indeed break out – is to attack very quickly and to attain

substantive and meaningful gains. That is the object. I do not
visualize any messing around with an extended war, developing war,
attrition etc. What I certainly do see – and this has relevance for
early decisions on our part, for our preliminary preparations and for
our readiness – is to carry out an offensive immediately.[30]

'Desert Cat' (in Hebrew *Chatul Midbar*) and 'Prairie Wolf' (*Ze'ev
Aravot*) were the generic code-names initially allotted to the most far-
reaching of the plans outlining the offensive operations which, in the
south and north respectively, were thus to constitute the summit of all
IDF operations in a future war.[31] What they envisaged was a massive
deployment of IDF armour – most of which would be manned by
reservists – far into enemy territory. But, as all Israeli military authorities
appreciated, the deep thrusts envisaged in both of these plans were
unlikely to be executed without some preliminaries having first taken
place. It was far more probable that the next war would commence with
an attack launched by Egypt and/or Syria, rather than by Israel. Hence,
the IDF had also to draw up a series of contingency directives which,
although ultimately designed to serve as preludes to such offensive
operations as 'Desert Cat' and/or 'Prairie Wolf' were in orientation
designed to 'contain' the enemy's initial thrust.[32]
Two clusters of contingency plans did in fact exist:

- The first was comparatively limited in scope, and was encapsulated in
  plans 'Dovecote' (*Shovach Yonim*) for the southern front and 'Chalk'
  (*Gir*) for the north. Conceived long before 1973, and formally
  reformulated and re-affirmed by the General Staff as recently as
  December 1972, 'Dovecote/Chalk' in effect provided for little more
  than holding operations. On receipt of warning of an imminent
  enemy attack, the regional commands were to reposition the
  armoured and infantry forces already in place on their fronts into
  pre-assigned locations, and to bring into line additional formations –
  most of which would consist solely of conscript troops. All such
  depositions were to be completed and the troops in place within 72
  hours of receiving initial warning.[33]
- Much more comprehensive in scope was 'Rock' (*Sela*). This
  envisioned responding to warnings of an enemy attack by a much
  larger, and lengthier, build-up of forces on both the northern and
  southern fronts – a process which would necessitate the mobilization
  and deployment of the main body of the reserves and which would
  take some five to seven days. During that period, the hostile offensive
  would have been contained (by the 'Dovecote/Chalk' formations).
  This would allow the troops massed by virtue of 'Rock' to take
  explicitly offensive action – first by smashing whatever resistance
  remained behind Israeli lines and then by carrying the battle to enemy
  territory and thus implementing 'Desert Cat'.

Thus outlined, IDF contingency plans for an enemy attack resembled a system of three inter-locking tiers,[34] each of which could be implemented independently or in sequence, depending on the manner in which events unfolded. What distinguished between these tiers was the scope and size of the forces which they encompassed. In this respect, the differences between plan 'Rock', on the one hand, and plans 'Dovecote/Chalk', on the other, are especially instructive.

Seen as an essential prelude to the full-scale offensives provided for in 'Desert Cat' and 'Prairie Wolf', plan 'Rock' called for the full mobilization of Israel's entire reserve capacity. In effect, what it envisaged was a virtual repetition of the scenario played out on the ground during the three-week long 'waiting period' of 15 May – 6 June in 1967. Then, too (as noted above), the implementation of the IDF's offensive plans had been preceded by the mobilization and deployment of the reserve forces upon which the execution of those plans had always been recognized to depend.

By contrast, the level of operational activity encompassed by plans 'Dovecote/Chalk' was entirely different. Their execution would be accomplished by activating little more than the standing army. The number of reservists to be mobilized would be relatively small, and limited almost entirely to a cluster of logistic and combat-support units. In other words, under the terms of 'Dovecote/Chalk' the IDF would expect to contain – or, even better, to deter – the attack with forces in being. That is basically what had occurred during the early and mid-summer of 1973, the last period of military tension prior to Yom Kippur itself. Fearing the possibility of an attack, even though the likelihood was rated 'very low' by AMAN, Elazar had then put into operation 'Blue-White' (*Kachol-Lavan*), in effect a variant of 'Dovecote'. In May 1973, when tension was at its height, the IDF deployed nearly 200 tanks on the Golan and almost 300 in the Sinai. Nevertheless, very few reservists were mobilized for this purpose; almost the entire burden was shouldered by standing forces. Similarly, most of the budgetary outlays attributed to 'Blue-White' (the famous 'sixty million lirot' which Elazar would be warned not to squander again early in October) were not the result of mobilizations but of speeded-up investments in the construction of new fortifications and additional forward depots.[35]

More germane than the differences which thus distinguished between the IDF's triple-tiered cluster of operational plans in 1973, were those features which they shared in common. All, in fact, were based on a core of at least four common assumptions.

- The first, and most obvious, was that the IDF High Command would receive adequate warning of an impending attack, and thereafter communicate that warning both to the regional commands and to the political echelon.[36]
- A second was that the regional commands would immediately

implement the first tier of plans ('Dovecote/Chalk'), and that the political echelon – at the IDF's request – would forthwith authorize the scope of reserve mobilization mandated by the next stage in the planning process ('Rock').

- The third assumption was that, should fighting break out before the reserve mobilization was complete, the regular forces in being – having been deployed in accordance with 'Dovecote/Chalk' – would, with the close support of the Israel Air Force (about which more below), meanwhile be able to contain whatever offensives the enemy could manage to mount.[37]

- Finally, it was assumed that all of the various stages of mobilization and deployment would be carried out smoothly and with the minimum of turbulence (the 'friction' of Clausewitzian fame).

As the next section of the present article will demonstrate, each of these assumptions would be put to the test in the final days before the outbreak of the Yom Kippur War – and each was to be found wanting.

APPLYING THE RESERVE CONCEPT

The Stage of Warning

In both their interim and final reports, the Agranat Commissioners emphasized the degree to which the absence of adequate warning contributed to the failure to mobilize the reserves in time. According to the commissioners, responsibility for this fault, which nullified the first of the assumptions upon which all IDF pre-1973 plans were predicated, lay with two specific persons. One was the head of AMAN, Maj.-Gen. Eli Zeira, who did not appreciate the extent to which an enemy offensive was imminent (a fault which the Commissioners attributed to his steadfast adherence to the prevailing 'conception' that the Arabs would not attack, and that all the signs indicating their preparedness to do so could therefore safely be ignored or discounted). The other individual whom the Agranat Commissioners found guilty of negligence was the Chief of Staff himself. Quite apart from his various other failings, General David Elazar was judged to have acted with insufficient caution in the light of such information as he did have to hand. Considering the vast numerical disparity between the IDF and its potential adversaries, the Agranat Commissioners determined that the Chief of Staff should have responded far more cautiously to even the slightest hint that an outbreak of hostilities was possible. Specifically: 'Given the circumstances, he [the COS] should have recommended partial mobilization of reserves as early as 1 October, when the [Egyptian] "exercise" commenced, or at the very latest on 5 October'.[38]

Whether or not Elazar and Zeira were in fact as culpable as the Agranat report maintained lies beyond the scope of the present article.[39]

What remains relevant is that, throughout the period specified by the Agranat Report, very little was in fact done to bolster the IDF's defences. True, at the initiative of the CO Northern Command (Maj.-Gen. Yitzhak Hofi), some steps were taken as early as 26 September to supplement the armoured forces maintained on the Golan Heights. True, too, that during the course of the following days the General Staff Operations Branch issued two sets of directives ('*ashur I*', on 1 October, and '*ashur II*' on 5 October), both of which specified various troop re-deployments in the light of the situation. Moreover, and also on 5 October, the Chief of Staff ordered that the entire IDF enter into the highest stage of alert ('Alert C'). All of these steps, however, were designed to do no more than implement the initial stages of 'Dovecote/Chalk' – i.e. the very first of the IDF's three operational tiers. Hence, they made no provisions whatsoever for the mobilization *of reserves*. On the contrary, some reservists were in fact released that week. Those manning the posts on the Suez Canal, for instance, continued with their accustomed rotation of leave; and even in the north (where staff officers seem to have been altogether more sensitive to the possibility of danger) most of the reserve brigade summoned to a pre-planned and routine call-up exercise which commenced on 30 September was de-mobilized the following day, only one battalion being kept behind.[40]

There is no gainsaying the *psychological* importance of the fact that, until as late as dawn on 6 October 1973, the IDF high command was totally unaware that an Egyptian–Syrian attack was planned for that day (and that even when confirmation was received, warnings relating to the precise time of the onslaught erred by a margin of some four hours).[41] Surprise, when it came, was so complete that it had a debilitating effect on all levels of command. Nevertheless, it still remains doubtful whether the absence of a warning ultimately possessed as much *operational* significance as the Agranat Commissioners suggested. On this point, their interpretation of events seems particularly biased. Focusing their attention on what they considered the Chief of Staff perhaps *should* have done, the Commissioners neglected to take sufficient account of what – given the constraints imposed by the structure of the IDF's reserve forces – he *could* have accomplished. A fresh look at the evidence suggests, in fact, that responsibility for the Chief of Staff's sins of omission in the week preceding 5 October does not rest solely with either AMAN's misinterpretation of the warning signals which it received, nor even with Elazar's own failure to check the sources for himself. Equally worthy of attention is his apparent ignorance of the constraints exerted on his freedom of operational manoeuvre by his entire concept of reserve forces and their use.

Even had Elazar been supplied with adequate warning that an attack was imminent and unavoidable, there is no reason to think that he would have used this information in order to bolster the IDF's defensive dispositions with reserve formations. None of the IDF's pre-war plans, it will be recalled, called for the mobilization of reserves for *defence*. Rather, mobilization was seen as a necessary prelude to *attack*. The 'Dovecote/Chalk' plans were predicated on that hypothesis – which (as noted above) is precisely why they were *not* implemented during Operation 'Blue-White' in May 1973. In this respect, nothing had changed by September–October 1973. Then, too, none of the plans entrusted the reserve with a defensive role.[42] Instead, once mobilized, they were to provide the forces for the massive offensive operations which Elazar always considered to be the key to victory. Virtually ignored in the Agranat Commission's explanation for the initial run of Syrian and Egyptian successes, this consideration was noted some years later with particular emphasis by one of the military experts who had worked on the Commission staff:

> If we attempt to reconstruct the mindset in the IDF prior to 1973, we find that even had the reserves been mobilized prior to the war – they would not have been fed into the defensive formation. Instead, they would have been kept for the shift to the offensive phase. In those years, even conscript forces, originally intended for defence, were in some cases pulled out of the line, so that they could be kept for the attack. Thus, for instance, the forward [defence] line in the Sinai, which was originally planned to be divided into three divisional fronts, was on the eve of war in fact divided into just two fronts – apparently in order to allow the third division to take part in the attack.[43]

The Stage of Decision

The magnitude of the constraints exerted on the IDF's freedom of strategic manoeuvre by its own pre-war concept of reserve dispositions became still more starkly apparent in the early hours of 6 October. What is more, the course of events that morning also indicated the extent of the fallacy in the second of the assumptions noted above: that the political echelon would automatically endorse whatever recommendation the COS might tender with respect to the mobilization of the reserves and their deployment.

The mobilization of reserves had always been a particularly sensitive issue in Israeli civil-military relations. Only in part was that because of the importance which (as has been seen) the country's security doctrine traditionally attached to the reserve component as the primary source of the IDF's military 'surge' capacity. Still more profound was the influence exerted by an awareness of the wider political repercussions to which mobilization might lead. After all, once mobilized, the reserves could not be kept in the field indefinitely. Inevitably, budgetary considerations would soon combine with societal strains to mandate that they either be disbanded or sent into battle forthwith. Whilst the former option was of course always possible, sensitivity to the fragility of Israel's security margins made the latter far more likely. Indeed, the pressure on Israel's policy-makers to move from mobilization to action could become well-nigh irresistible.[44]

That background explains why decisions affecting the mobilization of IDF reserves had never been taken lightly. Both the political and military components of Israel's security establishment had always appreciated that any such action threatened to narrow, rather than widen, their spectrum of strategic choices.[45] Even if mobilization was not tantamount to a declaration of war (as is said to have been the case in Europe in 1914[46]), it certainly substantively increased the probability of an outbreak of hostilities. For that reason, the entire process had to be carefully regulated and controlled. Indeed, it had long been an axiom of Israeli strategic thought that, other than in conditions of a clear-cut *casus belli*, the procedure of mobilization was best avoided altogether. As much had been explicitly pointed out by Elazar to the Prime Minister during the minor war-scare of May 1973: 'We neither desire nor advise the large-scale mobilization of reserves together with other measures which might get out of control and lead to war'.[47]

If Zeira's record is to be believed, the issue of authorization for a reserve mobilization in October 1973 first arose during the short Cabinet meeting called on 5 October. Since the probability of war was at that juncture still rated 'very low', most ministers understandably considered the issue of mobilization to be entirely hypothetical. Nevertheless, by the end of a brief discussion on the subject, definite constitutional ground rules had been laid down and clarified. Ideally, it was agreed, reserve mobilization was a matter for decision by the Cabinet as a whole. However, in the event of an emergency, the COS would bring his recommendation to the Defence Minister, Moshe Dayan, who would then seek authorization from the Prime Minister. Thus, in Dayan's own summary:

> If anything should happen on Yom Kippur [i.e. 6 October] – before the [regular] Cabinet meeting on Sunday [7 October] – we will make do with the decision of the prime minister on all matters, whether to mobilize the reserves or to begin a counter-bombing. I do not imagine that it will be possible to convene the Cabinet at the same speed. In any case, my working hypothesis is that it will be OK (in Hebrew: *beseder*) and legal etc.[48]

Designed as a time-saving mechanism, the procedure thus instituted was obviously based on the implicit understanding that the Prime Minister, Golda Meir, would in fact have to fulfil little more than a formal role. Representing the entire cabinet, she would merely have to sanction a policy on which Dayan and Elazar, her two senior military advisers, had already reached agreement. But what would her position be were the COS and the Minister of Defence to disagree? Would the Prime Minister, alone, then act as a last court of appeal? Or would she be duty-bound to consult with her entire Cabinet? These questions were apparently never discussed, probably because it was taken for granted that – on an issue so basic to Israel's security as reserve mobilization – divergences of opinion between the COS and the Minister of Defence were intrinsically unlikely to occur.

Under most circumstances, that assumption would undoubtedly have been warranted. Even though personal relationships between Dayan and Elazar were never particularly warm,[49] they did possess a record of intimate professional association which went back almost 30 years. What is more, both had internalized an even longer tradition of 'partnership' between Israel's civil and military elites, and had risen through the ranks at a time when the maintenance of a consensus at the most senior level of national security decision-making had widely been accorded the status of an ideological imperative.[50] The problem lay, however, in the fact that the circumstances which both men faced in the early hours of 6 October were exceptional in the extreme. And it was precisely because such was the case that the issue of reserve mobilization was most likely to generate friction.

Confronted with news that a massive attack on his forces was imminent, Elazar seems instinctively to have looked to immediate and large-scale mobilization as one of the means whereby he might turn the tables (the other was a pre-emptive air strike, on which see note 74, below). Only thus could he himself move, as planned, on to the offensive. Dayan's priorities were very different. At this stage, he was still thinking in terms of deterrence or, if deterrence failed, of defence. Hence, not only was he adamantly opposed to the notion of a pre-emptive air strike, he was also averse to any reserve mobilization larger than that required for Israel's territorial protection. A full-scale mobilization, he seems to have feared, might precipitate the very war which he still wished to avert. As he himself told Elazar in the course of what appears to have been an understandably tense exchange between the hours of 05.50 and 07.00 on the morning of 6 October:

> [I am] sceptical about mobilizing for a counter-attack in a war which has not yet begun. [On the other hand] if it is certain that war will break out, [we should] certainly mobilize reserves for defence. That is panic enough for the Syrians.[51]

In practical terms, this difference led to a disparity of numbers. Elazar, who had on his own initiative already ordered that Air Forces reservists be called up, now pressed for an immediate mobilization of almost 200,000 additional ground troops ('I want to be ready in minimal time to move on to a counter-offensive and destroy the Syrian army'). Dayan, however, refused to sanction any more than a total of some 50,000–60,000 personnel ('the Air Force, one division in the north and another in the south'). With their positions at such variance, both men eventually decided to refer the entire matter to the Prime Minister at 9am.

The Agranat Report strongly criticized Elazar for not taking what Dayan had offered. On the principle that half a cake is always better than none, the Commissioners argued, the COS should have immediately mobilized the 50,000–60,000 reservists for which he did have the Minister's authorization, leaving only the remainder for Meir's subsequent decision. Instead, he preferred to hold out for a much more extensive mobilization, and hence between 7 and 9am issued no additional summonses to duty at all. True (with what the Report noted to have been commendable alacrity), Meir did soon overrule her Minister of Defence, and at 09.25 gave Elazar the authorization for the large-scale mobilization which he had originally requested. Meanwhile, however, two vital hours had been wasted.[52]

Now that the emotional turbulence generated by the Yom Kippur War has begun to subside, it is perhaps possible to review the evidence somewhat more dispassionately. Elazar's decision not to set in motion a partial mobilization, it appears, cannot be attributed to a momentary lapse of judgement. Rather, it resulted from a deeper failure to comprehend the extent to which, under his aegis, the place allotted to the reserves in the IDF's overall order of battle had come to hold Israel's entire strategy in thrall. His fault, then, was to have predicated virtually all his operational thinking on the premise that the prime function of the reserves would be to mount an attack and that – once requested – political authorization for their use in that capacity would automatically be forthcoming. Notwithstanding his own lip-service on earlier occasions to the importance of diplomatic considerations in strategic planning, he seems to have lacked any true sensitivity for the degree to which his troop dispositions might be regarded as a constraint on the country's freedom of political action. Completely absent, therefore, was an appreciation of the possible need to prepare some alternatives courses of action. When most needed, no such alternatives were found to exist.

Analyzed from that perspective, the core of the argument between Israel's COS and the Defence Minister on the morning of 6 October appears to have been about much more than numbers. Even to portray their dispute as a clash between rival operational preferences (with Dayan advocating defensive action and Elazar an offensive campaign) is, it seems, to over-simplify a far more complicated situation.[53] A closer reading of what each man is reported to have said suggests, rather, that they were groping – very belatedly – for ways in which to articulate what each considered large-scale or partial mobilization to entail. At stake, in fact, was a divergent calculus of the strategic costs and benefits which the IDF's existing plans might entail. As befitted a COS, Elazar himself accorded priority to the immediate military risks of not mobilizing (so too, apparently even more forcefully, did Golda Meir: 'I have one criterion: if war really does break out, we have to be in the very best [military] situation'[54]). Dayan, by contrast – perhaps because he still hoped that war might anyway be avoided, and if not that its outbreak was still several hours away – emphasized instead the diplomatic price which a large-scale mobilization would entail:

> I think that even with many difficulties it is worth our while to begin [the war] in a good position from an international point of view, because we are not as free as were in 1967. As far as tonight is concerned [full or partial mobilization] will make no difference [to the fighting].[55]

The Role of the Air Force

Elazar fully shared Dayan's confidence that the extent of mobilization would prove immaterial in the first round of fighting. He had always expected the regular forces, together with such reserves as were engaged in routine duties, to be able to contain whatever onslaught the Arabs might launch against them without any further assistance. A war game ('Iron Ram'; in Hebrew '*Ayyil Barzel*') conducted by southern command as recently as August 1972 had seemingly confirmed that impression. In that game, the regular IDF forces, although given only 24 hours notice of an Egyptian onslaught on the Sinai peninsula, had successfully beaten back an Egyptian attempt to cross the Suez Canal – without any need for an extraordinary mobilization of additional reserves at all.[56]

Elazar's conviction that the results of that war-game could be reproduced in a real-life situation was based on his assessment that the IDF possessed two critical advantages. One was the inherent ability of the average Israeli soldier, whose superb fighting qualities were deemed to make him the equal of at least a dozen of his foes.[57] The other was the assistance which the ground forces could expect to receive from the Israel Air Force, the branch of service which had been chiefly responsible for the scale and speed of triumph in 1967. Ever since the Six Day War, the Air Force had been regarded in the IDF as a superb 'flying artillery',[58] capable of supplying close air support (CAS) to ground troops virtually on demand. More generally, it had also been considered Israel's ultimate 'insurance policy', and a safeguard against whatever mishaps might possibly occur. This concept, quite apart from being based on the operational reputation of the Israeli Air Force (IAF), was also rooted in the knowledge that its composition was far more 'professional' than that of most other Israeli military branches, and its dependence on reservists correspondingly slight. To all intents and purposes, therefore, the Air Force constituted a 'quick reaction force', whose ability to maintain a particularly high state of readiness and alert was especially pronounced.[59]

For whichever reason, the idea that the ability of the Air Force obviated the necessity for an immediate mobilization of the ground force reserves had long been considered axiomatic. Throughout 1973, in particular, this theme came to constitute a virtual mantra in Elazar's presentations. Thus, at the height of the May alarm, he informed the

Prime Minister that:

> The fact that the balance of ground forces is as I have described, and the fact that *we dare not to undertake a prior mobilization of reserves* [emphasis in original], derives from the ability of the Air Force to halt and contain [the enemy] in the event of an attack on one of the two fronts.[60]

Similarly, in July 1973, he justified the Air Force's receipt of as much as 52 per cent of the IDF's entire annual budget, on the grounds that:

> [The Air Force] can permit us to mobilize the IDF and concentrate the strength of the IDF reserves in the event of war. It is the Air Force which will close this gap [between the IDF and enemy forces] during the first 24 or 72 hours.[61]

As late as 5 October, the Chief of Staff was still justifying his resistance to the mobilization of the reserves by re-emphasizing his belief that:

> Should the worst thing possible occur, that is to say that a large-scale attack would be opened without so much as another word, then we shall have to contain it by means of the regular forces. That is to say, by means of the Air Force and all the forces which we have on the lines....'[62]

The great virtue of the strategy thus outlined by Elazar lay in its economy. It seemed to promise the IDF maximum success at a minimum cost. Israel would not need to mobilize its own ground reserves in order to defeat an enemy ground offensive. Instead, it could do so simply by exploiting to the full its proven superiority in the air. Therein, however, also lay the possible flaw in this line of thinking. In the last resort, it entrusted the Air Force with prime responsibility for the fate of the battle, certainly in its early stages. Should, for any reason, the Air Force be unable to rise to the challenge of providing the ground forces with the close air support which they required in order to repel an invader, then Israel's entire security concept would be in danger of collapse.

By 1973, there did indeed exist two principal reasons to fear that precisely such a condition now existed: one tactical; the other strategic. Although not necessarily related, these two flaws had combined to produce a situation which undermined much of the reasoning on which Elazar had based his confidence in the scale of CAS which he thought obviated the need to call upon the reserves to repel an attack.

The *tactical* flaw amounted to a fundamental lack of preparedness for the sort of air–land cooperation upon which the effectiveness of close air support to ground forces ultimately depends. This failure was manifest at several levels and affected virtually every echelon. Israeli pilots, for instance, had been trained to deliver simple, short-range attack sorties at undefended ground-force targets, and thus to fight under the sort of conditions which had prevailed in 1967. Very little thought had apparently been given to the possibility that the pilots might encounter massive enemy forces and heavy air defence resistance from a barrage of missiles and guns – which is exactly what happened in the first days of the war of October 1973.[63] To this must be added, second, the fact that the IDF altogether lacked a sophisticated targeting system. In the words of the report compiled by Cordesman and Wagner (altogether the most comprehensive of the available analyses on this particular topic):

> Israel had virtually no advanced targeting aids [and] relatively poor land-based sensors.... Israeli ground forces relied on line-of-sight, armoured reconnaissance, and slow arriving air reconnaissance.... No assets existed to adequately track Arab infantry forces, mobile SAMs, and radar-guided AA guns.... Forward air controllers were lacking and poorly trained and equipped.[64]

Above all, the IAF possessed no real air attack operations centre. To cite Cordesman and Wagner once again:

> Before 1973 the IDF failed to create an effective C³I system for attack missions to match its system for air combat. It relied on air superiority to give its attack aircraft freedom of action and on ground commanders to call in attack sorties with only limited central control. It was forced to create an improvised command staff after the war began and to develop tactics for planning and allocating sorties to take account of Arab SAM and other air defences in the midst of the fog of war.[65]

Whilst the tactical flaws vitiating Elazar's reliance on close air support did not become fully apparent until the Yom Kippur War had finally run its course, the *strategic* shortcomings in his thinking should have been evident some years earlier. Principally, this was because of the new dimension in local air warfare apparent ever since 1970, with the introduction into the middle east of the most recent generation of Soviet surface to air missiles (SAM-3s), whose presence in thick clusters on Israel's southern front at the end of the War of Attrition had become especially marked.[66] Confronted with this new threat to its freedom of activity over the prospective zone of fighting (later exacerbated by the introduction of large numbers of SAM-6 batteries and SAM-7 portable missile launchers into the Syrian and Egyptian air defence systems), the IAF had been compelled to revise its menu of basic mission definitions. In keeping with what had always been standard practice, the Air Force's first priorities remained:

- 'the defence of the state's skies' (i.e. the maintenance of an ability to prevent any enemy incursion of Israel's air space, principally by air-to-air combat);
- in case of war, the destruction of enemy air forces, principally by attacking their bases.

However, whereas 'close air support' (CAS) to IDF ground forces had traditionally come a close third behind these first two missions, since 1970 it had been pushed further down the ladder of priorities. In the most recent formulation of IAF mission statements, CAS was now to be preceded by 'the destruction of the enemy's anti-aircraft system'.[67] Indeed, the latter was recognized to constitute a *sine qua non* of assistance to ground forces. As recently as May 1973, representatives of the Air Force had warned both the COS and the Minister of Defence that, even under optimal conditions (i.e. adequate warning time) it might take them as long as two full days to complete the destruction of the enemy's air force as well as his missile umbrella.[68] Only once they had done so, would they be free to turn their attention to events on the ground. In Herzog's summary:

> The Israeli Air Force prepared for the coming war on the assumption that at the outbreak of the conflict it would be given adequate time to concentrate on the missile threat, without being involved in interdiction or close air support.... The Air Force was to enjoy a certain latitude without being obliged to care for ground forces.[69]

The implication of this situation, as Eli Zeira has recently pointed out with considerable passion and emphasis,[70] is that there existed no correlation between Elazar's timetable for the first stages of a future war and that of the IAF. Although intellectually aware of the implications of the missile threat,[71] the COS does not seem to have assimilated the information. Hence, his contingency plans for future war still counted on the immediate and massive use of air power in order to repel an invasion force. His air commanders, however, were thinking on very different lines. Since the IAF maintained only 14 fighter planes in a state of immediate readiness in order to guard against enemy intrusions of Israel's airspace (mission no. [i][72]), they now calculated that they would require a 'minimal' warning time of several hours to accomplish their second and third missions (the destruction of Arab air forces and missiles). Until they had done so, IDF ground forces would simply have to fend for themselves.

The inconsistencies in Elazar's assumption that Israel's air superiority obviated the need for a pre-emptive mobilization of the reserves became brutally apparent during the course of 6 October 1973. According to the Agranat Report, the COS's very first action after hearing (at 4.30am) that an attack was imminent was to contact the Air Force commander, Major-General Binyamin Peled.[73] Later that morning, the two men conversed at least four more times, twice face to face. But although Peled had taken the precaution of mobilizing some of his own reserves (mostly consisting of technical support units) the previous day, and received Elazar's immediate authorization to call up the remainder, it was now far too late to change the IAF's existing contingency plans.

Weather conditions permitting, the IAF was prepared to carry out a pre-emptive air attack on Syrian and Egyptian missile sites. Had political sanction been forthcoming, Peled might also have been ready to strike at one or the other of the enemy's air forces.[74] But, as both he and Elazar appreciated, the available force menus simply did not encompass the steps now most urgently required: either a pre-emptive strike against Arab *ground* concentrations or, failing that, immediate close air support to IDF troops in the event of an Arab attack. Hence, at a General Staff Operational Consultative Group (KEDEM) meeting held at 10am on the morning of 6 October, Elazar was forced to recognize that the IAF's battle priorities remained as before:

> action ... against the Syrian and Egyptian air forces, the Syrian and Egyptian missile systems, and in third order of priority, support to ground forces.[75]

As late as 11am Peled himself was still working under the assumption that such would be his sequence of actions, and only at 12.30 (when, by his own cautious estimate, there remained barely two and a half hours until the enemy attack would commence) did he give orders to change the armament on IAF jet fighters so that they might furnish the ground troops with whatever support they could. Even so, as he later admitted, 'there existed no clear picture as to who would cross [the frontiers], where and when'. Hence, he was reduced to improvising, or, in his own words: 'playing in accordance with the flow of events'.[76]

The results were very nearly disastrous. Instead of attaining immediate air superiority, the IAF was itself forced to fight a battle for its very survival. Under those conditions, there was little hope that it would be able to provide effective CAS (especially, as we have seen, because it was not tactically equipped to do so). In the last analysis, therefore – and contrary to all of Elazar's previous assumptions – the resort to air power could not obviate the use of reservists. If anything, the situation in the air made their immediate mobilization still more imperative.

Feeding Reserves into Battle

Orders for a large-scale mobilization of IDF reserves were ultimately issued, it will be recalled, at around 9.30am on 6 October. Given the failure of every other assumption on which Israel's pre-war planning had been based, all now depended on the speed and efficiency with which the reservists could be fed into the battle.

If there was one contingency for which the IDF was supposed to be prepared, this was it. Ever since 1949, the General Staff had invested considerable thought and energy in preparing for the mobilization of reservists under emergency conditions. Long before 1973, accordingly, there already existed an elaborate and frequently rehearsed system of call-up arrangements, which was designed to supply every reservist with an encoded mobilization summons and to ensure his speedy arrival at the designated assembly point. There, he was to find waiting the transports which would convey his unit and its necessary equipment to the assigned location on the battlefield.

In his autobiography, Ariel Sharon, who had only three months previously resigned from the IDF after three years as CO southern command, seeks to give an impression that on 6 October 1973 this aspect of IDF operations worked exactly according to plan. His own reservists, he reports, had begun to arrive at divisional headquarters since early morning. By mid-day,

> the trickle of reserves had become a stream and the place was bustling. The depots were open, and civilian reservists were busy getting themselves armed and supplied. In the motor pools, tank and truck engines were rumbling while mechanics worked to prepare the vehicles for action....
>
> ... As preparations shifted into high gear [i.e. once the sirens announced that the enemy attack had commenced shortly before 2pm], I walked around the base watching the soldiers cleaning and packing equipment; checking tanks, APC's and jeeps; loading ammunition; energetically doing all those things they were so well trained for.[77]

Although perhaps superficially persuasive, this picture of citizen-soldiers methodically and purposefully going about their business, even whilst the sirens wail, fails to pass any reasonable test of realistic accuracy. Quite apart from being inherently implausible (given the state of psychological shock which must have been induced amongst all the individuals concerned by the surprise nature of the Egyptian-Syrian attack[78]), Sharon's depiction is also flatly contradicted by all other available accounts of what actually transpired. These indicate that the mobilization of IDF reservists, far from being an orderly process carried out in accordance with pre-planned procedures, in fact became an administrative shambles, characterized by improvisation and dependent upon individual initiative. On this topic, the evidence collated by the Agranat commissioners is particularly informative, not least where it concerns Sharon's own division.

Foul-ups, it transpires, emerged at every single stage of the reserve mobilization and deployment process. In chronological sequence, the first problem was to ensure that personnel reached their designated assembly areas. ('I received many telephone calls from all over the country [complaining] that there were insufficient buses to transport the reservists to the base. We could have dispatched the force earlier had there been sufficient buses. ... That was a very serious foul-up [*puntcher*].')[79] Then, there was the delay caused by the need to register those troops who did manage to report for duty. ('The entire clerical procedure of absorption was very poor and took far too long. All the paper-work was a mess ... they didn't work fast enough.')[80] Third, much of the equipment which the reserves were supposed to draw from the emergency stores was either missing or unfit for use. ('I got to ____ and the picture there was awful. ... There were just two jeeps and two APCs for the entire command system'.[81] 'Instead of 46 tanks [that were supposed to be] at the depot, I found only 24.'[82]) Alternatively, the stores were in place, but there existed no means for extracting them from the depot. Thus, according to the Agranat Report: 'One [reserve] brigade suffered a delay of nine hours in the distribution of tank ammunition, principally because no steps had been taken to ensure the presence of sufficient forklifts.... Possibly, but for this delay, the severe crisis on the [northern] front in the first stages of the war might have been avoided.'[83]

Given the almost universal atmosphere of high tension (and in some cases panic), it is not surprising that fitting-out and deployment became a rough-and-tumble affair, which hardly corresponded to any military procedure – or even logic. Fitting-out, especially, turned into a catch-as-catch-can business ('We went to the tank training school ... and removed the communications sets from the tables in the classrooms, as we did also with some of the light weapons. Tank helmets were under lock and key in lockers in the cadet quarters [which we broke into]').[84] Dispatch to the front followed a similar pattern. Armoured units – and in some cases individual tanks – were sent on their way in small packets,[85] without any steps having been taken to ensure that they carried the full complement of ammunition and fire-arms, and without due consideration for the readiness of their organic support and logistic elements. Even then, there was no guarantee that the troops would reach their destinations with any speed. In some cases, as much as half of the complement of tanks dispatched to the front experienced mechanical breakdowns *en route*, often because a lack of sufficient tank transports compelled them to make long journeys on their tracks.[86] Others got caught up in the chaos of vast traffic jams.

> ... Mobilization was so hasty that we could not deploy properly - we had nothing to deploy with, and there was no control over the traffic on this particular route at all. ... [one of the armoured brigades] made its way to the front on tank transporters, whereas most of the force travelled on its own tracks. ... When the tank transporters began their return journey, it became evident that the road was too narrow to accommodate heavy traffic flowing in both directions at one and the same time.[87]

As the Agranat commissioners went to some lengths to point out, responsibility for so lengthy a succession of administrative mishaps cannot be attributed to any one cause – still less to any single individual. Rather, the shambles characteristic of IDF reserve mobilization in October 1973 must be considered an expression of what Clausewitz termed 'friction': the incremental loss of effort and intention caused by human fallibility compounded by danger and exhaustion[88] – and in this case by surprise too. True, the process of emergency reserve mobilization was made no easier by the fact that it had to be carried out on Yom Kippur, the one day in the entire year when Israel's national radio did not function and when its services could not therefore be employed in order to broadcast emergency summonses to duty. But that organizational disadvantage may possibly have been offset by the fact that Yom Kippur is also the one day in the year when most reservists could be most easily located – since they were likely to be either at home or in their synagogues. Moreover, traffic on the roads was likely to be so slight on Yom Kippur that, once summoned to duty by telephone or by personal messenger, they would be able to reach their bases in quick time.[89]

In retrospect, the failure of the IDF's process of reserve mobilization to function as smoothly as was necessary does not seem to have been the result of mere chance. Rather, it must be attributed to a cluster of deficiencies characteristic of the administrative system which was supposed to supervise the process.

For one thing, not once throughout the period between 1967 and 1973 had the IDF conducted a full-scale exercise of complete and immediate reserve mobilization, encompassing the entire spectrum of the process, from initial summons to ultimate battle-readiness. Perhaps the reasons for that particular neglect were budgetary (as some witnesses to the Agranat Commission maintained[90]); alternatively, they may have been psychological, and in that sense yet another expression of the prevailing 'concept' that war was inconceivable. Whichever the case, the Agranat commissioners were able to ascertain that in the years immediately preceding the outbreak of war in October 1973 the IDF had not conducted a single exercise designed to test transport arrangements (p.76); had established no clear demarcation of responsibilities between the various General Staff branches in the event of a surprise mobilization (p.95); had practised no division-size rehearsal of fitting out armoured units (p.101); and conducted no real test of the IDF's ability to ensure that mobilization summonses could reach all reservists in reasonable time (p.107).

The absence of sufficient training in full mobilization and deployment was especially serious in view of the low calibre of many of the personnel who were supposed to administer both procedures. Such failings were particularly marked amongst the conscript and regular troops charged with responsibility for maintaining the emergency depots and ensuring that they were properly administered. ('The people who work in the emergency stores [*yamachim*] are from the very lowest grade of IDF soldiers. Those sent to those tasks are drop-outs from combat and other units, or soldiers who for some physical reason have to serve near their homes. Those granted promotion in those units are also not of the very best quality, since they are promoted from that particular pool of personnel.'[91]) But similar deficiencies were also apparent in other areas too. This situation, exacerbated by what seems to have been a general aura of panic, might help to explain the extent of the collapse almost immediately suffered by the administrative system on 6 October ('Ultimately, we reached a situation in which the reservists simply went into the stores and [without pausing to fill out the regulation forms] just took whatever equipment they needed'[92]). It might also throw some new light on the dispute which, as noted above, erupted between Elazar and Dayan early in the morning of 6 October over large-scale or partial mobilization. On this issue, Dayan – who favoured only a partial mobilization – may have been even more realistic than he realized. Given its deficiencies, the administrative system might ultimately have produced better results had it been required to handle a smaller scale of personnel and equipment.

Still more fundamental, however, was the contribution made to the shambles by the most recent attempts to reform the IDF's force structure. Ever since taking office as COS in 1972, Elazar had invested much of his time and energy in efforts to augment the IDF's fire-power, principally by increasing the number of armoured brigades at his disposal and, in general, by transforming what had in 1967 largely been a brigade-based force into one constructed around a growing quantity of division-size mechanized formations.[93] Bureaucratic inertia and entrenched institutional conservatism apart, the principal obstacle to the implementation of this program (code-named, in 1972, '*Ofek-a*') was financial. Treasury pressure to reduce the defence budget (and also perhaps to reduce conscription terms) entirely ruled out the possibility that the pace of the growth in the overall size of the IDF would be matched by a parallel increase in the quantity of its available equipment. A time lag was inevitable. As the IDF Quartermaster-General informed the Agranat commissioners: 'There exists almost no correlation between the date of a decision authorizing the order of supplies [for a division] and the date by which the division is required to enter into the order of battle.'[94]

Not unexpectedly, the IDF's response to that situation had been to 'eat into capital'. As one commander later recalled: 'the policy [was] that it is preferable to establish a larger number of troops at a lower level of supply, than to establish less units at maximum supply levels'.[95]

As a result, not only were existing resources spread over a greater number of troops; in an attempt to meet what was hoped would be only a temporary shortfall in supplies, quartermasters also tended to draw for the everyday needs of the regular forces upon materiel originally ear-marked exclusively for the reserves or for emergency use only. The Agranat Report provides several individual examples of such practices (often referred to as 'lending and borrowing' arrangements), whose overall effect was to create a bureaucratic tangle which only the most pedantic of unit commanders even attempted to unravel. Most preferred to rely on the hope that equipment removed from the stores for a training exercise or for demonstration purposes in the instruction of new recruits (or in some cases, simply for a parade or march) would eventually be returned – and in good condition to boot. Little action seems to have been taken when such was not the case.

Worse still, virtually no thought was given to the inevitable consequences. As the Agranat Commissioners pointed out, precisely because the IDF was in such a state of organizational flux in 1972–73 – with equipment and personnel being transferred from older units to new ones still in the process of formation – accountancy-supervision should have been even more precise and regulations concerning the maintenance of a proper ratio between human and material assets enforced with particular rigor. In fact, the opposite was the case. Bureaucratic management, never the IDF's strongest point, became even more lax than was usually the case. In its rush to expand the absolute number of fighting divisions, the General Staff simply neglected to draw up an integrated plan which – whilst allowing for enlargement and re-allocation – nevertheless did not altogether deplete the resources of existing units. Instead, it was simply 'assumed' that 'the IDF's mobilization plans allowed for sufficient time to make up for discrepancies between the levels of equipment which regulations required and those which in fact existed'.[96]

The result was a logistic nightmare. When war did unexpectedly break out, reservists found that they had far less to fight with than they had been led to expect. Even when in good repair, much of the equipment which was put at their disposal had been cannibalized. Literally thousands of the items without which no force could even move – let alone fight effectively – were simply not where they should have been. Transport vehicles, maintenance tools, medical stores and – perhaps above all – weapons, were missing. Altogether 'in most of the emergency depots the shortfall of stores and combat equipment was somewhere in the region of 5–15 per cent.'[97]

CONCLUSION

Conventional wisdom maintains that the primary cause for the deficiencies which characterized the IDF's performance at the outbreak of the Yom Kippur War must be traced to the conceptual fallacies which underlay Israel's security thinking at that time. The purpose of the present article has been to add a corollary to that contention. More specifically, it has attempted to show that the range of faulty 'conceptions' was not restricted to gross under-estimates of either the ability or the willingness of Israel's immediate neighbours to wage war. Rather, it extended to an equally incorrect estimate of the ease with which the IDF's existing force structure could cope with whatever military challenges it might be called upon to face. Fundamental to Israel's strategic thought was the belief that a heavy reliance on reservists – quite apart from being mandated by budgetary and demographic

considerations – was also the framework best suited to provide the IDF
with the 'surge capacity' required in order to ensure a decisive victory on
the battlefield. Moreover, the martial triumph of 1967 had seemingly
demonstrated the skill with which the IDF could employ this particular
system and exploit the advantages which it conferred.

At initial glance, much of that faith seems to have been vindicated by
the Yom Kippur War too. After all, the reservists did eventually reach the
battlefield, where their performance proved to be in every way
outstanding. Without their skill, determination and valour, the IDF
could not possibly have recovered from the shock of the outbreak of war
and the initial run of defeats. What has to be recognized, nevertheless, is
that in many respects, that achievement was attained *despite* the reserve
system and not *by virtue* of its application in accordance with pre-
conceived plans. To put matters another way, the outcome of the war
reflected far more credit on the reservists as individuals than on the
framework of which they formed a part. Once the level of analysis is
extended to the systemic plain, it has here been argued, the Yom Kippur
War can be seen to serve as an example of the operational limitations of
the reserve structure, and not of its advantages.

Hence, the lesson of the Yom Kippur War is that reserve forces
constitute much less flexible agencies of force than they might initially
appear. Unless treated with extreme caution, they might narrow, rather
than widen, the options available to commanders and politicians. One
reason, long ago pointed out in another context by the late Dan
Horowitz, is their heightened sensitivity to shifts in societal moods. This,
he maintained, markedly restricts the types of missions which can be
entrusted to 'citizens in uniform' at times of domestic political discord
(such as occurred in Israel during the 1982–1985 Lebanon War).[98] But
even when such considerations do not apply – and they were to all
intents and purposes entirely irrelevant during the Yom Kippur War –
reserve forces can still be seen to possess other limitations.

- For one thing, the resort to a mobilization of reserve forces demands
  a particularly sophisticated calibration of political and military
  purposes. Consequently, it also mandates an especially high level of
  consensus between senior commanders and statesmen with regard to
  the desired 'match' of political ends and military means. Although
  highly effective as agencies of policy in 'black-and-white' situations
  (i.e. when fighting on a large-scale seems unavoidable), reserve
  mobilization can easily backfire when what is required is the
  projection of more subtle signals of intent. Under those
  circumstances, civil-military tensions at the level of supreme
  command are in fact likely to become particularly acute. In this
  respect, the dispute between Elazar and Dayan on the morning of 6
  October deserves to be regarded as an object lesson in the difficulty
  of tailoring the military need to mobilize reservists for offensive

purposes with the political requirements of a posture of defence and deterrence.

- Even more noteworthy, secondly, is the nature of the demands which the reliance on reservists imposes at the level of operational planning. Essentially, they mandate that all other components of the force accommodate themselves to the functions assigned to the reserves, to which their own plans of campaign have therefore to be subordinate. The failure to appreciate the extent of the burden which this limitation imposed (most markedly) on the Israel Air Force must, in this respect, be considered one of the IDF's most serious planning errors. At the very highest level, the General Staff apparently failed to assimilate the evidence (and warnings) that the post-1970 missile threat prejudiced the Air Force's ability to fulfil the CAS role which it was originally assigned, and without which the fighting effectiveness of the reserves would be seriously impaired. Hence, although reserve mobilization *within* the Air Force itself appears to have been efficient and effective, elsewhere in the IDF a situation of dissonance existed. Elazar, certainly, never seems to have drawn the necessary inference – that plans for the use of ground reserves in an offensive capacity and as the instrument of decisive victory might have to be revised. Instead, the COS gave in to the temptation of sticking to his pre-arranged plans, thereby allowing reliance on the reserves to hold his entire strategy in thrall.
- Finally, Israel's experience in the opening hours of the 1973 campaign also illustrates the particular organizational requirements of reserve forces. Even more than all other forces do they depend for their effectiveness on the support of a logistic infrastructure. Regular forces, especially when composed primarily of professional troops, can at least be expected constantly to maintain a minimum standard of battle-readiness, which might reduce the adverse impact of strategic military surprise. But reservists – even when as well trained and as experienced as the Israelis were – cannot be classified as 'quick-reaction' forces. If anything, they must be deemed especially sensitive to the organizational 'friction' which Clausewitz considered to constitute an integral feature of all military activity. As a result, their 'teeth' can only be effective if serviced by an especially lengthy – and efficient – logistic 'tail'. It is impossible to calculate the price which Israel paid as a result of the IDF's failure to ensure that this basic requirement was indeed satisfied.

ACKNOWLEDGEMENTS

This study was supported by a grant from the Ihel Foundation at Bar-Ilan University, whose assistance is gratefully acknowledged. The author also wishes to thank Mr. Ori Bagno for research assistance of a consistently high standard.

NOTES

1. This debate was renewed in the mid-1990s with the appearance of a memoir by the head of IDF Intelligence in 1973: Eli Zeira, *The Yom Kippur War: Myth Vs Reality*, Tel-Aviv: Yedi'ot Ahronot, 1993 (Hebrew). For summaries of the earlier literature see: Avi Shlaim, 'Failures in National Intelligence Estimates: The Case of the Yom Kippur War', *World Politics* 28/3 (April 1976), pp.348–80; Abraham Ben-Zvi, 'Hindsight and Foresight: A Conceptual Framework for the Analysis of Surprise Attacks', ibid., pp.381–95; and Michael I. Handel, 'The Yom Kippur War and the Inevitability of Surprise', *International Studies Quarterly* 21/3 (September 1977), pp.461–602. These studies were later supplemented by Janice Gross Stein, 'Calculation, Miscalculation and Conventional Deterrence', in Robert Jervis, Richard Ned Lebow and Janice Gross Stein, eds, *Psychology and Deterrence*, Baltimore: Johns Hopkins University Press, 1985, pp.34–88 and Moshe Bar-Kokhba, 'The Security Concepts and Dimensions of IDF Preparedness in the Test of the Yom Kippur War', *Ma'archot* 315–16 (1989), pp.7–11 (Hebrew).
2. This view permeates the Israeli military memoiristic literature of the times (much of which is cited below). It is also a prominent motif in such ostensibly non-partisan accounts as, e.g., Ze'ev Schiff, *Earthquake in October*, Tel Aviv: Zmora Bitan, 1974, pp.233–4 (Hebrew); Chaim Herzog, *The War of the Day of Atonement*, London: Futura, 1975; Dov Tamari, 'The Yom Kippur War – Concepts, Assessments, Conclusions', *Ma'archot* 276–7 (November 1980), pp.2–10 (Hebrew); and Anthony H. Cordesman and Abraham R. Wagner, *The Lessons of Modern War: Vol. 1: The Arab-Israeli Conflicts, 1973-1989*, Boulder: Westview Press, 1990, p.50.
3. Efraim Inbar, 'Israel's Strategic Thinking after 1973', *Journal of Strategic Studies* 6/1 (March 1983), pp.36–58.
4. Avner Yaniv, *Politics and Strategy in Israel*, Tel-Aviv: Sifriat Poalim, 1994, pp.280–2 (Hebrew).
5. See Stuart A. Cohen, 'Israel's Changing Military Commitments, 1981–1991', *Journal of Strategic Studies* 15/3 (September 1992), pp.330–50.
6. Stuart A. Cohen, 'The Israel Defence Force. From a "People's Army" to a "Professional" Force', *Armed Forces & Society* 21/2 (Winter 1995), pp.237–54.
7. Israel Tal, *National Security: The Few Against the Many*, Tel-Aviv, Dvir Publications, 1996, p.76 (Hebrew). During the Yom Kippur war, the author served as IDF Deputy Chief of Staff, and has for over 30 years played a prominent role in the formulation of national security policy.
8. For example, John Gooch and Eliot A. Cohen, *Military Misfortunes: The Anatomy of Failure in War*, New York: The Free Press, 1990, p.130.
9. The Report can only be consulted by prior arrangement with the custodians of the Israel Defence Forces Archives at Givatayim, Israel. A partial version of the Commission's interim report was published in Hebrew by Am Oved, Tel Aviv, in 1975. On 4 April 1994 the Cabinet authorized the release of additional portions of the *Agranat Commission Report*.
10. David Ben-Gurion, *Yehud ve-Ye'ud [Uniqueness and Mission]*, Tel Aviv: Am Oved, 1971, pp.99, 139–40 (Hebrew); cited in Ariel Levite, *Offence and Defence in Israeli Military Doctrine*, Tel Aviv: Jaffee Centre for Strategic Studies, 1989, p.34.
11. On this distinction see Shimon Peres, *The Next Stage*, Tel Aviv: Am Oved, 1965, pp.9–15 (Hebrew).
12. On the preference for pre-emptive strikes, see Levite, pp.39–45, 53–8. On the search for a military 'decision' see Avi Kober, *Military Decision in the Arab–Israeli Wars, 1948–1982*, Tel Aviv: Ma'archot, 1996 (Hebrew).
13. See Emanuel Wald, *The Curse of the Broken Vessels. The Twilight of Israeli Military and Political Power*, Tel Aviv: Shocken, 1987, esp. pp.159–79 (Hebrew).
14. Indeed, it had even been possible to de-mobilize some reserves as part of the deception ploy which preceded the Israeli onslaught of 6 June. See Janice Gross Stein and Raymond Tanter, *Rational Decision-Making: Israel's Choices, 1967*, Columbus: Ohio State University Press, 1980, pp.235–6.
15. Thus, according to one senior source: 'Had it not been for the three-week waiting period [of May–June 1967] – during which we repaired half-tracks, tanks, massed the reserves, and polished them up – we wouldn't have come through the Six Day War as well as we did in the Yom Kippur War. We would have been in a very sorry state!'

Major-General Avram Adan (Bren), cited in Hanoch Bartov, *Dado: 48 Years and 20 Days*, Tel Aviv: Ma'ariv, 1981, p.204 (Hebrew).

16. Yaniv, *Politics and Strategy*, pp.241–58, who concedes that at the *strategic* level, some revisions were made. For a particularly detailed indictment of inertia in operational thought, see Shimon Naveh, 'The Cult of the Offensive Preemption and the Future Challenges for Israeli Operational Thought', in Efraim Karsh, ed., *Between War and Peace: Dilemmas of Israeli Security*, London: Frank Cass, 1996, esp. pp.174–6.

17. On this aspect of the difference between the situation as affecting reserve mobilization before and after 1967, see Avraham Adan (Bren), *On Two Banks of the Suez*, Jerusalem: Eidanim, 1979, pp.63–4 (Hebrew).

18. On this episode see Yoel Ben-Porat, 'The Yom Kippur War: Mistake in May, Surprise in October', *Ma'archot* 299 (August 1985), pp.2–9 (Hebrew), and below p.79.

19. 'Since July the public had been reassured at every opportunity that an all-out war was unlikely in the next few years. ... Now general elections were scheduled to take place in a few weeks' time. If there were a general mobilization on Yom Kippur, the holiest day of the year, and it turned out to be a false alarm, the government – and especially the minister of defence – would become a laughing stock and an easy target for the opposition.' Bartov, *Dado*, pp.278–9.

20. On 'Rotem' see Ze'ev Tzachor, 'All Depends on the Air Force. The Rotem Incident of February 1960', in Ze'ev Lachish, ed., *A Decade Of Disquiet. Studies in the History of the Israel Air Force, 1956–1967*, Historical Branch of the IAF, Tel Aviv: Ma'archot, 1995, pp.225–48 (Hebrew). Uri Bar-Joseph, 'Rotem: The Forgotten Crisis on the Road to the 1967 War', *Journal of Contemporary History* 31 (July 1994), pp.547–66.

21. Cited in *ACR*, p.276, para.208.

22. Adan, *Two Banks*, pp.63–4.

23. One of the best descriptions is in Anthony H. Cordesman and Abraham R. Wagner, *The Lessons of Modern War. Volume 1: The Arab–Israeli Conflicts, 1973–1989*, Boulder: Westview Press, 1990, pp.36–43. On earlier disputes within the IDF High Command regarding the Bar-Lev line and its possible utility, see Ariel Sharon, *Warrior: An Autobiography*, New York: Simon & Schuster, 1989, pp.218–27 and Ya'akov Bar-Siman-Tov, 'The Bar-Lev Line Revisited', *Journal of Strategic Studies* 11/1 (March 1988), pp.149–76.

24. Which is not to say, of course, that AMAN had not been granted priority before 1967, too. In fact, ever since 1949, one of the axioms of IDF thinking had been 'Intelligence is our first line of defence'. See Lt.-Gen. (res.), Hayyim Laskov, 'Operations Team, 1949–1950', *Ma'archot* 191–2 (June 1968), p.43 (Hebrew).

25. Thus, one of the ground rules of the IDF war game 'Battering Ram' (*Ayyil Barzel*) held in the summer of 1972, stated that the General Staff 'received the briefest warning of Egypt's intent [to invade the Sinai] – not five to six days but merely forty-eight hours before the attack was scheduled to commence'. Bartov, *Dado*, p.167.

26. General Tal, cited in *ACR*, p.228, para.170. See also the following account of evidence given by the Quartermaster-general [*Rosh AGA*], (idem. p.95, para.2):
Question: '[Would you agree that] the implication is that from the IDF's viewpoint there existed no procedures for the case of mobilization in the event of a surprise attack[?]'
Answer: '[That is] 100 per cent [correct].'

27. *ACR*, p.285, para.217.

28. Kober, *Decision*, pp.313–26.

29. Elazar quoted in Bartov, *Dado*, p.209.

30. Cited in *ACR*, p.196, para.146. During the General Staff discussions on the defence of the Golan Heights, held on 26 April 1973, Elazar had similarly insisted: 'We should prevent the Syrians from attaining *any gain* [emphasis in original], both local and temporary. ... After a short phase on the defensive we should quickly carry the offensive into the enemy's territory in order to achieve the aims of the war, namely: the destruction of both the enemy's forces and his infrastructure.' Cited in Naveh, 'The Cult', p.186, n.36.

31. 'Desert Cat' was later re-named 'Stout-hearted Men' (*Abirei Lev*). There also existed two more limited variations of the planned counter-attack: 'Zefania' (*Tsefaniah*) and 'Valiant' (*Ben Hayyil*). See Bartov, *Dado*, pp.210–12.

32. For what follows see, *inter alia*, Bartov, *Dado*, pp.210–12; Adan, *Two Banks*, pp.44–5, 54; Gooch and Cohen, *Military Misfortunes*, pp.102–5; U. Milstein, *The Outbreak of*

War, Tel Aviv: Yaron Golan, 1992, p.61 (Hebrew); and *ACR*, pp.189–96.

33. On the origins of 'Dovecote', and for a discussion of the debate to which it gave rise, see Ze'ev Eitan, 'Shovach Yonim – Planning and Implementation under the Test of Fire', *Ma'archot* 276–7 (November 1980), pp.38–46 (Hebrew).

34. Or in some versions four, since within southern command itself, distinctions were sometimes made between 'large Dovecote' and 'small Dovecote'. See *ACR*, pp.195–6, para.144.

35. See Bartov, *Dado*, p.201 and Gooch and Cohen, *Military Misfortunes*, pp.119–20.

36. Dayan, *Story of My Life*, p.471, who further comments: 'It must also be added that the enemy forces launched their attacks with much greater efficiency than had been estimated when our plans were being devised.'

37. As recently as April 1973, Elazar had been absolutely confident that on the Golan, for instance, 'Before we mobilize our reserves all we need to do is deploy … no less than a hundred tanks; if we manage to do that[,] may God help the Syrians – against this number of tanks they are incapable of achieving anything. Whenever facing an operational problem, all we need to do is concentrate immediately a minimum number of tanks.' *The (classified) Report of the Nevo Committee: The Defence of the Golan Heights – Doctrines and Concepts*, IDF, 1974, as cited in Naveh, 'The Cult', pp.185–6, n.31.

38. *ACR*, pp.270ff., 277ff.

39. Elazar himself died before responding in any detail to the charges. For Zeira's detailed (and sometimes impassioned) defence, see Eli Zeira, *The Yom Kippur War*. At the personal level, Zeira makes two claims. First, he did provide more warnings than Agranat allowed. Second, responsibility for their interpretation was not his, but ultimately rested with the Defence Minister, Moshe Dayan. Neither claim reads particularly well. Penina Lahav, 'Israeli Military Leadership During the Yom Kippur War: Reflections on the Art of Reflection', in Kevin Avruch and Walter Zenner, eds, *Critical Essays on Israeli Society, Religion and Government*, Albany: SUNY Press, 1997, pp.171–86.

40. *ACR*, p.197, para.147.

41. The attack commenced at 14.00 hours, and not at sunset (18.00), as the latest intelligence reports eventually predicted.

42. The Deputy Chief of Staff, Tal, had been especially adamant on this point – which is why he had persistently insisted on the need to bolster the number of *regular* armoured divisions in the Sinai. 'It is no exaggeration to want three armoured divisions in Sinai for defensive purposes. Because I believe that if the enemy will be the first to commence an offensive, then … the regular forces in the Sinai have to be capable of reaching a decision – and that outcome cannot depend on the arrival of reinforcements from the centre of Israel.' Tal at meeting of Operational Consultative Group (KEDEM) of Operations Division, 19 May 1972, cited in *ACR*, p.230, para.171.

43. Ya'akov Hisdai, 'The Yom Kippur War. Surprise? Victory?', *Ma'archot* 275 (August 1980), p.9 (Hebrew). See the equally critical account in Zvi Lanir, *Basic Surprise: Intelligence in Crisis*, Tel Aviv: Ha-Kibbutz Ha-meuhad, 1983, p.30 (Hebrew). In contrast to the Agranat Report, Lanir argues that in 1973 (unlike in 1967) 'The IDF's strategic concept with respect to the conduct of the war was not decisively dependent on the definition of a minimal warning time'.

44. For an analysis of such pressures during the 'waiting period' which preceded the outbreak of war in June 1967, see Shlomo Nakdimon, *Towards Zero-hour: The Drama Preceding the Six Days' War*, Tel Aviv: Ramdor, 1968 (Hebrew).

45. Hence, Israel had always taken care to ensure that exercises designed to test full-scale reserve mobilization should not be misinterpreted by the Arab side. For a description of one of the instances when such precautions were deficient (a lapse which cost two members of the General Staff their jobs in 1959), see Yitzhak Rabin, *Service Record*, Tel Aviv: Ma'ariv, 1979, Vol.1, p.100 (Hebrew).

46. Mark Trachtenberg, 'The Meaning of Mobilization in 1914', *International Security* 15/3 (Winter 1990–91), pp.150–203.

47. Extract from protocol of meeting on 9 May, cited in *ACR*, p.278, para.212(2). The COS repeated virtually the same phrase on 5 October; ibid., p.279, para.212(5).

48. Zeira, *The Yom Kippur War*, pp.156–7. Compare Dayan, *Story of My Life*, p.477: 'I … requested that the prime minister be given authority to approve the mobilization of reserves if we should ask her to do so.'

49. Rumour has it that Elazar was not Dayan's first choice as COS when the appointment became vacant in 1972. Personally, the Minister of Defence would have preferred Yishayahu Gavish (then CO Southern Command) but bowed to the wishes of the Prime Minister, Golda Meir, who was herself under pressure from her Achdut Ha-Avodah coalition partners to appoint Elazar. See Amnon Barzilai, 'Generals and Gentlemen', *Ha'aretz*, 6 May 1998, B3.
50. On the background, see Yoram Peri, *Between Battles and Ballots: The Israeli Military in Politics*, Cambridge: CUP, 1983; and Yehuda Ben-Meir, *Civil-Military Relations in Israel*, New York: Columbia University Press, 1995.
51. *ACR*, p.33, para.29.
52. Interim Agranat Report (1974), p.11, para.15.
53. Compare Herzog, *War of Atonement*, p.52.
54. Meir's summary of her meeting with Elazar and Dayan, 6 October, 9.20am. *ACR*, p.43, para.32. For her later version, Golda Meir, *My Life*, Jerusalem: Steimatzky's, 1977, pp.358–9.
55. Dayan, in same meeting; idem. This is also the core of Dayan's defence in *My Life*, pp.464–5. 'I feared that such moves would burden our prospects for securing the full support of the United States. Forces needed for counter-attack could be mobilized a few hours later....'
56. Lanir, *Basic Surprise*, p.18.
57. For critical comments on this assumption, in an otherwise very uncritical article, see Tamari, 'The Yom Kippur War'.
58. See Herzog, *War of Atonement*, pp.252–3 and Sharon, *Warrior*, p.235.
59. The decision to 'professionalize' the IAF had been taken as early as 1957. See Tzachor, p.247. Although reservists still constituted a significant proportion of the Air Force's complement of pilots, engineers and air traffic controllers in 1973, the numbers involved were so small as to ensure that their mobilization could be accomplished with especial speed. See also Ezer Weizman, *On Eagle's Wings*, London: Weidenfeld & Nicolson, 1976, pp.273–6.
60. Elazar to Golda Meir, 9 May 1973, cited in *ACR*, p.278, para.212(1).
61. Elazar in General Staff meeting, 22 July 1973. Cited *ACR*, p.230, para.171 and in Aryeh Braun, *Moshe Dayan in the Yom Kippur War*, Tel Aviv: Eidanim, 1996, p.32 (Hebrew).
62. Elazar in Cabinet meeting, 5 October 1973 cited in *ACR*, pp.283–5, para.214. According to Herzog, *War of Atonement*, p.51, Elazar had two days earlier met privately with the editors of the Israeli press. Asked whether 'the regular forces would be adequate to deal with the attack should war break out', the COS 'answered that they would not at best together with the Air Force they could prevent a collapse in the event of a complete surprise'.
63. According to one source, 30–40 per cent of IAF close air support sorties flown between 6 and 8 October were lost to ground defences. Roy M. Braybrook, 'Is it Goodbye to Ground Attack?', *Air International* 10/5 (May 1976), p.245.
64. Cordesman and Wagner, *The Lessons of Modern War*, p.50. For a largely anecdotal account, which attributes this particular failing to the general over-confidence of the Force, see Ehud Yanay, *No Margin for Errors: The Story of the Israeli Air Force*, Jerusalem: Keter, 1993, pp.265–7 (Hebrew).
65. Cordesman and Wagner, p.94. Even Herzog's account, otherwise very sympathetic, notes the 'bedlam' characteristic of Israel air operations during the first days of fighting. *War of Atonement*, p.256.
66. Ya'akov Bar-Siman Tov, *The Israeli-Egyptian War of Attrition, 1969-1970*, New York: Columbia University Press, 1980, pp.125–7.
67. *ACR*, p.214, para.159(I). On the formulation of the consequent air plans, code-named 'Challenge' (*tagar*) and 'Model (*dugman*) – 5', both of which were designed to destroy the missiles 'layer after layer', see Yanay, *No Margin*, pp.254–5.
68. Assistant to the head of Air Command to Moshe Dayan, 22 May 1973, cited in *ACR*, p.215, para.159(4–5). See also the (undocumented) report of meeting between Maj.-Gen. Binyamin Peled (the newly-appointed IAF commander) and Dayan and Elazar on 13 May 1973, in Yanay, *No Margin*, pp.253–4.
69. Herzog, *War of Atonement*, pp.254–5.
70. Zeira, *The Yom Kippur War*, esp. pp.33–42, 66–7, 175.
71. See, e.g., comments in Bar-Tov, *Dado*, pp.205, 213.
72. This number could rise to 28 within half an hour and to 52 within the hour. *ACR*, p.214, para.159(2).

73. According to the log cited by the *ACR* (p.31), at 4.30am Elazar 'contacts the commander of the IAF and asks him [! – in Hebrew, *u-mkevaksho*] to prepare for a pre-emptive strike on enemy concentrations'.
74. Both in 1973 and thereafter, the issue of a pre-emptive air strike generated much debate. The possibility was first raised by Elazar at his meeting with Dayan at 5.50am on 6 October, and discussed in greater depth at their meeting with Meir some two hours later. On both occasions, it was rejected on political grounds. That decision was later criticized with considerable severity by, amongst others, a subsequent Chief of Staff. See Rafael Eitan, *Raful: A Soldier's Story*, Tel Aviv: Ma'ariv, 1985, p.146 (Hebrew). More dispassionately, the decision not to pre-empt has also been assessed on operational grounds, leading to the conclusion that an IAF attack that morning 'would have had a major impact both on subsequent aircraft losses and, still more significantly, on the mission effectiveness of the 10,000 ground-attack sorties flown in the course of the war'. Steven J. Rosen and Martin Indyk, 'The Temptation to Pre-empt in a Fifth Arab-Israeli War', *Orbis* 20/2 (Summer 1976), p.272. More recent estimates, however, adopt a more sceptical tone. (See, e.g., Gooch and Cohen, *Military Misfortunes*, p.122: 'Nor would a preemptive air strike have bought much more than psychological gains.'). The general consensus now seems to be that even had there existed an IAF plan to attack enemy ground forces before battle commenced, which is itself doubtful, there is no certainty that such an attack would have been effective. Interview with senior IAF commander, March 1998.
75. *ACR*, p.217, para.159(14).
76. Peled's remarks at meeting of commander's forum (*sapak*) on 13 February 1974, cited in *ACR*, p.219, para.159(19). See also Yanay, *No Margin*, pp.255–7 and Dayan, *My Life*, who describes his personal entreaties to Peled to change his order of priorities 'even if it meant losing planes' (pp.485–7).
77. Sharon, *Warrior*, pp.290–1.
78. In this respect, at least, Dayan's *My Life* reads far more realistically. 'The transition within twenty-four hours from desk, tractor and lathe to the battlefield is not at all easy. Going to war is not like putting out a fire, where you can rush with blaring sirens and do the dousing in one go.' (p.467).
79. Evidence by Col. Gideon of Sharon's division, *ACR*, p.173.
80. Evidence by Lt.-Col. Elyashiv, of Bren's division, *ACR*, p.149.
81. Idem.
82. Evidence by Lt.-Col. Hayyim Y., *ACR*, p.150.
83. *ACR*, p.96.
84. Evidence by Col. Hayyim, *ACR*, p.92. Similarly, 'We were not supplied with any lorries or APC's. So, whatever we found – we took. ... We took an old ZIL lorry, and loaded it with light ammunition [for tanks] and it followed in our tracks.' Evidence by Major Ami, ibid., p.176.
85. All observers noted the extent to which the initial Israeli armoured counter-attacks were made 'in drips and drabs'. E.g., Dayan, *My Life*, p.487 and Saad el Shazly, *The Crossing of the Suez*, San Francisco: American Mideast Research, 1980, pp.285–6.
86. *ACR*, pp.74, 103.
87. Evidence by Brig.-Gen. Tamari, cited in *ACR*, p.155.
88. 'The military machine ... is basically very simple. But we should bear in mind that none of its components is of one piece: each part is composed of individuals, ... the least important of whom may chance to delay things or somehow make them go wrong.' Carl von Clausewitz, *On War*, ed. and trans. Michael Howard and Peter Paret, Princeton: Princeton University Press, 1976, p.119. See Kathleen L. Herbig, 'Chance and Uncertainty in *On War*', in M.I. Handel, ed., *Clausewitz and Modern Strategy*, London: Frank Cass, 1986, pp.95–116; and Allan Beyerchen, 'Clausewitz, Nonlinearity, and the Unpredictability of War', *International Security* 17/3 (Winter 1993), pp.59–90.
89. Both considerations apparently surfaced at the meeting between Elazar, Dayan and Zeira on the morning of 5 October. On that occasion, the following dialogue reportedly ensued (Zeira, *The Yom Kippur War*, p.141):

Elazar: '... the problem is that on this festival everything is dead.'

Dayan: 'That's no bother.'

Elazar: 'Except in one thing, that if anything does happen, we want – plainly – to begin to concentrate forces or give warnings.'

Dayan: 'Do not move forces, unless something actually happens. The roads are empty today.'

Elazar: 'But we have no radio. We began to consider ordering the IDF radio to broadcast chapters of Psalms every two hours.'

Dayan: 'But then we would have to tell everybody now that they should listen to the IDF radio – that will generate tremendous panic. And anyway – who listens to Psalms? Those that do will not switch on the radio.'

90. Evidence by Brig.-Gen. Tzippori, *ACR*, p.101.
91. Evidence by Lt. Col. Brown, Chief of Staff, Northern Command, *ACR*, p.109.
92. Evidence by Lt.-Col. Elyashiv, of Bren's division, *ACR*, p.149.
93. Bartov, *Dado*, pp.200–1.
94. *ACR*, p.84.
95. Ibid.
96. Evidence by head of Quartermaster's Branch, *ACR*, p.90.
97. *ACR*, p.79.
98. Dan Horowitz, 'Strategic Limitations of a Nation in Arms', *Armed Forces & Society* 13/2 (Winter 1987), pp.277–94.

The Yom Kippur War:
Diplomacy of War and Peace

SIMCHA DINITZ

Any attempt to determine starting and ending dates for a review of a period in history is bound to be arbitrary. No historical event begins without relations to preceding events, or ends without directly influencing succeeding developments. Yet these arbitrary limitations must be made if we are to focus on a particular period without, of course, ignoring the events that led to it and the consequences that followed.

I arrived in Washington to assume office as Ambassador about six months before the Yom Kippur War. It was not easy to succeed Ambassador Yitzhak Rabin, who had come to the United States as the heroic Chief of Staff of the Six Day War. By virtue of his ability, background and standing, he succeeded in creating a new level of strategic relationship with the political, military and intelligence communities in the US. After the Six Day War, Israel was no longer the object of sympathy and compassion, but rather an important strategic asset to be reckoned with.

WAS THERE A MISSED OPPORTUNITY?

It is sometimes alleged that in early 1971 Egypt signalled a readiness to enter into a bilateral limited agreement with Israel. These claims are groundless. In fact, what Egypt hinted at was a readiness to accept a limited withdrawal of Israeli troops from the east bank of the Suez Canal, if it was done within a clearly laid down timetable that would guarantee total Israeli withdrawal from all the territories. All the territories included, in addition to the Sinai, the Golan Heights, the West Bank and East Jerusalem. President Anwar al-Sadat, then in the first year of his

Simcha Dinitz was Israel's Ambassador in Washington during the Yom Kippur War. This chapter is based on the author's forthcoming political memoirs.

presidency, was not yet ready to separate Egypt from the pan-Arab policies pursued since 1967. These policies committed all Arab countries to act in concert and to insist on a total Israeli withdrawal on all fronts.

Nowadays there are attempts to blame Israel and the United States for failing to take these signals more seriously, thus missing the opportunity for peace. This was not the case. Sadat's February 1971 speech did not mention peace at all, it only called for an Israeli withdrawal from the east bank of the Suez Canal, stating clearly that Egypt would not act alone, ignoring the other Arab territories (the West Bank, East Jerusalem, the Gaza Strip and the Golan Heights). Moreover, Sadat's move was designed to bring about the implementation of the Arab interpretation of all the provisions of Security Council Resolution 242.[1] The Arab leaders themselves, including President Sadat, stressed repeatedly that there was a precondition to negotiation. Before a dialogue with Israel was possible, even an indirect one, there must be guaranteed Israeli withdrawal to the pre-1967 lines. The memoirs of three of President Sadat's Foreign Ministers – Mahmoud Riad, Ismail Fahmi and Muhammed Ibrahim Kamel – further attest to this fact.[2] Sadat never tired of explaining, during the two years that followed his February 1971 speech, that what he had proposed meant a phased Israeli withdrawal from *all* the occupied territories (*all*, not only Sinai or part of it).[3] Significantly, in that very speech Sadat suggested not only the first withdrawal stage, but also swore not to give way on 'any of the Palestinian people's rights', which included the right of return of the Palestinian refugees to Israel. In May 1971, US Secretary of State William Rogers visited Egypt. On 20 May, President Sadat solemnly informed the Egyptian National Assembly that in his reply to Secretary Rogers he would say: '*The question of the opening of the Suez Canal is not a separate question and it is not a partial solution. This is a stage in the complete Israeli withdrawal, in accordance with a timetable.*'[4]

It is no wonder that under these circumstances neither Israel nor the United States could make headway with Sadat's 'proposals' of 1971 and 1972. Henry Kissinger describes this in detail in his memoirs.[5] In February 1973, Kissinger held talks with Sadat's National Security Advisor, Hafez Ismail. Ismail, too, rejected the limited Canal opening idea except as part of a plan for a complete withdrawal, to be carried out in stages over a brief period. Kissinger notes that, according to Ismail, '*Israel had to agree before anything else happened that it would return to its 1967 borders with all its neighbours.*' Arab control of East Jerusalem was '*essential and non-negotiable*'.[6]

Ambassador Yitzhak Rabin writes in his memoirs that Kissinger told him that, on the basis of his conversations with Hafez Ismail, Egypt might be ready to start negotiating if Israel acknowledged Egyptian sovereignty over all of Sinai. Rabin consulted with Prime Minister Golda Meir and told Kissinger that Israel authorized him to explore this approach. Egypt, however, was not interested.[7]

This subject was also discussed in detail in the meeting between Prime Minister Golda Meir and President Richard Nixon on 1 March 1973. I attended that meeting and heard Golda Meir enumerating to the President our continuous efforts and interests in exploring every avenue of negotiation. She specifically said that we were ready to enter into a partial agreement on the Suez Canal or into an overall settlement with Egypt. Such a settlement would include, as noted above, Israel's acknowledgement of complete Egyptian sovereignty over all of Sinai. As we know, all these approaches by Israel did not produce the proper response from Egypt. Indeed it took the Yom Kippur War, as will be shown, to change the basic attitude of Egypt to the peace negotiations. This change became evident during Sadat's historic visit to Jerusalem. Although he repeated all of Egypt's familiar policy lines in his address to the Knesset, he did not demand their acceptance by Israel as a precondition to peace negotiations.

THE EVE OF THE WAR

But here we stood on the eve of the Yom Kippur War. The self-confidence that had engulfed Israel after the Six Day War was reflected in its standing in Washington. Israel was viewed by the United States as a strong and united country, capable of withstanding any threat from the Arabs. There were voices which pointed out that the Arabs could not acquiesce to the existing situation, that they would have to avenge their 'humiliation' of 1967. But there was no serious assessment that predicted a military explosion. To the degree that American public opinion was at all interested in the Middle East, it reflected the spirit of complacency.

This attitude prevailed even among American Jewry. As a rule, American Jewry rallies round Israel in dramatic hours: a mass immigration, a daring military operation (Entebbe), a state of war, or a unique opportunity for peace. But at this point, none of these elements existed. American Jewry became more concerned with the needs of its own community and its future. Israel was regarded as safe and secure, not needing its particular attention or serious assistance. This distancing from concern for Israel was not only felt in the Jewish community, but also among liberal circles in America. Israel was no longer the underdog which required their care and sympathy. In fact, it was now occupying large territories and ruling millions of Palestinians. Israel was, in their eyes, David turned into Goliath. At the same time, the conservative elements in America, which were not traditionally sympathetic to Israel, now saw in it a new, strong ally, a strategic asset, that could help block Communist expansion in the Middle East.

The more Israel acquired conservative friends, the more it lost in liberal voices. When Golda Meir said, after visiting President Nixon, 'We have a friend in the White House', many eyebrows were raised among liberals. Had anyone else said this, they would have been condemned by the liberals forever, but Meir's position in America was such that even this was forgiven. So, on the eve of the Yom Kippur War, Israel was perceived in America as a strong country headed by a determined and forthright leader.

A week before the War, Golda Meir was visiting Austrian Chancellor Bruno Kreiski. The purpose of the visit was to convince Kreiski to reopen the Immigration Transit Centre at Schonau so that the Russian Jews could continue to pass through on their way to Israel. Arab pressure had persuaded Kreiski to close the transit station. The official explanation given by the Austrians was that it had been closed for 'security reasons'. Relations between Meir and Kreiski were problematic, to say the least. His pro-Arab policy was often interpreted as attempting to bend over backwards because of his Jewish origin. Meir's account of their meeting, as one at which he did not even offer his guest a glass of water, reveals the atmosphere that existed between the two socialist leaders.[8] In any event, Meir was not sure that she had succeeded in convincing Kreiski to reopen the transit station, and since this was crucial for continued Jewish immigration from the Soviet Union, she asked me to intervene with Kissinger and ask him to influence Kreiski. I arranged to see him that weekend.

It was Sunday, 29 September 1973 at noon when I received a call at my residence in Washington from our Military Attaché. He wanted to come and see me urgently with some information he had received from home. When he arrived at the residence he read me a report received from our Intelligence, saying that we observed Syrian concentration of troops on the northern front, and that the details had been passed to American Intelligence. Since the two Intelligence Services were examining the situation, the subject should not be raised with the political level at this stage. It was for my information only. I told him that I was to see Secretary of State Kissinger that afternoon, and while I would not bring the subject up on my own initiative, I would have to share this information with Kissinger and ask for his evaluation, if he were to raise the matter.

That afternoon I met with Kissinger at his office. The State Department looked pretty deserted. Weekend meetings with foreign diplomats were generally rare, except on emergencies. Kissinger, however, found weekends a good time to review cables and read Intelligence reports and position papers, uninterrupted by daily routine business. The subject of our unusual meeting was my intention to discuss with him the restrictions placed by Chancellor Kreiski of Austria on our transit facilities for Soviet Jews passing through Vienna.

This transit camp at Schonau was rented to the Jewish Agency by an Austrian countess, where the immigrants could be given information about Israel, were registered and classified according to their profession and received their preliminary guidance about the new life they were going to lead in Israel. The average stay of a family at this transit facility was only 2–3 days before they were taken to the airport and continued to Israel with El Al planes. I wanted Kissinger to use his influence with Kreiski to remove these impediments. The tension on the Israeli borders was not raised by either of us.

When I arrived at the Embassy to cable home a report on our meeting, the telephone rang. It was Kissinger on the line (no secretaries on weekends). He said that after I had left he went through the material on his desk and found some disturbing reports on the Syrian troop movements in the north. I told him that we had similar reports and that we were examining the situation. Kissinger asked for our immediate evaluation and requested to be informed, at any hour, on any development. I immediately sent an additional cable to Israel, this time marked 'most urgent', and requested, in light of the American interest, an immediate review of the situation. Within a couple of hours I received a reply stating that our evaluation is that these troop movements are designed for military exercises and have a political, rather than a military, aim. Our estimate, the cable said, is that the likelihood of war is remote. I phoned Kissinger, who had already left, but had asked his deputy at the NSC, General Brent Scowcroft, to await my reply. I passed our evaluation on to him. Scowcroft said that it corresponded exactly to their own Intelligence estimate. (How else? After all, the two Intelligence Services, as all friendly Intelligence Services do, had been exchanging information and evaluations with each other. After being reviewed by both Services, such Intelligence estimates are sent to the political level. When diplomats are asked to compare evaluations with foreign governments, they are 'surprised' to see that the estimates are usually identical.) Scowcroft requested that we stay in touch. I cabled home stating that while the evaluations were the same, the Americans were greatly concerned over developments and would like to be kept informed. I suggested close examination of developments and updating me.

Two days later my father passed away in Tel Aviv and I headed home for the funeral. Years later, reflecting on the Yom Kippur War, Golda Meir remarked to me: 'I wonder if the course of events would have been different had you remained in Washington that week, and together with Kissinger pressed for re-evaluation of the Intelligence estimate.' The fact is that Meir did order a re-evaluation that week, but the Intelligence Services came up with the same conclusion. She twice postponed her visit to my mother during that week of mourning for my father, because she said she was concerned over the situation at the front and had ordered a re-evaluation by the Intelligence.

In fact, Israel's Intelligence, known to be among the best in the world, was always able to supply crucial and accurate data on countless tactical moves and military movements by the enemy, but failed to predict in advance any of the wars, and the one peace that came about. This should remind us that Intelligence Service reports, however efficient, cannot, and ought not to be, a substitute for political decisions that should be analyzed and made by the elected leadership. The role that Intelligence data can play in diplomatic negotiations is in any event very problematic. The hard core information cannot be used for fear of revealing sources. What can be used is usually of secondary importance, watered-down material, and often such that has already been passed from one Intelligence Service to the other.

I recall that in 1967, prior to the Six Day War, I was serving as Minister at our Embassy in Rome. I received an Intelligence evaluation from Israel, to the effect that President Nasser's movement of Egyptian forces into Sinai was nothing more than military manoeuvres designed to create political pressure, and not intended to wage war. I was asked to compare this estimate with the Italian Intelligence. Conte Murari, then Italian Assistant Secretary of State for Middle East Affairs, confirmed to me that this was exactly the Italian estimate. The logic of both Intelligence Services was the same: Nasser was transferring his army and heavy equipment into Sinai in broad daylight in front of press and camera. Had he wanted to plan a secret operation, he would have done it at night, in secrecy away from the public eye. The logic of both Intelligence Services was right, but their conclusions were completely wrong.

By Friday, 5 October, Meir estimated that the war could start the following day and wanted me to leave for Washington as soon as possible. However, this was no easy matter. There were no commercial flights, and the Air Force planes had already been mobilized. An aircraft was found for me at the Israel Aircraft Industries, to be flown by a test pilot. It was to take my wife and me to Europe, where we could catch the first flight to the US. The time for departure was set for Saturday afternoon at two o'clock.

On Friday evening, the eve of Yom Kippur, which also breaks the *shiva* (seven-day mourning period for my father), my mother and I moved to my sister's home in north Tel Aviv. General Israel Leor, Meir's Military Secretary, called and informed me that disturbing reports were constantly coming in, but the crucial information would be received during the night, and that Meir had asked that I should be in close touch with the office and await instructions.

That night I went to the *Kol Nidre* prayer at the nearby synagogue. I did not wait until the end of the whole service, but left immediately after that prayer. I called Leor who said that the report was coming in and that it did not look good.

LATE ATTEMPT TO PREVENT THE WAR

Early on Saturday morning I received a call to come to the Prime Minister's Office at *Hakirya* in Tel Aviv immediately. When I arrived there I witnessed a great commotion in Meir's office. People were coming and going. Among them were Cabinet Ministers: Moshe Dayan,

Yigal Allon and Israel Galili; the Chief of Staff General David Elazar, and others. Meir told me that the information which had come in during the night had left no doubt that war would start that day. She had called in the American Ambassador Kenneth Keating, who would be arriving at any moment. She wanted me to stay for the meeting, then attend the Cabinet session which she had called for 11am, and then I should take off for the United States.

Before she had finished the last sentence, her secretary announced that the American Ambassador had arrived. Keating seemed alarmed and concerned when he entered the room. Ambassadors are not usually invited to see the Prime Minister on Yom Kippur. Golda got straight to the point: 'We have reports', she said to the Ambassador, 'that war will start today. We have refrained from mobilizing our reserves because we did not want to arouse tension, or cause our moves to be misunderstood in the Arab capitals. But now we have no choice and we have called up our reserves. I would like you to report this to your Government immediately, and ask them to make every possible effort to urge the Arab Governments to stop the oncoming war. The US should explain that the measures we have taken are defensive measures, that we have no intention of attacking them, but if they attack us they will bear the full responsibility for the outcome.' Meir added, to the startled Ambassador, that she had refrained from authorizing a preventive strike in order to avoid ambiguity or misunderstanding as to who had started the war.

The Ambassador was shocked. He said that he would rush back to his office and cable immediately. He did not want to ask any questions because he did not want to lose any time. He was not a young man, but he seemed to be physically running as he left Meir's office. After the Ambassador had left, Meir entered the adjacent Cabinet Room. The Cabinet met regularly in Jerusalem, but this room was used for emergencies and for the rare occasions when meetings had to take place in Tel Aviv.

Golda told the Cabinet that we had information that war would start that day. She then asked Minister of Defence Dayan and Chief of Staff David 'Dado' Elazar to brief the Cabinet on the security and military situation. They both pointed out the dangers, but assured the Cabinet that we could overcome them. Dado Elazar excused himself after his briefing, to join his troops. Dayan remained for the discussion. He explained to the Cabinet Ministers that it was going to be a tough battle but that he had full confidence in our capacity to win, even without taking a preventive strike. Meir emphasized the political importance of avoiding a preventive strike. 'We will need the assistance of the Americans with equipment and military supplies as well as their political and diplomatic support. All these', she said, 'will not be given to us if the notion is that we started the war'. She said that she had asked both Dayan and Elazar whether Israel could absorb the first strike and still win the war, and they had both assured her that Israel could. Dayan, who was still at the meeting, confirmed this and the Cabinet decided to approve the mobilization (already under way), and to approve the avoidance of a pre-emptive strike.

By then it was 1pm and I had to leave for the airport. I sent two separate notes, one to Golda Meir and the other to Moshe Dayan, asking them an identical question: 'I am now leaving for Washington. What is the most urgent thing you want me to do?' I received an identical reply from both: 'Get the items (or the tools) we need urgently.'

I left the Cabinet meeting for the airport, stopping at my sister's house to pick up my wife Vivian. In the streets young men were coming out of the synagogues with their prayer shawls on, rushing to their cars or to buses and trucks parked at various corners. There was no panic in the streets but rather, in an inexplicable way, an atmosphere of order and discipline. People moved determinedly as if they knew exactly where they were going. The Government may have been surprised, the people perhaps not.... On some street corners you could see young couples lingering with a last hug, a last kiss, a final good-bye. Some parents escorted their children and some children escorted their fathers. I thought to myself: Some will probably never see each other again. But, little did I know how many.

RETURN TO WASHINGTON

At exactly 2pm we arrived at the military terminal of Lod Airport. Precisely at that moment the air raid sirens began to sound and the radio in the car announced that the fighting had begun. It was a very terrible feeling to be leaving the country at that particular moment. I tried to comfort myself, not with great success, that at a time like this everyone should be where he can do the most good. We boarded the small, unarmed civilian plane and took off into a sky already crowded with military aircraft engaging in the first air battles. I sat next to the pilot and could observe this and the Egyptian coastline on the radar screen of the small plane. I was glad that my wife was sitting in the back and could not see the drama.

We landed safely in Rome, but there was no immediate connecting flight so we continued with the aircraft to London, where we took the first plane to Washington. All during the flight I thought to myself that all I had learned and all the experience I had gathered must now be mobilized and tested in the crucial battle I was about to face in Washington. I prayed that I would have the wisdom and the power to accomplish the task.

By Sunday afternoon, a couple of hours after we landed, I was already in Kissinger's office relating to him the recent developments and the Cabinet's decision not to pre-empt with a military strike. I emphasized that Meir's decision not to pre-empt had been a very difficult decision, placing an additional burden on us. Its purpose was to avoid confusion in America as to who had started the war, since she was sure we would need American assistance in military supplies as well as in political support . I explained this to the Secretary of State and told him that it placed heavy responsibility on our American friends to see to it that the military supplies Israel requested be sent immediately, to help us combat the unprovoked, surprise attack by Syria and Egypt. Kissinger pointed out that some attempts had already been made to place the responsibility for starting the war on Israel, but he had dismissed them. He promised to be helpful and asked that we remain in very close contact.

That night, attending a previously scheduled event at the home of the Anti Defamation League representative David Brodie, I met with a group of Senators and Congressmen, headed by Republican Senator Bob Packwood of the Foreign Relations Committee, as well as a group of Jewish leaders. I briefed them on the situation and emphasized our urgent need to receive the military supplies requested. The following morning I met in Washington with key representatives of the Presidents' Conference of Major Jewish Organizations. This is an umbrella organization of some 37 national Jewish organizations in the US. I described the situation to them and left them with the same urgent message.

THE BATTLE FOR THE AIRLIFT

This started an intensive political and diplomatic struggle in Washington to get the military supplies to Israel and eventually, the airlift. It ended a week later with America conducting the biggest airlift operation in its history (larger than the Berlin Airlift). A number of people and factors were involved in that decision. The controversy over who delayed the airlift and who pushed for it and why, lingers until today. Some analysis of all the factors involved is therefore required.

The week leading to that historic decision was the most crucial week in the relations between the United States and Israel. I had to face a combination of factors never before assembled together: the difficult decision by the US to allow American aircraft to land in a battle zone; the threat of an Arab oil embargo that would cause a severe blow to America's allies and hurt the American economy; political pressure on the US by its European allies, Japan and the Third World; the danger of extreme Soviet reaction and the dangers to the future of détente; the shaky position of President Richard Nixon amidst the Watergate crisis; the reluctance of the Pentagon to part with sophisticated equipment in its own stockpile, and the traditional pro-Arab sentiments in some quarters of the State Department and the Pentagon.

As I waged this battle against so many odds, I knew that every day, in fact, every hour that the supply was delayed, caused us additional casualties. I was helped in the struggle to overcome these obstacles by the moral force of our case, public opinion – by and large sympathetic to

Israel, the influence of the Jewish community, and the all-important Congressional support. The central and crucial factor was the person and standing of Secretary Kissinger. As one who had lost 13 members of his family in the Holocaust, he was not about to let another catastrophe befall the Jewish people. As American Secretary of State he tried at first to minimize American involvement in the war and keep a low profile. Like many others in the Administration, recalling the pattern of the Six Day War, he did not believe that this war would last more than a few days. He therefore thought in terms of *long range* military supplies to Israel to retrieve the losses, rather than the necessity for an immediate airlift. But, by the third day, when the extent of the Israeli losses had become evident and the massive Soviet supplies to Egypt and Syria by air and sea were apparent, he was pressing for a quick delivery.

By Tuesday, Kissinger was able to announce to me that President Nixon had decided to supply Israel with all the losses it had incurred during the War. 'Thus', added Kissinger, 'you are able to use all the equipment you have, without concern for replenishing it'. Kissinger advised me to urge my Government to go on the offensive as quickly and as strongly as possible, because he did not know how much time we had before pressure would be mounted to freeze the situation. This Presidential decision was indeed important, but it did not provide an answer to our immediate need arising from a costly and protracted war.

From the very beginning, we had been managing to ship small equipment and ammunition on El Al planes. We were able to make some 30 shipments of this nature, but only after we had painted out the Star of David on the tails of our aircraft, at the insistence of the Pentagon. This incident indicated the reserved and cautious mood at the Defence Department. President Nixon, when informed of this, said: 'It was unthinkable that Israel should lose the war for lack of weapons, while we were spraying paint over the Star of David. "Tell (Secretary of Defence James R) Schlesinger to speed it up"; I told Kissinger.'[9]

However, the need for re-supply was immediate and great and could only be satisfied by an airlift operation. From that point on, it became clear that the real decision would have to be the authorization of American planes to fly into the battle zone carrying American military supplies. But there was a reluctance at first to use American aircraft in a combat zone, and the Pentagon was charged with the task of finding charter planes which could do the job. That brought no results.

Kissinger realized that the delay in military supply to Israel might affect the outcome of the war and thus destroy his entire strategy. From the very beginning Kissinger believed that Israel should not be allowed to suffer a defeat. An American ally using American arms, which is attacked by countries allied to the Soviet Union using Soviet arms, should not be allowed to lose. Israel must prevail in this war, was his strategy, but Egypt should not be allowed to be devastated. Egypt should suffer the consequences of its attack enough to realize that war does not pay; and that alliance with the Soviets does not assure security; but Egypt should not be destroyed and Sadat should not be humiliated, so that he could be a party to the negotiations that would follow the war, under American guidance.

In addition, the President, caught up in the Watergate scandal, was anxious to score a diplomatic victory and end the war. He began to press Kissinger to achieve an early cease-fire. On Wednesday, 10 October, Nixon was inclined to accept the Soviet offer for a cease-fire in place. I urged Kissinger to resist this move, which was totally unacceptable to us. I questioned what strategic benefit there would be to the United States in freezing a military situation which would give control to the Russians on both sides of the Canal. I suggested to Kissinger that he respond negatively to the Russian suggestion and instead propose a cease-fire, based on the return to the *status quo ante*. If the Russians rejected this, then let us wait for the military outcome on the ground. At 10:00pm that day Kissinger called to tell me that he had succeeded in convincing Nixon to delay his answer to the Russian cease-fire proposal.

Kissinger himself was reluctant to stop the war before Israel could achieve a clear military advantage. To achieve this Israel had to receive the essential military supply of the airlift. Thus, the delay in military supplies to Israel was contrary to Kissinger's own strategy, and to the wish of President Nixon. Kissinger's anger at the Pentagon for its delaying tactics was not *pro-forma* as some suggested, but rather a recognition that such delaying tactics could destroy the whole post-war strategy of peace.

Secretary of Defence Schlesinger, who had always regarded Israel as an ally against the Soviet threat in the Middle East, did not treat Israel as an ally in the battle for the airlift. He feared a strong Arab reaction, including an oil embargo and an Arab threat not to refuel the 6th Fleet in the Mediterranean. He was reluctant to use American pilots and equipment in a battle zone. He was under pressure from his aides not to part with equipment from the stockpile of the US army and air force. He entrusted his deputy, Under Secretary Clements, an oil millionaire with strong ties in the Arab world, with the task of finding charter planes instead of American military aircraft. Under Secretary Clements displayed less than great enthusiasm for accomplishing this difficult task, and thus contributed to further delay in the decision on the airlift.

Since the beginning of the political battle for military re-supply, I had been trying to get a meeting with Secretary of Defence Schlesinger. While the main thrust of my efforts was directed at the Secretary of State and the National Security Council (NSC), it became apparent that the Defence Department was being far from helpful. The meeting with Secretary Schlesinger was being postponed from day to day. The unofficial explanation given to us by his aides was, that as long as there was no clear-cut decision handed him by the White House or the NSC, there was no sense in meeting the Secretary of Defence. On Wednesday,

Schlesinger's spokesman suggested cancelling yet another meeting set for Thursday, because 'the Secretary did not think that the publicity attached to such a meeting was helpful'.

I met with Kissinger on Thursday afternoon to further press for the speedy delivery of Phantoms and Skyhawks. I told him that Secretary Schlesinger kept postponing the meetings with me. I said that I was considering suggesting to Prime Minister Golda Meir that she come for an urgent meeting with the President. Kissinger's reaction was quick and emphatic: 'There is no point in that. There is nothing we can possibly give the Prime Minister which we don't give you. You know the situation in Washington, and you know what we are up against.' Obviously, Kissinger (and specially Nixon) did not need Golda Meir in Washington at that time. A public confrontation with Israel was not exactly what Nixon needed. I was aware of this, and my suggestion had its effect.

Towards the end of the week, a special 'guarded telephone' was installed by our security people at the Embassy so that I could talk to Israel on a 'secure' line. We nicknamed this telephone 'SILON' – the 'jet'. It was inaugurated by a conversation from Golda Meir to me. Her first words were: 'I understand that the voices come through this telephone in a whining tone. Do not be alarmed. The situation is tough, but not as bad as it sounds on the phone.' Then she proceeded to give me a pretty gloomy description of the situation. 'Our offensive in the north has not been very successful. Our losses are very heavy. There are voices among us who are considering the possibility of a cease fire. Check with Kissinger and see how he views this possibility.' I checked with Kissinger and he replied that it was the worst possible time to ask for a cease-fire: 'One does not ask for a cease-fire when one's back is to the enemy.' He strongly recommended that we do not ask for it. He urged us to go on a full military offensive and I replied that this was difficult to do while the arms shipments to Israel were being delayed.

I saw Schlesinger on Friday morning, 12 October. I took our Military Attaché, the late General Motta Gur, with me. The meeting was held in a very tense atmosphere. Schlesinger said that it had been decided to supply us with 16 Phantoms, at the rate of two a day. After a couple of days there would be a pause to gauge Arab reaction and the continued supply would be determined accordingly. As to the airlift, they were experiencing great difficulty in mobilizing charter planes.

I responded very strongly to the Secretary's remarks. I explained the seriousness of the situation and added that it was not what I expected of an ally in time of emergency. I went to see Secretary Kissinger and informed him of the outrageous reply I had received from the Defence Department. Kissinger was shocked. He said that he had heard President Nixon instructing Schlesinger to get things moving. He called in General Scowcroft and then telephoned Schlesinger to say that the delay in supply would affect Israel's ability to go on the offensive. He said that he believed Clements was sabotaging the moves and his efforts to get the charters was, at best, half-hearted. Kissinger went on to say to Schlesinger that from the point of view of American diplomacy, they needed the Israeli offensive, and that their whole strategy would be destroyed if Israel would not be able to perform effectively on the front.

Kissinger hung up and told us that the Pentagon would immediately ship us the ten huge C-130 transport planes loaded with the essential cargo. Kissinger said that Schlesinger had admitted that they had not put enough pressure on the airlines which owned the charters. I said to Kissinger that we could not continue this game. That in this battle of 'passing the buck' between the State Department, the Pentagon, and the NSC we were paying with human lives. Every hour, every minute of delay was crucial. I told him that I was spending 90 per cent of my time fighting for the airlift and 10 per cent of the time preventing our friends from attacking the President. I added that if the airlift did not start that night (Friday), I would consider it an unfriendly act on the part of the United States towards my country, with all it implied. Kissinger telephoned General Alexander Haig, then Chief of Staff of the White House, related our conversation to him and added that elements in the Pentagon were operating against the Presidential decision. Haig promised to deal with the matter forthwith.

At around midnight, shortly after I had returned from the meeting, Kissinger called to say that the Defence Department had received a Presidential order to start the supply to Israel immediately, and that I could inform Prime Minister Golda Meir of this decision. I used the guarded telephone – the SILON – to inform Meir of Nixon's decision. This time my voice and her reaction did not sound whining. After midnight I went home. It was the first time I had been home since the beginning of the War. I said to Vivian: 'The airlift is starting' and collapsed on the bed. After six extremely pressured days I fully understood the meaning of the seventh day of rest.

The following morning I accompanied our Foreign Minister Abba Eban, who had arrived from New York, to a meeting with Kissinger, where we were officially informed of the decision on the airlift.

President Nixon had to hold another meeting with General Haig, Secretaries Kissinger and Schlesinger, and others, to execute the decision. The various options were presented to the President. Nixon endorsed Kissinger's recommendations, but decided to increase the military supplies recommended by Kissinger and overruled the objections of Secretary Schlesinger. Nixon said: 'We would take just as much heat for sending three planes as for sending thirty'. Turning to Schlesinger, Nixon said: 'Whichever way we have to do it, get them in the air now'. And when he heard that there was disagreement in the Pentagon about which kind of plane should be used for the airlift, Nixon became totally exasperated and said to Kissinger: 'Goddam it, use every one we have. Tell them to send everything that can fly.'[10] When Secretary Schlesinger continued to enumerate the difficulties involved in executing the order,

Nixon said to Schlesinger (according to one of the participants) that either he did it, or he would have to find another Secretary of Defence.

Once the political decision had been made, the American machine, including, of course, the military arm of the Pentagon, executed it not only with efficiency and precision, but with a great feeling of solidarity and friendship.

A recent publication, *Operation Nickel Grass* by Kenneth K Robertson, offers a detailed account of the American airlift.

> According to the Harmon Trustees, it was 'one of the greatest airlift operations in history'. Further, it was arguably the most significant the US had performed since the Berlin airlift of 1948. Compared to the US effort to aid Berlin, the Israeli airlift *achieved five and half times more ton miles per day to Israel than to Berlin.*[11]

A 'ton mile' is the weight of one ton being used one mile, one time. Among other things, the equipment brought to Israel included all kinds of ammunition including 2,000 TOW missiles; 14,800 rounds of 105 mm APDS (powerful armour piercing ammunition); 16,256 LAWs (light anti-tank weapons); 11,500 rounds of 105 mm HEAT (high explosive anti-tank ammunition); and on a more humane side 100,000 morphine Syrettes.[12]

In addition, according to secret documents recently declassified, it is known that on board two Israeli ships departed from Germany there were 65 M-60 tanks and 23 M-109 self-propelled howitzers and on other carriers, some 400 M-54 trucks. In all there was a total of 567 missions flown by C-5s and C-141s, and those missions transported a total of 22,000 tons of war supplies.[13] Kenneth Patchin offers some comparisons to the Russian airlift to Egypt and Syria, which were flown concurrently with *Operation Nickel Grass*:

> On the Russian Airlift, with the best estimates available, their 935 missions over a distance of 1,700 miles moved in about 15,000 tons during a 40 days period. In short, MAC airlifted one fourth (sic) more cargo with a little more than half the missions, over a route that was three times greater.[14]

It is difficult to estimate the financial value of the equipment supplied to Israel. It is important to note, however, that during the war President Nixon authorized a special appropriation to Israel for $2.2 billion which was supposed to cover the cost of this equipment.

The airlift had a great military, political and psychological impact. Militarily, it replenished the heavy losses of Israeli tanks, planes, missiles and above all, ammunition. It is reported that Meir decided to postpone the crossing of the canal until the beginning of the airlift. A lot of equipment arriving in Israel was dispatched directly to the front, especially ammunition. It is difficult to assess whether their absence would have changed the course of the war, but it is obvious that their presence facilitated a quicker and more decisive victory and a less costly one in terms of loss of human life.

Politically, it acted as a deterrent to the Soviets against contemplating intervention in the war, signalling that the US was capable of massive movement of equipment and in taking strong political decisions, even at a time when the President was heavily involved in the Watergate crisis. A tank was loaded on one of the planes to demonstrate to the Soviets that if need be the US could airlift to Israel tanks as well. It also signalled politically to the Arabs that the US was not about to abandon its ally, Israel.

Psychologically, it was extremely important for the morale of the soldiers and the people of Israel, who were undergoing difficult hours. Contrary to some reports, at no time was the question of the nuclear capability of Israel mentioned in course of conversations with the US during the war, or used as leverage to expedite the US arms supply.

When the American planes and pilots landed in Israel, Golda Meir went to greet them. She telephoned me from the airport, describing the warmth and love with which the American pilots were received. Her voice was choked: 'This is a great day, an historic day for our two democracies', she said. There was not a dry eye at the airport, nor at the Embassy.

The good relations with leaders of the Congress were also of great importance in winning this battle. Many of them called the White House and the Secretaries of State and Defence to urge for the supply of military equipment to Israel. Senator Henry 'Scoop' Jackson, a leading member of the Armed Services Committee, was particularly close to Secretary Schlesinger and wondered why Schlesinger, as a Jew, should not be more helpful in getting the supplies for Israel. I pointed out to Scoop that Schlesinger had converted twice. 'How many times', I inquired, 'does a Jew have to convert before you stop referring to him as a Jew?' Scoop said: 'Once a Jew, always a Jew.'

Senator Frank Church, a senior Democrat on the Senate Foreign Relations Committee, was extremely helpful when the US was searching for a route to transfer the equipment to Israel. No European country would allow American aircraft to land for refuelling on their way to Israel. America needed to use its base in the Azores islands, but the Portuguese Government had conditioned its consent on the US Senate lifting the sanctions imposed on the Salazar regime by the Church Amendment. I went to speak to Senator Church and he agreed to do this in order to facilitate the emergency aid to Israel.

By now, the tide of the war had turned. Israel was crossing the Suez Canal into Egypt. President Sadat became alarmed about the fate of his Third Army, and the road to Cairo was now wide open to Israeli troops.

THE CEASE-FIRE

The timing for a cease-fire became a controversy. The Russians, who had been postponing earlier attempts at reaching a cease-fire, to stop the

Egyptian offensive, were now pushing hard for it in order to stop the Israeli advance. President Nixon, at the height of the Watergate crisis, did not want another crisis with the Soviet Union. He dispatched Kissinger to Moscow on 20 October, with instructions followed by full authority, to conclude an immediate Cease-Fire Agreement right then and there. Israel was not interested in calling a halt to its advance. The Agreement on the Cease-Fire was reached in Moscow faster than anticipated, but not fast enough to save the Egyptian army from encirclement by the Israelis. Kissinger flew from Moscow to Tel Aviv to explain the predicament that had forced him to conclude the Agreement on Cease-Fire with Russia so quickly. By 22 October, the United Nations Security Council approved the Cease-Fire. Since the Egyptians continued to shoot, thus violating the Cease-Fire, Israel took advantage, completed the encirclement of the town of Suez and sealed the closing on the Egyptian Third Army. That move by Israel was a subject of great controversy and dispute between the United States and Israel.

Kissinger claimed that by this move, concluded after the Agreement was reached with the Soviet Union and approved by the United Nations, Israel had created a new strategic situation which did not exist when the United States and the Soviet Union signed their agreement. This, he contended, was not a technical violation of the Cease-Fire, but a major strategic change, in violation of a written commitment between the two superpowers, and President Nixon would not stand for it. In addition, he argued, the destruction of the Third Army would be the greatest act of humiliation to Egypt and might even bring about the collapse of Sadat's regime. That too, was contrary to American strategy which aimed at bringing the two sides to the negotiating table.

When I retorted that it was the Egyptians who had first violated the Cease-Fire, and that we were not seeking to 'destroy' the Third Army, but to disarm it and send it back to Egypt, Kissinger replied that it amounted to the same thing: 'Sadat will not survive the marching of 20,000 barefoot, unarmed soldiers into the streets of Cairo. It is worse than taking them prisoner.'

This was at the basis of the United States' efforts to avoid starvation or liquidation of the Third Army. At one point, they even raised the possibility of American planes flying food and medical supplies to the besieged army. But at no point did Kissinger entertain the possibility of a joint action with the Soviet Union, or allow a unilateral Soviet action.

THE NUCLEAR ALERT

The Soviets, who were not sure about the wisdom of Egypt and Syria initiating the war in the first place, gave them full support once the war started. Moreover, surprised and encouraged by the early success of their clients, they saw in it an opportunity to extend and enhance the Soviet influence in the Middle East and curtail that of America. But that hope quickly evaporated as they realized that the military reversals of their clients threatened the very regimes of both Sadat and Asad, and the Arab world was turning more and more to Washington for assistance and guidance. If Moscow was essential for the conduct of war, Washington became pivotal for the diplomacy of peace. For the Russians, the encirclement of the Third Army and the possible collapse of Sadat would signal a total collapse of their ally which they had equipped and supported. If this was to happen, they would have liked that Egypt at least place the blame on the United States.

It is in this light that we must view the desperate note sent on 24 October by Leonid Brezhnev to Nixon threatening to take unilateral action in the Middle East if the United States did not agree to a joint action to curb the Israelis. This Russian threat produced the American nuclear alert (25 October 1973, Defcon III), described as the most serious potential confrontation between the superpowers since the Cuban Missile Crisis. The US response was to place American forces on military alert, even before sending the written reply to Brezhnev. 'Let the Soviets learn of our intentions by picking up the signals in the radar screens', said Kissinger to me, 'that way they will treat our Note that follows more seriously'.

I was one of the few at the time who were shown the actual Russian message. Kissinger called me late in the afternoon to the White House to await the National Security Council decision on the Soviet note. I advised Golda Meir of this dramatic development, and she called for an emergency meeting of the Cabinet in Jerusalem. Later in the evening, still at the White House, I was informed of the NSC decision, as Haig and Kissinger were going upstairs to inform the President and receive his approval. The Soviet threat and America's reaction were a subject of a great domestic controversy, which to some extent lingers until today. Was the Russian threat serious? Did America overreact? Was the National Security Council decision, taken without the presence of President Nixon, motivated by Watergate and the domestic situation?

Because I had actually seen the Russian note, I was the focus of many inquiries regarding the justification of the American reaction. I answered that the wisdom of the American reaction ought to be judged by the results it produced. Since Soviet unilateral intervention, or a nuclear confrontation, did not take place, obviously the American reaction was the right one. We will never know whether the Soviets really meant to do what they had threatened to do. The only thing we do know is that they didn't and thus the reaction of the US was justified.

At the beginning of the war, Foreign Minister Abba Eban was sent by Golda Meir to New York to watch over the United Nations. Meir did not want Eban to leave New York and did not want me to leave Washington. Eban requested that I brief him on the rapid developments in Washington. Finally, Meir okayed a brief trip for me to meet Eban in New York. We arranged a lunch on Wednesday, 10 October, at 1:30pm in Manhattan. I took the 12:00 noon shuttle plane to New York, accompanied by my bodyguard. As we landed in La Guardia, I received a message to call my office in Washington very urgently. I called my deputy, Minister Mordechai Shalev, who in a choked voice said: 'Come right back, "The Bears" (meaning the Russians) are threatening again. Golda says you should return to Washington immediately.' I sent the driver to the restaurant with a note of apology to Abba Eban, turned around and took the 1:00pm shuttle right back to Washington. My bodyguard, who was sitting next to me and had not opened his mouth the whole trip, was unaware of the reason for the sudden return. Finally he said: 'Of course, it's none of my business, but why are we travelling back and forth on the shuttle?' I looked at him and said: 'You know what a tense period this is. Some people take a drive to relax. I take a flight.'

I was hardly relaxed for the rest of the flight. The threat by 'The Bears' was a threat by the Russians to send missiles over Israel, if it did not accept their proposal and withdraw to the cease fire line. It created quite an alarm when General Scowcroft informed Minister Shalev of it, and caused an emergency night session of the Cabinet in Jerusalem. When I got to Washington and saw Kissinger, it became clear that the Russians had been bluffing. We did not withdraw and they did not send missiles.

DIPLOMACY OF PEACE

Now that the cease-fire was on, the Egyptian Third Army encircled, the Syrian army pushed back from the Golan and beyond, and Israel within 60 miles of Cairo and 30 miles of Damascus, the US was prepared to launch its diplomacy. Even while the war was on, Kissinger began to plan the diplomacy of peace. This explains some of his seemingly contradictory and controversial moves both in the Arab–Israeli context as well as in the Soviet–American sphere.

In the Middle East arena Kissinger, as was stated earlier, wanted Israel's victory over Egypt. But at the same time Kissinger did not want a vanquished Egypt, a destroyed and humiliated Egypt that might even endanger the continued regime of President Sadat. He wanted a Sadat despaired of the option of war and ready for peace negotiations; he did not want a Sadat despaired of America and filled with a notion of revenge. He wanted a Sadat angry at the Russians for not assisting him sufficiently in the military sphere to defeat Israel, but grateful enough to the Americans for preventing Israel from subordinating him completely. He wanted the Arabs to end the oil embargo, not because they had succeeded in intimidating America but because they needed America's goodwill. We were fully aware of this strategy and were in basic agreement with it. Our difficulties and arguments lay with some of its tactical implementation.

In the Soviet sphere, Kissinger wanted to diminish Soviet influence without destroying cooperation; to take away the initiative from the

Russians in the Middle East while giving them the feeling that they were still partners; to limit their freedom of action without provoking them into intervention. In brief, to win the Cold War confrontation without destroying détente.

All this had to be done during a period of great anxiety and turmoil in America. For Watergate was not only a domestic upheaval but a great danger to American posture and leadership in the world. Everything had to be planned as if America was in full control of its moves, and headed by a strong and credible leader in navigating world events. The Russians might have underestimated the impact of Watergate, the Europeans might have belittled its seriousness, but Kissinger knew the truth. Every student of the Washington scene could detect a president who functioned only partially; a Congress completely occupied with Vietnam and Watergate; and a press driven to explore Watergate to the end and later consumed with the desire to put an end to Nixon's presidency.

In spite of Kissinger's attempt to minimize it, Watergate did have an effect on the conduct of American foreign policy in general and on Nixon's relations to Israel. Nixon's attitude to Israel and the Jewish people had always been dichotomous. On the one hand, he had a great admiration for Israel as a nation, which, defying all odds, defended itself successfully against hostile neighbours. An Israel, which had become a strategic asset and bulwark against Russian expansion in the Middle East. But at the same time, Nixon distinguished clearly between the 'gutsy' Israeli and the 'liberal' American Jew for whom he had little regard. He thought that those Jews practised double standards by being critical of him on the use of force in the Far East and yet demanding strong American intervention policy in the Middle East.

His overestimation of Jewish control and influence in the financial world and the media, bordered on the notion of the *Protocols of the Elders of Zion*. He was convinced, for instance, that Watergate was a Jewish conspiracy against him and he called Bob Woodward and Carl Bernstein of the *Washington Post* – 'Woodstein'. It was indeed inexplicable that the man who had ordered a tenfold increase of military supplies in the airlift to Israel could be the same man who later issued injunctions against military supplies to Israel during the post-war negotiations; that the man who had approved $2.2 billion as emergency aid to Israel during the war would consider sanctions against Israel in the post-war diplomacy; that the man who admired the Jewish State and its leader could advise his daughter (on the White House tapes) not to associate with Jews, artists and homosexuals when she visited New York; that the man who had hired Henry Kissinger as his close National Security adviser and then his Secretary of State, could question his objectivity on the Middle East situation. As when Kissinger had given a briefing at the National Security Council, Nixon told the participants: 'Now let us hear an *American* point of view' (emphasis added).

It was under these constraints that the post-Yom Kippur War diplomacy must be viewed. Kissinger initiated the step-by-step diplomacy in order to lead the way from total belligerency to partial peace. That suited the Egyptians who were not ready for a full-fledged peace, and it suited the Israelis who were not prepared for a full-fledged withdrawal. This course of diplomacy produced the first Disengagement of Forces Agreement with Egypt, the Disengagement Agreement with Syria, and the Interim Agreement with Egypt. All this was achieved not without ups and downs and serious crises with Russia, Egypt and Syria, and especially with Israel.

It was during one of these crises with the US that Republican Senator from New York Jacob Javitz was visiting Israel and met with Golda Meir. Assuming that she would ask him to help in this crisis, he wanted to set the record straight and said: 'You must remember that I am an American first, a Senator second and a Jew third'. 'That's OK with me', said Meir, 'in Hebrew we read from right to left'.

The new realignment of the political forces in the Middle East was a source of concern and suspicion for Israel. The pre-Yom Kippur War Middle East was neatly divided between countries under American influence and those under Russian. The demarcation lines were clear: the United States was an ally of Israel; and the Soviet Union that of Egypt and Syria. And while there were other Arab countries [Jordan, Saudi Arabia and the Persian Gulf countries] who were within the US sphere of influence, they were not *directly* involved in that war or for that matter in the diplomacy that followed.

Now there was a new alignment in the post-war Middle East. The US was also a patron of Egypt and even, to some extent, of Syria. They both relied on it to pressure Israel and extract political advantages from the war they lost. The United States was anxious to demonstrate to them that they could rely on it instead of on Russia. 'You can get better declarations of support from the Russians', was the voice from Washington, 'but action you can get only from us'.

This was not the United States Israel knew. It was now an ally turned arbitrator. It explains some of the tension inherent in the effort to translate the victory of a costly war into a risky peace. For Israel knew that what it had to put on its side of the bargaining table were concrete elements such as territory, and settlements, while what was required from the other side were promises and pledges. In such an equation the name of the game is trust and confidence and this could only be built step by step.

One of the major crises between the United States and Israel came in the dispute over where the line of Israel's withdrawal in the Sinai should be to facilitate the Interim Agreement with Egypt. When Israel resisted American pressure to fix the line west of the strategic Passes in the Sinai, Kissinger left the area in anger, publicly blaming Israel, and advising President Gerald Ford to declare a reassessment of American policy towards Israel.

A fierce diplomatic battle followed in America between the Administration and Israel to gain public sympathy and Congressional support for their respective stands. Kissinger flew to see Senator James William Fulbright, a known critic of Israel, then Chairman of the Foreign Relations Committee of the Senate. I went to see Senator Church and other members of the same Committee, trying to explain our case. Secretary Kissinger severed all contacts between us, except through the 'mediation' of Lawrence Eagleburger, Under Secretary of State, and Kissinger's able and loyal aide. Leaks began to appear in the press that the White House and State Department were reconsidering Israel's requests for assistance. When over 70 Senators signed a letter to the President in support of Israel, Kissinger sent me a message that the President would never forgive or forget 'the incitement of Congress against him'. It became clear that in the battle that was raging between the two allies, so disproportionate in size and might, there would be no victors or vanquished. The only forces which could benefit from such a rift would be the Soviet Union and radical Arab states who opposed diplomatic progress towards peace.

Prime Minister Yitzhak Rabin, who formerly served as Ambassador in Washington, realized that we had to find a way out of the deadlock. On his instructions I flew on a secret mission to talk to Secretary Kissinger who was on vacation at the Rockefeller retreat in the Virgin Islands. Larry Eagleburger arranged an unmarked White House plane to fly us both to Kissinger's hideout. Not until we got on the plane at St. Andrews Air Force Base did I know where we were heading. When I asked Larry what I should bring with me, a sweater or a raincoat, he said: 'Bring a shirt, but be careful not to lose it during the meeting...'. We landed on one of the islands where a coast-guard boat took us to St. John's Island. As we arrived at the Rockefeller's retreat the sun was setting, and I could see the wooden hut where Kissinger and his wife were staying, lit by lux lanterns and with some of the window screens torn. Kissinger greeted me and I said to him: 'I guess one must be very rich to live so very poor'. (Only later did I understand that when on vacation, rich people like to rough it and poor people look for luxury).

We negotiated the whole night over the suggestion I had brought, that American observers with the proper equipment be stationed in the strategic Mitla and Gidi passes of the Sinai to monitor the Egyptian movements, so that we could retreat to a line beyond the Passes. By sunrise, we agreed on the plan, which was now to be brought for approval to President Ford and to Prime Minister Rabin. Kissinger said that he saw no chance that President Ford would approve it. Being acquainted with his vocabulary, I knew that 'no chance' meant that there was a good likelihood that the President would approve it. The President did and so did Rabin. The understanding we had reached that night facilitated the signing of the first political agreement between Egypt and Israel in September 1975.

Early in the morning, Larry and I reached the unmarked Presidential plane that was to take us back to Washington. After sitting on the ground for half an hour and knowing that we were not expecting any other passengers, I asked Larry to check with the pilot why we were not moving. Larry came back from the cockpit with the incredible story that the gasoline station attendant at the small airport was refusing to refuel the White House plane because it had no markings on it, and was demanding payment in cash. None of us had $3,500 in cash, and Larry was now anxiously calling General Scowcroft at the White House. General Scowcroft said to the pilot: 'Order him to fill the plane but don't identify yourself'. 'I tried', said the pilot 'but it didn't help'. 'OK', said the General, 'We'll take other measures'.

Twenty minutes later, I was to understand what 'other measures' meant in White House terminology. From the window of the plane I could see an armed personnel carrier flying the American flag, followed by a huge gasoline tanker, approaching us. The attendant at the gasoline pump rushed to the station and locked himself behind the door, sure that the United States had decided to invade his territory. That indeed was a military contingent brought from a nearby American military base. The Presidential plane was refuelled and we took off leaving the attendant still locked in the station. I turned to Larry and said: 'Regarding the agreement we have just initialled with Henry, you really think we can trust American monitoring observers in Sinai, if you can't be trusted with refuelling your own Presidential plane?'

Shortly afterwards (July 1975) I flew to join Prime Minister Rabin and Secretary Kissinger at an American military base in Germany, to conclude the last details of the suggested draft to the Interim Agreement with Egypt. Two months later, and after another round of talks with Kissinger in the area, the Interim Agreement with Egypt was signed in Jerusalem and Alexandria (1 September 1975).

This first political Agreement signed between Israel and an Arab country laid the foundations for the continuation of the peace diplomacy which culminated in the Camp David Agreements and which laid the foundation for the continued peace diplomacy until the present day. It was terrible indeed, that the Yom Kippur War was needed to create the necessary conditions for peace.

For the Egyptians, their military successes in the early stages of the War restored to them (and to some extent to the Syrians), the confidence they had lost, and helped them overcome the trauma of the humiliating defeat of 1967. They now felt as equal partners. But that on its own would not have been sufficient. Had the tide of war continued in their favour and they had been able to defeat Israel, they would have had no need or incentive to negotiate. However, the fact that the war had ended with the Israeli army 60 miles from Cairo and 30 miles from Damascus indicated to them that in spite of their early successes, in spite of all the odds working for them – surprise attack, oil embargo, massive Russian support, Arab solidarity – they were still not able to overcome Israel. It was the combination of these two factors – the restoration of Arab pride and the realization that force would not retrieve their land – that made them turn to the diplomatic option which facilitated negotiations.

For the Israelis too, the war created the incentive for negotiation. It became clear to them that the victory of 1967 did not provide insurance against future wars; that *status quo* could not be a substitute for a political solution, that military power on its own could provide only partial security, and that a compromise was necessary in order to achieve recognition and peace in the Middle East.

It was the wisdom of American diplomacy, which knew to combine all these elements and convert the results of the war into a negotiation for peace. Had there not been a strong diplomatic initiative, the opportunities created by the war would have remained dormant until the next violent eruption. It became clear that while the United States could not and ought not make the necessary concessions for the parties, it could make the parties feel more secure and confident in taking the risks that any negotiation demands.

NOTES

1. BBC Monitoring Service 6.2.71, and other references which appear in the well documented article by Mordechai Gazit, 'Egypt and Israel – Was a Peace Opportunity Missed in 1971?', *Journal of Contemporary History* 32/1 (1997), pp.97–115.
2. Mahmoud Riad, *The Struggle for Peace in the Middle East*, London: Quartet Books, 1981, pp.194–8; Ismail Fahmi, *Negotiating for Peace in the Middle East*, Baltimore: Johns Hopkins University Press, 1983, p.283; and Muhammed Ibrahim Kamel, *The Camp David Accords*, London: KPI Ltd., 1986. It should be remembered that Ibrahim Kamel refused to participate in the signing of the Camp David Agreements because of his objection to a separate agreement which did not involve Israel's commitment on the other fronts.
3. Gazit, 'Egypt and Israel', p.100.
4. Ibid., p.102.
5. Henry Kissinger, *White House Years*, Boston: Little, Brown, 1979, pp.1280–2, 1287, 1288.
6. Henry Kissinger, *Years of Upheaval*, Boston: Little, Brown, 1982, pp.214–15.
7. Yitzhak Rabin, *Pinkas Sherut* [*Service Record*], Tel Aviv: Ma'ariv, 1979, p.389 (Hebrew); Yitzhak Rabin, *The Rabin Memoirs*, Boston: Little, Brown, 1979, pp.216–17; and Kissinger, *Years of Upheaval*, p.221.
8. Golda Meir, *My Life*, New York: G.B. Putnam's Sons, 1975, pp.418–19.
9. Richard M. Nixon, *The Memoirs of Richard Nixon*, New York: Sidgwick and Jackson, 1978, p.924.
10. Ibid., p.927.
11. Kenneth L Patchin, *Flight to Israel: A Historical Documentary of Strategic Airlift to Israel, 14 October–14 November 1973*, Office of the MAC (Military Airlift Command), History, Scott AFB, Illinois, 30 April 1974, (Revised 1 July 1976), quoted in Kenneth K. Robertson, *Operation Nickel Grass*, Dover, Delaware, 1998, p.263.
12. Robertson, *Operation Nickel Grass*, p.57.
13. Patchin, *Flight to Israel*, pp.249–50.
14. Ibid., pp.249–55.

The Soviet Union and the Yom Kippur War

GALIA GOLAN

The Yom Kippur War was a war that the Soviet Union did not want. The period preceding the war had been one in which Moscow had sought to deter both the Egyptians and the Syrians from their war plans. Indeed, it was a period in which the relationship with the Arabs had deteriorated in large part because of these Soviet efforts. Moscow had invested quite heavily, both politically and militarily, in Egypt and, to a somewhat lesser extent, in Syria, primarily in order to obtain and maintain a system of air bases and naval facilities important to its Mediterranean naval squadron and disposition *vis-à-vis* the American sixth fleet (and its Polaris components). The Soviets had taken the unprecedented (for Moscow) step of placing close to 20,000 military personnel and advanced defensive missiles in a non-Marxist, non-contiguous, Third World country, Egypt, in order to shore up the government of Gamal Abdul Nasser, which had made possible this Soviet military and political challenge to western power in the region. In so doing, the Soviets came close to destroying the nascent détente emerging with the West, and particularly the United States, in the early 1970s. It was both to preserve this détente and, most importantly, to avoid the risk of military confrontation with the United States that Moscow sought to deter Egyptian President Anwar al-Sadat and Syrian President Hafiz al-Asad from initiating a new Arab–Israeli war. A military crisis in the Middle East, where both superpowers were heavily and directly committed, was deemed by Soviet experts as one which could easily, if not inevitably, escalate to global proportions, not only destroying détente but precipitating a superpower conflagration.[1]

Thus, even as the Soviet Union armed its Middle Eastern clients, it argued that these arms should be used as a bargaining chip – to negotiate

Galia Golan is Jay and Leoni Darwin Professor at the Department of Political Science, The Hebrew University of Jerusalem, Israel.

from strength – in what should be purely political efforts to achieve the return of Arab territories from Israel. More to the point, Moscow repeatedly postponed delivery of various types and quantities of arms, in particular the offensive weapons such as the Scud ground-to-ground missiles and MiG-23 fighter planes deemed necessary for an Arab attack. Soviet promises of arms and failures to fulfil these promises have been amply documented, in particular by Sadat. It was finally these three connected factors, the continued delay of such arms deliveries, Moscow's opposition to a war and the deepening of superpower détente, that led to Sadat's expulsion of the Soviet military advisers from Egypt in July 1972 and a serious deterioration in Soviet relations with Egypt and eventually also Syria.

What was apparent at this time was a dualism in Soviet policy which sought to serve perhaps contradictory purposes. There was the clear Soviet interest in the Arab world, for both military and political reasons, and, therefore, a need to preserve and strengthen the relationship. At the same time, there was not only the interest in avoiding military confrontation with the United States but also the important development of détente, not least of which for economic reasons, that could hardly be served by increased polarization and tension between the superpowers. To some degree this dualism was reflected in if not actually caused by differing opinions within the Soviet regime, with hard-liners, that is, those in favour of an expansionist policy and opposed to détente, versus doves, that is, those who, favouring détente, were concerned about involvement in the Third World. These were not totally defined camps, nor were the parameters all that clear, for there were those who favoured expanding Soviet influence for ideological reasons but were highly sceptical about the reliability of non-Marxist regimes, while others, including parts of the military, worried both about placing advanced Soviet arms in unstable regions or countries and about the danger of military confrontation with the United States. Whether the result of a juggling of the two main attitudes within the Politburo or simply the effort to pursue two important but potentially incompatible policies at the same time, Soviet Third World policy in general and Middle East policy in particular assumed a dualistic nature. Leonid Brezhnev himself appeared to believe that one could 'divide détente', limiting it to the superpower sphere, while expanding (defined as pleasing your clients) in the Third World. The Middle East was one of the areas where such a division of détente was particularly problematic.

The expulsion of the Soviet advisers from Egypt led to a serious reevaluation in Moscow of its Third World policies, but, following six months of what Sadat later described as 'frozen relations' and a suspension of all arms deliveries to Egypt, the Soviets decided to restore the relationship, resuming arms supplies and returning some 1,500 military advisers to Egypt in February 1973 (although nowhere near the previous numbers). The suspension of arms supplies had not changed and certainly had not improved Soviet–Arab relations, and there was a growing possibility that Sadat would find his way to the Americans.[2] As far as can be determined, the Soviets were aware at this point of Sadat's plans to go to war in 1973, although they may have believed that the year would pass much as Sadat's 1971 'year of decision' had passed without a military action. It is also possible that Moscow believed that by continuing to deny the Arabs at least some of the advanced offensive weaponry and by keeping under direct Soviet control that which they did provide (Scuds), they could prevent the war.

According to some Soviet sources, Brezhnev and others in the Politburo did believe that resumed arms supplies would create greater Soviet ability to influence Sadat's decisions and prevent war.[3] This is substantiated by the fact that the Soviets continued to try to dissuade both Sadat and Asad from going to war, arousing their anger and even open polemics, creating a seriously strained atmosphere in the months prior to the outbreak of the war.[4] While it could be argued that this was part of a disinformation campaign, designed to deceive Israeli intelligence which may have estimated that Egypt would not go to war without Soviet backing, there was and has been no indication either before or since the Yom Kippur War that anything but serious disagreement existed between Moscow, on the one hand, and Egypt and Syria on the other, over the plan to go to war. What did, to some degree, deceive Israeli intelligence, though not intentionally as far as can be determined, was the continued withholding of almost all of the offensive equipment sought by Egypt and Syria.

On 3 October Sadat informed the Soviet Ambassador Vladimir Vinogradov that war was 'imminent' without specifying the day or time, and on 4 October Asad informed the Soviet ambassador in Damascus, Nureddin Mukhitidinov, that the battle would be in a few days. Only on the morning of 6 October did both Sadat and Asad inform the respective Soviet ambassadors of the hour (Sadat more vaguely than Asad). Actually Sadat's 3 October communication, albeit vague, was sufficient to prompt the Soviets to begin evacuating their civilians – an act which they conducted through a far from secret airlift which threatened to destroy the element of surprise (and did raise alarm in Jerusalem). Although Egyptian military were angry over what they considered to be a breach of secrecy, the Soviets do not appear to have planned to thwart Arab plans by this form of indirect disclosure.[5] At this stage, they apparently believed it was too late to change anything, only offering Sadat, once again, the advice that a political solution was preferable.

With the outbreak of war, the dualism and dilemmas characteristic of Moscow's Middle East policy became acute. Soviet behaviour would have sought to serve two primary objectives: (i) the preservation of relations with Egypt and Syria; and (ii) the preservation of détente and avoidance of military confrontation with the United States. Each of these objectives would prove most difficult; both together would prove impossible. Clearly an early cease-fire would be highest on the Soviet agenda so as to avoid what they believed would in fact be an Egyptian defeat. Soviet military leaders, still smarting from the abrupt expulsion of 1972, had little regard for Egyptian military capabilities and expected an Arab defeat. According to Victor Israelyan, Soviet military leaders initially relished the idea of such a defeat (proof that Egypt could not win without the Soviets) and whether out of this sentiment or in defence of their low estimates of Arab capabilities, they reportedly withheld from the Politburo information on Israeli losses.[6] Political leaders, including Brezhnev, also believed the Arabs would lose, so together both the presumably pro-détente, dovish forces and the anti-détente, hawkish forces – insofar as they could actually be categorized this way – all saw the need for a speedy cease-fire, both to prevent discrediting of Soviet arms and, more importantly perhaps, to forestall any need to respond to an Arab call for direct Soviet involvement. Similarly, were there any who believed Israel was heading for defeat – and apparently there were none initially – it could equally be argued that an Israel facing defeat would call in the Americans, which in turn would necessitate Soviet involvement. Either scenario spelled relative disaster. Yet the first objective could not be ignored: the Arab allies could neither be neglected nor short-changed.

The first result was a Soviet effort to gain Egyptian and Syrian agreement to a cease-fire. This was pursued from the earliest hours of the conflict, although Ambassador Vinogradov succeeded in seeing Sadat only in the evening after the battle had begun. His efforts continued on 7 and 8 October, incurring Sadat's increasing anger. The Egyptian leader's ire was augmented by Vinogradov's insistence that Asad had agreed to a cease-fire, which, according to Israelyan, was the case as of the evening of 7 October.[7] However, prior to the war, Asad had discussed with Soviet Ambassador Mukhitidinov a plan whereby the battle would last only 48 hours, after which the Soviet Union would propose a cease-fire at the United Nations.[8] There is some discrepancy between ex-Soviet and Arab versions of this discussion, but it would appear that whoever made the suggestion in the talks with the Syrians on how operative that plan was or was not, Sadat refused to believe that Asad was ready for a cease-fire. Without Egypt's agreement, Moscow refrained from joining the US in a call for a cease-fire, particularly since the US version called for withdrawal of the Arab forces, which to the Soviets' surprise were registering successes. There was the added, though secondary problem, that Moscow's competitor China would veto any proposal the Arabs rejected. The Soviets did, however, draw up a resolution to be presented to the UN Security Council at some point and continued to press Sadat for agreement.

Moscow published its first official reaction to the beginning of hostilities only on the evening of 7 October – following the two days' unsuccessful attempts to gain Sadat's approval of a cease-fire. While the official statement itself made no mention of a cease-fire, presumably out of deference to Egypt, it nonetheless exhibited some elements of restraint aimed mainly at portraying the conflict as a local and limited event, which by implication should not involve the superpowers or harm détente. The following day, however, some of the disagreements in the Politburo surfaced in what were two quite different characterizations of the war. In a speech honouring visiting Japanese Premier Tanaka, Brezhnev emphasized and praised the relaxation of world tensions and the trend towards détente, viewing the Middle East war as something of an exception. Brezhnev described the conflict in purely local terms, making no reference to 'imperialist' or American culprits. In contrast, on the same day, *Pravda* carried an article by Defence Minister Andrei Grechko (on the thirtieth anniversary of the battle of the Caucasus) which pointed directly to the war waging in the Middle East as proof of the continued aggressiveness of the imperialists – a formulation clearly associated with the anti-détente position.

At this stage, the two views did not represent differing opinions upon how the Soviet Union should proceed with regard to the war. Inasmuch as the military, including Grechko, did not believe the Arabs could win, they were not at odds with what was generally the more pro-détente interest in ending the war as quickly as possible. Yet there were two events which seemed to contradict this interest and, actually, assist in prolongation of the war. The first was a message sent by Brezhnev to a number of Arab leaders calling for 'Arab solidarity' and support for Egypt and Syria in their 'hard fight against the Israeli aggressor'.[9] Such a call certainly gave the impression that Moscow was seeking to expand the war and thereby also prolong it, thus contradicting the policy adopted by the Politburo. In fact, however, the letters were a response to queries made by Algerian President Houari Boumedienne to all the permanent members of the Security Council immediately after the beginning of hostilities.

According to the one letter published, that which was sent to Boumedienne the evening of 8 October, the Soviets not only emphasized the need for Arab solidarity, but also added that the Algerian leaders 'understood' the complexity of the situation. The strong suggestion, subsequently confirmed, was that Moscow was putting the ball back in the Arab court, that is, responding that it was the Arab rather than Soviet responsibility to assist, particularly in view of the risks of a superpower getting directly involved. Indeed, Soviet leaders reportedly told Boumedienne during his 14–15 October visit to Moscow that 'the Arab countries should be worrying about solidarity with Egypt and Syria rather than lecturing the Russians on how to help them'.[10] Nine years later, after the Israeli invasion of Lebanon, the same Soviet message to the Arab world was even more explicit and clear.

Moscow had not intended for this exchange of messages to be published, nor was it particularly anxious to receive answers, for the

Arab ambassadors had great difficulty in getting appointments to see Foreign Minister Andrei Gromyko in the next days. The only exception to this were the Iraqis, from whom Moscow was in fact seeking direct transfer of aid to Syria. Iraqi Foreign Minister Murtada Abdul Baqi made a trip to Moscow on 9–10 October and met with Soviet President Nikolai Podgorny. According to Mohamed Heikal, Baqi asked the Soviets to intervene with the Shah of Iran to relax tension on the Iran–Iraq border so as to free up Iraqi troops to fight with Syria. Podgorny reportedly commented in these talks that he was surprised that the Arab states, particularly Iraq and Algeria, were not using their Soviet-supplied equipment to do more for Egypt and Syria.[11] The request to Iraq to send aid, particularly tanks, was part of a larger effort which was the second event to stand in apparent contradiction to the attempt to end the war quickly: the massive sea and air lift of equipment begun on 9 October.

There was reportedly little debate or controversy within the Politburo over the initial decision to send military aid at this point.[12] It may have been remembered that Moscow had been severely criticized, at least in Egypt, for not providing supplies of any kind during the 1967 Six Day War. It was important for Soviet credibility as a reliable ally to provide some kind of assistance. And the accidental Israeli bombing of the Soviet cultural centre in Damascus on 9 October may well have strengthened the disposition to help. The decision to commence the air and sea lifts was taken on 7 or 8 October (there are conflicting accounts), but Sadat complained to the Soviet ambassador on 9 October that the airlift had not begun.[13] In fact some planes did arrive that day, both to Egypt and Syria.

The intention of the air and sea lifts was not, however, indirectly to intervene and thereby prolong the battle, but, rather, the assistance was based upon the assumption that the Arabs were going to lose. The Syrians had halted their advances – inexplicably in the eyes of Soviet military experts – and had already suffered some reversals from the Israeli counter-attack. In addition, estimates of Egyptian capabilities were still quite low, despite the early victories. On this front too, the Arabs were digging in rather than advancing as the Soviet military would have advised them to do. Soviet military leaders, still expecting Arab defeat, were quick to point out that neither Soviet military doctrine nor advice was being applied.[14] Additional signs of Soviet concern over the Arabs' expected fate could be seen in the stepped up alert in the Soviet airborne forces reportedly begun on 8 October, and the following day a Cosmos satellite (launched on 3 October) was returned to earth, six or seven days earlier than the usual period in space, revealing, perhaps, the extent of Israeli action on the Golan. In view of this situation, the airlift might have been initiated in order to shore up the Arab armies until a cease-fire could be established, averting an Arab disaster that would precipitate a call for direct Soviet intervention. Moreover, the aid might strengthen Moscow's hand in gaining Sadat's agreement to a cease-fire.[15]

While the initial decision to send aid, presumably to stabilize the battlefield until a cease-fire, was not contested, some differences of opinion reportedly did appear as the Arab situation began to deteriorate. Sadat for his part complained that the equipment was not coming as scheduled; he also complained about the items being sent, maintaining that Moscow was merely fulfilling existing contracts, and more bitterly, he claimed that the Soviets were asking for hard currency payment, including the payment of $80 million interest due on past deliveries.[16] Asad's negative response came in the form of simply ignoring any mention of the Soviet Union when thanking various states (all Arab) for their help, in a speech he gave in the midst of the war on 15 October. Boumedienne maintained that actually the first days' airlifts consisted only of medical supplies, blankets and the like, changing only after he visited Moscow 14–15 October and provided cash payment (reportedly $100 million each for Egypt and Syria) for Soviet weapons.[17] The airlift did, indeed, virtually triple after 15 October, but that may have been due to the situation on the battlefield rather than Boumedienne's funding.

The issue in Moscow, according to Israelyan, was not the money but the quantities and types of weapons to be sent. Sadat's claims were partially confirmed by these arguments, for the issue was whether to go beyond the long-standing bilateral agreements in resupplying Egypt and Syria or to stay at existing levels.[18] There was growing concern, among the military as well, that the weapons would simply be lost, advanced weapons systems falling into Israeli hands, when in fact the Arabs had more than enough arms, and that still more arms would prolong the war. Nonetheless there was also the growing concern that without increased supplies, the Arab armies would collapse. It was on this point that military leaders, such as Grechko, found themselves in a dilemma – supporting a cease-fire because of the concern over defeat, but favouring increased Arab might and the possibility of an Arab victory for the glory of Soviet arms. While there is no direct evidence of Grechko or other military leaders arguing for increased arms *instead* of a cease-fire, a lone article in the army newspaper, *Krasnaya zvezda*, on 13 October spoke of a prolonged war – suggesting that this opinion may have had some supporters. Indeed Grechko is said to have spoken favourably, later, of a prolonged war of attrition following the successful Israeli counter-offensive of 14 October, but according to another source, he nonetheless approved of an immediate cease-fire.[19]

Soviet efforts for a cease-fire continued even as the air and sea lifts got under way. On 10 October the Soviets informed Washington that they would not block a cease-fire proposal at the United Nations, suggesting that a third party make the proposal and the US and Soviet Union abstain. The reason for this was the failure of Vinogradov's renewed attempt to gain Egyptian approval for a cease-fire. His efforts in this direction were in fact meeting with still greater anger from Sadat, who insisted the Soviets were lying to him about Syrian interest in a cease-fire.[20] Nonetheless, the Soviets, mainly through their ambassador in Washington, Anatoly Dobrinin, were now in daily contact with the Americans. They were actively seeking a way to introduce a cease-fire resolution in the UN, through the British, without Egyptian approval, and without harming Soviet–Egyptian relations. These efforts continued from 10 to 13 October, at which time the British ambassador to Egypt Sir Philip Adams paid an early morning call on Sadat with the Soviet–American proposal for a cease-fire. It is not clear that the Soviets, or the Americans, had intended the British to seek Egyptian agreement, but, in any case, Sadat responded angrily, noting that once again Moscow was trying to deceive him regarding Syria's position.

Even as this Soviet-initiated cease-fire attempt of 10–13 October was unfolding, Moscow's tone, particularly domestically, underwent a change. The shift was most likely caused by the successful Israeli counter-offensive on the Golan Heights, which brought forward units of the IDF within 35 kilometres of Damascus, and, more directly, the sinking of a Soviet merchant ship in the Syrian port of Tartus on 12 October. The Soviets published a harsh governmental statement which constituted the first official warning to Israel of this war. Less harsh perhaps than warnings delivered during the Six Day War and far less harsh than that of the Suez War of 1956, Moscow spoke of 'grave consequences for Israel itself' should it not desist immediately from 'bombings of peaceful towns in Syria and Egypt' and strictly obey 'the norms of international law, including those regarding the freedom of navigation'.[21] It was only in this statement that the Soviets revealed that some of their citizens had been killed in the 9 October bombing of the Soviet cultural centre, evidence that Israeli interference in the Soviet resupply effort to Syria, and, presumably, the breakthrough of Israeli forces near Damascus, were of greater concern than the earlier loss of Soviet civilian lives. At this time, 13 October, Moscow informed the United States of an alert in its airborne forces. It was in response to the official warning that Israel agreed early on 13 October to the ostensibly British cease-fire proposal, even though stopping the battle at this point would have left Egyptian forces on the eastern side of the Suez Canal.

Accompanying the Soviet statement was the commencement, one week after the beginning of the war, of protest meetings and public 'demonstrations' against Israel, as well as a stepped up and quite harsh propaganda campaign against Israel and, to a much lesser degree, the United States. It was at this point, and somewhat alarmingly, that *Krasnaya zvezda* published its comment about a prolonged war and the economic difficulties that Israel would face from a long mobilization-war of attrition. While this commentary may well have reflected the thinking of some in the military, opposing a swift cease-fire, it was an isolated comment, typical of the army paper's tendency to be more hard-line than the rest of the Soviet press. Nonetheless, it was soon to be echoed, reportedly, by Grechko in Politburo deliberations following the Israel counter-offensive against Egypt on 14 October.[22]

The delay in the domestic campaign around the war may have been due to an interest in avoiding alarm among the public, particularly over what was apparently an unpopular war.[23] The regime was interested in promoting détente and, therefore, reluctant to draw attention to events that might contradict the prime basis of détente, that is, that one could reach agreements with the West, that peace was possible. Moreover, Moscow was about to play host to a large international conference of the World Peace Council, meant to be a demonstration of the success of Soviet peace efforts, namely détente. Sensitivity to damage that might be done to détente was also evident in the Soviets' willingness to continue and even slightly increase limited Jewish emigration even during the war – despite Chinese accusations, for example, that this was treason to the Arabs' cause and a source of Israeli military manpower. Jewish emigration was a matter of Soviet–US relations and a delicate part of détente at this time.[24]

Part of Moscow's general tone of restraint with regard to the war was the effort to portray it as a local aberration limited in scope (and hopefully duration). For this reason, apparently, Soviet statements and even propaganda barely mentioned the Palestinians, speaking only of the Arab states' right to have their territories returned. Aside from a brief mention in the 7 October official statement, there were no references to the Palestinians in any subsequent official pronouncements during the war, for example, the 12 and later, 23 October, warnings to Israel, Alexsei Kosygin and Brezhnev's speeches during the war, Ambassador Yakov Malik's speeches to the UN, or Grechko's comments. The Palestinians were even absent from the reports of most of the resolutions and statements produced by the protest meetings as well as official Polish, Hungarian, Bulgarian and Czechoslovak statements on the war.[25] Although TASS and the Soviet press periodically reported Palestinian 'military operations', the Palestinians were generally excluded from the lists of those Arabs aiding the Egyptian and Syrian war effort, despite the fact that Yasir Arafat (according to him) had been included in Brezhnev's appeal for Arab solidarity.[26] The only exception to this was the Trade Union paper *Trud* and its boss, Aleksandr Shelepin, who, in 1969, had been the first Soviet leader publicly to express support for the PLO. Only after the war did Brezhnev resume the pre-war formula calling not only for Israeli withdrawal from the occupied territories but, also, 'justice' for the Palestinian people.[27]

Thus it was only when the efforts to reach a cease-fire were meeting with repeated failure and the situation on the ground becoming one of serious concern, including concern over strikes against Soviet targets abroad, that the tone of Soviet pronouncements, both domestic and international, changed. Even then, however, there was a good deal of caution when referring to the United States. Possibly implying their own anti-détentists, but clearly to defend a continued policy of détente, Soviet media spoke positively of the failure of 'western hawks' to disrupt détente with their calls for greater support for Israel.[28] In his speech welcoming Danish Prime Minister Jorgensen, for example, Kosygin, a supporter of détente, spoke directly of the efforts of opponents of détente in the West to use the war to disrupt détente, and, aside from a vague reference to 'outside protectors' of Israel, Kosygin's remarks contained nothing negative towards the Americans. Similarly, a report on the new US Vice President's views on the Middle East quoted Gerald Ford on America's efforts to seek a cease-fire and his opinion that a possibility existed for a cease-fire. These were typical of Soviet reporting during the war, even as American assistance to Israel was nonetheless mentioned.

While there were Soviet military advisers with both Syrian and Egyptian forces during the war, their numbers were quite small and they were not introduced into actual battle. The Soviets also maintained intelligence surveillance by satellite, by MiG-25 reconnaissance planes, and from the sea, but there does not appear to have been on-going sharing of this information with the Arabs. With the outbreak of the war, the navy had moved its ships in the Mediterranean away from the battle area, to a point off the island of Crete – where the Americans were also deployed. The Soviet navy did, however, gradually introduce more vessels. By 13 October their numbers reached 70, ten more than the maximum ever present previously, consisting of ships on their way back to the Black Sea from Africa and the north, as well as ships sent to shore up the Soviet naval presence during the hostilities. Following the sinking of the Soviet merchant ship, Moscow dispatched a destroyer northeast of Cyprus to protect merchant vessels en route to Syria. By the end of the war, the total of Soviet ships in the Mediterranean reached 96, including 29 surface combatants and 23 submarines.

The commander-in-chief of US Naval Forces in Europe, Admiral Worth Bagley, later said of this Soviet build-up: 'In fact the Soviets weren't overtly aggressive. It looked as though they were taking some care not to cause an incident. On the whole, their overt posture was restrained and considerate.'[29] The numbers may have been intended to impress the Arabs that Moscow was ready for action if necessary, and doing no less than the US which had also augmented its fleet in the Mediterranean. Yet the Soviet ships had no tactical air capability and only limited resources for an infantry landing. A 'modest' total of 1,800 or even less Soviet marines from the also modest total of 18,000 marines in the Soviet armed forces could not be taken for a serious intervention threat, especially in view of the 300 aircraft and 3,000 marines of the American Sixth Fleet at the time.[30]

Up until 14 October the major, or at least most immediate, Soviet concern was over the Syrian front and the possible threat to Damascus. On 14 October, however, their concerns turned to a different direction. On this day Egyptian forces began to move eastward from the positions they had initially gained and held on the first day of the war. In Israel's counter attack, Egypt lost over 500 tanks. The next day, 15 October, the American airlift to Israel began, and the Politburo debated options that evening until almost dawn of 16 October. A small Israeli force managed to cross the Canal during the night of 15 October, to be followed by a more serious contingent the next day, but the Politburo deliberations of the night of 15 October occurred before these events. Thus, Moscow's concern was over the collapse of the Egyptian line and, therefore, the potential for an Israeli move across the Canal, particularly now that Israel was receiving American aid.

According to Israelyan, there were two lines of thought at the meeting, with Brezhnev, Kosygin and Gromyko – the pro-détentists – in favour of sending a high-level emissary (Kosygin) to Cairo to persuade Sadat to agree to a cease-fire. Also in favour of such a trip, but more hesitant about pressing Sadat, were Grechko, but also KGB Chief Yuri Andropov and President Podgorny, the last two reportedly out of concern over the future of Soviet–Arab relations. As noted above, Grechko appeared ambivalent at this time, leaning toward the idea of a war of attrition, recommending therefore that Kosygin merely explore Sadat's position. Brezhnev, on the other hand, reportedly instructed Kosygin to warn Sadat of a possible Israeli crossing of the Canal and to remind the Egyptian leader 'that Cairo is not far away from the Canal'.[31] Brezhnev reportedly also instructed Kosygin to 'be flexible, manoeuvre, do anything required so as not to quarrel with the Arab world. We must not provoke Sadat to declare that we are undermining friendship with the Arabs', but he also told Kosygin to inform Sadat that Moscow could not go on indefinitely sending replacements for Arab losses. Brezhnev is also reported to have referred to the expulsion of the Soviet advisers from Egypt as one of Sadat's many 'mistakes' and suggested that Kosygin remind Sadat that Moscow had always warned him about the grave consequences of going to war.[32] The objective of Kosygin's mission was to obtain Sadat's agreement to a cease-fire.

The trip itself was not particularly successful, and apparently not all that friendly on the Egyptian side. Just hours before Kosygin's arrival Sadat delivered a speech clearly indicating that he had no interest in a cease-fire, warning Israel that Egypt had surface-to-surface missiles, the scuds, aimed at Israeli cities.[33] In his talks with Kosygin between 16 and 19 October, Sadat's main interest was in assuring that Israel would withdraw entirely from the lands occupied in 1967. He did not believe the Soviet warnings about a deterioration on the battlefield, nor did he take seriously the now larger Israeli crossing of the Canal on 16 October. By 18 October, Kosygin reportedly had photographs flown in indicating the scope of the Israeli breakthrough, but Sadat remained unconvinced. Instead, he complained about the Soviet re-supply effort, although in fact Soviet deliveries had increased to somewhere between 70 and 80 flights a day. Moscow also sent a number of troop carriers into the Mediterranean on 17 October.[34] Kosygin, nonetheless, reportedly told

Sadat that Moscow firmly opposed prolongation of the conflict, believing that a protracted war would be counterproductive.[35]

In his final attempt to persuade Sadat, Kosygin reportedly spoke of the Soviet military attaché's estimate that not only was the road to Cairo virtually open for an Israeli advance on the virtually undefended city, but that Egypt's best troops, in the second and third armies, were exposed and might be cut off on the eastern side of the Canal.[36] Israelyan was present in the room when Kosygin made his telephone report to Brezhnev. According to his account, Brezhnev was not at all happy about Kosygin's conduct of the meetings with Sadat, angry, apparently, that the Soviet message to Sadat had not been clear enough. In fact, it would appear that Sadat was not interested in the Soviet message. Supplies were arriving in large quantities, even if not the quantities or types necessarily that had been requested. Most likely, however, Sadat's rejection of Kosygin's urgings was Sadat's chronic distrust of the Soviets (which dated back to the 1956 conflict), particularly in view of Moscow's opposition to Arab plans to go to war and Vinogradov's repeated efforts to gain a cease-fire from the earliest hours of the conflict. Moreover, Sadat was not convinced that Israel had now gained the upper hand, including a growing offensive on the western bank of the Canal. Whether this was out of faulty intelligence or simply refusal accurately to evaluate what intelligence was available, including the photographs provided by Kosygin, is not certain. What is certain is that Kosygin was unable to gain Sadat's approval to a cease-fire resolution, be it one including a demand for an Israeli withdrawal or otherwise, although the issue of guarantees for an Israeli withdrawal to the pre-1967 lines was a Sadat demand.

There were rumours that Kosygin went to Damascus from Cairo to meet with Asad, but, in fact, he went directly back to Moscow on 19 October, without Egyptian agreement to a cease-fire. The next Soviet step was directed at the Americans. On the same day Kosygin was dispatched to Cairo, Brezhnev sent a long message to the United States urging restraint and continued détente, along with the need for a cease-fire to be based on a demand for full Israeli withdrawal from the territories occupied in 1967. This missive, while mild in tone, even with regard to Israel, nonetheless opposed the idea of a cease-fire resolution that would only vaguely refer to Resolution 242 rather than explicitly call for full Israeli withdrawal. And the Soviets' draft of a cease-fire resolution attached to this message called for staged Israeli withdrawal over the shortest time possible.

Following the failure of Kosygin's mission, the Soviets decided upon a meeting with the Americans. Secretary of State Henry Kissinger told Foreign Minister Abba Eban that he had been surprised by a message from Moscow calling for an urgent meeting, either of Gromyko in Washington or Kissinger in Moscow. Kissinger told the Israelis that he opted to go to Moscow so as to buy time for the Israeli army, now in all out effort to take the western bank of the Canal.[37] Both the US and the Soviet Union announced Kissinger's trip on 20 October and talks began immediately upon Kissinger's arrival at 9:15pm, rather than the following day as had been requested by Kissinger. Kosygin, discredited after his failure in Cairo, was not included in the talks.

The Soviets' opening position in the talks with Kissinger was that conveyed to Richard Nixon in Brezhnev's message of 16 October, namely cease-fire tied to a commitment for Israeli withdrawal. In the talks which resumed the day after Kissinger's arrival in Moscow, however, the Soviet position changed. Kissinger offered a proposal for a cease-fire to be followed by the beginning of implementation of Resolution 242 and peace negotiations, under appropriate auspices, for a peace agreement on the basis of Resolution 242. Brezhnev agreed to this formulation, thereby abandoning his earlier insistence upon Israeli withdrawal, including a timetable and so forth. The reason for the change in the Soviet position may have been a series of telephone calls from the Soviet ambassador in Egypt conveying Sadat's concern, finally, over the Israeli crossing and Sadat's request for a cease-fire as soon as possible in place. Both Sadat's willingness to agree to a cease-fire in place and the obvious urgency of the battlefield situation led Brezhnev and his Politburo to agree to the Americans' draft of a resolution. Once this hurdle was out of the way, the talks with Kissinger were easily concluded.

Whether Moscow would have made this compromise had Sadat not made his call for a cease-fire, in place, is a moot point. The Soviet military were alarmed by the situation in the field, convinced that the Egyptian army might collapse and concerned that large quantities of Soviet equipment were falling into Israeli hands. Nor did they have any faith in the Syrians' plans for a counter-offensive on the Golan. As for the political level, the invitation to send Kissinger to Moscow and the urgency with which Brezhnev approached the talks, even prior to Sadat's acquiescence strongly suggest that the Soviet leader would have agreed to a compromise with Kissinger in any case. Thanks to satellite photographs as well as aerial reconnaissance the Soviets were well aware of the dangerous situation for the Egyptian army and capital. The risk of hurting Soviet–Egyptian friendship, therefore, would presumably have been preferable to total Egyptian collapse, which certainly would not have improved Soviet–Egyptian relations. Fortunately Moscow did not have to face that kind of choice by the time talks with Kissinger resumed on 21 October.

The remaining points were quickly worked out both by Kissinger and Brezhnev and by Kissinger and Gromyko. It was agreed that the two superpowers would propose a joint cease-fire resolution; the cease-fire was to begin 12 hours after passage of the resolution (Kissinger's effort to buy time for the Israelis) and, in a separate note of understanding, it was agreed that 'appropriate auspices' meant Soviet and American involvement. Their respective UN representatives were ordered to cooperate in presenting the resolution, and both states undertook consultations with their allies. For Moscow this would not be an easy task.

Sadat received the news of the US–Soviet agreement favourably, inasmuch as he had finally grasped the seriousness of his situation. Asad, however, was another matter. In a 29 October speech, the Syrian leader claimed that he had not been informed of the joint resolution and that there had been no consultations with him; the first he learned of the resolution, he claimed, was when it was brought to the United Nations Security Council.[38] This claim is contradicted by Israelyan's account, which states that Asad was informed through the Soviet ambassador in Damascus immediately after the Brezhnev–Kissinger talks.[39] Asad also claimed that Sadat, informing him of the Soviet–American resolution, assured him that the proposal to which he, Sadat, had given his approval included Soviet–US guarantees of total Israeli withdrawal.[40] Sadat, according to Asad, claimed that the Soviets too, had given him assurances. The Syrians, like the Egyptians, had not been entirely satisfied with Soviet supplies during the war, but their major objections were to the cease-fire proposal, on two counts: first, Asad was planning a counter-offensive, now impossible, and second, Syria had never agreed to Resolution 242, which was now to be part of the cease-fire resolution. Indeed, it was only after Sadat sent his Prime Minister to Damascus on 23–24 October that Syria accepted the cease-fire and, implicitly with it, Resolution 242. Nor did Syria participate in the peace negotiations begun in Geneva after the war as dictated by the cease-fire resolution, Security Council Resolution 338.

Additional Arab states, along with the Palestinians, were also displeased with Resolution 338. Iraq reportedly held Soviet interest in détente directly to blame for the cease-fire, accusing Moscow of colluding with the Americans.[41] This was the line taken by Libya as well, which added that Kissinger and Kosygin were working for the Zionists.[42] In an interview to *Le Monde*, 23 October, Libyan leader Qadhafi called Resolution 338 a 'time bomb', arguing that Moscow and Washington would surely propose stationing their troops on the borders between Israel and the Arab countries, and 'thus we will be submitted to the neo-colonialism of the two superpowers'. Algeria and Kuwait also expressed their opposition to the cease-fire resolution and the PLO attacked it for, among other things, its reference to Resolution 242, and, of course, the absence of any reference to the Palestinian issue or the occupied territories. The Chinese added their criticism, which was in line with their anti-Soviet propaganda throughout the war, and they did not participate in the Security Council vote on the resolution.[43]

In their propaganda to the Arab world, the Soviet media defended the resolution by offering their own interpretation, namely that the reference to Resolution 242 meant that Israel would finally withdraw from the occupied territories.[44] They also explained, defensively, that Resolution 338 was the result of 'serious and difficult' high-level contacts between the Soviet Union and the Arab states directly concerned, and only lastly between the Soviet Union and the United States. Noting Egypt's satisfaction with the resolution (and challenging Libya's right, as a non-combatant in the war, to judge Moscow's actions), the Russians pointed to their long record of support for the Arabs.[45]

One strange form of assistance, never mentioned by the Soviets, was related to the Scud missiles Moscow had given Egypt prior to the war. On 22 October, just before the cease-fire was to go into effect, two Scud surface-to-surface missiles were launched by the Egyptians in the direction of Israel. They landed in the northern Sinai without doing any harm, but the launching remained something of a mystery until Israelyan provided some explanations in his 1995 book. According to Israelyan, Sadat had earlier urged Moscow to permit the Egyptians to control the use of the Scuds, but the Soviets not only refused but Gromyko actually vetoed an Egyptian military order to permit a strike against El Arish where the US was unloading supplies for the Israeli army. In Moscow, the military was reportedly inclined to permit a firing of the Scuds, but the Politburo opposed the idea. On 22 October the Egyptians once again sought permission to launch the Scud missiles before the cease-fire went into effect, presumably to impress Israel that Egypt possessed and could, if necessary, use such weapons. Ambassador Vinogradov sought to consult with Gromyko but was unable to reach the Foreign Minister. Instead, then, he called Grechko, the Defence Minister, who, according to Israelyan, immediately replied: 'Go the hell ahead and fire it'. Which they did. Just a few minutes later Gromyko contacted Vinogradov and was outraged upon learning of the order, but it was too late to prevent the firing of the Scuds. The entire incident was quite strange and belied Moscow's attempts to avoid direct involvement or provocative behaviour. Yet, coming as it did just prior to the cease-fire, and failing to reach target or cause any damage, the firing of the Scuds had no effect on events in the Middle East, and was not in fact a deliberate Soviet act.

A major problem with Resolution 338, aside from most of the Arabs' dissatisfaction with it, was the absence of any mechanism for implementation or supervision. This became particularly relevant when Israel continued its advances to take all of the western bank of the Canal despite the cease-fire, which officially began at 6:52pm local time on 22 October. The Soviets, for their part, had their own means of supervision: they launched a Cosmos satellite on 20 October and they had their MiG-25 reconnaissance flights over the region. This did not, however, change the situation on the ground, and Moscow was faced with a serious dilemma.

What ensued remains something of an enigma even 25 years later. Moscow's credibility was once again at stake as Israel continued to violate the cease-fire negotiated by Moscow. There was an additional problem for Brezhnev, though not necessarily his primary concern. The World Peace Council, a Soviet front, was about to hold a major international Peace Congress in Moscow, with an address by Brezhnev at its opening. The Soviet leader could hardly go before this massive, highly publicized gathering in praise of détente and peace, with war still raging in the Middle East – and despite Soviet cooperation with the United States. During a meeting in the Kremlin the evening and night of 22–23 October, various Soviet options were discussed, including a suggestion by Grechko that the US and the USSR use their armed forces to ensure the cease-fire, while Gromyko suggested the two superpowers restrict their arms supplies to the belligerents. Brezhnev reportedly responded that Gromyko's idea would take too long but perhaps the Soviet airlift could be temporarily halted to see what the US reaction would be. Grechko's proposal reportedly was not discussed.[46] The only operative decision at this meeting apparently was to send an urgent note to Kissinger from Brezhnev, along with a more general personal note from the Soviet leader to Nixon.[47]

During the next day, 23 October, as Israel continued its advances, which threatened to leave the Egyptian Third Army cut off on the eastern bank of the Canal, Sadat urgently requested Soviet and US enforcement of Resolution 338. The Egyptian leader called for a reconvening of the Security Council to provide a force for implementation of the cease-fire, while he assailed the Soviet ambassador with complaints about Moscow's failure to fulfil what he believed to be the Soviets' obligation to guarantee the cease-fire. The notes agreed upon at the previous night's meeting were sent to Washington, expressing Moscow's concern and anger over Israel's actions, which were characterized as 'unacceptable' and deceitful. One of the notes also implied American–Israeli collusion, at least according to Nixon's interpretation.[48] At the same time, responding to Sadat's pleas, Brezhnev proposed that the superpowers introduce a second resolution calling for UN observers to be dispatched to the area in order to supervise the cease-fire. The result of this was a second joint resolution proposed by the United States and the Soviet Union, Security Council Resolution 339.

In addition to the communications to Washington and the new joint resolution in the UN, Moscow also issued a warning to Israel. This was contained in a statement by the Soviet government which protested Israel's violations of the cease-fire and warned 'the Government of Israel of the gravest consequences that the continuation of its aggressive actions against the Republic of Egypt and the Syrian Arab Republic will entail'.[49] This warning, however, was no stronger than that issued on 12 October and, indeed, less threatening than those issued at the close of the 1967 war when Israel had disregarded a cease-fire decision and pressed on against Syria. It also fell far short of the warning sent Ben-Gurion at the close of the 1956 Sinai Campaign, when Moscow had warned that Israel might cease to exist as a state. Yet, on this day in 1973, the Soviets refrained from sending the by now daily contingent of transport ships from Odessa, and the airlift was also stopped. This would suggest that Moscow was not in fact exceedingly concerned that the cease-fire would not hold, perhaps counting on American pressure to restrain Israel. The Arabs did, however, hold Moscow responsible for the cease-fire, and given the opposition expressed in various Arab quarters – supported by Chinese attacks on the Soviets' position – the Soviet leadership must have felt it incumbent upon themselves to take a strong public stand. Such a stand, clearly reflected in Soviet UN representative Malik's comments to the Security Council and presumably in the other communications between the two superpowers, would also, and perhaps most importantly, press Washington to restrain Israel.

The Kremlin discussions during the day of 23 October had focused on various means of ensuring implementation of the cease-fire. According to Israelyan, no one proposed sending Soviet troops or even sending Soviet observers unilaterally, but, rather, Kosygin proposed a joint observers team of 200 to 250 military personnel each from the US and USSR. Chief of Staff Marshal Kulikov reportedly objected even to this proposal unless Israeli and Egyptian forces were first disengaged, lest Soviet military become involved in the fighting.[50] The compromise reached was reflected in Resolution 339's call for observers to be dispatched from UN forces already in the Middle East, along with the demand for Israeli forces to return to the lines held when the cease-fire went into effect, 6:52pm on 22 October.

The call for the return to the earlier lines was the result of the alarming new situation developing on the front: the isolation of the 20,000 strong Egyptian Third Army. By the next day, 24 October, Israel was virtually in control of the city of Suez, and following a failed attempt by the Third Army to break out, this Egyptian force was left with no supply lines, for water, plasma or any other means of survival, completely encircled by Israel. With the Cairo–Suez road cut off and almost no Egyptian force standing in the way of a move on Cairo, the atmosphere in the Egyptian capital was one of near panic and confusion.[51] The militia was called up to protect the city, and Sadat sent urgent messages to both Washington and Moscow to send forces to stop Israeli advances. Sadat requested a joint Soviet–American force, though he viewed his patron-ally, Moscow, as primary guarantor of the cease-fire, particularly since the Soviets had raised his ire throughout the war by pressing for a cease-fire long before he was ready for one.

Thus on 24 October, one day before he was supposed to open the World Peace Congress celebrating the strength of détente and the peace forces of the world, Brezhnev had to cope with what threatened to be disaster in the Middle East. At 3pm Washington time, 24 October, the United States rejected Sadat's call for a joint force, at 9:35pm it received a note from Brezhnev, and at 11:41pm the White House decided to declare a DefCon3 nuclear alert. Just what role Moscow played in this development, that is, what the Soviets did to precipitate such a move, or more simply, what caused the American alert – perhaps the second most dangerous crisis of the Cold War – is one of the questions that remains unanswered to this very day, some 25 years, numerous memoirs and interviews, intensive (good) research and speculation later.

The various alleged or real Soviet moves which have been said to have precipitated the US alert include: an alert in four to seven of Moscow's airborne divisions, an in-flight command post established for them in southern Russia, with preparations on the ground for their departure including troop trains heading for Soviet airfields; a break in the Soviet airlift which theoretically freed the large Antonov-22 aircraft for the transporting of the airborne divisions, followed by the detection of some ten Soviet planes en route to Egypt;[52] the dispatch of two Soviet amphibious ships from the coast of Syria to the direction of Egypt and the entry into the Mediterranean of Soviet troop carriers; a reported alert of Yugoslav forces in response to a Soviet request to overfly troops; a report that Soviet nuclear materials had been delivered to Alexandria (or was on its way there) for use with the Scud missiles; and, finally, a letter from Brezhnev to Nixon threatening unilateral Soviet intervention, with a direct threat to destroy the State of Israel, which followed Soviet support at the UN for Egypt's request for military enforcement of the cease-fire.

There was indeed an alert of the Soviet airborne divisions, lending credence to the possibility of Soviet military intervention. This alert had been in effect throughout the war and, according to US Defence Secretary James Schlesinger, had been known to the US for at least five or six days, if not more. One western account claims that the airborne troops were placed on alert on 11 October, with one of them going on to a higher level of alert ('ready to move' status) on 24 October, while another western source claims that three divisions were on 'ready to move status' as of 10 October, with the remaining four moving to that status on 24 October.[53] The total of seven airborne divisions would have included 50,000 soldiers and almost double that number in the rear. In any case, Schlesinger said at a press conference immediately after the war that the alerts in the Soviet airborne forces had not been the reason for the US DefCon3 alert.[54] In fact, the dispatch of such a large Soviet force and placement in the field could not have been carried out within less than a week in the war conditions prevailing in the area at the time – far too late to save the Third Army or even an attack on Cairo.[55] The albeit small contingent of Antonovs headed for Egypt was a cause for concern, according to Schlesinger, but this would indicate concern not over the dispatch of a large, intervention force but rather of a symbolic, political action of no more than one or two divisions to be placed perhaps around Cairo.

It was soon realized, however, that the planes contained cargo and not troops (with further planes carrying 70 Soviet observers arriving the next day). It was also most unlikely that the Soviets would make a new overflight request to the Yugoslavs, specifically for troops, when in fact they had been landing supply planes there throughout the war; actually the Yugoslav alert had been in effect since the beginning of the war because of the movement of warships in the Mediterranean. There were indeed Soviet troop carriers in the Mediterranean at the time of the 24–25 October crisis, some apparently even entering at this time, but the total of troop carriers was four (and tank carriers another four), one of which had come from the coast of Guinea and most probably had no troops aboard. Two of these ships were in fact awaiting passage through the Dardanelles back to the Black Sea, and the grand total of eight such landing ships (or ten with the two that came from Syrian coast) was actually less than the total of 14 present in earlier non-war periods. Moreover, the entire Soviet marine force was the size of the US Sixth Fleet, and Moscow had no aircraft carriers in the area which could have provided air cover for a landing force.[56] It is interesting also, that the Chief of Staff, Marshal Kulikov, was occupied on the morning of 24 October with a visiting Finnish military delegation, received in the presence of a guard of honour from the Moscow garrison. This would not suggest expectation of an imminent, unprecedented Soviet military action in the Middle East.[57]

As to the claim that nuclear materials were dispatched to Egypt, there was a report to the White House that such material had passed through the Bosphorus. According to one most reliable, confidential source, however, the report dated back to two days earlier and reached the White House only the morning of 25 October, hours after the DefCon3 alert was called. Several other reliable sources claim that the report did reach the White House before 25 October but was not considered important or relevant to the US alert decision. This was presumably because nuclear material was often transported to the Soviet naval squadron in the Mediterranean.[58] Moreover, if such material were indeed warheads intended for use against Israel in the present emergency, transportation by air rather than via a three to four day sea journey through the closely monitored Turkish Straits would have been more appropriate. And, further, US government analysts undoubtedly estimated that the Soviet Union, a generally conservative nuclear power, was most unlikely to dispatch nuclear warheads, even under Soviet control, to a Third World, non-Communist, non-contiguous country, engaged in a war in the Middle East. The only time Moscow had taken even a partially similar step was in 1962 to Cuba, where the nuclear warheads were not only strictly under the Soviets' sole control but were intended as a component of the Soviet–US strategic balance (even if presented *post factum* as a means of defence for a Communist ally).

What remains, therefore, as the major cause of the US alert was the letter sent to Nixon by Brezhnev. Yet, this letter did not contain a direct threat to Israel; more importantly, it was couched in careful, even qualifying terms.[59]

Let us together, the USSR and the United States, urgently dispatch Soviet and American military contingents to Egypt, to ensure the implementation of the decision of the Security Council of October 22 and 23 concerning the cessation of fire and of all military activities and also of our understanding with you on the guarantee of the implementation of the decisions of the Security Council. It is necessary to adhere without delay. I will say it straight that if you find it impossible to act jointly with us in this matter, we should be faced with the necessity urgently to consider the question of taking appropriate steps unilaterally. We cannot allow arbitrariness on the part of Israel.[60]

Indeed it was the letter, however qualified, that prompted the American alert according to the various White House participants in the crisis, including President Nixon. The Antonovs preparing to depart for Cairo were detected only shortly after the decision to call the alert. More to the point, however, was actually the disappearance of the Soviet air transport command Antonovs – the break in the airlift – which, together with the alert in the airborne divisions and the letter, led the CIA and the military to believe some Soviet action was likely. Others in the National Security Council believed this was merely a Soviet bluff and that there would be no intervention. Estimates varied, but the key player, Kissinger, along with others in the White House, expected, if anything, merely a limited, symbolic Soviet force rather than a full-scale intervention. The US alert, at least from the point of view of the White House, was to make a strong point with Brezhnev that the US would not permit Moscow to gain either a political or military advantage in the Middle East at this time.[61]

The Russians provide a somewhat different picture. Israelyan's account appears to be the most authoritative to date, although interviews with other former Soviet officials provide some conflicting information and speculation. The Politburo met in the evening of 24 October (roughly around the time the United States was announcing its rejection of Sadat's call for Soviet and American enforcement of the cease-fire). The first decision of the meeting, in response to Sadat's call, was to send a group of 70 Soviet military observers (including 20 interpreters). This was followed by a long discussion of Sadat's request for troops. Kosgyin reportedly repeated his proposal to dispatch several hundred American and Soviet observers, but participants in the meeting regarded this option as unrealistic given the Americans' rejection of the idea of a joint force of any kind. Kulikov reportedly commented that by the time a joint force, or even a unilateral Soviet force reached the area and achieved battle readiness, Cairo would have fallen and the war would be over. Other accounts claim that the joint force idea, contained in the crucial letter to Nixon, was a serious Soviet proposal. In 1956, when Nikita Khrushchev proposed such an idea to the US at the close of the Suez War, it was so preposterous that US Ambassador Charles Bohlen was hesitant even to pass the proposal on to Washington.[62] In 1973, however, détente was the by-word, and Soviet–American cooperation had been achieved to some degree. According to some sources, there had even been signs of American willingness in 1971 to send a joint peace-keeping force to guarantee an Arab–Israeli settlement.[63] Now, apparently, Brezhnev's interpretation of the Soviet–American cease-fire resolution, and especially of the clause which called for negotiations 'under appropriate auspices', was that the Soviets and Americans were jointly committed to ensure the peace (which coincides with the interpretation Sadat claimed to have received from Brezhnev).

With the joint force idea apparently regarded as unrealistic (because of American opposition), the discussion focused on unilateral Soviet action. The idea of unilaterally sending troops found no support among the Politburo participants. There was no decision to send Soviet troops. No decision was taken to threaten such an action. Moscow was unwilling to become militarily involved in the conflict, yet it had to respond to Sadat's desperate situation. The option adopted was to bring pressure on the Americans to press Israel to observe the cease-fire, and thereby save the Third Army as well as avoid any threat to Cairo and total Egyptian collapse. The form of the pressure was to be a letter implying that if the US were not willing to send a joint force, Moscow 'would not exclude the possibility of unilateral action', according to Israelyan.[64] The message to Nixon was reportedly purposely drafted, by Gromyko, cautiously, even employing the word 'contingents' rather than 'troops' so as to render the message somewhat vague. Nonetheless, the message concluded with the ominous, albeit conditioned, threat to consider unilateral steps. According to one account, this sentence was not in the draft prepared by Gromyko but added directly by Brezhnev, just before dispatch. There was, as far as can be determined, no intention to do anything more than pressure the United States; there was no support for or even discussion of actually implementing the Soviet threat.

There was no discussion at the meeting of military measures to be taken to provide credibility to the threat, although it has been claimed that it was not unusual for Brezhnev to leave such matters to Grechko without bringing them to the Politburo. Reportedly, when on 25 October Grechko was asked about the various military measures that had been taken, namely the alerts, the movement of ships, and the like, Grechko reportedly replied that these had been routine military measures.[65] General Yuri Yakovlevich Kirshin told Lebow and Stein that military leaders were indeed asked to prepare contingency plans for the optimal use of the Soviet airborne troops.[66] And Aleksandr Kislov, a Middle East expert who was then Director of the Institute for World Economy and International Affairs, also said that there were contingency plans, to save the Third Army, by sending 'a minimum of two to three divisions. A battalion would have been insignificant. We needed enough troops to make an impression.'[67] Admiral Nikolai Amelko, deputy chief of the

Soviet navy at the time, later said that transfer of so many paratroop divisions, for which the Soviets had only limited transportation, would have required air, logistical and marine support which would have taken some time.[68] Gromyko said, in a 1989 interview, that the Soviet Union had seriously considered sending troops to form a cordon around Cairo, but, 'On the other hand, we were anxious not to get involved in the fighting. Some of my colleagues might say that this [Brezhnev's letter] was only a form of political pressure.'[69] A diplomatic comment that probably tells the whole story, Gromyko's reference to political pressure as the real meaning of the Soviet threat is confirmed by a number of Foreign Ministry officials who were present at the Politburo discussions. Israelyan is adamant about it, citing Chief of Staff Kulikov's opposition to sending even observers until there was a disengagement of Israeli and Egyptian troops, whatever contingency plans the military might have had.[70]

CONCLUSION

My own conclusions, then and now, coincide with those of Israelyan and other Russian and western observers.[71] The Politburo, meeting on 25 October, was surprised by the strong American reaction, failing to grasp that the White House could have taken the 'threat' so seriously or that the American move was even connected to the letter. Anti-détentists in the Politburo predictably interpreted the alert as unprovoked imperialist aggressiveness while Brezhnev and others were simply surprised as well as indignant. In the ensuing four hour discussion on the appropriate Soviet response, the Politburo rapidly and unanimously rejected the idea of military confrontation with the Americans. Grechko, reportedly somewhat hesitantly, raised the idea of sending troops to the Middle East, but this option was soundly rejected by Kosygin and Gromyko on the grounds that it would merely lead to American intervention and escalation. Grechko suggested mobilizing 50,000–70,000 Soviet troops and others recommended raising the state of alert in several Soviet military districts. Ultimately all agreed that only a political response should be made, and Brezhnev decided the best course would be to ignore the American alert. The cease-fire was indeed holding, Nixon had just communicated to the Kremlin that Washington was pressing Israel to observe the cease-fire, and it was agreed with the United States that a UN peace-keeping force (exclusive of Security Council countries) would be sent. The DefCon3 alert was called off at midnight 25 October, and Brezhnev went on to address the World Peace Congress, one day late.

The message Brezhnev gave to the World Peace Congress and in subsequent statements pointed to the experience during the war as proof that détente was both necessary and possible, even claiming on at least one instance that it was détente that had saved the world from conflagration.[72] At the same time, he spoke of the Soviets' firm stand behind its Arab allies, specifying the dispatch of 70 'representatives' to supervise the cease-fire.[73] Yet Moscow emerged from the war on the defensive with regard to both issues and what might be seen as the contradictory nature of its two objectives from the beginning of the war: to maintain détente and prevent confrontation with the US; and to maintain (or improve) relations with the Arabs. It was perhaps the very pursuit of both these objectives, simultaneously, that is, Moscow's dualistic policy, that led to the failure to achieve either.

The efforts to achieve an early cease-fire in the interests of preventing escalation or need to intervene, with all the risks involved, angered Sadat. The joint Soviet–American effort to reach a cease-fire, an effort made possible by détente, drew the ire of Syria and other Arab states, portrayed by some as superpower collusion. At the same time, Soviet assistance to Egypt and Syria, intended to shore them up and demonstrate Soviet loyalty to its Third World friends raised serious doubts in the West about Soviet loyalty to détente. More to the point, the war drew to a close with an American nuclear alert, provoked, however innocently or not, by the Kremlin in its effort to fulfil its commitments to the Arabs. Thus both détentists and anti-détentists in Moscow could point to the war as proof of their positions.

But the real loss for the Soviets was on the ground in the Middle East. Whatever plans Sadat may or may not have had prior to the war with regard to the Soviets, whom he had long distrusted, Egypt was to turn fully to the United States after the war. While Syria did not follow suit entirely, Asad's anger with the Soviets eventually did lead to a slight improvement of relations with Washington and a diversification of Syrian military suppliers. While the Soviet Union made a significant effort to remain a player in the region, primarily by trying to be part of any peace negotiations and supplying arms to Syria, their relations and standing in the Arab world declined as the Americans became increasingly dominant. By the 1980s Moscow could do little more than try to prevent a Pax Americana in the region.

NOTES

1. See V.V. Zhurkin and E.M. Primakov, *Mezhdunarodnye konflikty*, Moscow: Mezhdunarodnye otnosheniia, 1972, p.19.
2. According to Evgeny Prylin, Soviet intelligence had copies of US–Egyptian exchanges, although there were varying interpretations in the Soviet leadership as to tactical versus strategic nature of the budding US–Egyptian relationship; Ned Lebow and Janice Stein, *We All Lost the Cold War*, Princeton, NJ: Princeton University Press, 1994, p.169. The KGB, and especially the KGB chief in Cairo, did believe Sadat was turning to the US, while the Soviet ambassador to Cairo, Vinogradov, and ultimately the Politburo were more confident of Sadat's loyalty and/or dependence upon Moscow. Victor Israelyan, *Inside the Kremlin During the Yom Kippur War*, University Park, PA: Pennsylvania State University Press, 1995, p.9.
3. Interviews with Victor Israelyan and Vadim Zagladin in Lebow and Stein, *We All Lost the Cold War*, pp.170–1.

4. Moshe Maoz, *Syria Under Hafiz al-Asad: New Domestic and Foreign Policies*, Jerusalem Peace Papers, 1975. The strains were not helped by the poor performance of Soviet SAMs in Syria when the Israeli Air Force downed 13 Syrian MiGs on 13 September 1973.
5. *Al-Hawadess*, 16 August 1974.
6. Evgeny Prylin, *Some Observations (Memoirs) About the Arab-Israeli War (1973)*, unpublished memorandum commissioned for Lebow and Stein, *We All Lost the Cold War*, p.184; and Israelyan, *Inside the Kremlin During the Yom Kippur War*, pp.31–2; 53–6.
7. Israelyan, *Inside the Kremlin During the Yom Kippur War*, p.44.
8. *Al-Safir*, 16 April 1974; and the speech by Vinogradov, *Journal of Palestine Studies* 3/4 (1974), pp.161–4.
9. *Le Monde*, 11, 13 October 1973; *New York Times*, 10 October 1973; and *Al Nahar*, 10 October 1973.
10. Riad N. El Rayyes and Dunia Nahas, *The October War*, Beirut: An Nahar Press Services, 1973, p.95.
11. Heikal, 'The Road to Ramadan', *Ma'ariv*, 15 May 1975; and Galia Golan, *Yom Kippur and After: The Soviet Union and the Middle East Crisis*, Cambridge: Cambridge University Press, 1977, p.84.
12. Israelyan, *Inside the Kremlin During the Yom Kippur War*, pp.57–8.
13. Ibid. pp.47, 57; Golan, *Yom Kippur and After*, p.85.
14. Israelyan, *Inside the Kremlin During the Yom Kippur War*, p.55.
15. Interview with Leonid Zimyatin, in Lebow and Stein, *We All Lost the Cold War*, p.186.
16. *DPA*, 13 April 1974 (Sadat interview to *Der Stern*). See also *Le Monde*, 31 March – 1 April 1974, 18 April 1974; Sadat interviews, *MENA*, 22 September and 8 October 1974.
17. Ibid. According to Heikal, Abu Dhabi too informed Egypt on 11 October that it was providing Moscow with a $100 million for the war effort.
18. Israelyan, *Inside the Kremlin During the Yom Kippur War*, pp.58–60.
19. Prylin, *Some Observations*, p.12; Israelyan, *Inside the Kremlin During the Yom Kippur War*, p.91.
20. Golan, *Yom Kippur and After*, pp.76–7; and Ismail Fahmy (Egyptian Foreign Minister at the time of the war), *Negotiating for Peace in the Middle East*, London: Croom Helm, 1983, pp.25–6.
21. *TASS*, 12 October 1973.
22. Prylin, *Some Observations*, p.12.
23. Actually neither Soviet overseas involvement nor wars that might bring some kind of hardship on the Soviet public or standard of living were ever popular among the Soviet public; nor were the Arabs particularly popular in the Soviet Union.
24. *New York Times*, 9, 11, 13 October 1973; and *Le Monde*, 18 October 1973.
25. For samples of the east European statements, see *TASS*, 8 and 9 October 1973. For protest meetings see, for example, the meeting in Patrice Lumumba Friendship University, *TASS*, 19 October 1973.
26. *Pravda*, 17 October 1973.
27. Moscow Domestic Radio, 26 October 1973.
28. For example, *Pravda* and Moscow domestic radio, 14 October 1973.
29. Interview, *US News and World Report*, 24 December 1973, pp.27–8.
30. Ibid.
31. Israelyan, *Inside the Kremlin During the Yom Kippur War*, p.91.
32. Ibid., pp.92–3.
33. *MENA*, 8 October 1974.
34. *New York Times*, 19 October 1973 (US Defence Department briefing of 18 October 1973).
35. Israelyan, *Inside the Kremlin During the Yom Kippur War*, p.105.
36. Ibid., p.108.
37. Personal interview with an Israeli official.
38. *Al Anwar*, 30 October 1973.
39. Israelyan, *Inside the Kremlin During the Yom Kippur War*, p.140.
40. Fahmy, *Negotiating for Peace in the Middle East*, p.28.
41. *Iraqi Radio*, 25 October 1973.
42. *Tripoli Radio*, 22 October 1973.

43. For example, *Jen-Min Jih-Pao*, 8 October 1973.
44. For example, *Moscow Radio* in Arabic, 22 October 1973.
45. *Moscow Radio* in Arabic, 23 October 1973; and *TASS*, 23 October 1973 directly responding to the Libyans.
46. Israelyan, *Inside the Kremlin During the Yom Kippur War*, pp.153–4.
47. Henry Kissinger, *Years of Upheaval*, Boston: Little, Brown, 1982, p.570.
48. Richard Nixon, *The Memoirs of Richard Nixon*, New York: Grosset and Dunlop, 1978, p.936; and Kissinger, *Years of Upheaval*, p.570.
49. *TASS*, 23 October 1973.
50. Israelyan, *Inside the Kremlin During the Yom Kippur War*, pp.162–3.
51. Fahmy, *Negotiating for Peace in the Middle East*, p.27 and western press accounts at the time.
52. Some accounts say eight planes, other as many as 12.
53. Raymond Garthoff, *Détente and Confrontation: Soviet–American Relations from Nixon to Reagan*, Washington, DC: The Brookings Institutions, 1985, pp.377–8; Douglas Hart, 'Soviet Approaches to Crisis Management: The Military Dimension', *Survival* 26/5 (September-October 1984), pp.214–22; and Bradford Dismukes and James McConnell, *Soviet Naval Diplomacy*, New York: Pergamon Press, 1979, p.202.
54. *New York Times*, 26 October 1973.
55. For airlift and sealift limitations, see J.L. Moulton, 'Seaborne and Airborne Mobility in Europe', *US Naval Institute Proceedings* 100/5 (855), 1974, pp.127–30 and Dismukes and McConnell, *Soviet Naval Diplomacy*, pp.60, 193–213, 347–51.
56. Dismukes and McConnell, *Soviet Naval Diplomacy*, p.60. The lack of aircraft carriers, the construction of which began only in the late 1960s, was one of the reasons for Soviet air bases in Egypt and Syria, that is, to provide air cover for the Soviet Mediterranean squadron and ASW.
57. *TASS*, 24 October 1973.
58. Garthoff, *Détente and Confrontation*, p.378n; Alan Dowty, *Middle East Crisis: US Decision-Making in 1958, 1970, and 1973*, Berkeley: University of California Press, 1984, p.275 (interviews with Thomas Moorer, chairman of the Joint Chiefs of Staff, CIA Director William Colby, and Helmut Sonnenfeld of the National Security Council).
59. For an excellent analysis of this, as well as other Soviet threats, see Francis Fukuyama, 'Nuclear Shadow-Boxing: Soviet Intervention Threats in the Middle East,' *Orbis* 25/3 (Fall 1981), pp.579–605. See also Galia Golan, 'The Soviet Union and the Suez Crisis', in S.I. Troen and M. Shemesh, *The Suez-Sinai Crisis, 1956: A Retrospective and Reappraisal*, New York: Columbia University Press, 1990, pp.274–88.
60. *Washington Post*, 28 November 1973; and Kissinger, *Years of Upheaval*, p.583.
61. For a thorough account of the American decision, see Lebow and Stein, *We All Lost the Cold War*, pp.246–51, along with Kissinger, *Years of Upheaval*, pp.575–90; Nixon, *The Memoirs of Richard Nixon*, p.938; Barry Blechman and Douglas Hart, 'The Political Utility of Nuclear Weapons', *International Security* 7/1 (Summer 1982), pp.132–56; Bruce Blair, 'Alerting in Crisis and Conventional War', in Ashton Carter, John Steinbruner and Charles Zraket, eds, *Managing Nuclear Operations*, Washington, DC: Brookings Institution, 1987, pp.75–120; Alexander Haig, *Inner Circles: How America Changed the World, A Memoir*, New York: Warner Books, 1992, pp.415–16; William Quandt, *Soviet Policy in the October 1973 War*, Santa Monica, CA: Rand Corporation, 1976, R-1864, p.197.
62. Charles Bohlen, *Witness to History, 1929-1969*, New York: Norton and Co., 1973, pp.432–3.
63. In response to Sadat's proposal, made through Secretary of State Rogers (Lebow and Stein, *We All Lost the Cold War*, p.237).
64. Israelyan, *Inside the Kremlin During the Yom Kippur War*, p.168.
65. 1992 interview with Israelyan, in Lebow and Stein, *We All Lost the Cold War*, p.235; 1992 interview with Brezhnev's assistant Andrei Alexandrov-Agentov, ibid., p.235; Prylin, *Some Observations*, p.235.
66. Ibid., p.237.
67. Ibid.
68. 1991 interview, ibid, p.479n.
69. Ibid., p.237.
70. Ibid., p.238.

71. Golan, *Yom Kippur and After*, and Galia Golan, 'Decision-making in the Yom Kippur War, 1973', in J. Valenta and W. Potter, eds, *Soviet Decision-making for National Security*, London: George Allen and Unwin, 1984, pp.185–217.

72. To the World Peace Congress, in view of the just ended US alert and, therefore, in deference to anti-détentists, Brezhnev spoke of aggressive, imperialist circles but nonetheless praised détente. The standard line, however, became that expressed by Kosygin 14 November 1973 and Brezhnev in India 29 November 1973 who said: '... matters would look quite different were it not for this factor of détente in the world, which emerged in the last two or three years. If the current conflict had flared up in a situation of universal, international tension and aggravation of relations, say between the United States and the Soviet Union, the clash in the Middle East might have become much more dangerous it might have assumed a scope endangering world peace.' *Izvestia*, 1 December 1973.

73. *Moscow Domestic Radio*, 26 October 1973.

From Crisis to Change:
The Israeli Political Elites and
the 1973 War

GABRIEL SHEFFER

Various observers of the Israeli scene have argued that due to its particular historical evolution, small elites played a pivotal, or even an exclusive, role in shaping the Jewish State's political structure and behaviour. These observers have added that during its fifty years of existence these elites also determined the patterns of political change.[1] Despite the prevalence of this view, it is based on questionable premises. In this vein, there is at the least an alternative approach to questions of development and sources of change in Israel that has not adequately been examined. Essentially, this alternative approach postulates that in the long run, rather than elites, grassroots and organized social groups have played significant roles in the emergence of societal and political arrangements and patterns of activities.[2]

Though such a general re-examination is highly warranted, the present chapter will not re-assess these two contentious approaches and their main arguments concerning the development of the entire Israeli polity since the establishment of the Jewish State. This chapter rather focuses on one aspect of that general question of political development and deals with changes of the Israeli elites during and immediately after the 1973 War.

Within this framework, the present chapter examines the changes that occurred in elites' composition, roles and political behaviour during that crucial period in Israel's history. Its starting point is that while the 1967 War indeed constituted a crucial turning point in the social, economic and political development of Israel, it was the 1973 War that caused a major shift in the nature of Israeli polity, including its political, bureaucratic and military elites. More specifically, this chapter intends to examine whether due to their problematic performance on the eve and during the first stages of that war and in its aftermath major changes

Gabriel Sheffer is Professor of Political Science at the Hebrew University of Jerusalem.

occurred in the composition, attributes and behaviour of national level
elites.

This chapter also explores the extent to which these changes were
entirely generated within an insulated political system and instituted by
the political elite itself. Therefore, it examines the connection between
that war and deeper and wider changes that occurred in Israel's society,
political culture and political arrangements. And finally it examines the
extent that these cumulative changes contributed to the appearance of
new characteristics of the political elites and to the redefinition of their
power, position and roles in the social and political systems.

The analysis here is based on the theoretical approach that political
culture and resultant political arrangements are in fact answers to social
needs.[3] Following this approach, the chapter will examine the impact of
shifting social loyalties and inclinations on the Israeli consociational
arrangements that had been carried over from the pre-state Yishuv
period. The main hypothesis here is that in the 1970s this arrangement
was replaced by neo-corporatist arrangements. With upheavals and
reversals these arrangements influenced later political development,
including the elites' transformation.

SOCIETY, POLITY AND POLITICAL ELITES UNTIL THE LATE 1960s

As suggested above, there is a wide consensus that the results of the 1967
War expedited structural changes in the Israeli society and polity.[4]
Although there is an ongoing debate about the nature and scope of Israeli
consociationalism during the 1950s and 1960s,[5] nevertheless, after the
establishment of the Jewish State in 1948, its polity, especially that of the
Jewish sector, demonstrated a number of consociational features and
attributes. Most prevalent were the arrangements that Israel inherited
from the Yishuv and through it from the Zionist movement.[6]

To evaluate these processes it is appropriate to frame them in
a comparative perspective. Thus, from the late 1940s until the mid-
1960s, some essential aspects of the Israeli political regime resembled
arrangements which were evident in countries that probably matched
more fully the formal consociational model, such as Holland, Belgium,
Austria and Switzerland. Like some of these consociational systems,
the Israeli society was deeply segmented along ideological lines. This
social structure generated a multi-party system. The relative size,
electoral strength of these parties and the need to regulate their relations
created a need for broadly based parliamentary coalitions. In turn
these parties coalesced and formed distinct ideological camps (or to use
consociational terminology – pillars). But unlike some other
consociational systems, the leaders of these camps were unwilling and
unable to form grand coalitions. Each of the partners in these coalitions
held a mutual veto power that was intended to guarantee that none of

the camps and parties would be outvoted by a hostile majority when its vital interests were at stake. This system was governed by arrangements whereby most national resources were allocated according to a pure proportional principle, uncontrolled conflicts were avoided (yet when such conflicts occurred, the elites could manage them) and the autonomy of the major camps was maintained.

The espousal of these basic consociational arrangements was mainly a response to the needs of the various Jewish segments. If at all, only in the second place these arrangements were instituted as a response to the needs of the Israeli Palestinian community. In other words, the adoption of these arrangements was tailored to the deeply segmented Jewish society.

The origins of these cleavages were in the deep-rooted social structure of the Yishuv. The creation of Israel did not alter much in this sphere. Consequently, after the establishment of the state, the Jewish community in Israel still demonstrated a number of superimposed ideological, social and economic cleavages that had fully emerged during the mandatory period. Although the Labour bloc and its small top elite, which dominated all coalitions and governments until the late 1970s, tried to foster integration and promote an etatist approach (*mamlachtiut*), nevertheless, the old segmentation patterns that characterized the Yishuv period prevailed.

The result was the uninterrupted existence of three loosely organized and superficially united political camps or blocs – the Labour, the Religious and what was known as the Civic bloc (or the Third bloc). Unlike the segmentation patterns in other consociational polities, the *raison d'être* of these three blocs had been their divergent ideologies. Unlike its socialist image, in fact the Labour bloc's mainstream followed a social democratic ideology. Internally this ideological orientation was responsible for the introduction of an elaborate welfare system that, in turn, contributed to the emergence of a highly centralized state. Middle class groups in the loosely organized Civic bloc adopted a traditional liberal economic and social platform. The Herut party that was part of this camp shared that liberal orientation toward economic and social issues, but it had adopted a nationalist ideology in regard to the protracted Arab–Jewish conflict. Other groups in this camp adopted a moderate position on these matters.

The religious bloc was composed of parties that held different shades of religious ideology, ranging from orthodox to ultra-orthodox views especially in regard to the position and role of religion in the Jewish segment. At that formative period in Israel's history, the religious bloc adopted a moderate posture toward the Arab–Israeli conflict. This camp was less liberal regarding religious affairs. Essentially, it was determined to maintain the Jewish Orthodox tradition in personal matters. This was anchored in what has been known as the Status Quo Agreement. This agreement prevented the separation of state and religion and guaranteed the observance of religious practices, such as kosher food in state agencies including the Israel Defence Forces (IDF), religious holidays, and religious burial, marriages and divorces. It was also agreed that the orthodox and ultra-orthodox religious parties and rabbinate would control all religious services, and that these services would be provided only by agencies that they headed.

Other cultural, social, economic and occupational cleavages were superimposed on these three diverse ideologies. These divisions defined the borders of the various blocs, and determined their goals, political orientation and main patterns of political action. The basic tenets of the specific operative ideologies of each of these three blocs also determined the degree and scope of their respective organization. Thus the social-democratic Labour bloc was the most organized, and the liberal civic bloc was the least organized camp. Each bloc provided its members with a supportive framework for action and blocs also supplied cultural, social, economic and political services necessary to cater for the needs of the members of its constituent parties and factions.

In return for the various services and benefits that members received through their blocs and constituent parties, they were committed to demonstrate loyalty toward their blocs and leaders. Firm loyalty and discipline were required to prevent defection from the bloc (the reason was clear – maximal membership guaranteed a proportionally maximal share of national resources) and to prevent spontaneous and uncontrolled clashes between members of the various camps on the grassroots level. Such clashes could have wrecked the entire political boat.

Until the mid-1960s most members of the blocs showed loyalty to their respective camps and leaders. Since these leaders were capable of maintaining impressive levels of discipline, preventing mass defections and avoiding undesired conflicts and clashes, they gained power, prestige and respect. These arrangements explain the remarkable overall systemic stability, which was reflected in the electoral results throughout the Yishuv period and during the first two decades after the establishment of the state. Moreover, these arrangements explain the longevity of the Labour bloc hegemony and the predominance of its elites.

Again like other consociational regimes, Israel was a pure *proporzdemokratie*.[7] That is, most national resources were allocated in accordance to the principle of proportionality. The blocs' leaders decided on the specific actual allocation of these resources behind closed doors. This was a major source of their power. To avoid any spark that might cause undesired spontaneous clashes between the various blocs, by design the Israeli parliament was weak. While the parliament constituted only a junior partner in the national level policy making process, considerable powers were invested in the executive, which was staffed and firmly controlled by the political elite.

In this type of political regimes, elites, and especially what is known as the 'elites cartel', play an essential role in the daily operation of the entire political system.[8] Members of that elite cartel perform significant functions on the system's macro-level, as well as on intra- and inter-bloc level of activities. The following are some of these functions. On the level of each of these blocs, these elites are expected to protect the camps' borders and resources; they are engaged in strategic and tactical decision-making pertaining to all major matters affecting the well-being of the blocs, especially the allocation of available resources; are to prevent defection from the bloc and ensure recruitment of new members; are to regulate the relations between the various factions in the bloc, and supervise the services which are supplied to the camps' members. On the level of inter-bloc relations, the elites' tasks include monitoring the activities of the other social-political blocs; making adequate preparations for coping with social and political conflicts, conducting negotiations with other members of the elites-cartel and participating in coalition and government formation. On the systemic macro-level, the members of this elite-cartel play important roles in policy making, in avoiding undue tensions and conflicts and in a number of related functions.[9] From this viewpoint, power sharing among the elites was the basic norm that dictated internal developments within the blocs.

All these consociational features were present in the Yishuv and Israeli political systems. Yet in order to maintain stability, continuity and the hegemony of the Labour bloc, certain additional mechanisms were needed. Thus, as if in accordance with the stipulations of the academic consociational model, the elite 'invented', inculcated and promoted an overarching symbolic structure that was intended to ensure national solidarity, but also compliance with the national leadership. Among these symbolic mechanisms they emphasized respect toward the flag and the national anthem, old and new national myths, 'authentic' Israeli food, 'Israeli folklore', etc.

At the same time, the elite augmented control mechanisms (such as the need for maintaining high degrees of public mobilization and for maintaining disciplined behaviour in view of purported external threats) over the entire society and especially over members of their camps. Moreover, the elite made and implemented public policies that were intended to create minimal friction and adverse ripple effects thereof. Thus, for example, the Labour elite agreed to allocate national resources to parties of the Civic bloc that were traditionally excluded from the governing coalitions (though less than their strict proportional share in accordance to their weight in the entire electorate). By the same token, the Labour camp and its coalition partners opted for maintaining the religious Status Quo Agreement. In sum, the consociational arrangement was an essential contributing factor to Israel's political development during the first decades after its establishment.[10] But it also resulted in 'dynamic conservatism', that is, political development and adaptation to changing circumstances within almost rigid structures.[11]

In any event, this political arrangement allowed Labour leaders and their coalition partners to adopt and implement hard-line policies in regard to the Arab–Israeli conflict and the Israeli Palestinians. In a different sphere of activities it allowed them to adopt and implement a non-selective immigration policy that, during a short period, increased more than threefold the Israeli Jewish population. They implemented a state sponsored social integrationist policy in regard to the waves of incoming immigrants. They introduced state capitalism and applied this approach to Israel's economic development. And it allowed them to simultaneously implement expansionist economic policy and a policy of provision of universal welfare services.

A review of the performance of the elites in Israel until the 1967 War shows that indeed the small and almost unchanging groups of leaders had undertaken all these functions, and that to the best of their ability they tried to implement the main stipulations of their operative ideologies. It resulted in some major achievements and a relatively smooth operation of the polity. Although like in other similar polities, in Israel too there were rifts, disagreements and frictions, these were not serious enough to frustrate the system's initial impressive achievements. These achievements included the establishment of the state, the military victories in the 1948 and 1956 wars, the arrival of large waves of Jewish immigrants and their economic integration, and fast economic development.

These accomplishments, which were coupled by hopes for further personal, group and national gains, ensured a further relatively reasonable degree of systemic stability. In turn this aura of growth on the one hand and stability on the other hand, fortified the position of the ruling elites. At the same time these also strengthened the opposition leadership that nevertheless participated in the elite cartel.

From the point of view of its party affiliation, the actual ruling elite was composed of the most senior leaders of what was known the 'historic partnership'. It was composed of the bloc, especially the senior leaders of the 'hegemonic' Mapai,[12] the religious-Zionist parties, and some leaders of the General Zionists and Progressives. Because of its predominant position in the Labour bloc and through it in the coalition, Mapai's leadership held a pre-eminent position in the entire elite cartel. During the first two decades after 1948, this leadership consisted of two generations of founding fathers of the Jewish State.

Until the early 1960s, the most prominent Israeli leader was Mapai's chief and Prime Minister David Ben-Gurion. He is still regarded by most of the Israelis as the most powerful and influential Israeli leader ever.[13] Although he probably deserves the admiration that many Israelis have been showing toward him, and although he demonstrated charismatic qualities and forged considerable political power, by no means was he an absolute ruler. His power was restricted by the coalitional structure of his own party and of the entire system. He was further constrained by the group of leaders that surrounded him and that as a group guided Mapai, the Labour camp and through them the entire system.[14]

Until the mid-1950s, the party leaderships consisted of two distinct camps. The first was an activist (hawkish) group, led by Ben-Gurion, and the second was a moderate group that had been led by Moshe Sharett. The latter's ouster from power in 1956 did not mean that the moderate group totally disappeared. Yet it meant that a new group of leaders came to the forefront. This was a less ideological, middle of the road and a more pragmatic political elite. At the centre of this group was a group of four: Levi Eshkol and what was known as the Troika – Golda Meir, Zalman Aran and Pinhas Sapir. By then Ben-Gurion's faction was composed of veteran supporters of the 'old man' and 'Mapai's Youngsters'. Moshe Dayan and Shimon Peres were the most visible personae in this group. In the early 1960s, however, neither the Ben-Gurion faction nor Eshkol's camps inside Mapai were homogeneous. Actually, each of these two groups within Mapai was a coalition of various individuals and ideological factions.

Consequently toward the end of his premiership, even the great Ben-Gurion lacked the ability to dictate all policies and moves of the Israeli government, or to continue to shape Israeli society. Eventually, the internal struggle that was triggered by the Lavon Affair led to the political demise of Ben-Gurion and his followers in the mid-1960s.[15] The result of this reshuffle was Eshkol's and the Troika's ascendance to power. This pragmatic and less hawkish group gained the support of some of the moderates, that had supported Sharett, and of some former followers of Ben-Gurion. Thus, the new Mapai leadership was a coalition of moderates, pragmatists and activists. In more than one sense this was an internal elite cartel in Mapai.

While most of the founding fathers could have been characterized as *transformational* leaders, the next generation, led by Eshkol, should be viewed as *transactional* leadership.[16] Thus, the generational transition from Ben-Gurion's to Eshkol's and the Troika's generation of leaders marked not only the upcoming of a 'new' group of leaders, but also the transition from one type, style and patterns of leadership to a qualitatively different type. This transition had an evident impact on later developments in Israel and especially on developments on the eve of the 1973 War.

Simultaneously, a similar transformation was occurring in the other coalitional camps and parties that had been part of the 'historical partnership' with Mapai. Thus, for example, a similar shift was taking place also in the religious Zionist party Mizrahi. During this period some of the veteran and moderate leaders of this party, like Moshe Shapira, were losing their clout on the party, and were gradually replaced by younger leaders, like Yosef Burg, who like their counterparts in Mapai were less ideological and more pragmatic. Their leadership style resembled the transformational character of their partners in Mapai. This generation of leaders established itself in the late 1960s. By the early 1970s they firmly held the reins in their separate parties and through these parties and participation in the Mapai-led coalitions in the entire polity.

During the interim period between the 1956 and 1967 wars two other elites gradually accumulated power and were building impressive power bases in the social and political system. These were the military and the civil bureaucratic elites. Among these two groups, the more powerful and influential was the military elite.

The military elite gained its influential position not only because of the centrality of the security issue in Israel's history, but also due to its symbiotic connections to the political leadership. In any case, this elite gained considerable prestige and hence influence as a result of the impressive military victories in the 1948, 1956 and 1967 wars. Because of the continued salience of the defence issue, gradually this elite enjoyed not only recognition and prestige, but also obtained control over a substantial chunk of national resources. This elite had been groomed and encouraged by Ben-Gurion and his younger disciples.

The result of the struggle between Ben-Gurion and his followers on the one hand and Eshkol and the Troika on the other hand, led to the temporary demise of Dayan and Peres. When Ben-Gurion established his activist party, Rafi, the two joined him. Since there is no vacuum in such crowded political systems, these two politicians were replaced by a new elite in the Ministry of Defence and also the IDF. Thus, for example, until the 1967 War Eshkol himself held the Defence portfolio. As could have been expected, the new political leadership promoted IDF officers who, so they thought, were ideologically closer to their own views. One of the main criteria for the promotion of these officers was their loyalty to the political elite. This explains the appointment of Rabin as Chief of Staff under Eshkol and Elazar when Golda Meir became Prime Minister after Eshkol's death in 1969.[17]

Simultaneously to the military elite's much enhanced position, the civil bureaucracy also was rapidly gaining power in the system and influence over policy making. This was connected to the shift from the previously fragmented structure of power to a highly centralized national government.[18] This transition was accompanied by a change in the recruitment patterns to this elite. During the first two decades after the establishment of the state, many senior members of the bureaucratic elite were recruited from among the second and third echelons of the political elite. This pattern of political recruitment of senior bureaucrats was regarded as legitimate since it tallied well with the logic of the consociational arrangement, according to which positions in the bureaucracy should be allocated proportionately. Accordingly not only the ministries but also the senior bureaucratic positions in these ministries were perceived as part of the legitimate political spoils. The ministers, who were representatives of the coalitional parties and acquired their portfolios strictly according to that consociational principle, were able to appoint their allies or followers to senior positions in the ministries that they controlled.[19] These patterns resulted in a great proximity, almost symbiosis, and a distinct similarity between the political and official elites.

The power of the bureaucratic elite grew not only because of the patterns of their recruitment and their intimate proximity to the politicians. Their growing power and influence should be attributed also to the gradual decline in the power of what Horowitz and Lissak termed as 'the traditional centres of the secondary fields of authority' in the Israeli consociational arrangement. That is, the bureaucracy's growing importance should be attributed to the decline in power of the blocs' institutions as well as of the parties themselves and the trade unions.[20]

The increase in the power of the national centre and the simultaneous decline in the power of these secondary centres were far from being accidental. It was closely related to Mapai and Ben-Gurion governments' intentional etatist policy of transferring authority and power from the various sectors' organizations and concentrating it in the hands of national institutions. Power and authority were transferred and concentrated mainly in the hands of the Government and its bureaucracy. The Arab–Jewish wars, the perception of constant danger created by Israel's enemies and the control over the inflow of material resources from the Jewish Diaspora, foreign governments and international organizations facilitated this shift in power and authority. The shrewd bureaucrats were not slow in realizing what was expiring in this sphere. They became engaged in extending their own scope of authority, strengthening the central government at the expense of the blocs and local authorities, and marshalling additional resources.

This was a gradual but a very effective process. Consequently, on the eve of the 1973 war, both the military and civil bureaucracies occupied a central position in the system. Though IDF officers and the officials of the defence establishment enjoyed greater prestige, the less prestigious civil officials mastered considerable powers too.[21]

In the wake of the great military victory in the 1967 War the Israeli economy was growing rapidly (though at a slower pace than that during the period between 1957 and 1965). The immense expenditures on the IDF's reorganization and its redeployment in the vast occupied territories, the vast civilian investments in these territories, a new wave of immigrants, the economic connections with the territories, the new openness and the general aura of euphoria, contributed to that impressive growth. Consequently, unemployment was reduced, exports increased, and the service sector grew. But at the same time, inflation raised its head, the trade deficit increased and the budget deficit grew too.[22] This relative economic boom facilitated the emergence of yet another new elite – the economic elite. The veteran officials of the economic ministries, the senior staff of the Bank of Israel, directors in government industries and in the private sector were making their initial steps on the way to greater influence in Israeli society and politics. This elite, however, would garner enough power only in the early 1990s.

'SYSTEMIC COMPLACENCY' ON THE EVE OF THE 1973 WAR

The participation of Menahem Begin and his Herut/*Gahal* bloc in the national unity government, which had been forced on Levi Eshkol on the eve of the 1967 War, created expectations that some fundamental changes would occur in the ruling political elite. This was the case since for a while after joining the Eshkol government on the eve of the 1967 War, it seemed that Begin and his party finally succeeded in gaining the political legitimacy that Ben-Gurion and his colleagues had denied them. Begin, his colleagues and followers had hoped that their participation in a government led by the Labour bloc would contribute to their rapid integration into the political elite, and consequently enhance their chances to win a national election. For the time being these hopes remained unfulfilled. Thus, while they gained some respect and legitimacy, Begin's and the *Gahal's* withdrawal from the government in 1970 (as a result of profound disagreements concerning American and United Nations peace initiatives) temporarily stopped their full inclusion in the ruling elite. Structural changes in the elite were staved off. These occurred only after the 1973 War 'earthquake'.

Indeed in the wake of Begin's withdrawal from the government, the Labour party and its 'historical partners' closed ranks and restored their predominance in the political elite. Thus the senior politicians of the Labour camp and their traditional partners were responsible for the developments leading to the 1973 War. Eventually, this elite would pay heavily for its role in these stormy events.

In more than one sense on the eve of the 1973 war the Israelis and the Israeli political elite were still in a state of exhilaration. This was due to a combination of events and processes. The military victory in the 1967 War, the occupation of the territories, the continued status quo and the rapid economic development contributed to the Israelis' contentment. A lot has been said and written about the Israelis' consequent enhanced sense of security; the pride in their new 'vast empire' (resulting from the occupation of the Golan Heights, the West Bank and Gaza, and the entire Sinai); and the sense of invincibility that contributed to what might be called 'systemic complacency'.[23] Therefore, there is no need to elaborate on these factors here. Yet there is a need to add certain factors that were relatively neglected in previous analyses, but influenced those developments and eventually the future of the political elite.

The first factor was connected to the behaviour of the political elite in regard to the domestic social and economic situation. Despite the growing gap between rich and poor, the growing dissatisfaction and protest of oriental Jews (which was very well demonstrated in the emergence and activities of the Israeli Black Panthers and the Tents' Movement in Jerusalem) and the growing signs of corruption in government, Prime Minister Golda Meir achieved a 76 per cent approval rating and her popularity was not affected by her positions and denigrating statements about oriental Jews. Similarly, Moshe Dayan was at the height of his popularity as the hero of the 1967 War. This posture of the leading political personae favourably affected the position of the IDF and civil bureaucracy. The hegemony of these elites seemed unchallenged.

The second factor was connected to the behaviour of the military and civil bureaucratic elites. Encouraged by the complacency of the politicians and by the sense that Israel would be able to indefinitely maintain the status quo, the military and civilian elites were deeply engaged in creating the bureaucratic arrangements and the physical infrastructures for holding on to the territories and for managing the general economic boom that Israel experienced during that period. These two bureaucracies did not heed various signs coming either from Israel's Arab neighbours that they would try to disturb the regional status quo, or from large dissatisfied segments in the Israeli public.

THE 'CONCEPTION'

The nature and composition of the Labour elite that dominated the ruling coalition contributed to the emergence of the 'conception'. In turn that conception, the systemic complacency and the Arab states' deception caused the Israeli military debacle during the first stages of the 1973 War. More specifically, the conception itself had been a result of a combination of mistaken political-military strategic and tactical considerations made by that elite. Thus, the assumption here is that the 'human factor', rather than the IDF's organizational structure, deficient weapon systems, or the impossibility to predict the moves of the Arab opponents (the 'deception') was at the root of the system's behaviour.

Concerning the long-term strategic considerations, Israeli political and military planners adopted the view that Israel's perceived overwhelming victory in the 1967 War enhanced its strategic military deterrence. This view was not altered even during and after the 1968–1970 War of Attrition, that had shown that the Arab rulers were ready to risk their own security and military interests to attain certain political and economic gains. By the same token, the purported Israeli nuclear capability at that time did not enhance that coveted deterrence. Presidents Anwar al-Sadat and Hafiz-al Asad must have taken this factor into their own risk calculations when they decided to initiate the 1973 War. Apparently they decided to ignore this potential Israeli threat. In retrospect it seems that they had good reasons to do so. Eventually Dayan's panicky suggestion to use nuclear weapons in view of the initial military reversals was rejected by Golda Meir and her close advisers.[24]

Another part of the 'conception' was the view that the occupation of the territories had created sufficient strategic depth to prevent Arab governments from launching a successful attack on Israel. The Israeli planners thought that this territorial factor, combined with the Israeli superiority in the air (especially in view of the huge investments in the Israeli Air Force after its stunning attainment in the 1967 War), ensured the relative protection of Israeli civilian centres. There was a second aspect to this strategic posture: Israeli strategic planners postulated that any Arab attempt to launch ground attacks into the Sinai or onto the Golan Heights would only result in the destruction of the invading Arab troops; the vast territories of the Sinai especially were regarded as a potential death trap for any Egyptian troops crossing the Suez Canal.

During the late 1960s and early 1970s the Israeli politicians had not endorsed any plans for a withdrawal from the Suez Canal line, where Israeli and Egyptian forces were directly facing each other. Such arguments for establishing a flexible line of defence away from the waterline had been suggested by Dayan and a number of Israeli military senior commanders, including Ariel Sharon, Israel Tal and Benjamin Peled, who had criticized the 'Maginot Line mentality' that was created by the Bar-Lev fortifications. Consequently, the defence establishment fortified the Israeli positions on this line and built what became known as the Bar-Lev Line. This massive static line of fortifications that had provided reasonable protection to Israeli troops during the War of Attrition infused an additional sense of complacency into the Israeli policy making system. In view of the tremendous planning, financial and professional investments in the Bar-Lev Line, the defence establishment was not ready to change its positions. Moreover the severe criticism waged at the Israeli political strategic planners was enhanced by the fact that the Egyptians conducted repeated series of successful military manoeuvres simulating the crossing of the Suez Canal, did not alter that ingrained view.

Furthermore, the Israeli political and military elites made some mistaken assumptions about the Israeli and Arab states' relative military capabilities. These elites maintained that in view of the victory in 1967 the IDF should invest most of its resources in further developing its air force, armoured corps and navy. Consequently they decided to invest less in the IDF's infantry. These decisions, which were based on 'lessons' from the 1967 War without taking into account possible future changes in the battlefield, proved wrong in view of the nature of the forces that the Arab states eventually used in the initial stages of the 1973 War and the nature of their surprise attack across the Suez Canal. To further exacerbate these decisions the same planners had as a working assumption that the Arab states would complete their armies' reorganization and re-equipment only by the end of 1975. This mistaken assessment was based in turn on a wrong mirror image that air forces would be the most important elements in an Arab attack. Again in retrospective, these assessments were proven wrong since the Egyptians and Syrians, reportedly assisted by Soviet planners, thought in an innovative fashion, correctly assessing the weaknesses of the Israeli strategic posture. Thus the Arabs based their surprise attack that was launched on Yom Kippur on an infantry attack.

Furthermore, not only did the Israelis rely on the Bar-Lev line for the defence of their forces deployed on the waterline east of the Suez Canal and were not well prepared for simultaneous infantry attacks across the Canal and on the Golan Heights, but conceptually they were preparing for an all-out full-scale war. The Egyptian and Syrian politicians and military strategists had understood also these positions and on their part they planned and launched only a limited war on the Israelis. This strategic concept that accurately fitted their capabilities was examined in the repeated manoeuvres carried out during the two years before the war.[25] On the one hand these preparations enhanced the success of the deception during the initial stages of the war, and on the other hand confused the Israeli civilian and military elites.

These strategic miscalculations were accompanied by a host of tactical mistakes that added to the military debacle during the initial stages of the war. Yet before describing these factors, it should be noted that early in 1973 there was a round of new appointments in the IDF. Relevant to our discussion here are the facts that the IDF Chief of Staff, the Head of Military Intelligence, the officer responsible for intelligence on the Egyptian front and the Commander of the Southern Front, were all new appointees. All of them, who had reached their senior positions during the euphoric period after the 1967 War, had neither enough time nor an inclination to dramatically alter the IDF's organizational structure and deployment, nor the strategic evaluations of the Arabs' capabilities and military plans. In short, they were not ready to seriously reconsider the presumptions of the Israeli strategic 'conception'.

Now it is possible to turn to some tactical problems that were connected to the contemporaneous behaviour of the Israeli elites. From 1972 to the beginning of the 1973 War the IDF's chiefs had plenty of information about the Arab military preparations and movements. Thus, in view of the alarming Arab military exercises conducted in May 1973, the IDF mobilized the reserves and deployed them in preparation for a possible surprise attack but the Arabs did not launch their attack then. Apparently, the fact that the Egyptians and the Syrians did not launch such an attack only enhanced the Israelis' sense of security. To avoid further costly and embarrassing mobilization and deployment in response to false alarms, the Israeli chiefs were reluctant to do so on the eve of the 1973 War, when they had valid information about the real surprise attack that was in the offing. Moreover at the time, the Israeli politicians and press used to ridicule the Arab leaders and their preparations for war, and, for example, President Sadat was then portrayed as an indecisive hesitant leader who wanted to extract Israel's withdrawal from the Sinai by empty military threats.

Within that mind-set of complacency which prevailed among the Israeli elite on the eve of the 1973 War, which was based on a sense of superiority *vis-à-vis* the Arabs and self-assurance about Israel's invincibility, the IDF did not publicize these preparations. The reasons for downplaying all these factors were connected to Israeli domestic politics. For it should be remembered that at that time Israel was in the midst of the 1973 general election campaign and the Labour's elite did not want to wreck its chances of winning by publicizing such military preparations, thus giving them credence.

To this factor another one should added: the Prime Minister's reluctance to launch an Israeli first strike when it became clear that a major Arab attack was in the offing. The official explanation of this was that the Israeli government had no intention to frustrate its close relations with the American administration that opposed such a pre-emptive strike.[26]

THE ELITES' BEHAVIOUR DURING THE 1973 WAR

The surprise attack launched by the Egyptians and Syrians on the Day of Atonement caused an immediate collapse of intelligence gathering and reporting systems. Hence the response of bewildered Prime Minister Golda Meir and of her advisers – the minister of defence, a minister without portfolio and senior IDF officers – was to create a smoke screen. This was intended to conceal the initial military debacle to facilitate the next moves of the IDF. Yet it was also intended to prevent adverse reactions inside Israel on the one hand and to boost the Israelis' morale on the other hand. All these elements were clearly present in Meir's famous radio broadcast on the afternoon of Saturday, 6 October. Dayan followed her and used a similar language. Then the Chief of Staff surpassed these two politicians and said on the radio: 'our aim is to teach [the Arabs] a lesson and to win a decisive and significant victory, in short, to break their bones'. Later a few generals adopted similar postures and made boastful statements. These reactions reflected the exceedingly poor adaptation to the new situation. Moreover, reacting this way they repeated the mode of operation of the government and IDF during the first stages of the 1967 War. They resorted to this mode of operation since under the circumstances they either could not or did not want to consider the implications of the actual calamitous situation.

Their public statements, however, did not fool the Arab politicians and military chieftains. Nor did they fool the Israeli public. Apparently, the Arab politicians and military chieftains were surprised by the success of their attack and later regretted their decision to launch merely a limited war. Yet, unlike the Israelis, they were perfectly aware of the results and the implications of the initial stages of the war. In retrospect, Egypt achieved its strategic goals. On the other hand, the rapid unveiling of the simultaneous and successful Syrian and Egyptian attacks and the IDF failure shocked both the Israeli public at large as well as the political and bureaucratic elites.

As far as it is possible to judge the psychological sources of the reactions of the Israeli elites, it seems that their members began to face the facts about the new realities with utter disbelief and helplessness. It took them quite a while to digest what was happening. Therefore their actual operative decisions continued to be directed by past experience. In short, they were slow to fully adapt to the new circumstances and this explains the first Israeli desperate reaction to the initial attack: the use of the air force to stop the Arab infantry attack. As should have been expected, because of the massive deployment of Soviet missiles west of the Suez Canal, in this first counterattack the Israeli air force suffered heavy losses. Moreover the air force attacks could not stop the orchestrated Egyptian and Syrian infantry and armour attacks.

Realizing the limited effect of the air force operations, the Israelis tried to simultaneously recapture the Bar-Lev line and the lost territory on the Golan Heights. When these immediate quasi-automatic responses that had been conducted according to outdated Standard Operating Procedures (SOPs) failed, the IDF tried to launch a major counter attack, which was intended to break the front that the Egyptians succeeded to establish and uphold east of the Suez Canal (in fact, east of the Bar-Lev line). Thus nobody in the political and military elites tried to devise and implement innovative solutions to the severe problems created by the early Arab successful deception and surprise attack on the one side and by the Israeli military debacle on the other side. The utmost that they were capable of doing was to use again and again routines and SOPs that had been formulated on the basis of the previous sense of invincibility and ability to maintain the status quo that prevailed in the wake of the 1967 War.

Inertia and lack of imaginative ideas dictated some further decisions that were taken by these elites. Despite the setbacks during the first three days of war, the system still continued to act according to its traditional conceptions, strategies and tactics. The Israeli military moves in the battlefield during the first week of fighting were one example of reactions in accordance with previous strategic conceptions. The patterns of mobilization and defence of the civilian population was another such example.

When these routines and quasi-automatic responses proved ineffective in repulsing the Egyptian and Syrian invading forces and in concealing the full dimensions of the intelligence and initial military failures, the elites demonstrated a considerable degree of confusion. The strategic and tactical confusion was reflected in the conduct of futile military operations. Only then Meir and her few close advisers became doubtful about the ability of the chain of command to perform well in repulsing the Arab armies and to launch a successful counter-offensive. This confusion and lack of trust in senior commanders resulted in the appointment of retired generals to supervise the activities of the minister of defence and the active commanders on the battlefield. Thus for example, the former Chief of Staff, Chaim Bar-Lev (who held a ministerial position in Meir's government) was dispatched by the Prime Minister to visit the northern front to evaluate the plans suggested by Dayan and the officers. Bar-Lev indeed recommended a drastic change in Dayan's plans, and his recommendations – rather than those of Dayan – were executed. Consequently Israel concentrated its efforts on the northern front. Later Bar-Lev was appointed the supreme commander of the Southern Front over the head of General Shmuel Gonen, the commander of this front. Other officers, like former chief of military intelligence, Aharon Yariv, were also called back to active service. Yariv was appointed as chief military spokesman, and he was involved in military decision-making and later conducted the negotiations with the Egyptians at KM 101.

On certain occasions these retired generals improved the quality of decision-making and introduced a greater sense of confidence. Yet on other occasions they only added to the general sense of confusion that characterized the military elite during the first phase of the war. Considerable confusion characterized not only the military but also the political and civilian bureaucratic elites. This was reflected in contradictory and unclear decisions regarding various matters, including the burial of soldiers who were killed in the battlefield.

That confusion deteriorated into alarm. One of the most senior members in the political elite, the hero of the 1967 War, the then Minister of Defence Moshe Dayan, acted under the impact of this alarm. First, he was reluctant to shoulder responsibility for the actual operations, and told the IDF commanders that all he was willing to do was to offer them 'ministerial advice'. Later some of his policy recommendations were coloured by even greater alarm. These included his suggestion to withdraw from the Golan Heights (which, as noted above, was reversed by Chaim Bar-Lev's recommendation). Another such proposal was to deploy Israel's nuclear weapons for possible use. It was reported that Dayan had suggested it to prevent the destruction of 'the third temple [the state of Israel]'.

Action as a result of confusion and alarm characterized the Israeli elite decisions in regard to urgent requests addressed to the US for the immediate supply of large quantities of weapons. These requests were utilized by US Secretary of State, Henry Kissinger, to exert substantial pressure on the Israeli government regarding its political moves. The massive airlift to Israel, that according to some observers was not absolutely warranted, proved highly costly.[27] A similar alarmist decision was to buy in the free market large quantities of oil at a very high price and because of the OPEC boycott. Analysts have argued that the Israeli alarmist move contributed to the tremendous increase of oil price.[28]

To these psychological and attitudinal factors that had adversely affected the decisions of the senior Israeli ruling elites one should add some organizational difficulties. The traditional 'fiefdom arrangement' that characterized the Israeli government and the consequent high degree of its compartmentalization (that characterized also other consociational governments) had a marked impact on the problematic *modus operandi* of the elites. Thus Prime Minister Golda Meir, who was regarded and regarded herself as 'the only virile man' in her cabinet, acted in almost a vacuum. Except for her closest confidants such as Minister without Portfolio Israel Galili, former Chief of Staff Bar-Lev, Director General of her office Mordechai Gazit, and Israel's Ambassador in Washington Simcha Dinitz, other ministers and senior officials either deserted her or were excluded from decision taking.

Thus during the first stages of the war the various mechanisms of deliberation and consultation almost totally collapsed. There was a lack of organized flow of information, evaluations and strategic and tactical proposals directed to the Prime Minister and the cabinet. Those who were responsible for providing these inputs were either stunned or busy assisting the field commanders in the desperate conduct of military operations. These difficulties were further exacerbated by the fact that there was no alternative source for strategic evaluation to the military intelligence. Later, in fact, the Agranat Commission of Inquiry recommended establishing two alternative mechanisms – a kind of a National Security Council and a unit in the Ministry of Foreign Affairs. On another level of analysis the confusion, alarm and focus on the military situation isolated the Prime Minister and the political elite. Therefore regardless of the protest movement that had emerged at that time,[29] the decisions taken by the Prime Minister and her government were not influenced by the public mood.

Golda Meir's personal reaction to the unveiling of the scope of Israeli casualties and costs in the war – over 6,000 killed and wounded soldiers, hundreds of POWs, and a devastating economic toll amounting to $7 billion – was influenced by the traumatic experience during the first stages of the war. It is not clear to what extent she fully recognized the long-term ramifications of that war. Thus for a while she overcame her immediate emotions and headed the Labour campaign in the delayed general elections. Because of a combination of factors that are out of the scope of analysis here, the Labour party lost some seats in the Knesset, but with 51 seats it still maintained its dominance in the Israeli political system. Based on these results Meir could form and head a new government. Yet her government's days were numbered.

The immediate reason for Golda Meir's resignation and the end of her long political career was the Agranat Commission's Report. The Commission, headed by Supreme Court Justice Shimon Agranat, had been established after the war to examine the complex question of responsibility for the debacle. The commission submitted its report in April 1974. Essentially, the report did put the onus for the failure on the chief of staff, the military intelligence and the commander of the southern front. The report was ambivalent about Meir's and Dayan's responsibility.

Many Israelis expressed their outrage at what were regarded as unbalanced conclusions pinning all responsibility on the IDF officers. Yet the publication of the report caused a host of resignations of officers, among them the chief of staff, the chief of military intelligence and the commander of the southern front. Thus, the report was a severe blow to the military elite. In turn the report's indictments and the resignations that followed it further exacerbated the public's mood.

The opposition Likud party sensed this rebellious mood, and tabled a motion for a vote of no-confidence in Meir's government. Anticipating a defeat in this vote of no-confidence, partly because of lack of support of some members in her own party, Meir submitted her resignation. Apparently, Meir's move was a result of a belated, but probably not a full, recognition of the disastrous consequences of the 1973 War. She must have realized the numerous fatalities, the massive destruction of weapons and other military equipment, the public's depressed mood, the loss of self-confidence, the loss of economic resources, the diplomatic isolation, the galloping inflation, and the reduction of immigration to Israel.[30]

Meir's resignation marked the end of a leadership generation. With her departure from political life veteran politicians, like her close adviser, Israel Galili, accompanied her. Eventually, their departure from active political life would be followed by withdrawal of other senior and junior political figures.

After a short struggle inside the Labour party, essentially between Yitzhak Rabin and Shimon Peres, the former, who had not been involved in the conduct of the War, was elected by the party to succeed Meir. Shimon Peres was appointed Minister of Defence. The advent of these two pragmatic politicians and the removal and replacement of the former military elite marked a new phase in the political development of Israel, including its political, military and bureaucratic elites. First and foremost it signalled the disappearance of the Labour's centrist faction that had come to the political forefront two decades earlier. In the longer-term this paved the way to the belated Likud victory in 1977, and the establishment of the first Begin government.

THE EMERGENCE OF NEW ELITES

On the level of Israeli macro-politics the 1973 War expedited the transition from the consociational to a neo-corporatist arrangement. As noted, this transition had begun in the late 1960s and there were a few contributing factors for this particular direction of social and political development. The first of these factors was a rapidly growing inclination of the rank and file to alter their main patterns of reliance on political institutions and agencies. Rather than relying on the traditional social-political blocs, the old parties and state agencies for the achievement, protection and promotion of their interests, the rank and file turned to social, political and economic interest groups. The problematic performance of the political, military and bureaucratic elites during the 1973 'earthquake' only enhanced this tendency.

Other factors that contributed to that transition derived from some basic social changes. Thus grassroots political affiliation shifted and their action was freed from the firm control of the traditional ideological camps. Parties and especially their elites were part of that transition. This process was accelerated by the growing scepticism about the efficacy of the established elites after the 1973 War. This was even further enhanced by the inclination and ability of wider social groups to participate in policy making and influence its outcomes. The relaxation of the highly centralized power structure, and the consequent decentralization of policy making were such contributing factors to this change. These were accompanied by more elaborate patterns of consultation between the elites that represented specific and specialized interests. As a result of these developments the grassroots felt freer to defect from the traditional blocs and parties. In the long run the main loser in this gradual process of defection from the established camps was the Labour bloc. The other side of the same coin was that these processes enhanced popular support for the rightist, nationalist and religious parties, who were less identified with the 1973 debacle than Labour.

The deterioration of the traditional political blocs and parties, the rapid expansion of groups engaged in interest articulation and aggregation that had begun during the late 1960s and early 1970s, motivated those Israelis, who still felt a compelling need to rely on well-organized groups for the fulfilment of their needs, to turn to established and newer interest groups. Subsequently more Israelis joined these groups hoping that they would promote their well-being and protect their interests. Indeed since then there has occurred a discernible increase in the number of single-issue and multi-purpose interest groups in Israel. A similar development took place in regard to the scope of their membership, and consequently also of the volume of their activities.[31] This trend paved the way for the introduction of the next social-political arrangement.

A by-product of the transition to neo-corporatism was an increase in the importance of 'peak organizations', such as those of the industrialists, bankers, large commercial firms, organized labour and professionals. There occurred also, but to a lesser degree, an increase in the volume, scope and intensity of the activities of regional and local-municipal interest groups, at what is known as the mezzo-corporatist level. These peak organizations and regional and local interest groups became indispensable and assertive partners in public policy making. Because of their previous predominance in nation level policy making and since their power was not immediately and substantially eroded, for a while, the veteran elites remained the senior partner in public policy making. Yet the power of these elites continued to dwindle. Also in all these developments Israel showed great similarity to other former consociational democracies that made the transition to the neo-corporatist arrangement.

Consequently during the late 1970s there emerged a system of representation in which the most significant interests were organized into hierarchically ordered and functionally differentiated entities. By then too, some of these neo-corporatist associations were formally and informally recognized by the state as significant partners in public policy making. To a certain extent each of these groups, or corporations, maintained or acquired representational monopolies within their respective spheres of interest and activity. In this capacity they became active in the realm of national public policy making. Thus, for example, the heads of the large banks formed an informal interest group, or more accurately a 'bankers' elite cartel' that had enjoyed substantial influence on policy making in this sphere. The 'capitalists' (that is, the industrialists, commercial and professional) associations were only loosely organized, and their peak organizations were based on federal arrangements. While these peak interest groups recognized the 'first among equals' status of central government in the public policy making process, they succeeded in limiting its veto power and ability to mediate between capitalists and labour. Moreover, each of these organizations formulated policies on their own, that is, without prior consultation with other corporations, and then set out to implement them.[32] Again, as in other neo-corporatist polities, under the emerging Israeli neo-corporatist arrangement, the character of national level policy making reflected the relative strength of those corporations.

Essentially since the mid-1970s, the Israeli political arrangements accurately reflected an early description of the main features of neo-corporatism. According to this portrayal, this arrangement is

> more than a peculiar pattern of articulation of interests. Rather it [is] an institutionalized pattern of policy-formation in which large interest organizations cooperate with each other and with public authorities not only in the articulation, or even in the 'intermediation' of interests, but also – in its developed forms – in the 'authoritative allocation of values' and in the implementation of such policies. It is precisely because of the intimate mutual penetration of state bureaucracies and large interest organizations [that] we are dealing with an integrated system of 'societal guidance'.[33]

Like the previous consociational arrangement, the main purposes of the neo-corporatist arrangement were to achieve social and political stability, maximal degree of social integration, economic growth and efficient political performance in an otherwise potentially unstable polity functioning in hostile external environments. From the point of view of national level public policy making, the main purpose was to build a pluralist consensus concerning pressing social and especially economic policies. Much as in the previous arrangement, in the neo-corporatist arrangement consensus building was also attempted on the level of elites, but in this instance among the leaders of the peak associations. Moreover, and in a way resembling the 'elite-cartel' in the consociational arrangement, these elites struggled to maintain their hegemony and freedom of action.

Consequently, the main pattern of decision-making was that of bargaining leading to business-like compromised agreements about policy packages, especially, but not only, in the economic sphere. These patterns of public policy making have not been limited to spheres such as wages and employment. Rather, the basic political arrangements, the policy making style and the patterns of behaviour that they produced had spill-over effects in other spheres, such as welfare policies, municipal matters, and even in the sphere of military industries.

This transition enhanced the ascendance of a new type of leader. It first occurred in the deteriorating Labour camp and later also in the Likud. Rabin and Peres were the archetypal examples of the new transactional leadership in the centre left bloc. The 1977 critical elections in Israel brought to power the Likud under Begin's leadership. Begin and some of his colleagues who served in his government still belonged to the same leadership generation of Golda Meir and her associates. Yet, the transition to neo-corporatism and the type of the elites that this arrangement entailed was evident also in the Likud governments. Thus side by side with veteran leaders like Begin himself, Jacob Meridor and Yitzhak Shamir, a new group of transactional political leaders, like Moshe Arens and Simcha Erlich, appeared also in the Likud, and in the early 1980s these leaders would play an important role in the Likud and its governments.

CONCLUSIONS

In a historical perspective it seems that the 1973 War occurred when the Israeli society was in the midst of a major social and political transformation. During that period large groups in the Israeli society were shedding their previous allegiance to the three major camps and parties. These camps and parties, which had been formed during the Yishuv period and maintained during the two decades after the establishment of the Jewish State, forged a certain ability to control the development of Israeli political arrangements. Though not fully fledged sub-cultures, the existence of three camps created a consociational system that resembled other similar polities. In this arrangement the elites that frequently form an 'elite cartel' play a decisive role in policy making and implementation. Since the Labour camp was the largest and most organized, it dominated the system, and its elite controlled the government and its policy making. The Israeli stunning military victory in the 1967 War and the consequent euphoria and self-confidence on the one hand, and the economic growth and enhanced openness on the other hand, enhanced processes of change. Thus the 1973 'earthquake' dealt only a severe blow to the previous political arrangement.

Among other things, during the early 1970s veteran elites, who were mainly identified with the Labour camp and were responsible for the 1973 debacle, showed clear signs of decline. After that war the disillusioned public especially altered its perceptions of the previously prestigious military elite. The public was searching for new arrangements and for new leadership. Gradually the 'old regime' was giving way to the emerging neo-corporatist arrangement that was based on and nurtured by a new breed of political, economic and military leaders. From a theoretical viewpoint, the analysis here points at the significance of profound social change to the appearance of a new political arrangement and eventually to the emergence of new elites. Thus it has been argued that a severe external blow causing a national trauma is not a sufficient factor in causing major shifts. These can only expedite processes that are brought into existence by developments at the grassroots level.

NOTES

1. See for example, Emanuel Gutmann and Jacob Landau, 'The Political Elite and National Leadership in Israel', in George Lenczowski, ed., *Political Elites in the Middle East*, Washington, DC: The American Enterprise Institute, 1975; Yonathan Shapiro, *An Elite Without Successors. Generations of Political Leaders in Israel*, Tel Aviv: Sifriat Poalim, 1984 (Hebrew); Dan Horowitz and Moshe Lissak, *Trouble in Utopia, The Overburdened Polity of Israel*, Albany: SUNY Press, 1989; Alan Arian, *The Second Republic. Politics in Israel*, Tel Aviv: Zmora Bitan, 1997 (Hebrew); and Eva Etzioni-Halevi, *Elites and Elitism in Israel*, Tel Aviv: Tcherikover, 1997 (Hebrew).
2. Gabriel Sheffer, 'Structural Change and Leadership Transformation', in David Levi-Faur, Gabriel Sheffer and David Vogel, eds, *Israel: The Dynamics of Change and Continuity*, London: Frank Cass, 1999; Gabriel Sheffer, 'Political Change and Party System Transformation', paper presented at the conference on 'Parties, Elections and Cleavages: Comparative and Theoretical Perspectives', The Hebrew University, Jerusalem, 3 June 1998.
3. S. Welch, *The Concept of Political Culture*, Basingstoke: Macmillan, 1993.
4. David Nachmias and David Rosenbloom, *Bureaucratic Culture: Citizens and Administration in Israel*, New York: St. Martin's Press, 1978.
5. Emanuel Gutmann, 'Parties and Camps – Stability and Change', in Moshe Lissak and Emanuel Gutmann, eds, *The Israeli Political System*, Tel Aviv: Am Oved, 1977 (Hebrew); Lissak and Horowitz, *Trouble in Utopia*; Michael Shalev, *Labour and the Political Economy in Israel*, New York: Oxford University Press, 1992; Gabriel Sheffer, 'Structural Change'; and for a divergent view see Peter Medding's paper presented at the conference on 'Parties, Elections and Cleavages: Comparative and Theoretical Perspectives', The Hebrew University, Jerusalem, 3 June 1998.
6. Shmuel N. Eisenstadt, *Israeli Society*, Jerusalem: Magnes Press, 1967 (Hebrew); Dan Horowitz and Moshe Lissak, *The Origins of the Israeli Polity*, Tel Aviv: Am Oved, 1977 (Hebrew); Gutmann, 'Parties and Camps'; Sheffer, 'Elite Cartel, Vertical Domination and Grassroots Discontent in Israel', in Sidney Tarrow *et al.*, eds, *Territorial Politics in Industrial Nations*, New York: Praeger, 1978; Horowitz and Lissak, *Trouble in Utopia*; Peter Medding, *The Founding of Israeli Democracy 1948–1967*, New York: Oxford University Press, 1990; Arend Lijphart, 'Israeli Democracy and Democratic Reform in Comparative Perspective', in Ehud Sprinzak and Larry Diamond, eds, *Israeli Democracy Under Stress*, Boulder: Lynne Reinner, 1993; Alan Dowty, 'Israel's First Decade: Building a Civic State', in Ilan Troen and Noah Lucas, *Israel, The First Decade of Independence*, Albany: SUNY Press, 1995.

7. Gerhard Lehmbruch, *Proporzdemokratie: Politisches System und Politische Kultur in der Schweiz und in Österreich*, Tübingen: J.C.B. Mohr, 1967.
8. Arend Lijphart, *The Politics of Accommodation*, Berkeley: University of California Press, 1968; Arend Lijphart, 'Consociational Democracy', *World Politics* 21/2 (1969); Arend Lijphart, *Democracies: Patterns of Majoritarian and Consensus in Twenty One Countries*, New Haven: Yale University Press, 1984; Kenneth McRae, ed., *Consociational Democracy: Political Accommodation in Segmented Societies*, Toronto: McLelland and Stewart, 1974.
9. Erik Nordlinger, *Conflict Regulation in Divided Societies*, Cambridge, MA: Centre of International Affairs, Harvard University, 1972; and Sheffer, 'Elite Cartel'.
10. Troen and Lucas, *Israel*.
11. Eisenstadt, *The Transformation of Israeli Society*.
12. Yitzhak Galnoor, 'The Crisis in the Israeli Political System: The Parties as Dominant Factor', in Moshe Lissak and Baruch Knei-Paz, *Israel Towards the Year 2000*, Jerusalem: Magnes Press, 1996 (Hebrew); Reuven Hazan, 'Presidential Parliamentarism in Israel', *Electoral Studies* 15/1 (1996); Reuven Hazan, 'Party System Change in Israel 1948–98', in P. Pennings and Jane Lane, eds, *Comparing Party System Change*, London: Routledge, 1998.
13. See, for example, a *Yedi'ot Ahronot* survey conducted on this issue.
14. G. Sheffer, *Moshe Sharett: A Biography of a Political Moderate*, Oxford: Oxford University Press, 1996.
15. Eliahu Hassin and Dan Horowitz, *The Affair*, Tel Aviv: Am Hassefer, 1981 (Hebrew); Hagai Eshed, *Who Gave the Order?*, Tel Aviv: Idanim, 1979 (Hebrew); Shabtai Teveth, *Ben-Gurion's Spy. The Story of the Political Scandal that Shaped Modern Israel*, New York: Columbia University Press, 1996.
16. See, for example, James MacGregor Burns, *Leadership*, New York: Harper, 1979; Bernard Bass, *Bass and Stodgill Handbook of Leadership*, New York: The Free Press, 1990; P. Gronn, 'Greatness Re-Visited: The Current Obsession with Transformational Leadership', *Leading and Managing* 1/1 (1995).
17. Edward Luttwak and Dan Horowitz, *The Israeli Army*, New York: Harper and Row, 1975; Yoram Peri, *Between Battles and Ballots, Israeli Military in Politics*, Cambridge: Cambridge University Press, 1983; Moshe Lissak, 'Paradoxes of Israeli Civil-Military Relations', in Moshe Lissak, ed., *Israeli Society and its Defence Establishment*, London: Frank Cass. 1984; Moshe Lissak, 'Boundaries and Institutional Linkages Between Elites: Some Illustrations from Civil-Military Relations in Israel', in G. Moore, ed., *Research in Politics and Society, Vol. I: Studies of the Structure of National Elite Groups*, 1985.
18. Dan Horowitz and Moshe Lissak, *Origins of the Israeli Polity*.
19. Hillel Schmid, *Thirty Years of the Governmental and Public Senior Officialdom*, Jerusalem: the Israeli Government, 1979; David Dery, *Politics and Civil Service Appointments*, Jerusalem: The Israel Institute of Democracy, 1993; Aharon Kfir and Jacob Reuveny, 'Transitional Processes', in Aharon Kfir and J. Reuveny, eds, *Public Administration in Israel Towards the 2000's*, Tel Aviv: Tcherikover, 1998.
20. Horowitz and Lissak, *Troubles in Utopia*.
21. Nachmias and Rosenbloom, *Bureaucratic Culture*.
22. Nadav Halevy and Ruth Klinov-Malul, *The Economic Development of Israel*, Jerusalem: Acadamon, 1975; Yair Aharoni, *Structure and Performance in the Israeli Economy*, Tel Aviv: Tcherikover, 1976 (Hebrew); Haim Barkai, *The Cost of Security in Retrospective*, Jerusalem: The Falk Institute, 1980 (Hebrew); Haim Barkai, *The Formative Years of the Israeli Economy*, Jerusalem: The Falk Institute, 1983; Ira Sharkansky, *The Political Economy of Israel*, New Jersey: Transactions, 1987.
23. Ze'ev Schiff, *October Earthquake: Yom Kippur 1973*, Tel Aviv: University Publishing Project, 1974 (Hebrew); Chaim Herzog, *The War of Atonement*, Boston: Little, Brown, 1975.
24. Yair Evron, 'The Relevance and Irrelevance of Nuclear Options in Conventional Wars: the 1973 October War', *The Jerusalem Journal of International Relations* 7/1-2 (1983); Avner Yaniv, *Deterrence Without the Bomb: The Politics of Israeli Strategy*, Lexington, MA: Lexington Books, 1987; and Amnon Sela, 'Strategic Depth, Electronics and Negotiations', in Lissak and Knei-Paz, eds, *Israel Towards the Year 2000*.
25. On the Arab preparations and military operations see, for example, *The October War*, Beirut: A-Nahar, 1974; and Mohammed Heikal, *The Road to Ramadan*, New York: Quadrangle Books, 1975.

26. William Quandt, *Decade of Decision: American Policy Toward the Arab-Israeli Conflict*, Berkeley: University of California Press, 1977.
27. Quandt, *Decade of Decision*; Matti Golan, *The Secret Talks of Henry Kissinger*, New York: Quadrangle Books, 1976.
28. J. Kaikati, 'The Arab Oil Boycott', *California Management Review* 3 (1978); and O. Feuth, 'The Oil Weapon De-Mystified', *Policy Review* 15 (1981).
29. Since other chapters in this volume deal with protest and protest movements in Israel after the 1973 War this chapter is not discussing this issue.
30. Golda Meir, *My Life*, Jerusalem: Steimatzky, 1975 (Hebrew); and Meron Medzini, *The Proud Jewess: Golda Meir and Israel's Vision*, Tel Aviv: Idonim, 1990 (Hebrew).
31. Yael Yishai, *Interest Groups in Israel*, Tel Aviv: Am Oved, 1987 (Hebrew).
32. Shalev, *Labour and the Political Economy in Israel*, 1992.
33. Gerhard Lehmbruch, 'Liberal Corporatism and Party Government', *Comparative Political Studies* 10/1 (1977).

The Domestic Fallout of the Yom Kippur War

SUSAN HATTIS ROLEF

While the Yom Kippur War plays a central role in the military history of Israel and as an opening in the evolution of the Arab-Israeli conflict, one should not ignore its psychological effect or belittle its significance in the social, political and economic development of the state. This review tries to outline the social, political, economic and psychological effects of the war. Naturally, in such a review it is impossible to go into any detailed analysis. However, by trying to present a general, minimalist sketch, the monumentality of the total effect comes to light. Nevertheless, it is also impossible to escape the conclusion that except perhaps for the immediate psychological effects and the longer term economic effects, the Yom Kippur War was, on the whole, much more of a catalyst for various developments, which would have occurred even had it never taken place, than the perpetrator of these developments.

THE PSYCHOLOGICAL EFFECT

Twenty-five years after the Yom Kippur War, most Israelis still refer to it as an earthquake that changed the course of the state's history. In psychological terms there is no doubt that the war was a traumatic experience, which warrants the use of the term 'earthquake'. In the most immediate and extreme form the psychological effects were suffered by over 2,000 soldiers and officers – regulars and reservists – who, both during and soon after the war, developed symptoms referred to by the professionals as 'combat reactions', and required professional treatment. In none of Israel's previous wars were there so many casualties of this type. The reactions were especially severe due to the fact that the war had come as a total surprise, the mobilization of reserves (the bulk of the fighting force) was rather chaotic, in the course of the war several 'holy

Susan Hattis Rolef is a political scientist and freelance writer.

myths' regarding IDF preparedness, morale and the quality of its strategy were broken, and perhaps worst of all, the competence of many top and middle rank commanders was called into question.[1]

On the national level the state of shock should be understood against the background of the fact that on the whole, the six years between June 1967 and October 1973 had been considered 'good years' by the majority of Israelis and the Israeli leadership. Economic prosperity, domestic tranquillity and the absence of *major* external threats to national security created an impression that things were well under control. It was not that anyone thought for a moment that the Arabs had forgotten their dream of defeating Israel or of trying to make it vanish from the face of the earth, but the prospects of the Arabs having enough power to realize this dream seemed remote.[2] What further complicated the situation was the fact that in the period immediately before the war, the media, out of a false sense of 'public responsibility' and a desire to avoid creating 'unnecessary' panic within the public, failed to report important developments, such as major Syrian and Egyptian troop movements near Israel's borders, even though such information was available and had been published abroad.[3]

The Israelis were, thus, totally unprepared for the outbreak of the Yom Kippur War, and what made things worse was that it very quickly became apparent that both the political and military leadership had totally misread the situation before the outbreak of the War. Furthermore, it later transpired that in the course of the war the leadership had chosen to lie to the public about the actual situation.[4] It is not that the Israeli leaders had previously been completely truthful with the public or inclined to give it an accurate picture of reality at any given moment of time.[5] However, this time the lies seemed to result more from confusion and doubts than from cunning and confidence. Doubts started to creep into the minds of many of the political leaders regarding the wisdom of past policies and the assumption of Israel's unfailing military superiority and invincibility,[6] while the 'Wars of the Generals', which accompanied and followed the Yom Kippur War, highlighted the doubts within the military.[7]

THE EMERGENCE OF A PROTEST MOVEMENT IN ISRAEL

One of the first reactions to the new national mood in the aftermath of the war was the emergence of several protest movements. These were not peace movements. Their main message was not that war had broken out because the Israeli Government had failed to pursue peace, but that the decision-making process and conduct of the Israeli leadership before the war and after its outbreak proved that major changes were urgently required both in the political and social systems. In a sense this reaction was more reminiscent of the public demand for constitutional changes, which were to follow the fall of the Yitzhak Shamir Government in

March 1990, and the ugly political horse trading that preceded the formation of a new Government at the time (what Yitzhak Rabin termed 'the stinking manoeuvre'), than of the demands for a more positive approach by the Israeli Government to the peace negotiations with Egypt that followed the visit of President Anwar al-Sadat to Jerusalem in November 1977, by the 'Peace Now' movement.

Yisrael Shelanu

The best known protest movement to emerge after the Yom Kippur War was Yisrael Shelanu (Our Israel) which was established by demobilized reservists, who had served on the front lines and felt that the establishment was totally detached from the people and the men on the front.[8] The movement, headed by Motti Ashkenazi, was made up predominantly of middle class, educated Ashkenazim. The roots of the movement, or the dissatisfaction which gave rise to it, may be found in the period before the Yom Kippur War, and manifested itself in growing alienation of large sections of the population from the political leadership and their feeling that they had no influence over it.[9]

The movement, whose immediate demand was the resignation of Minister of Defence Moshe Dayan, and whose vaguer, longer term demands included the introduction of a constitution and changes in the *modus operandi* of the system, had an extremely strong public impact. But as an organization it vanished almost as rapidly as it had emerged. This was largely because of organizational problems and a failure to define practical goals, but also because Prime Minister Golda Meir resigned on 11 April 1974, and with her the rest of the Government.[10] The last mass demonstration of Yisrael Shelanu, which had started to operate in February 1974, took place on 25 April 1974.[11]

However, even though Yisrael Shelanu, and the other protest movements, soon vanished from the scene, the dissatisfaction which they had expressed and the general demands that they had raised, remained. Furthermore, from an extra-parliamentary political-historical point of view, the protest movements broke the operative national consensus in an unprecedented manner, and created a negative peripheral consensus towards the centre.[12] The human make-up of 'Yisrael Shelanu' and similar movements was predominantly middle class and Ashkenazi. Nevertheless, one of the general demands that they raised, within the framework of the changes which they claimed were necessary in the Israeli society, was for the closing of socio-economic gaps within the Israeli society. However, an attempt by Yisrael Shelanu to cooperate with the 'Black Panthers' on such issues was a total failure.[13]

The Black Panthers

The Black Panthers were a protest movement, founded in 1970 by poor neighbourhood activists of Muslim country origin, many of them with criminal records. The background to the foundation of the Black Panther movement had been the cease-fire of August 1970, which ended the War of Attrition. For the first time since June 1967 the Israeli society entered a period of relative calm in the security sphere, which was accompanied by rapid economic growth and the introduction of the electronic media (especially television). As a result of these developments public attention was diverted from foreign affairs-security issues to internal-welfare ones. In addition, this was also a period in which there was substantial immigration from the Soviet Union, and the poorer old-timers (mostly of Muslim country origin) resented the extensive benefits bestowed on the new immigrants.[14]

The Black Panthers won 1.6 per cent in the Histadrut elections which took place on 11 September 1973, mostly at the expense of the Alignment (the joint list made up of the Israel Labour Party and Mapam).[15] However, even before the Yom Kippur War, the movement came across organizational and personal difficulties, while the war itself temporarily reversed the national order of priorities, with security concerns and general dissatisfactions related to the way the country was being run, replacing social protest with an ethnic background. The Black Panthers, and another five 'Oriental' lists that ran in the general elections to the 8th Knesset, which were held on 31 December 1973 (see below), didn't even manage to get passed the 1 per cent qualifying threshold. This was largely due to the decline in the interest which these lists generated,[16] but also to fragmentation. A uniting of forces in the elections might have led to a different result. When the ethnic aspects of the social problem in Israel once again started to gain momentum as a political issue towards the elections to the 9th Knesset in 1977, it was the Likud which benefited electorally – not radical protest movements such as the Black Panthers.[17]

THE DECEMBER 1973 GENERAL ELECTIONS AND THEIR AFTERMATH

The elections to the 8th Knesset were to have been held on 27 October 1973, but because of the outbreak of the war were put off. On 24 October, the last day of the war, the Knesset Labour Party faction held a first discussion on the implications of the war and its effect on the approaching elections. Minister of Justice, Ya'acov Shimshon Shapira, argued that the elections ought to be further put off by at least a year, in order to give the public the chance to digest the true significance of the recent events and consider, in a more relaxed manner, who ought to lead the state. At the same time he demanded that Minister of Defence Moshe Dayan, who was seen by the general public as the symbol of the Government's failure to foresee the approaching military attack, should resign, in order to clear the atmosphere. Other members objected to putting off the elections, arguing that such a long delay would damage the prospects of the Alignment, and did not feel that Dayan ought to go.[18]

As it were, the elections were held on 31 December. It is difficult to know what would have happened had the elections been put off, as demanded by Shapira, or had new lists, that had not previously registered, been allowed to run in the elections. However, the decision to hold the elections without any further delay, on the basis of the lists that had registered for the elections before the war, one week after the opening of the historic Middle East Peace Conference in Geneva, undoubtedly benefited the ruling Labour-Mapam Alignment, headed by Golda Meir.[19] 'Considering that they were exhausted, mourning their dead, and having difficulty in digesting recent events or comprehending the significance of them, the voters were merciful toward the Labor Party', Yitzhak Rabin wrote in his memoirs.[20]

According to opinion polls held at the time, even had the war not broken out and had the elections been held on time, the Alignment, which had lost 3.7 per cent in the Histadrut elections held in September 1973, would have lost several seats in the Knesset, and the results would have been quite similar to what they actually were.[21] The Alignment received 51 out of the Knesset's 120 seats – down from 56 in the elections to the 7th Knesset held in October 1969, but certainly not a result which pointed to a political earthquake. While the public was clearly in a state of shock after the war, the full implications of what had happened had not yet fully filtered into its consciousness, and despite the fact that Meir insisted on keeping Moshe Dayan, whose popularity was at a low ebb, by her side,[22] a large section of the public was still willing to swallow the slogan 'The Alignment Anyway'.[23]

Nevertheless, there were some indications that the earth was starting to move. The first was the fact that the Likud increased its Knesset representation by close to 26 per cent – from 31 to 39 seats[24] – to a certain extent due to the personal popularity of Ariel Sharon – one of the initiators of the Likud, who had emerged a hero from the Yom Kippur War.[25] The second was that Shulamit Aloni, running for the first time at the head of her own list, the Civil Rights Movement (Ratz), unexpectedly received three seats, drawing some of the 'protest votes', which in the 1977 were to pour in much larger numbers to Yigael Yadin's new Democratic Movement for Change (Dash). Finally, while the Alignment emerged the clear winner from the elections, Golda Meir had difficulties forming a new coalition, and for the first time since the establishment of the State, the status of the labour movement parties, as the pivotal bloc (the only group of parties capable of forming a coalition around itself), was called into question.[26]

The broader implications of the Yom Kippur War started, however, to manifest themselves one month after Golda Meir finally managed to form a coalition, with the Independent Liberals and the National Religious Party, on 10 March 1974. The publication of the interim report of the Agranat Commission, though it blamed the military leadership rather than the political leadership for what had happened, caused Meir to resign together with the rest of the Government, a month and a day after it had been formed, turning it into the shortest lived government in Israel. A whole generation of political leaders, including Meir herself, Pinhas Sapir, Abba Eban and Moshe Dayan were sent into the wilderness.[27] These resignations, together with the death of Israel's first Prime Minister, David Ben-Gurion, on 1 December 1973, was much more than just a symbol of a changing of the guard in the Labour Party.

Meir's resignation enabled a new generation of Labour leaders, headed by the 51-year-old Yitzhak Rabin and the 50-year-old Shimon Peres, to take over. After a leadership contest between these two – the first of four – Rabin became Prime Minister and Peres Minister of Defence. 'The wounds of the Israeli people were still fresh and painful after the recent war, and deep fissures undermined its faith in its leaders and government', was how Rabin described the public mood at this juncture.[28]

Despite some impressive achievements in the peace making process, the sphere of security and in the economy, this was to be the Labour Party's last government for a while, ending 29 years of uninterrupted Labour (and before that Mapai) leadership. By 1977 the Israeli public was ready for a change, and the Labour Party, worn out and bedevilled by financial scandals,[29] was sent into opposition. The Yom Kippur War was not considered by analysts at the time as one of the direct causes of this political 'upheaval', though its long shadow certainly took its toll.[30]

EFFECTS ON THE RELATIVE POWER OF SPECIFIC GROUPS IN ISRAELI SOCIETY

The Return to Religion

One of the major effects of the Yom Kippur War, both on the society and politics of Israel, was in the religious sphere. On the one hand the shock of the war strengthened a phenomenon which had emerged in the aftermath of the Six Day War – that of penitence, or the return to religion. 'The Six Day War reminded people of their past and heritage, and the Yom Kippur War, caused a shock and raised general existential questions.'[31] On the other hand, it caused a radicalization in the political positions of the younger generation of leaders in the National Religious Party, who were more strongly influenced by the halachic rulings of various rabbis, especially regarding the integrity of 'Eretz Israel' and the future of the 'occupied territories'.[32] The National Religious Party (NRP), and other national-religious circles, started placing greater emphasis than before on a religious-halachic definition of the Jewishness of the State of Israel, and advocating positions that emphasized ethnocentric isolationism, with clear xenophobic characteristics, which gained ground within certain sections of Israeli society.[33]

Feminism

In the early 1970s a feminist movement started to develop in Israel, and one of its leading spokeswomen was Marsha Friedman – an immigrant from the United States.[34] In the December 1973 elections Friedman entered the Knesset, not so much because of her feminist message but because she had been placed in third place on Shulamit Aloni's new list Ratz, which had attracted part of the frustrated protest vote.

Nevertheless, observers of the feminist scene in Israel agree that the Yom Kippur War gave the feminist movement a certain moral push forward, especially since the war emphasized the weakness of the public consciousness regarding the status of women in Israel, and the movement's activists became more determined than before to bring about a change in the situation.[35] To a certain extent the appointment in 1976 of MK Ora Namir (Labour) by Prime Minister Yitzhak Rabin to head a commission of inquiry on the status of women in Israel and the absence of equality for women in most spheres of Israeli life was the result of the new found determination.[36]

The Israeli Arabs

The Yom Kippur War also played an important role in the politicization of the Arab minority in Israel. The war encouraged this development from two completely different angles. The first was that by weakening the Israeli political leadership, the war also reduced its power to regulate disadvantaged groups in the Israeli society – the Arab minority included. The Arabs now started to avail themselves of the various methods of struggle resorted to by the Black Panthers, the post-Yom Kippur War protest movements and Gush Emunim.[37] The Land Day demonstrations of 30 March 1976, which ended with six Arabs being killed at the hands of the Israeli law enforcement forces, was a direct outcome of this change, and the beginning of the open struggle by the Israeli Arabs for equality.

The second was the growing Palestinization of the Israeli Arabs and their identification with the PLO as an organization fighting for Palestinian self-determination. This development resulted from the upsurge of Palestinian nationalism and the breakthrough of the PLO into the international political consciousness after 1973 as more than just a terrorist organization.[38] The change in the status of the PLO was not the result of the Yom Kippur War itself, but rather of the renewed interest in the Middle East peace-making process, which followed. The moment the issue of Middle East peace talks became a practical item on the international agenda, one of the questions to which an answer had to be given was: who should represent the Palestinians in such talks? Despite Israel's formal insistence, until September 1993, that the Hashemite Kingdom of Jordan should speak for the Palestinians, it soon became evident that most of the rest of the world believed that this role should be reserved for the PLO. This was clearly manifested by the invitation to

Yasir Arafat to address the UN General Assembly in November 1974 –
one month after the Rabat Arab Summit Conference declared the PLO
to be the sole legitimate representative of the Palestinians in negotiations
about the future of the West Bank and Gaza Strip.

The PLO, in turn, responded by adopting a more pragmatic and
positive approach towards the Palestinian Arabs who had chosen to
remain in Israel after the 1948/49 war, and towards contacts with Israelis
– both Arab and Jews.[39] This resulted in meetings starting to take place
between PLO representatives and Arab MKs from the New Communist
List (Rakah) in the beginning of 1975, simultaneously with similar
meetings, which they held with former MK Uri Avnery and some of the
leading personalities amongst the Black Panthers.[40]

The Generals

While the outbreak of the Yom Kippur War was seen, to a very large
extent, as a failure on the part of the military men (even though its final
outcome was, without doubt, a military victory), in the aftermath of the
Yom Kippur War the influence of reserve generals in Israeli politics
grew.[41] Four 'new' reserve generals entered the Knesset in the December
1973 elections – two within the framework of the Labour Alignment
(Lieutenant General Yitzhak Rabin and Major General Aharon Yariv)
and two within the framework of the Likud (Major General Ariel Sharon
and Major General Avraham Yoffe – the first retired generals to enter the
Knesset on the Likud ticket), joining the 'old timers' Lieutenant General
Moshe Dayan, Major General Yigal Allon and Major General Moshe
Carmel.[42]

While the four had been placed on the respective Alignment and
Likud lists before the war (in other words, there was no connection
between their election and the fact that one – Sharon – emerged from the
Yom Kippur War a war hero, another – Yariv – had played an active role
in attaining the cease fire with the Egyptians, while the remaining two
were 'untainted' by the war, because they had not played an active role
in it), there is no doubt that in the political situation that emerged in the
aftermath of the war (especially negotiations involving the
relinquishment by Israel of territory), the views of the generals were
considered of vital importance. Within half a year one of the four –
Rabin – was to become Prime Minister.

Nevertheless, for the sake of historical accuracy one should point out
that the entry of the four into politics was much more a function of the
fact that a growing number of Israeli generals were reaching retirement
age and seeking an outlet for a second career, than an immediate
consequence of the Yom Kippur War itself. To a certain extent one
should also see their cooption into politics as part of a trend within the
parties to select more attractive 'electable' candidates for their lists – a
trend that in later years was to lead to the primaries system.[43]

THE CRYSTALLIZATION OF DIFFERENT APPROACHES TO THE
PROSPECTS OF PEACE

Introduction

The Yom Kippur War and its aftermath resulted in a sharpening of
diametrically opposed positions in Israel regarding the prospects for
peace and the price that Israel ought to be willing to pay for it. Also
before the Yom Kippur War there were those who believed that Israel
ought to be willing to return all the territories in return for peace with
its neighbours, and those who believed that Israel should not be willing
to give up a single inch of 'liberated' territory. However, in light of the
Arab policy, as it was formulated at the Khartoum Arab Summit
Conference of September 1967, which declared that there would be 'no
peace with Israel, no negotiations with it and no recognition of it', the
Israeli 'peaceniks' could do little more than dream of better days while
the 'Greater Israel' camp had little to worry about. The majority
appeared to agree with the approach of Moshe Dayan to the effect that
Israel should sit back and wait for a phone call from the Arabs.

The Yom Kippur War shook everyone out of complacency. The
peaceniks could now argue that the option of 'waiting for the Arabs to
call' had failed, and were also encouraged by the appearance of a more
pragmatic approach towards the peace-making process on the Arab side.
The 'Greater Israel' people could no longer take it for granted that no
Israeli Government in the foreseeable future would be willing to
consider handing territories captured in June 1967 back to Arab
sovereignty, while the majority could no longer just sit back and enjoy
the post-Six Day War economic prosperity.

Within this amorphous majority, some concluded from what had
happened in October 1973, that despite Israel's military victory, time
was not playing in Israel's favor, and that a psychological 'window of
opportunities' had been created, which enabled the first steps to be taken
in a slow and tortuous peace making process.[44] Others reached the
opposite conclusion: that the Yom Kippur War had proven that the Arabs
did not want peace, and that Israel should not only be much more alert
than before regarding its security, but should start acting more decisively
to prevent a wholesale return of territories.[45]

As we shall see later on, the more dramatic results of the war in this
respect were the emergence of Gush Emunim, which rejected any sort of
territorial concession, on the one hand, and a radical 'peace camp',
which spoke not only of the need for Israel to be prepared to give up the
territories it had occupied in 1967 in return for peace, but also of the
need for it to come to terms with the PLO, on the other. However, in
historic terms the more significant development was the beginning of an
extremely slow change in the approach of the ruling Labour Party – a
change without which the breakthrough on the Palestinian front 20 years
later would not have been possible.

The Labour Party

From its foundation in January 1968 and until October 1973, the Labour Party held numerous debates on the issue of a future peace settlement with the Arabs, but never reached any concrete conclusions – what Yossi Beilin, the initiator of the Oslo process on the Israeli side, termed 'the paralysis of the Israeli political initiative'.[46] The general assumption of the leadership following the Six Day War was that if Israel consolidated its control of the occupied territories and increased its military superiority over its neighbours, the Arabs would finally realize that they had no alternative but to recognize Israel and conclude peace with it.[47] The Yom Kippur War seemed to disprove this assumption, and while the Israeli Government continued in its policy of consolidating Israel's control of the occupied territories and increasing its military power, much more serious attention was now given to the need to also start taking steps in the direction of some sort of accommodation with the Arabs, on the basis of a step by step approach.

At a meeting of the Labour Party Central Committee on 5 December 1973, Prime Minister Meir demanded that the forum approve an 11-point peace plan towards the Geneva Conference, which was to open 16 days later. The plan included a call for the attainment of peace within secure boundaries on the basis of a territorial compromise and the preservation of the Jewish nature of the State of Israel, but rejected a return to the borders of 5 June 1967. While expressing support for interim agreements and territorial withdrawals by Israel, it stated that the Palestinian identity should be realized within the framework of a Jordanian-Palestinian state, living side by side with Israel.[48]

Under American pressure Golda Meir was then pushed into participating in the Geneva Conference, which convened on 21 December 1973, and agree to disengagement agreements with Egypt (16 January 1974) and Syria (31 May 1974),[49] attained through the good offices of US Secretary of State Henry Kissinger. The disengagement agreements were based on both the 'territories for peace' and the 'peace by stages' principles. This slow shift to a practical approach towards the peace-making process continued after Yitzhak Rabin became Prime Minister.

Soon after the Rabin Government was formed on 3 June 1974, a major policy debate on relations with Jordan and the Palestinian issue – the first of its kind – was held in the Government. Even though the resolution adopted by the Government at the end of the debate on 21 July 1974 did not include the 'Yariv–Shemtov formula', which had first been presented to the previous government by Minister of Transportation Aharon Yariv and Minister of Health Victor Shemtov,[50] it was innovative. The resolution, repeatedly quoted by Israeli government spokesmen in the next three years, stated:

> Israel will continue to strive for peace agreements with the Arab states about defensible borders, which will be attained in

negotiations without any preconditions. The Government will promote negotiations with Jordan. Peace will be based on the existence of two independent states only – Israel with its capital united Jerusalem, and an Arab Jordanian-Palestinian state east of Israel, within boundaries, which will be determined in negotiations between Israel and Jordan. In this state the self-identity of the Jordanians and Palestinians will manifest itself, within the framework of peace and good-neighbourliness with Israel.

The resolution ended by reiterating that the Government adopted the statement made by the Prime Minister in the Knesset when he presented his new government, to the effect that 'the Government of Israel will not hold negotiations with terrorist organizations whose declared goal is the destruction of the State of Israel'.[51] Though no progress was made at the time by the Rabin Government regarding an agreement with the Jordan and the Palestinians,[52] it did sign a second agreement with Egypt based on 'territories for peace' – the Interim Agreement of 4 September 1975.

The slow change in the official Israeli policy regarding the peace-making issue was not affected so much by changes in public opinion, as much as the latter was affected by changes in the policy, and one might observe a gradual, extremely slow but clear shift in public opinion: especially on the issue of 'territories for peace' and beliefs regarding the readiness of the Arabs to reach a peaceful solution of the Arab–Israeli conflict.[53]

The Land of Israel Movement and Gush Emunim

While the changes in the Government's peace-making policy, resulting from the Yom Kippur War, were hardly revolutionary, they did turn on a red light in right-wing circles in Israel. The territorial maximalists, headed by the Land of Israel Movement (LIM), emerged from the war strengthened in their belief that the post-Six Day War borders had saved the Jewish state from destruction, and were strengthened in their determination never to relinquish any land. Especially after the establishment of the Rabin Government, they became worried that under pressure from US Secretary of State Henry Kissinger, whom they regarded as a self-hating Jew and a very serious threat to the safety and integrity of the State of Israel, the new Government would continue making territorial concessions, such as those begun by the previous Government – concessions which the LIM magazine *Zot Ha'aretz* compared to those made by Chamberlain to Hitler in 1939 at Munich. What was needed, the LIM ideologues argued, was a massive settlement of Jews in the territories.[54]

However, the most significant development amongst the territorial maximalists in this period was the emergence of the religious Gush Emunim ('Block of the Faithful') in March 1974. The founders of Gush Emunim, all former students of the *Merkaz Harav* Yeshiva in Jerusalem, whose spiritual leader was Rabbi Zvi Yehuda Kook, were determined to oppose further territorial concessions and to bring about the application of Israeli sovereignty over the occupied territories. Even though the territorial issue had caused much concern to the graduates of *Merkaz Harav* in the years immediately after the Six Day War, they dared not go against the Government, which at the time enjoyed much prestige. It was the new situation created in the aftermath of the Yom Kippur War which brought about the change.[55]

Gush Emunim was not a spontaneous phenomenon, but rather a group with deep ideological roots, which made no efforts to compromise over its position in order to win over supporters.[56] At first, Gush Emunim was a faction within the NRP, which was a member of the coalition at the time. But the faction, which included MKs Zvulun Hammer and Yehuda Ben-Meir, soon gave up its party affiliation, in order to broaden its support base to non-religious circles, and started placing greater emphasis on settlement activities rather than politics. Very rapidly Gush Emunim turned into one of the most active and effective extra-parliamentary groups in Israel.[57] Though the movement tried to emphasize its strong attachment to secular Zionism, it was, from the very start, strongly rooted in religious dogma.

According to Ehud Sprinzak, the thinking of many of the original members of Gush Emunim was strongly influenced by an essay written in the immediate aftermath of the Yom Kippur War by Rabbi Yehuda Amital of the *Har-Etzion* Yeshiva, on the war's significance.[58] Rabbi Amital tried to explain, from a religious perspective, why the Yom Kippur War, with all the suffering that it brought, was necessary after the Six Day War, whose divine purpose had been the liberation of parts of the Land of Israel that had been under foreign occupation. His answer was that it could have but one meaning, which was to bring together, refine and purify the Jewish society – to shock it in order to bring the people together.[59]

According to Amital the Yom Kippur War had exposed a deep crisis in Herzlian (i.e. secular) Zionism, which sought to solve the problem of the continued existence of the Jewish people on the one hand, and the problem of antisemitism on the other. But neither problem was solved through the establishment of the State of Israel, and now was the chance for the other Zionism – the Zionism of redemption – to have its day. The goal of this Zionism was not the normalization of the people of Israel in order to become a nation like all the nations, but to help it revert to being a holy people, the people of God, whose centre is in Jerusalem with the Temple at its heart.[60]

The Peace Now Movement

It is a common mistake to assume that the Peace Now movement emerged at this time. Peace Now, founded in 1978, was the outgrowth of the apparent stalemate in the peace process following the visit of

Egyptian President Anwar Sadat to Jerusalem in November 1977, not an outgrowth of the Yom Kippur War. Nevertheless, the Yom Kippur War did bring about, even if indirectly, a certain shift and radicalization in what one may term the 'Israeli peace movement'.

In the case of those Israelis who had always believed that Israel must seek peace with its neighbours, on the basis of mutual concessions regarding maximalist national and territorial demands, the Yom Kippur War strengthened this belief. But the Yom Kippur War did something else. If after the Six Day War the Arab response was the 'three noes' resolution of the Khartoum Arab Summit Conference, after the Yom Kippur War the beginning of a shift in the previously rigid positions of certain Arab states, circles and individuals started to become discernible, both because the war was not perceived as having resulted in a total Arab defeat and because the perception of Israel's invincibility had been shattered.

The change which was most significant from the point of view of the Israeli 'peaceniks', however, was that which started to occur in the PLO, even though the Palestinian organization had not been directly involved in the War. Due to certain ideological and tactical developments in the PLO following the Yom Kippur War, which resulted from the PLO's desire to be a partner in the peace process which began in the Geneva Conference,[61] Israeli peaceniks started changing their attitude towards the PLO. If before the Yom Kippur War there wasn't a single Israeli peacenik who advocated talks with the PLO,[62] now there was a core group, which started advocating the importance of meeting with PLO representatives.

The first significant set of meetings of this nature took place in January 1975 between MK Uri Avnery and the PLO representative in London, Said Hammami.[63] A year later the Israeli Council for Israeli–Palestinian Peace was established by Avnery, Eliav, Matti Peled, Ya'acov Arnon, Me'ir Pa'il, Yossi Amitai, Amos Kenan and others, and continued the meetings with the PLO representative in Paris, Issam Sartawi.

ECONOMIC EFFECTS

The origins of economic effects of the Yom Kippur War were of two kinds. The first was related to the economic cost of the war, the second to an upgrading of the implementation of the Arab boycott against Israel. In the course of the Yom Kippur War, the US Administration airlifted to Israel enormous quantities of arms, ammunition and spare parts. This very generous assistance – in many respects a lifesaver for Israel – had to be paid for, and together with the further upgrading of the Middle East arms race, which followed the war,[64] imposed a very heavy burden on Israel's external debt, which in the years 1973–1984 increased from 30 to 40 per cent of GNP.[65] In addition to the external debt, a considerable internal debt was also accumulated, resulting in debt repayment and service reaching an unprecedented portion of the Israeli budget – a predicament which persists to the present day.

The Yom Kippur War, together with the oil crisis which accompanied it (though it was not caused by it) was a crossroads in the development of the Israeli economy, which, in addition to the increase in the internal and foreign debt, moved sharply from rapid growth to stalemate, with an upsurge of the rate of inflation[66] – problems that the Israeli economy is still contending with, 26 years after the war.

The upgrading of the Arab boycott had a different effect. The Arab boycott was first introduced by the Arab League in January 1946 – almost two and a half years before the establishment of the State of Israel.[67] However, the oil crisis, for which the outbreak of the Yom Kippur War served as a catalyst, greatly increased the economic power of the Arab oil producing states, which were now more willing than before to use this power to try to harm Israel. Israel's reaction was to establish new apparatuses in order to confront the problem, and to open a vigorous, worldwide anti-boycott campaign.[68] The difficulties which Israel came across in this campaign, even in the United States,[69] without doubt strengthened its 'the whole world is against us' complex.[70] While it is impossible to calculate the effect of the boycott on the Israeli economy,[71] there is no doubt that it had a major effect on its development in the 1970s, as it did before and after.

CONCLUSION

In the aftermath of the Yom Kippur War many changes took place within the Israeli society and economy, and in its political arena. However, except perhaps for the deep state of shock caused by the war and its immediate economic cost, all the other developments would most certainly have taken place sooner or later even if the war had not broken out. Thus, the war and its aftermath should be regarded more as a catalyst that speeded up the arrival of certain social and political changes in Israel than as their direct cause.

Even had the war been averted, or had the Israeli political and military leadership been better prepared for its outbreak, a changing of the guard would have taken place in the Labour Party, the hegemony of the labour movement in the Israeli political system would have come to an end (if for no other reason than the demographic make-up of the country no longer justified such a hegemony), and the Israeli public would have learnt to regard its leaders with greater criticism and scepticism, and less awe.

In addition, as the role of ideology weakened and Israel, as the rest of the western world, entered a period in which there seemed to be more questions than answers, a certain return to religion could be expected. The feminist movement would have reached Israeli shores, and women were bound to start calling the bluff of the myth regarding equality between the sexes in Israel. Also the Israeli Arabs, finally freed in 1966 from the Military Administration, would have started to demand equality, and a growing number of retired generals would have started entering Israeli politics. A peace movement would have emerged, and simultaneously the advocates of 'Greater Israel' would have become more radical.

In fact, a strong case might be made for the statement that it was the Six Day War which served as the mover of major changes in the Israeli reality and attitude, while the Yom Kippur War was its natural corollary – the accelerator of some of these changes and a brake on others. The Six Day War placed Israel in a certain optimistic day dream; the Yom Kippur War, though it might itself have been avoided, constituted an unavoidable awakening from this dream.

NOTES

1. Michel Granak, Eliezer Witztum, Amihai Levy and Moshe Kotler, '*Tguvot Hakrav Bemilhamot Yisrael, 1948-1973 – Helek V: Milhemet Yom Kippur, 1973*' [Combat reactions in the Israeli wars, 1948-1973 – part 5: the Yom Kippur War, 1973], *Sihot* 5/1 (Nov. 1990), pp.53–9; and I. Levav, H. Greefeld and E. Baruch, 'Psychiatric Combat Reactions during the Yom Kippur War', *American Journal of Psychiatry* 136/5, pp.637–41. Note should be taken, however, of a new study by the sociologist Edna Lomsky-Fedder, *Ke'ilu lo Hayta Milhama* [As if there had been no war], Jerusalem, Magnes Press, 1998, which found that on the whole the Yom Kippur War did not have a long term traumatic effect on those who fought in it. However, the study (Lomsky-Fedder's Ph.D. thesis) was based on 67 interviews only, primarily with middle class, secular Ashkenazi men born in 1952–54, in other words, those who during the Yom Kippur War were still in regular military service – not the reservists, who were not in uniform when the war broke out, did the brunt of the fighting and were much better able to grasp the enormity of the 'screw up'.
2. Michael I. Handel, 'Perception, Deception and Surprise: The Case of the Yom Kippur War', *Jerusalem Papers on Peace Problems*, No. 19, (Jerusalem: The Leonard Davis Institute for International Relations, 1976), p.40.
3. See Moshe Negbi, '*Ha'tsenzura Ha'atzmit shel Va'adat Ha'orchim*' [The self-censorship of the Editors' Committee], *Namer shel Niyar* [Paper tiger], Tel Aviv: Sifriyat Hapo'alim, 1985, in Binyamin Neuberger and Ilan Ben-Ami, eds, *Demokratia Ubitahon Beyisrael* [Democracy and security in Israel], Tel Aviv: The Open University, 1996, pp.477–8, and Ze'ev Schiff, '*Meida Bitzvat Habitahon*' [Information in the tongs of security] *Me'et Katavenu Hatzva'i* [By our military correspondent], Tel Aviv: The Journalists' Association, 1990, in Neuberger and Ben-Ami, *Demokratia Ubitahon Beyisrael*, p.489.
4. Granak *et al.*, '*Tguvot Hakrav Bemilhamot Yisrael, 1948-1973*', p.53. In Yeshayahu Ben-Porath, Yehonatan Geffen, Uri Dan, Eitan Haber, Hezi Carmel, Eli Landau and Eli Tavor, *Hamehdal* [The culpable blunder], Tel Aviv: Special Publication, 1974, the authors state: 'The soldiers on the front say: "the Egyptians have learnt from the IDF how to fight – the Israelis have learnt from the Egyptians how to lie".' p.269.
5. Anyone who reads the biography of David Ben-Gurion, Israel's first Prime Minister, cannot but be impressed that 'transparency' and truthful reporting were not exactly hallmarks of the culture of government in Israel in the heyday of this great Israeli leader.
6. Ze'ev Schiff, *Re'idat Adama Be'october – Milhemet Yom Hakippurim* [An earthquake in October – the Yom Kippur War], Tel Aviv: Zmora, Bitan, and Modan, 1974, pp.243, 253.
7. 'The Wars of the Generals' relate to mutual recriminations publicly exchanged, in the course of the Yom Kippur War and in its aftermath, amongst senior commanders in the IDF. The recriminations started with complaints that Major General Ariel Sharon was

disobeying orders. Sharon responded by accusing many of the other commanders of incompetence. Later the recriminations also dealt with certain military events, which took place on 8 October 1973, in one of the battles on the Egyptian front, in which the IDF lost close to 190 tanks.

8. All the information regarding the post-Yom Kippur War protest movements comes from Moshe Livne, '"Yisrael Shelanu" – Aliyata Veshki'ata shel Tnu'at Meha'a' ['Our Israel' – the rise and fall of a protest movement], MA thesis submitted to the Hebrew University of Jerusalem, June 1977. See p.15.

9. Ibid. pp.4, 28.

10. Ibid., p.11.

11. Ibid., p.15.

12. Ehud Sprinzak, *'Politika Hutz Parlamentarit Beyisrael'* [Extra-parliamentary politics in Israel], in Shmuel Stempler, ed., *Anashim Umdina – Hahevra Hayisraelit* [People and state – the Israeli society], Tel Aviv, Ministry of Defense Publishers, 1989, p.228.

13. Livne, *'Yisreal Shelanu'*, pp.44–5.

14. Dvora Bernstein and Yohanan Peres, *'Mehavurat Rehov Litnu'a Hevratit – Hapantherim Hash'horim'* [from street gang to social movement – the Black Panthers], in Yohanan Peres, ed., *Yahasei 'Edot Beyisra'el* [relations between ethnic groups in Israel], Tel Aviv, Sifriat Po'alim and Tel Aviv University, 1977, p.161.

15. Asher Arian, *The Elections in Israel – 1973*, Jerusalem: Jerusalem Academic Press, 1975, p.10.

16. Ibid. pp.168, 174–5, Dvora Bernstein, *'Hapantherim Hashhorim: Conflict Umeha'ah Bahevra Hayisra'elit'* [The Black Panthers: conflict and protest in the Israeli society], in Moshe Lissak (compiler), *Edah, Le'om Uma'amad Bahevra Hayisra'elit* [Ethnic group, nationality and status in the Israeli society], a reader, Vol. II, Tel Aviv: The Open University, 1989, p.77 and Sammy Smooha, *Israel – Pluralism and Conflict*, London: Routledge & Kegan Paul, 1978, p.166.

17. Dan Horowitz and Moshe Lissak, *Metzukot Be'utopia* [Unrest in utopia], Tel Aviv: Am Oved, 1990, p.119. In the elections to the 10th Knesset in 1981 many of the ethnic protest votes went to Aharon Abuhatzeira's predominantly Moroccan party Tami, and since the elections to the 11th Knesset in 1984 it has been the ultra-religious Sephardi party Shas, which most benefited from the continued feelings of discrimination and dissatisfaction within the population of Muslim country origin.

18. Meron Medzini, *Hayehudiya Hage'a – Golda Me'ir Vehazon Yisrael* [The proud Jewess – Golda Meir and the vision of Israel], Tel Aviv, Edanim, 1990, pp.461–2.

19. See, for example, Na'omi Kies, *'Hashpa'at Mediniyut Tziburit 'al Da'at Ha'kahal: Yisrael 1967–1974'* [The influence of public policy on public opinion: Israel 1967–1974], *Medina, Mimshal Veyahassim Beinleumiyim* [State, Government and International Relations], No.8, 1975, in Neuberger and Ben-Ami, *Demokratia Ubitahon Beyisrael*, p.579.

20. Yitzhak Rabin, *The Rabin Memoirs*, Boston: Little, Brown, 1979, p.236.

21. In the 1969 elections the Alignment received 46.2 per cent of the vote. Opinion polls for April 1973 showed it receiving 43.0 per cent, for August 1973 – 40.4 per cent and it actually received 39.8 per cent. See Yochanan Peres, Efraim Yuchtmann-Yaar and Rivka Shafat, in Arian, *The Elections in Israel – 1973*, p.195.

22. Medzini, *Hayehudiya Hage'a*, pp.462–3, 465.

23. Abraham Diskin, *Elections and Voters in Israel*, New York: Praeger, 1991, p.27.

24. The 31 were made up of 26 for Gahal, 3 for the State List and 2 for the Free Center, all of which joined the Likud.

25. In the 1973 election Sharon still enjoyed greater popularity in the public than Likud leader Menahem Begin (see Rachel Tokatli, 'Image Modification and Voters Behavior', in Arian, *The Elections in Israel – 1973*, p.182).

26. Ibid., p.181.

27. Of the four Dayan was the only one who later made a comeback, as Minister for Foreign Affairs in the Begin Government in 1977, and regained some of his prestige as one of the participants in the making of peace with Egypt.

28. Rabin, *The Rabin Memoirs*, p.242.

29. Amongst these scandals was the Asher Yadlin Affair (which ended with Yadlin's conviction and imprisonment), the Avraham Ofer affair (which ended with Ofer's suicide), and the Rabin US bank account affair (which ended with Yitzhak Rabin's resignation from the premiership).

30. See, for example, Shevah Weiss, *Hamahapach* [The upheaval], Tel Aviv: Sifriyat min Hamoked, Am Oved, Tarbut Vehinuch, 1979. In his book, Weiss, who is both a Knesset member and a Professor of Political Science, presents the views of numerous observers regarding the reasons for Labour's fall. The Yom Kippur War is mentioned only once, in connection with the results of the 1973 elections.

31. Shaul Mayzlish, *Hazara Bitshuva* [Penitence], Tel Aviv, Masada, 1984, p.73.

32. Horowitz and Lissak, *Metzukot Be'utopia*, p.98.

33. Ibid., p.290.

34. See Dafna Sherfman, *Nashim Upolitika* [*Women and Politics*], Haifa, 'Tamar' Publishers, 1988, pp.83–6.

35. Ibid., pp.87–8.

36. Ibid., p.90.

37. Sammy Smooha, *The Orientation and Politicization of the Arab Minority in Israel*, monograph series on the Middle East No. 2, University of Haifa, The Jewish-Arab Center, Institute of Middle Eastern Studies, second edition, 1983, p.160.

38. Ibid., p.159.

39. Experts in Israel differ in the importance they attribute to the Yom Kippur War as a catalyst in this respect, but they all agree that in the aftermath of the war the attitude of the PLO towards the Israeli Arabs changed. See Ori Stendel, *Arviyei Yisrael – Bein Patish Lesadan* [The Arabs of Israel – between Hammer and Anvil], Jerusalem: Academon, 1992, p.304. Stendel argues with Dr. Asher Susser of the Dayan Center at Tel Aviv University, about whether the Yom Kippur War was or was not a turning point.

40. Guy Bechor, *Lexicon Ashaf* [PLO dictionary], Tel Aviv: Ministry of Defense Publishing House, 2nd edition, 1995, p.172.

41. Amos Perlmutter, *Israel: the Partitioned State*, New York: Charles Scribner's Sons, 1985, p.233.

42. Gabriel Ben-Dor, 'Politics and the Military in Israel: the 1973 Election Campaign and its Aftermath', in Arian, *The Elections in Israel – 1973*, p.131.

43. See, for example, Gad Ya'acobi, *The Government of Israel*, New York: Praeger, 1982, p.36.

44. Schiff, *Re'idat Adama Be'october*, p.258.

45. See Horowitz and Lissak, *Metzukot Be'utopia*, p.153. In a debate held in the Knesset on 4 January 1995, on motions for the agenda presented by eight different Members of Knesset, on the occasion of the publication of most of the secret section of the Agranat Commission Report of 1974, it became apparent that all these various conclusions regarding the implications of the Yom Kippur War were still prevalent (unedited Knesset minutes).

46. Yossi Beilin, *Mehiro shel Ihud – Mifleget Ha'avoda 'ad Milhemet Yom Hakippurim* [The price of unity – the Labor Party until the Yom Kippur War], Tel Aviv: Revivim Publishing House, 1985, p.14.

47. Ya'acov Bar-Siman-Tov, *Israel and the Peace Process – 1977-1982*, New York: State University of New York Press, 1994, p.50.

48. Medzini, *Hayehudiya Hage'a*, p.466.

49. Yitzhak Rabin and Shimon Peres took part in the negotiations with Syria; Rabin, p.240.

50. The Yariv–Shemtov formula stated that 'Israel will carry out negotiations for peace with Jordan and with any Palestinian factor which will be willing to make peace with it and will not engage in terrorism'.

51. Statement by Minister for Foreign Affairs Yigal Allon, *Divrei Haknesset*, Vol. 71, 23 July 1974, p.2389.

52. Minister for Foreign Affairs, Yigal Allon, tried to initiate a 'disengagement agreement' with Jordan (better known as 'The Jericho Plan'), based on the 'territories for peace' principle, but following the Rabat Arab Summit Conference of October 1974, the idea fell (See Susan Hattis Rolef, 'Jericho Excavations', *Jerusalem Post Magazine*, 24 February 1984, and Sheila Hattis Rolef, *'Tohnit Yeriho – Hagirsa shel Yigal Allon'* [The Jericho Plan – Yigal Allon's version], *Davar*, 30 August 1994).

53. See e.g. Na'omi Kies, pp.576–82.

54. Ehud Sprinzak, *The Ascendance of Israel's Radical Right*, New York: Oxford University Press, 1991, pp.64–5.

55. Sprinzak, *'Politika Hutz Parlamentarit Beyisrael'*, p.230.

56. Ibid., p.229.

57. Sprinzak *The Ascendance of Israel's Radical Right*, pp.65–6, and Myron J. Aronoff,

'The Institutionalization and Cooptation of a Charismatic, Messianic, Religious-Political Revitalization Movement', in David Newman, ed., *The Impact of Gush Emunim – Politics and Settlement in the West Bank*, London: Croom Helm, 1985, p.49.

58. Sprinzak, *The Ascendance of Israel's Radical Right*, p.116.

59. Rabbi Yehuda Amital, *Hama'alot Mim'amakim* [The Emergence from Depths], Jerusalem: Agudat Yeshivat Har-Etzion, 1986, p.28.

60. Ibid. pp.41–3. It is interesting to note that in the 1988 elections, this very same Rabbi Yehuda Amital ran at the head of a moderate religious party by the name of Meimad, which was willing to accept a territorial compromise in return for peace. Meimad failed to pass the qualifying threshold. Amital joined the Government which Shimon Peres formed in November 1995 – after the assassination of Yitzhak Rabin – as Minister without portfolio.

61. See, for example, Aryeh Y. Yodfat and Yuval Arnon-Ohanna, *PLO – Strategy and Tactics*, London: Croom Helm, 1981, pp.48–67 and Guy Bechor, *Lexicon Ashaf*, p.170.

62. For example, as late as May 1974 Major General (Res.) Mattityahu (Matti) Peled, one of the first Jewish Israelis to start meeting with PLO representatives in 1975, still objected to talks with the PLO, arguing that the PLO did not represent the Palestinian population in the territories, and that Israel should let this population elect its true leadership, with which Israel should hold negotiations within the framework of peace talks; Matti Peled, *'Mi Meyatzeg et HaPalestin'im?'* [Who Represents the Palestinians?], *Ma'ariv*, 24 May 1974.

63. Uri Avnery, *My Friend, the Enemy*, London: Zed Books, 1986, pp.40–1.

64. In the period 1969–1981 Israel's defence expenditure reached an average of over 25 per cent of GNP, reaching around 30 per cent in the aftermath of the Yom Kippur War. In comparison, the average rate for all the western countries except the United States was below 5 per cent, and below 10 per cent for the United States. See Eitan Berglas, 'Defense and the Economy', in Yoram Ben-Porath, ed., *The Israeli Economy – Maturing through Crises*, Cambridge, MA: Harvard University Press, 1986, p.173.

65. See Nissan Liviatan and Sylvia Peterman, 'Accelerating Inflation and Balance of Payments Crises 1973–1984', in Ben-Porath, *The Israeli Economy*, p.323.

66. See Yossef Yuran, *'Dynamica shel Anti-Tzmiha – Hameshek Hayisra'eli Le'ahar Mashber Haneft Umilhemet Yom Hakippurim'* [The dynamics of anti-growth – the Israeli economy after the oil crisis and the Yom Kippur War], in Shmuel Stempler, ed., *Anashim Umdina*, p.348.

67. See for example, Gil Feiler, *From Boycott to Economic Cooperation: The Political Economy of the Arab Boycott of Israel*, London: Frank Cass, 1998, Chapter 2, 'The History of the Arab Boycott and its Administration'.

68. Susan Hattis Rolef, *Israel's Anti-Boycott Policy*, Policy Studies No. 28, Jerusalem, the Leonard Davis Institute for International Relation at the Hebrew University of Jerusalem, 1989, pp.33–45.

69. Feiler, Chapter 7, 'The Policy of the United States'.

70. This complex was also strengthened by the refusal of most of the west European states to let the US use their territory in the course of the arms airlift in the Yom Kippur War, and later by the growing understanding in the world for the demands of the PLO and the automatic anti-Israel majority in the UN, which made the passage of the 'Zionism equals Racism' resolution (Resolution 3379) by the General Assembly in November 1975 possible.

71. Feiler, *From Boycott to Economic Cooperation*, Chapter 11, 'The Boycott's Effectiveness and Cost'.

Perception, Image Formation and Coping in the Pre-Crisis Stage of the Yom Kippur War

GABRIELLA HEICHAL

Perception will be defined in this work as the discerning of detail, relating to political, military or other intentions of the rival. Perception does not include interpretation of a certain fact but only the knowledge about its existence. The act of perception is dependent on values, anticipation and drives, experiences and cultural and operational environment in which the actor is immersed.[1] As will be discussed perception is dependent on intentions and the literature explains these intentions as created by the rival states. This is a direct derivation of the treatment of the state as a unified actor. The diagram does not specify whose intentions are or are not perceived. This is intentional. As decision-makers may have distinct perceptions, image's relativity should be taken as given.

A democratic pluralistic state is liable to have an elite of decision-makers whose values, anticipation and drives are different. This may be the case in an authoritarian regime too, though the divisions of opinions may be latent. A variety of values may influence individual decision-makers in a routine situation. The cultural and operational environments are liable to influence interpretations. As perception is automatic it is the image of the political rival or ally which largely enables the formulation and implementation of foreign policy. The importance attached to a fact so that it registers as an item of knowledge determines whether the information will be assimilated by the decision-maker or disregarded.

In contrast to perception, the image includes an interpretation of the facts as viewed by the perceiver. The interpretation of a fact is dependent on the same variables which initiated the occurrence of the perception process, while a clear desire of the perceiver is to create harmony between incoming information and that which he already knew. Hence

Gabriella Heichal is Research Fellow at the Harry S. Truman Research Institute, The Hebrew University of Jerusalem.

image formation is an important stage in which the reliability of the understanding or distortion of a fact is decided.[2]

THREAT PERCEPTION

The time that elapses between the time a threat has been issued and the time the threat has been perceived is of critical importance to the effective management of a crisis. There are no rules as to the length of this time span, which differs from personality to personality. A threat perception is dependent on both objective and subjective factors. The objective factors include the amount of noise in the system.[3] 'Signals' and 'noise' are differentiated only by hindsight and by the verification of their correctness and falsity. The quantity of deception present during a crisis may influence the image of threat provided that one assumes that the higher the acceptance of a norm of truthfulness in that system, the higher will the threat perception be.

On the other hand, subjective factors include the belief system, cognitive ability, flexibility and the decision-maker's world view, which includes his appreciation of the relative capabilities of his rival. The world view is composed of cultural values, which are a part of the belief system. The cognitive ability and flexibility of thought influence the world view. Thus they play a major role in the interpretation of the decision-maker of the international environment. For example, for a decision-maker belonging to a culture which glorifies war, threat will have a different meaning than for a pacifist. Frequently, decision-makers fail to recognize the build-up of a crisis in time.[4] This may have dire repercussions, as it shortens the time span available for them to search for alternatives and for the making of decisions, once they recognize it. This phenomenon is especially prevalent if false alarms occurred frequently enough to reduce the credibility of the early warning system, as happened prior to the Yom Kippur War.[5]

The possibilities that are theoretically open to a decision-maker concerning threats are accurate and timely perception, late perception, coping, coping avoidance and misperception. The cases potentially involving the most hazardous situations for the state are coping avoidance and misperception. To cope with something means according to the Webster dictionary to 'strive to contend [with] successfully or on equal terms' and thus, coping activity means that a person deals with a challenge successfully.

According to Irving Janis and Leon Mann, coping behaviour 'results in thorough information search, unbiased assimilation of new information, and other characteristics of high quality decision-making'.[6] When routine decisions are undertaken coping behaviour is expected to take place, as no stress is involved. On the other hand, there is a possibility that instead of coping behaviour, coping avoidance will take place during crisis.

COPING AVOIDANCE

Coping avoidance will be defined here as the tendency to avoid the making of a decision and this usually involves the need to approach a negative goal.[7] As the perception of a threat is more often than not a negative occurrence, there is little wonder that coping avoidance is liable to occur. Consequently, one of the tendencies of the relevant decision-maker will be to retract or withdraw from making a decision. If the other alternative offered is equally appalling, the vacillation will be characteristically to a pattern labelled avoidance-avoidance conflict.[8]

Janis and Mann specify four psychological conditions, which constitute this pattern. They are:

- Awareness of a threat of serious losses from failing to take preventive action.
- Awareness of a threat of serious losses from changing to any of the available alternative courses of action.
- Lack of hope of finding a solution that will keep the risks at a tolerable level.
- Lack of deadline pressures for announcing a definite decision to which the decision-maker will be committed.[9]

The first two conditions demonstrate that coping avoidance occurs only when there is no other worthwhile alternative to be approached. This is emphasized by the third condition, which involves difficulties for empirical research, as it is doubtful whether it may be proven. Regarding the fourth condition, though deadline pressures aggravate the need to reach a decision, this may be disregarded by way of transferring the responsibility or by the hope that the difficulty will be solved without the need to reach a decision, that is, hope that the forecast is incorrect.[10]

If the alternatives are equally appalling vacillation among them will be a characteristic of a pattern called avoidance-avoidance. One famous example given by Lazarus is of the donkey, hesitating between two piles of hay and starving to death of hunger.[11] Such a situation may evolve, if the alternatives are (a) the loss of resources in a major conflict, or (b) the loss of immense amount of public support at home.[12] One of the alternatives is to search for new information, or in a worse case, distort incoming information.[13] Another way to deal with the situation is to decentralize authority, by finding someone else to take the decision, and the possible blame afterwards. The third option is to dismiss the danger imminent in the situation. While the first two alternatives may cost time, which is usual in crisis situations, the third is even more dangerous, as it offers a fertile ground for the construction of misperception.

Perception is treated here as a variable dependent on capabilities and intentions. The image is formed on the basis of the existing perceptions and their interpretations, and coping, dependent on both, is a means to formulate rules of behaviour. Some of the known decision-makers in history were coping avoiders.[14] Does coping avoidance apply to the Yom Kippur war?

MISPERCEPTION AS A WAY TO COPE WITH THREATS

Interpretation of facts previously known creates images and these, in turn, trigger the response pattern open to the decision-maker. Hence the way a fact is presented and the contextual background of its becoming a part of the knowledge of the actor becomes important.[15] The usual process of information assimilation is by adjusting it to pre-existing beliefs and images. Thus, incongruent information may be distorted or regarded as unimportant; these are defence mechanisms used for the sake of possible dissonance reduction.[16]

Jervis discussed the unfortunate consequences of misconceptions, which evolved due to pre-existing belief systems:

> If the decision-maker thinks an event yields self-evident and unambiguous inferences when in fact these inferences are drawn on pre-existing views and he will grow too confident of his views and will prematurely exclude alternatives because he will conclude that the event provides independent support for his beliefs. People frequently fail to realize that evidence that is consistent with their hypothesis may also be consistent with other views.[17]

One addition must be made: the fault is not always, and not exclusively, that of the decision-maker. Distortion of information may occur at an earlier stage, that is, before it reaches the decision-maker, by the collector or disseminator of the information. It seems that the conclusion to be drawn from a concept of relativity applied to the analysis unto this point is that rational decision-making does not necessarily have to be based on a zero-sum game. The more actors involved, the higher the possibility that different decision-makers will decide according to a different price rationale and it will become complicated to distil the 'correct' answer needed for the particular solution.

Can a misperception change, and be corrected to become an accurate perception? The impediments to such a process are many, especially when time during a crisis is short.[18] A correction may occur if somehow the actor is convinced that he used an inappropriate concept and another one has to be used for the sake of a better definition of the situation. Another possibility is the understanding that the motives of other actors were different from those previously assumed. This is dependent on the receipt of additional, new information, which for certain reasons cannot be ignored or distorted. The most difficult situation arises when an actor lacks the concepts needed for understanding a given situation.

Hypothesis No 1:

The intent and the threat are perceived by the receiver according to his understanding of the rationality of the initiator.

A foreign policy system includes a large number of components, which may be classified as inputs and outputs. The source of the inputs evolves in the operational environment and is transferred through communication channels, trickling into the psychological environment.[19] The operational environment forms the background for decision-making in foreign policy and it may be divided into two main components: an external environment which includes constraints, conditions and relationships operating outside the borders of the state involved and occur at three levels: systemic, sub-systemic and bi-lateral. On the other hand the internal environment includes the political structure, military and economic capability, competing elites, interest groups and public opinion.[20] The output of these variables in the psychological environment is evident in the decisions undertaken which provide feedback to the operational environment.

Events in foreign policy can be perceived as triggered by decisions of decision-makers, self-perceived as acting in a rational way.[21] The anticipation of possible moves by different actors is a requisite to decision-making in international relations. As the presumption that decision-makers act rationally exists there is no need to clarify the concept.

What is a rational way of action? The literature on rational action is adequate for such an analysis. The most common definition equates rational action with efficiency, that is, maximizing profits and minimizing losses.[22] Still, there is a difference between rationality and efficiency as sometimes it may be rational not to maximize profits, for example, for the sake of enlarging consensus, or avoiding risks. Hence, another definition for rationality is needed. A definition used in economic analyses of rationality is maximizing profits while minimizing risks.[23]

The advantage of this definition, which will be used here, is that it implicitly includes the supposition that the need to optimize is not a *sine qua non* of the definition, as an optimal decision may involve high risks. This is important as it partly bridges the gap between objective and actual rationality. According to Herbert Simon, objective rationality cannot be achieved.

- Rationality requires a complete knowledge and anticipation of the consequences that will follow on each choice. In fact, knowledge of consequences is always fragmentary.
- Since the consequences lie in the future, imagination must supply the lack of experienced feeling in attaching value to them. But values can only be imperfectly anticipated.

- Rationality requires a choice among the possible alternative behaviours. In actual behaviour, only very few of all these possible alternatives ever come to mind.[24]

If the condition of optimality is relaxed, the third condition of objective rationality no longer holds, and hence the gap between actual and objective rationality is smaller.

A maximization of profits involves a ranking of preferences, objectives or goals. Still, the possibility exists that a foreign policy action is undertaken for the sake of achieving simultaneously a number of goals, all of which have different rankings of preference.[25] In such a case the prioritizing of the goals to be pursued will be helpful in determining which action has to be undertaken for the sake of deciding the way rational policy is to be formulated. The assumption that foreign policy is rational corresponds to the criteria delineated in the definition. The decision about efficient foreign policy includes the ranking of goals and ordering of preferences, including considerations about the probabilities of the rival's response.[26] On the other hand, a particular activity must not necessarily be rational, as it may be an action, which was decided upon by lack of information, compromise or satisfying. The term satisfying was first used by Simon, who remarks it was revived from a Scottish word.[27] The meaning of the term is that 'instead of requiring that the pay off be maximized, we require only that the payoff exceed some given amount'.[28] In other words, satisfying means adjustment to the level of aspiration.[29]

Satisfying has far-reaching consequences for understanding of rational decision-making; the trade-offs and aspirations of different decision-makers may differ. If the requirement is only 'that payoff exceeds some given amount' a different ordering of preferences, or in other words a different readiness to pay a certain price may cause different decision-makers in the same situation to arrive at different rational decisions. This may be due to a different estimate of the payoff or to a different level of aspiration. The problem is compounded in foreign policy as the 'rational' decision is based on an estimate of the response of other actors, which may have different belief systems and different values to guide them while making their decisions. A decision-maker has to decide according to the options as he understands them, and these options include an estimate of the actor with whom he deals.'[30] This estimate can be done only according to values of which he is cognizant. If the leader opposing him has other values upon which he is not knowledgeable he has no possibility of making a rational decision.[31]

Thus the assumption that foreign policy is rational is a necessary but not a sufficient condition. 'Irrational foreign policy may even be chosen as a method, when a leader decides to act as a crazy state or by brinkmanship.'[32] This is the case in which the decision-maker decided that the expected inutility is higher than the price of the risks he takes.[33]

Another case in which foreign policy may seem irrational to an observer occurs when the goal has priority, which evolves from the beliefs, or core values of the decision-maker. In such a case it is possible that the estimate of the risk is distorted, due to the influence of such values on the decision-maker's decision.

Theoretical models of pure economics assume that the needed information is given. In contrast to economy, belief systems and core values, which mould the actions of leaders, have to be taken into account in international relations. Hence a complex set of possibilities, including actions and reactions of possible rivals and allies, has to be anticipated as information can never be complete. The leader has to rank the probabilities according to his definition of the situation, and to the level of his knowledge about other actors. A further complexity arises when the foreign policy to be formulated deals with different cultures. The values of western civilization differ from those of Islamic or Chinese civilizations. Therefore, a high likelihood exists that rankings of preferences as to the means to be used and goals to be achieved will differ.[34]

When such differences exist, the decision-maker needs to be informed about them; otherwise he will not be able to anticipate the steps taken by his adversary.[35] This information may influence his perception of options open to him. The better the knowledge the decision-maker has of the differences, the higher the likelihood that his decision will maximize profits and minimize risks. To summarize, rational decision-making in this study is defined as maximizing profits while avoiding risks. This is not identical with optimization, but it is incongruent with satisfying because sometimes optimization can be reached only at the cost of taking risks. As people differ, depending upon their level of aspiration, their belief systems and the trade-offs they are ready to make, rational decisions may differ for dissimilar actors or for the same actors in different situations.

To create a correct order of preferences,[36] the decision-maker has to be knowledgeable and cognizant about the values of other actors. This knowledge may influence his perceptions and anticipation of the intentions and threats of his rivals and hence his calculation of likely outcomes.

THE YOM KIPPUR WAR

These points will be examined through hypotheses formulated as their derivatives, with the Yom Kippur War as the case study. The case study will focus on some of the concepts discussed unto this point. These are:

- Different rationalities and their influence on the formulation of foreign policy.
- Is there a connection between misperception and coping avoidance?
- How does the lack of information influence the decision-maker?

What are the impediments involved and how does the lack of feedback influence the decision-makers concerning follow up decisions?

- How is a 'deviant' person treated by the group of decision-makers?

Every one of these points was analyzed both theoretically and empirically by the comparative case study method.

On 6 October 1973 a combined attack of Egypt and Syria against Israel took place. Prior warnings about the possibility of an impending attack were discredited. Though the Israel Defence Forces (IDF) expected a Syrian reprisal to an earlier Syrian–Israeli air combat, misperceptions regarding Egypt's motives existed unto the very start of the hostilities. There was a consensus that an Arab attack would be irrational. The political rationality of a limited war, according to the Soviet war doctrine, was overlooked by Israeli decision-makers and the rationale leading the Arab leaders to attack was not grasped by the Israelis.

The different hierarchies involved in the decision-making process were the intelligence, the Chief of Staff, the Defence Minister and the Prime Minister. As in every democratic country, the military is under civilian control. In Israel this means that the Defence Minister had a broad area of authority, which might be enlarged or shrunk, depending upon the power relationships between the Prime Minister, the Minister of Defence and the Chief of Staff. As warning of an impending attack spread, an unusual decision was made in a partial cabinet meeting on 5 October according to which Prime Minister Golda Meir, Defence Minister Moshe Dayan and Chief of Staff David Elazar, would have the authority to mobilize the reserves, even without a prior cabinet decision.[37] A decision to mobilize the reserves was made only four hours prior to the attack. The information dissemination processes, the bureaucratic processes involved and the contribution of personality characteristics due to coping processes of the leaders involved will be analyzed, to verify if some general conclusions may be arrived at.[38]

BASIC POSTULATES OF THE ISRAELI SECURITY DOCTRINE AS OF OCTOBER 1973

One of the gravest mistakes of strategic planners was that they had basic postulates that were not reviewed critically time and again. One of the reasons for the evolving misperceptions and conceptions is that they were not questioned often enough by the top decision-makers.

Not all the postulates regarding Israeli security doctrine which were held are relevant to this research. Thus, only six of them will be recounted here.

1. A situation of status quo is better than a dynamic change, which may have implications for the interrelationships of Middle Eastern states.

This postulate needs to be qualified. First, the usual image held by top military leaders is that in case an armed conflict is approaching it is worthwhile to pre-empt before the opponent is ready.[39] On the other hand, during 1967–1973 it was believed that the world would get used to Israel's presence in the Sinai desert, which was never before a part of Egypt. Hence in this case and for this politico-military reason a situation of *status quo* was deemed to be favourable to Israel.[40]

2. The Israeli military power is superior to that of the Arab forces[41] and any Soviet interference will be balanced by the US. Dayan's preoccupation with the damage the Soviet Union could inflict on Israel was well known.[42] The premise that the US would interfere was a derivative of the belief that Israel had been a solid and reliable ally of the US in the Middle East.

3. In any case of a confrontation between Israel and the Arab states, an immediate confrontation was preferable to a delayed one,[43] especially if new types of weaponry had been acquired by the Arab states.

4. The regular army would suffice until the reserve forces got involved in the battle.[44] Manpower in Israel is limited, thus the regular army has the duty to take care of prevailing security needs during routine situations. This postulate was based on necessity and not on an ideal-type arrangement.

5. The Israeli intelligence organization would have timely knowledge, and everybody concerned would be warned in time.[45]

6. There existed a definite need for air superiority for the purpose of launching a war.[46]

These assumptions are true for small states, but as everyone who has dealt with second strike capability knows, they are not a *sine qua non* for the huge area included under the label 'the Arab states'. Decision-makers in Israel based this assumption on the 1956 and 1967 wars, and tended to forget earlier lessons such as Pearl Harbour or even the Israeli War of Independence. In short the problem may be explained in terms of the relations between a small state, many rivals and a superpower. Both in 1956 and 1967 Israel was forced to use a pre-emptive strike. In 1956 the need arose as a measure of self defence against the entry of the USSR to the area as an active actor. In this regard the 1956 war failed, especially as Bulganin's threats combined with Eisenhower's fury compelled Ben-Gurion to retreat quickly. The 1967 war was different. The whole world knew Nasser's threats and much public and international support was voiced. Efforts to reopen the Tiran straits were fruitless. Long mobilization periods would have ruined the economic structure of Israel.[47] Hence the IDF had to use its first-strike capability.[48]

The case was somewhat different in 1973 as the top decision-makers believed the Sinai area provided enough strategic depth and the state would gain more support from the US if no pre-emptive strikes were undertaken.[49] To these basic postulates, which might be termed misconceptions, because the situation is never one of status quo in the Middle East, the notion that Israeli and Arab forces would be automatically balanced by the superpowers was no more than wishful thinking. The escalation in new types of weaponry has turned the Middle East into a weapon laboratory of the kind Spain was on the eve of the World War II, and the quality of the regular forces might not suffice one day, especially as sophisticated 'smart' weaponry can compensate for a certain amount of lack of quality. As to the timely knowledge of Israeli intelligence, it included a fail-safe presumption that was incorrect, for by definition any human being is liable to mistakes and distortion. To all these one has to add the latent assumption which is a common denominator to the first five: the value of lives of Israeli soldiers, as common in western civilization as opposed to the value of human life in the Muslim culture. According to the Arab world-view, life is only a means to an end,[50] while according to the perception of a state where many of the decision-makers were holocaust survivors, life is a sacred gift, not to be taken according to the bible in certain cases even in a defensive war.[51]

Though one may argue that this treatment of the value of life differs for different Arab states, for example according to the amount of religiosity involved, the writer is not aware of a study on the subject and will not conduct a detailed analysis of it here.[52] The component, however, has to be considered when calculating the likelihood of a rational decision. The cultural value of religion, used by politicians should be treated as an ideology.

BACKGROUND: 1972 – A YEAR OF COMPROMISE OR THE DECISIVE WAR?

On 13 January 1973, Egyptian President Anwar Sadat declared, on the eve of his meeting with Yugoslav President Tito, that 'Egypt has decided to wage against Israel the fiercest battle in history. Even the bombs on North Vietnam would pale compared to that battle.'[53] Sadat clearly had some definite plan in mind already and according to various Egyptian generals the decision to launch the war against Israel was made in November 1972. The situation in the Middle East should have been understood as complicated and open to changes. Were Sadat's threats empty? From his point of view the stalemate in the Middle East was unbearable.[54] What price could be rational for him for the sake of creating change? Did the different value attached to human life apply in Sadat's considerations? What was the influence of the religious duty involved in the Muslim concept of a holy war or *jihad*?[55]

Is it possible to weigh the influence of this factor? However, the rationale for the behaviour of Sadat was very simple: survival is achieved by struggle. Whoever fails has no right to continue to exist. This is shown in Sadat's autobiography, when he describes a conversation he had with Nasser. Having been told that Amer took his life because of the Israeli victory in 1967, he (Sadat) replied that Amer was right doing so.[56] Thus, Sadat seems to belong to the approach-approach type of coping, that is, to the achievers, and certainly had a motive to change Egypt's position in the world. Bernard Reich summed up Sadat's way of behaviour very succinctly: Sadat's policy had a multitude of purposes combined with a minimalist air of achievement in the military issue area.[57] This motive is evidenced by the change of the content and quality of the relationships he had with the Soviet Union, while simultaneously threatening Israel that if the status quo was maintained concerning the Egyptian territories occupied by Israel, a war would break out.

Israel's overt reaction was to raise the alert of the army. This was not the first time Israel raised its level of alert, and not the last one in 1972–73. The reason for this, and for the 'cry wolf syndrome' is explained by Mohammed Heikal: 'For six years these (Egyptian and Syrian) armies had to live with the shame of defeat. They had trained as few armies had trained before ... now they had a chance to prove not just their courage but their skill and it was a chance which each officer and man seized almost with rapture.'[58]

Israel's rational behaviour was very different from the one employed by Sadat. As Golda Meir recounts, Sadat tried to convey to her that he wanted to hold negotiations with Israel. This message involved a visit by Golda Meir to Romania in 1972.[59] As to the rationality of Israeli behaviour, every effort to achieve peace was considered valuable, provided certain existential preconditions were fulfilled. These preconditions included, for example, changes to be inserted in the Palestinian Charter. This was to play a role in September 1973, when Israel was led to believe that the Arab states wanted some kind of talks, which was to be disproved, again, at the beginning of October.[60]

If this was the political elite frame of reference, the situation looked different for the decision-makers in the Israeli army. The Israeli army mobilizes its forces on certain dates that are liable to be dangerous, given the PLO's wish to exploit certain 'anniversary' dates for propaganda. In addition, warnings started to accumulate that something was stirring on the rival's side and thus in May, information arrived concerning the build-up of forces at the borders of Syria and Egypt. The army mobilized its forces, though the intelligence estimated that the likelihood for war was low.[61] Mohamad El Gamasi made an interesting observation: 'On the strategic, operational and tactical levels, surprise was accomplished by deceiving the most up to date enemy intelligence systems'.[62]

The long range planning department of the IDF warned at the end of March that a war was very likely, because of politico-strategic considerations. This warning was remembered in May, though it is difficult to prove that it was considered to be very significant. Writing on the situation on the Israeli–Syrian border in September 1973 Ze'ev Schiff observed: 'Israel succeeded in convincing the American CIA that no war will start.... Inside the general staff was a division of opinion. The head of the northern command, General (Yitzhak) Hofi, spoke of a possible attack by Syria. Dayan said something had to be done to satisfy the general. General Hofi himself said: "Even though I was worried it might happen, I did not believe it would".'[63]

There is no wonder that Israel's security doctrine was influenced by a sense of having strategic depth, which, it was presumed, would be enough to defend the state until mobilization started. The euphoria of winning in 1967 is to be blamed for the fact that certain intelligence collection mechanisms were not checked again.[64] In 1973, the political military situation was more complicated and harder to analyze as the relationships between the Soviet Union and the Arab states were less clear. President Richard Nixon, on the other hand, gave Secretary of State Henry Kissinger a free hand. The outcome was devastating from the Israeli point of view. 'Those whose duty it was to decide did not feel what was happening, not only from the point of view of the enemy's intentions, but even as to its capabilities.'[65] In short, discussion developed up to this point, the rational calculations of Sadat were not understood by the Israeli decision-makers.

EGYPT'S WARNINGS AND ISRAEL'S ACTIONS: MISPERCEPTION OR COPING-AVOIDANCE?

A threat might be accepted as such or distorted, depending on the perceptions and images of those involved. The characteristics of threat acceptance or rejection involve some disagreement about interpretation. These may include, in the case of Israel, the following specifics, which may be treated as patterns: the image that the Egyptians would not attack because they lacked air superiority. The intelligence branch was always seen to be representing the most up to date material, its concomitant idea because the conclusions of the intelligence branch have to be accepted as the central element in decision-making. It has to be appreciated that 'those whose duty it was to decide did not grasp what is happening not only from the point of view of the enemy's intentions, but also as to his capabilities and possibilities'.[66]

All these variables involve some amount of coping, which is demanded from the decision-makers. As to the personal traits of Dayan, he certainly was not as strong as public image of him had been for many years. Dayan was charismatic, as his appointment in 1967 proved, but his personal traits were of a weak loner and his influence in Meir's cabinet depended on some affinity of ideas with Golda Meir. When asked if he would leave his party and join Rafi, Dayan hesitated so long that he was called a 'fence sitter'. Asked about this by a reporter, he replied: 'I admit with pride that I hesitated before deciding to join Rafi. No, it was not just that I could not make up my mind. I hesitated and carefully weighed various things. I would have continued to hesitate and weigh.'[67]

Indeed it may be that the behaviour of Dayan could be called denial, and not only coping avoidance. Yitzhar Smilansky who was a close acquaintance of Dayan for many years remarked: 'Every one who knew Moshe Dayan has to remember the hours of melancholy, the boredom and pessimism, the sitting on the fence and the surprising hesitation and unexpected fog'.[68] Likewise political commentator Yoel Markus observed: 'Dayan always needed number one: to depend on, to give him his ideas and to manipulate him.... I suspect he knew he is not fit to be a prime minister in Israel, where a prime minister has to be a politician, a leader and a unifying diplomat.'[69]

The political signals of Sadat did not go unnoticed and neither did the Egyptian military preparations. The Minister of Defence, however, felt that Israel should not escalate the situation. Should it come to the worst, the military was ready to execute the routine plans and there was no need to mobilize additional reserves. Thus it may be concluded that the Minister of Defence acted in a way of least possible resistance, that he did not assimilate the threat, as it was not in correspondence with his images as to the danger to which Israel was exposed, and was disregarded until a later date. At the end of July, Dayan was quoted as saying: 'During the next ten years the borders of Israel will be stabilized according to the existing lines, and there will be no outbreak of a major war'.[70] On 10 August Dayan said: 'Our military superiority is a consequence of both the weakness of the Arabs and our strength. Their weakness depends on factors which will not easily be changed.'[71] One should remember that on 13 September there already was a continuous movement of Soviet weaponry to Syrian ports. On 26 September during a visit at the Golan Heights Dayan remarked: 'The surface-air missile constellation on the Syrian side is higher than any thing known in the whole world. Israel is cognizant of the situation.'[72]

The Agranat report concluded that during the days preceding the war the intelligence branch (research) had enough knowledge provided to it by the collecting agencies in the state but they were not weighed correctly as the 'conception' predominated the thinking of the people.[73] On 3 October in a partial Cabinet meeting, no one disputed the assessment of the military intelligence that the likelihood of war was low. According to Schiff, Prime Minister Meir agreed to the distinction made between Syria and Egypt and that it was not worthwhile for Egypt to attack Israel.[74] On that day, the Soviets were already pulling their families out of Egypt and Syria.[75] On 4 October the Chief of Staff assessed that there was no high likelihood that war would break out.[76]

Though Israelis have a working knowledge of the Arab belief system, instead of working according to the worst case analysis, somebody, or some organization, did not cope. Who was it and why? One of the possible explanations for coping avoidance was given by Shlomo

Breznitz. According to him, if a true alarm is used many times, and the needed steps are taken, thus preventing the rival from taking the steps envisaged, there is a large difficulty in alerting those who have to be alarmed, and the possibility that steps will be taken half heartedly grows.[77] The larger the amount of former success of the correct alarm, the more it will sound to the decision-makers as a false alarm, not understanding that steps made by them trigger the mechanism which falsifies it. This is another version of the 'cry wolf' approach. This fact, besides the fact that an Arab attack may be executed for the sake of limited political military goals, should be taken into account along with the coping process.

The Egyptian posture had become one of attack. This situation was not considered to be grave enough for Dayan to decide on mobilization of the reserves. Though Elazar said that 'We have no proof that the enemy is not going to attack' but decided the highest alert possible in the IDF, Dayan opposed complete mobilization of the reserves on the day the war began.[78] The time from 4:30am until 9.30am was lost because of his obstruction. Elazar had no right to call the reserves without civil authorization, and this was not given by Dayan. Indeed the best factual proof of the disregard of the threat, and non-coping by Dayan, can be found in the mobilization at a very late stage and against his expressed wish.

One of the difficulties was that the central decision-makers did not relate to the possibility of early co-ordination between the Soviet Union and the Arab states. This may be attributed to a misunderstanding of the practical limitations of détente, or to a mistake in the calculations about the immediacy with which the US would decide to interfere as a result of Israel's readiness to refrain from pre-emptive strike. Schiff was correct in asserting that 'most of the IDF officers saw what happened but surrounded themselves by a psychological defence barrier'.[79] Such a barrier has many historical precedents during the first and second world wars and the Korean war. It seems clear that while the Arabs planned a limited war in which they were ready for military losses to secure political gains, Dayan saw Israel as a major power in the Middle East. Information that contradicts such an image may trickle usually only slowly, in small amounts and many times in a distorted form. Hence the coping avoidance of the threat was a simple process, which did not demand new adjustment and did not create a dissonance due to conflict. When the sirens began at 13:50 hours the Minister of Defence was standing before a special meeting of the Cabinet explaining why a war threat was not credible.

Was this a situation of misperception or coping avoidance? During the argument between Dayan and Elazar about the extent of mobilization, it was Elazar who urged the Prime Minister to decide. Dayan did not fix the date for the meeting, and hence he avoided making a decision.

All the criteria for coping avoidance are fulfilled.

- Awareness of the threat of serious losses from failing to take preventive action is evident during the discussion between Dayan and Elazar on 6 October when both disagreed on the need for mobilization.
- Awareness of the threat of serious losses from changing to any of the available alternatives is evident when Dayan asked Elazar what would a hundred thousand people do if they were mobilized and the war did not commence.
- Lack of hope of finding a solution was evident when Dayan spoke about a meeting between Meir, Elazar and himself against full mobilization and did not suggest any alternative.

To conclude, as the case fits both the definition and conditions regarding coping avoidance we are not confronted here with a misperception.

FIGURE 1
PSYCHOLOGICAL FACTORS INVOLVED IN DECISION-MAKING

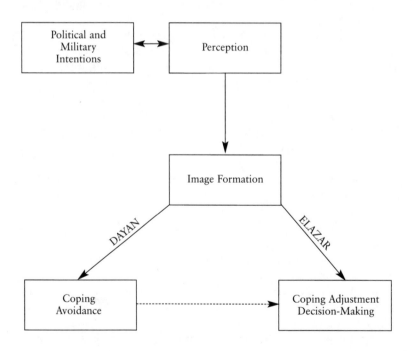

A comparison of the responses of M. Dayan and D. Elazar during the period
2–5 October 1973

Hypothesis no 2:

The more one relies on a single source of information the greater the possible distortion of available information for the decision-makers.

Talking and writing about intelligence is always shrouded in mystery. One of the obvious reasons is that intelligence professionals are in a situation in which it is quite difficult to defend themselves. Another is that it is complicated to get access to hard, inside evidence, which cannot be disproved by some rumour or story. The question whether the rumour is correct, or is fabricated to defend a source will not be discussed here.

Another question is 'how much is enough', or, to speak plainly, how much evidence is needed in order to convince senior officers in the intelligence community that there exists a possibility that they are mistaken, that another interpretation of the material is possible and, furthermore, that somebody higher up in the ladder of authority should be convinced about the possibility that the policy decided upon is mistaken. Generally, intelligence may be collected in public sources.[80] At least one estimate is that 70 per cent of the needed intelligence is to be found in such publications, and that the USSR has a backlog of two to three months due to this immense amount of information that is collected openly.

A classification, which is to be found in the literature on intelligence, is between 'suppliers' and 'consumers'.[81] This classification needs to be elaborated upon. How does a supplier decide that his information is reliable? Why does he decide that a certain source is better than another? This question is important to answer the questions posed by the decision-makers, if and when they are explicitly asked.[82] This question raises an even more important consideration: Does one intelligence unit have all the needed information? The question has important implications as 'Rationality requires a complete knowledge and anticipation of all consequences that will follow on each choice. In practice, knowledge is always fragmentary.'[83] Who are to decide what the value of certain information is?

The personnel in the intelligence department may have a certain feeling about the state he deals with. On the other hand, the consumer, and only he, can evaluate and interpret the value of a certain piece of information for the question on which he has to make a decision. Hence, a conclusion is warranted: if weighing information has to be close to reality, and an answer to the question which bothers the decision-maker, the intelligence community has to take part in the evaluation process.[84] It is preferable, if possible, that men whose country desk is involved will be consulted directly, as their knowledge of specifics may provide the decision-maker with a direct answer to the question which bothers him.

The risks in this procedure should be obvious: The more people who have the duty to evaluate and interpret the greater the likelihood that their images and prejudices will contribute to the creation of misconceptions.

Different perceptions, images, life experiences, knowledge, interests – private and organizational – and coping behaviour contribute to the process of distortion that may be unintentional or conscious. One should remember that a crisis is a period in which evaluations on the assessment of the situation and alternatives are growing needs. The question which comes to mind is whether more processing of information increases the chances of warnings about future events reaching the senior decision-makers in time. Considering the research done by Roberta Wohlstetter, Charles Herman, Janice Stein and others,[85] this writer would counter the common wisdom: the more the processing the smaller the chances that the senior decision-maker will get the correct information. Though there is no necessary correlation between raw and correct information this impediment to timely evaluation, assimilation adjustment and coping behaviour has to be discussed.

Wohlstetter addresses this point in the following way: 'The attempt to make ONI (Office of National Intelligence) into a new collection agency had serious consequences that Naval War Plans refused to acknowledge in 1941: for when the job of collecting information is separated from the job of assessing its meaning, the fundamental motive or incentive for collection information disappears.'[86] The claim made here is that this difficulty may be overcome. Though manpower and price are relevant considerations, the method has a direct influence on arriving at a rational decision from the point of view of the decision-maker involved.

ASSIMILATION OF INFORMATION: PROBLEM OF EFFICIENCY VS ACCURACY

The difficulty involved in coping is, to a certain degree, dependent on the flow of information. Though different people have different styles of decision-making, everyone is likely to decide according to the culture in which he lives and the norms and values imbued in him since childhood. The form and timing, as well as the amount and quality of the information, are decisive elements in the process of choice. This is a choice the Prime Minister or the Chief Executive has to make. How does information arrive to the decision-maker? Kennedy was known to cut through the lines of communication; Truman was different. His remark was recorded by Richard Neustadt: 'I sit here all day trying to persuade people to do the things they ought to have enough sense to do without my persuading them ... that's all the powers of the president amount to.'[87] This is certainly not a style that entails cutting lines of communication. Neither is it a style which shows energetic taking of the initiative. Truman emerges from this quote as a president who persuades, and does not command.

The question as to the way in which information is accepted or rejected has to be discussed to understand if there is a way to improve the dissemination methods of intelligence. Intelligence has to be timely. If it is processed many times it is likely to become outdated. Even if it remains timely, the fewer people it goes through, the fewer the interpretations that may be indiscernible from the information itself. Maybe one way to overcome this difficulty is by separating the intelligence material from its evaluation, mechanically, so that the reader will be able to differentiate the intelligence material from interpretations.

When the possibility of the eruption of a crisis emerges, the need for information grows and hence the flow of intelligence is bound to grow. This will, inevitably, contain a mixture of signals and noise. The mixture is liable to influence the image of the consumer even if he gets the raw material separated from the evaluation of the supplier. Where separation is marked, the possibility of distortion may be smaller. Thus, it seems that for the sake of accuracy some amount of possible efficiency involved in the writing of position papers has to be sacrificed. On the other hand, to prevent the triggering of the 'cry wolf' syndrome, consecutive warning based on the same source should be minimized unless new evidence comes up.

It is paradoxical that while it is important to transmit all the signals immediately, in the hope that the image of the decision-maker will be as accurate as possible, this may undermine to a certain degree the efficiency of the process of transmitting the information. As a result 'usually subordinates have the power to decide what information to pass on to the higher superiors; and it is usually argued that they withhold a disproportionate amount of discrepant information'.[88] Thus, a tendency toward groupthink tends to be magnified.[89] After the war Elazar complained that there were hundreds of intelligence pieces that never reached him and were scattered in the different research branches.[90]

The process of intelligence collection and evaluation is very similar in different democratic states and amounts to distilled and filtered assessment of the situation. C.L. Cooper describes the process in the US concerning preparation of a National Intelligence Estimate (NIE) in the following way:

> Each National Intelligence Estimate is written after due consideration of contributions submitted by intelligence analysts both within and outside the agency, but the final wording bears the unmistakable stamp of one's style of composition and analysis. What emerges is a mass of distilled information, a painstaking search for the most just and an assiduous effort to co-ordinate the views of the appropriate elements of the intelligence community. And when all is said and done what emerges is an opinion, a judgement.[91]

It seems from this interpretation that the situation is grave indeed. The decision-maker gets raw material only occasionally. What they get is an evaluation and, hence, nothing protects them from distortion which may occur along the way. In the US there is a custom of adding dissension opinions to the different estimates by the different agencies, but no mechanism whatsoever assures that these dissenting opinions will arrive at the decision-maker's desk. Thus it would be recommended as a method of improvement that instead of one, distilled and filtered estimate, every agency would transmit its own material including the dissents. It was shown by Phillips and Rimkunas that the image, weight and interpretation of the agencies are different.[92] Different interpretations should reach the decision-makers so that they will be able to have freedom of choice, and not choices dictated to them by unified, integrated and distilled interpretation. While it is possible that the analyst of the agency will be cognizant of intentions, there is a possibility that the decision-maker will be more cognizant of expectations. Hence the importance in diversity of material, and the knowledge about different interpretations, have to be known to the decision-maker to avoid as far as possible the creation of a closed mind set, which furthers self fulfilling prophecies.

The pre-crisis stage of the Yom Kippur War can be understood only when one remembers the largest misperception held by the military was that an alarm of at least 48 hours would precede any Arab attack. Intelligence distortions by different agencies were responsible for the transmission of information to the decision-makers. Why the IDF organizational plans were not activated both on the operational and on the tactical levels can be understood with the same misperception of minimal alert time. This was not fulfilled due to the cry wolf syndrome. The theory of false alarm states that the credibility of a warning will be depreciated in direct correlation with the number of alarms which have been disproved before. Such alarms were activated at the end of 1972 and in May 1973.[93] It was subsequently apparent that the alarm of May 1973 was not false and President Sadat planned an attack but postponed it.[94]

A false alarm has two main effects: (a) the amount of sensitivity to the same kind of threat is depreciated; and (b) the activity undertaken in response to a subsequent alarm is lessened, and there may be a tendency to relate to the expenses involved. The facts as published show that both kinds of consequences had their influence on Dayan, Elazar and head of the Military Intelligence Eli Zeira.[95] As they were the heads of the different hierarchies, their convictions were of major importance. Both Dayan and Elazar deliberated about the need to mobilize the reserves because of the frequency of the mobilizations and their economic cost. Their conclusions were different at the end: Elazar pressed for maximal mobilization, and Dayan decided there was no need to mobilize.

Military organization is hierarchical by definition. This fact is very significant for suggestions of decisions brought to the attention of the decision level, and especially when the central decision-maker objects to the strategic image underlying those suggestions. Hence, though all suggestions brought up were rational from the point of view of the individual suggesting them, the rationale guiding each individual was different. In other words, as in any other human group, the military system is confronted with different views and images. But in contrast to other groups, the military is a hierarchical organization and hence decision is always taken according to the ideas of the man at the top, in this case, Dayan. The differences of opinion in the military hierarchy are best exemplified in a time table, showing explicitly the pulling and hauling in the system, according to the intelligence, or rather, the part of it which was assimilated.

The outcome of consecutive warnings was a hindering factor of full mobilization until 6 October. The possibility that mobilization might contribute to escalation in the Middle East and serve the political goals of the rival states may have been a contributing element to this decision. This conception was accompanied by an overestimate of the capability of Israel's regular army.[96] Hence, the alternative chosen, namely, no mobilization and high alert in the regular army, seemed most rational to the decision-makers involved.[97] In other words, the assimilation of accumulating information and the understanding of its implications were deficient.

PRESENTATION AND ANALYSIS OF THE DATA

Different echelons of the intelligence hierarchy accumulated information, including signs, which indicated that war was about to begin.[98] On 30 September 1973, General Hofi, commander of the northern command, warned that the Syrian forces were poised for an offensive and hence a reinforcement force was sent to the Golan Heights.[99] On 1 October Lieutenant Siman-Tov, the field intelligence officer of the southern command, wrote to his superior that according to his checklist, the Egyptian manoeuvre was a cover-up for the initiating hostilities. His commander told him his estimate contradicted the assessment of the intelligence branch and he should erase his conclusion. That was done, but on 3 October a second report was prepared that reiterated this grave warning.[100] The commander, Lieutenant Colonel Yona Bandman, did not transmit Siman-Tov's estimate and did not include it in his report.[101]

On 5 October the head of the Syrian desk said in a conference of intelligence officers that Syria was ready for war but he was silenced and it was intended to reprimand him on 7 October.[102] On 4 October information arrived that the Soviets were removing their advisers and families from both Egypt and Syria.[103] Before the Six Day War, this was a sign that war was about to start. Civilians reading this information in *Ha'aretz* started to worry. As for the Intelligence establishment, they explained the removal of the Soviet advisers from Syria as a further deterioration in Soviet–Syrian relations.[104] This did not explain the evacuation from Egypt. According to Janice Gross Stein, there were three possible interpretations:

First, the Soviets knew of an impending attack, and anticipating the military consequences of a counter attack by Israel was withdrawing their personnel. Such an interpretation was alarming in its implications. Alternatively, if Soviet–Syrian relationships have deteriorated badly, as some speculated, Syria might have requested all Soviet advisers to leave, but this would not explain why Soviet personnel were being withdrawn simultaneously from Egypt. Third, it was possible that the Soviet Union had accepted Syrian allegations, broadcast repeatedly in the last days that Israel was about to attack. Again, however, if this were so, Moscow would have asked Washington to warn Israel against attack and no such warnings were delivered.... In a series of briefings the next morning (that is, 5 October) he (Zeira) presented all three interpretations ... but accepted none, explaining he did not know why Soviet personnel were withdrawn and that he is awaiting further information.[105]

Until 5 October the predominant consideration in the military system, furthered by the central decision-maker, Dayan, was that the earlier mobilizations in May 1973 seemed to be futile.

It has to be remarked again that discussion about mobilization was held while knowledge about the exit of the Soviet military advisers already existed. This raises the question whether another agency, which attached more weight to political considerations, would have alerted the decision-makers to the vast importance of this political signal. It seems that the self-confidence of the decision-makers was so high that even such a political signal did not lead to integration of movement of the forces in the field with it.

The Agranat commission maintained that the military intelligence was the only centre for the evaluation of military intelligence in the state, and the sole guardian of information accumulated by them from their collection agencies, those of the Mossad and other collection agencies. While the branch of intelligence disseminates processed information including its evaluation as 'intelligence' to other agencies, it decides who will get what and how much.[106] Therefore, there was only one evaluation that was brought to the attention of the chief of Staff, the Defence Minister and the Prime Minister.

There is a need for the existence of several independent agencies, which may arrive at different conclusions and interpretations. If those who differ from the interpretation of the establishment are allowed to be heard, there is a small chance they will be considered. This chance should not be overlooked, the practical claim, often heard, that Israel cannot allow itself to have an optimal number of independent intelligence agencies is not valid. This claim contradicts the basic goal of the survival of the state.

SUMMARY

The analysis of Hypothesis 2 shows the dangers involved in an integrated, filtered and distilled evaluation handed to the central decision-makers. As there is no way that all the raw material can be handed over to the decision-makers, some arrangement has to be made whereby an optimal amount of raw material will be passed on, separate from the interpretation and evaluation. This material must consist not only, as is the practice, of evidence to support the current interpretation at a given time, but some sample of contradictory interpretation. Thus the decision-maker will be able to form his own reading and interpretation of the situation.

Since the Yom Kippur War was no surprise for the decision-makers, why did they refrain from timely mobilization and a pre-emptive strike? What was the consequence of usage of only one channel of communication to recommend further action to the central decision-makers?

It was shown how taking the correct steps to prevent war later turned into a component of the cry wolf syndrome. It is surmised that coping processes play the role of an independent variable in determining the pace of such a process. Meanwhile the Chief of Staff of Israel Mordechai Gur found himself in a similar situation when he disbelieved the seriousness of the Sadat initiative. He was not alone. Management of the peace negotiations by Kissinger contributed to the turning of a severe situation into a peace process and created a major change in Egyptian–Israeli relations, later to be followed by another peace accord with Jordan, Hence the outcome of the war was turned into a considerable gain for those involved in the conflict except one major actor – Syria – where, because of Asad's inflexible attitude, the dialogue did not prove to be fruitful. Another channel of political research operates now from the foreign office. Though a step in the right direction even this is not enough. It is imperative that the Prime Minister's office create an independent database for its political-military decisions; this may shift the emphasis and open other alternatives for the formulation and application of policy with a short and long-term perspective.

NOTES

1. J.S. Frank, *Sanity and Survival: Psychological Aspects of War and Peace*, New York: Random House, 1967, p.4: the author says that these variables decide which of the characteristics of the environment will attract the attention of the decision-maker, what amount of importance will be attached to the incoming information, and the way he describes it to others. Also see E.R. Hillgard, *Introduction to Psychology*, New York: Harcourt, 1967.
2. 'People individually or collectively view the occurrence of events in a perspective formed as much by a prevailing climate of opinion as their past experiences and their perception', K. Deutsch and R.L. Merritt, 'Effects of Events on National and

International Images', in Herbert C. Kelman, ed., *International Behaviour: a Social Psychological Analysis*, New York: Holt, Reinhart and Winston, 1965, pp.151–2.

3. Michael Handel, *Perception, Deception and Surprise: The Case of the Yom Kippur War*, Jerusalem Papers on Peace Problems, Jerusalem: The Leonard Davis Institute, 1976, p.7.

4. Oren R. Young, *The Politics of Force*, Princeton: Princeton University Press, 1968, p.20.

5. Shlomo Breznitz, 'False Alarms: Their Effects on Fear and Adjustment', unpublished paper (n.d.) p.128.

6. Irving L. Janis and Leon A. Mann, *Decision Making*, New York: The Free Press, 1977, p.52.

7. Richard S. Lazarus, *Patterns of Adjustment and Human Effectiveness*, New York: McGraw Hill, 1969, p.181.

8. There are three possible ways of action regarding a conflict of coping: approach-approach means both alternatives are equally desirable, and hence the conflict, Avoid-avoid means a conflict in regard to which both alternatives are equally negative, and approach-avoid means a conflict in which both alternatives are equally positive and negative.

9. Janis and Mann, *Decision Making*, p.109.

10. Lazarus, *Patterns of Adjustment and Human Effectiveness*, p.194.

11. Ibid., p.181.

12. This was the case with Truman's policy toward China during the civil war. Truman did not make even one decision regarding support of the nationalist Chinese withdrawal thereof. When at last he wanted to make the decision to stop sending ammunition he let himself be convinced by Republican Congressman Arthur H. Vandenberg not to do so.

13. See Janis and Mann, *Decision Making*, p.88. See also Saul Friedlander and Raymond Cohen, *The Personality Correlates of Belligerence in International Conflict: A Comparative Analysis of Historical Case Studies*, Jerusalem: The Leonard Davis Institute for International Relations, unpublished paper, n.d.

14. French Prime Minister Raymond Poincare, Czechoslovak Prime Minister Beck and Italian Prime Minister Crispi are only some examples of coping avoiders. For details see Friedlander and Cohen, *The Personality Correlates of Belligerence in International Conflict*.

15. See Warren R. Phillips and Richard V. Rimkunas, 'A Cross Agency Comparison of US Crisis Perception', in J.D. Singer and M.D. Wallace, eds, *To Augur Well Warning Indicators in World Politics*, Beverly Hills: Sage Publications, 1979, pp.238–9.

16. See discussion of this point in Leon Festinger, *Conflict Decision and Dissonance*, Stanford: Stanford University Press, 1957, p.96.

17. Robert Jervis, *Perception and Misperception in International Politics*, Princeton: Princeton University Press, 1976, p.181.

18. See discussion of the variable of time in Charles F. Herman, 'International Crisis as a Situational Variable', in James N. Rosenau, ed., *International Politics and Foreign Politics*, New York: Free Press, 1969, pp.409.

19. For the differentiation between operational and psychological environment see Michael Brecher and Janice Gross Stein, 'A Framework for Research on Foreign Policy Behaviour', *Journal of Conflict Resolution* 13/1 (March 1969), pp.75–101.

20. With the exclusion of public opinion these variables are enumerated in Brecher and Stein, ibid.

21. A qualification has to be made: sometimes events are triggered by multinational corporations or terrorist groups and not by governments. Another qualification deals with events evolving of nature like flood or draught.

22. See, for example, Herbert A. Simon, *Administrative Behaviour*, New York: The Free Press, 2nd ed., 1957, p.65; A. Downs, *An Economic Theory of Democracy*, New York: Harper and Row, 1957, p.58; J.C. Harsanyi, *Rational Behaviour and Bargaining Equilibrium in Games and Social Situations*, Cambridge: Cambridge University Press, 1977, p.19; and Glen H. Snyder and P. Diesing, *Conflict Among Nations*, Princeton: Princeton University Press, 1977, p.80.

23. See, for example, Samuel L. Popkin, *The Rational Peasant*, Berkeley: University of California Press, 1979.

24. Simon, *Administrative Behaviour*, p.81.

25. Janis Gross Stein 'Can Decision Makers Be Rational and Should They Be? Evaluating the Quality of Decisions', *The Jerusalem Journal of International Relations* 3/2-3 (Winter-Spring 1978), pp.316–39.

26. Harsanyi makes an exceptional differentiation between game theory and decision-making, writing that decision-making theory deals with the expectations of the decision-makers themselves and not of their rivals. Harsanyi, *Rational Behaviour and Bargaining Equilibrium in Games and Social Situations*, p.10.

27. Herbert A. Simon, 'Theories of Bounded Rationality', in C.B. McGuire and R. Radner, ed., *Decision and Organization*, Amsterdam: North Holland Publishing Company, 1972, p.168.

28. Herman A. Simon 'Rational Choice and the Structure of Environment' in Herman A. Simon (ed.) *Models of Thought,* (New Haven: Yale University, 1979) p.13.

29. Herbert A. Simon, 'Theories of Bounded Rationality', p.8.

30. See, for example, Ole R. Holsti, 'The Belief System and the Native Image', in Rosenau, *International Politics and Foreign Policy*, p.544.

31. In his *The Active Society*, New York: Colliers and Macmillan, 1968, Amitai Etzioni treats this problem by stating: 'The inputs of a decision include the knowledge of the actor, used to chart alternative routs and to explore the unexpected consequences, the actor's consciousness of himself and others.' p.250.

32. For a discussion of a crazy state see Y. Dror, *Crazy States*, Tel-Aviv: Ma'archot, 1973 (Hebrew), pp.45–9. As to brinkmanship see Alexander L. and Juliette George, *Woodrow Wilson and Colonel House*, New York: John Day Company, 1956, pp.167, 170–1.

33. For a discussion of the influence of the belief system on the decision-maker see, for exampl,e S. Verba, 'Assumptions of Rationality in Models of the International System', in Rosenau, *International Politics and Foreign Policy*, p.229.

34. Thus, for example, the concept of a holy war which is prevalent in Islam no longer exists in the values of western culture. See also David Chan, 'Rationality, Bureaucratic Politics and Belief Systems: Explaining the Chinese Policy Debate 1964–1966', *Journal of Peace Research* 16/4 (1979) p.335; and Davis Bobrow *et al.* 'Understanding How Others Treat Crises', *International Science Quarterly* 21/1 (1977).

35. See, for example, the threat made by Sadat in 1972, about his readiness to sacrifice a million soldiers in battle with Israel, which implies a different value of human lives for Egypt and Israel.

36. The word preference is used instead of options as unliked options may be distorted.

37. H. Bartov, *Dado, 48 Years and 20 Days*, Tel Aviv: Ma'ariv, 1978, p.319.

38. Personality of leaders involved in crises has been widely researched: specific crises in which this factor has been analyzed are the Cuban Missile Crisis (1962) Johnson's intervention in Vietnam, Kissinger's influence on the development of the Arab–Israeli conflict, sometimes labelled 'shuttle diplomacy', Carter's mishandling of the hostages in Iran, and Reagan's efforts to regain Lebanon's sovereignty, which did not amount to a crisis due to Israeli constraints.

39. The war of 1956 is an example of such a premise which applies of course to postulate no 3.

40. Bartov, *Dado*, p.244.

41. *Agranat Commission Report*, p.40.

42. Michael Brecher, *The Foreign Policy System of Israel*, London: Oxford University Press, 1972, p.336.

43. Shabtai Teveth, *Moshe Dayan*, Tel Aviv: Shocken, 1974, p.562 (Hebrew).

44. *Agranat Commission Report*, p.40.

45. Ibid., p.60.

46. Ibid., p.19.

47. Shimon Peres, *Kela David [David's Sling]*, Jerusalem: Wiedenfeld & Nicolson, 1970, p.190 (Hebrew).

48. Chaim Herzog, *The War of Atonement*, Tel Aviv: Idanin, 1975, p.12 (Hebrew).

49. Golda Meir, *My Life*, Tel Aviv: Ma'ariv, 1977, p.311 (Hebrew).

50. 'Shahid', in C.E. Bosworth *et al.*, *Encyclopaedia of Islam*, Leiden: E.J. Brill, 1995, Vol.9, pp.203–7.

51. Meir, *My Life*, p.311.

52. For a short explanation see John Laffin, *The Dagger of Islam*, London: Sphire Books,

1979, ch.6., especially pp.39–40 that explains the Islamic image regarding Presidents Jimmy Carter and Sadat after the signature of the peace treaty with Israel. Current political implications of suicidal groups were evident in the Lebanon war, 1983. See for example 'The Suicide Organizations from Ba'al Beck: Terror against the Devil', *Ma'ariv* 16 December 1983, pp.13–14 and *Iran Times* (Washington), 7 October 1983.

53. Arie Hashavia, *The Yom-Kippur War*, Tel Aviv: Davar, 1974, p.11 (Hebrew).
54. Anwar el Sadat, *In Search of Identity*, Jerusalem: Edanim, Yedi'ot Ahronot, 1978, p.158 (Hebrew).
55. This concept brought the Muslims to Spain, where they ruled from 711 to 1031 AD. 'Believers do not make friends with any man other than your own people. They will spare no pains to corrupt you. They desire nothing but your own ruin.' Sura III, Laffin, *The Dagger of Islam*, p.40.
56. Sadat, *In Search of Identity*, p.158.
57. Bernard Reich, *Quest for Peace*, New Jersey: Transaction Books, 1977, p.270.
58. Mohammed Heikal, *Sphinx and Commissar*, London: Collins, 1979, pp.256–7.
59. Meir, *My Life*, pp.290–1.
60. Ibid.
61. Herzog, *The War of Atonement*, p.52.
62. 'The Military Strategy of the October 1973 war and its repercussions on world strategy', International Symposium on the 1973 October War, Cairo, October 1975 proceedings, p.31.
63. Ze'ev Schiff, *Earthquake in October*, Tel Aviv: Zmora Bitan Modan, 1974, p.13 (Hebrew).
64. The entrance of Egyptian forces into the Sinai peninsula on 5 May 1967 came as a 'surprise' to the top decision-makers of Israel as this step was not predicted.
65. *Agranat Commission Report* , p.18.
66. Schiff, *Earthquake in October*, p.65.
67. Dayan quoted in Michael Brecher, *The Foreign Policy System of Israel*, p.323. The term 'fence sitter' is originally taken from M. Kohn, 'Moshe Dayan Why I Joined RAFI', *The Jerusalem Post*, 10 September 1965.
68. Yitzhar Smilansky, 'The Artist of the Short Line', *Ma'ariv*, 27 November 1981.
69. Joel Markus, 'He Was No Leader', *Ha'aretz*, 23 October 1982.
70. *Time*, 23 July 1973, quoted in Bartov, *Dado*, p.273.
71. *The Jerusalem Post*, 11 August 1973.
72. Schiff, *Earthquake in October*, p.12.
73. Yeshayhu Ben Porat *et al.*, *Hamechdal* [The Failure], Tel Aviv: Hotza'a Meyuchedet, n.d., p.18 (Hebrew). Conception, in this context, means a stereotyped way of thinking which predominates and thus hinders the creation of new images.
74. Schiff, *Earthquake in October*, pp.18–19.
75. Ibid., p.20.
76. Bartov, *Dado*, p.305.
77. Breznitz, *False Alarms*, p.130.
78. Schiff, *Earthquake in October*, p.19.
79. Ibid., p.51.
80. Interview with an intelligence officer in the Israeli Army, Washington, DC, 1982.
81. C.L. Cooper, 'The CIA and Decision Making', *Foreign Affairs* 50/2 (January 1972), pp.223–36.
82. H. Heyman Jr. and A.P. Williams Jr., 'Possibilities for Research on Intelligence Needs for National Security Decision Making', D-19784 ARPA, 29 December 1969, p.2.
83. Simon, *Administrative Behavior*, p.9.
84. Cooper, 'The CIA and Decision Making', pp.223–36.
85. Roberta Wohlstetter, *Pearl Harbour: Warning and Decision*, Stanford: Stanford University Press, 1962; Glen D. Paige, *The Korean Decision*, New York: Free Press, 1968; Charles F. Herman, *Crisis in Foreign Policy*, New York: Bob Merrill, 1969; and Janice Stein 'The 1973 Intelligence Failure: a Reconsideration', *Jerusalem Quarterly* 24 (Summer 1982), pp.41–54.
86. Wohlstetter, *Pear Harbour*, p.319.
87. Richard Neustadt, *Presidential Power*, John Wiley and Sons, 1980, p.9.
88. Jervis, *Perception and Misperception in International Politics*, p.143. See also William J. Banks, 'Intelligence and Foreign Policy Dilemmas of a Democracy', *Foreign Affairs* 47/1 (January 1969), p.286.

89. An elaborate discussion of this subject is done during the analysis of the fifth hypothesis in the full research. See also Irving L Janis, *Victims of Groupthink*, Boston: Houghton Mifflin, 1972.
90. *Ma'ariv*, 13 June 1975.
91. Cooper, 'The CIA and Decision Making', pp.224–5.
92. Warren R. Phillips and Richard V. Rimkunas, 'A Cross Agency Comparison of US Crisis Perception', in J.D. Singer, ed., *To Augur Well*, Beverly Hills: Sage, 1979, pp.237–70.
93. Herzog, *The War of Atonement*, pp.53, 60.
94. Stein, 'The 1973 Intelligence Failure', p.49.
95. Herzog, *The War of Atonement*, pp.248–9.
96. *Agranat Commission Report*, p.60.
97. The description of this approach can be found in Y. Erez, 'How Dado Saw it', *Ma'ariv*, 7 February 1975.
98. *Agranat Commission Report*, pp.19–20.
99. Schiff, *Earthquake in October*, p.13.
100. Ibid., p.15.
101. Herzog, *The War of Atonement*, p.55.
102. Schiff, *Earthquake in October*, p.22.
103. Ibid., p.46.
104. Stein, 'The 1973 Intelligence Failure', p.44.
105. *Agranat Commission Report*, p.20.
106. Ibid., p.28.

The Air Force and the Yom Kippur War: New Lessons

SHMUEL L. GORDON

This article seeks to address some of the hitherto unexplored issues that offer new understanding about the role and importance of the Israel Air Force (IAF) during the crucial phase of the war. To focus on these lessons and to prevent diversion, it will concentrate on the most dangerous day to the existence of the State of Israel – 7 October 1973. This work begins with description of the 7 October crisis and afterwards it illustrates the pre-war preparations of the IAF. Then, it analyses the IAF roles and deeds during the long and fateful day, and suggests lessons to be learned for future air operations.

The third day of the hostilities, 8 October – the day when the first Israel Defence Forces' (IDF) counter-attack had failed – is often considered as the most critical day of the Yom Kippur War. However, the most dangerous day of the war was the day before, when both fronts – the Egyptian and the Syrian as well – were almost empty of any IDF units. Reserve units were organized deep inside Israel, the regular units were worn out, and the 'gates' to the heartland of Israel were open to the penetrating Arab armies. The IAF considers that day the most frustrating point of the war because of the colossal failure of its counter-attack against the Syrian surface-to-air missiles (SAM) systems along the Golan Heights. Many high ranking military officers as well as civilian analysts have berated the less than expected performance of the IAF during the war because of its failure to achieve air superiority against the SAM systems.[1] The famous statement of the present President of the State and former commander of the IAF, Ezer Weizman, amplified that assessment loud and clear:

Dr Shmuel L. Gordon is a Colonel (Res.) in the IAF.

The IAF didn't overcome the Syrian and Egyptian SAM arrays on time... and couldn't be involved with its full strength in the containment of the penetrating enemy armies on the two fronts... The missile has bent the aircraft's wing in this war – This is a fact that should be analyzed very carefully, in order to deduce important lessons.[2]

That recommendation, to learn and deduce the lessons, is the main goal of this study.

PREPARATIONS FOR THE WAR

The main claims against the IDF preparation for war before the war included:

- An atmosphere of serenity, and over-confidence.
- The level of readiness was quite low.
- The preparedness for war was unsatisfactory.
- The emergency stocks of equipment were in a very bad condition.
- The training of the regular units and the reserves did not match the requirements of the modern battlefield.
- The doctrine was not suitable to the next war.[3]

Are these accusations appropriate? Since the Six Day War, the IDF did not confront the Arab counterparts in large operations and hence its axis of reference was the main campaigns of the Six Day War. On the other hand, the IAF had encountered, during the War of Attrition, the enemy SAM systems, supported by Soviet professionals. In this intense operation, for the first time, the IAF commanders and pilots did not achieve a decisive victory as in the past. The unfinished battle made them worried and sceptical about their abilities to destroy massive, modern SAM systems. The three years following the War of Attrition were devoted to the development of new tactics, weapon systems, exercises, conferences and studies. They were focusing on a sole goal: to re-acquire the capability to achieve battlefield air superiority. The appearance of a new SAM system – SAM-6 – sharpened and intensified the IAF efforts. The building of extensive and hardened aircraft shelters by the Arab air forces further accelerated the IAF development of tactics and weapons against airfields and other components of the air force infrastructure. Despite its success during the War of Attrition where two dozen enemy aircraft were shot down for each aircraft that Israel lost, the air-to-air combat tactics of the IAF had also improved. These improvements were proved useful in the Yom Kippur War. In short, the intensity of the fighting during the War of Attrition prevented the IAF from being too confident about the next conflict.

The IAF was in a high state of *readiness* before the war. About ten days before the war broke out the IAF had been strengthened towards meeting an optional attack of the Arab armies. Afterwards, on Yom Kippur morning, the IAF was on full alert, ready to attack the Syrian SAM systems or airfields. That pre-emptive attack was cancelled by the prime minister's decision, not by lack of readiness of the IAF.

The *preparedness* was also quite satisfactory. The logistic organization had met its requirements before and during the war, and no complaints had been recorded concerning the lack of essential equipment. Even though dozens of aircraft arrived during the emergency airlift, the pre-war size of the IAF was decided by the US Government that limited the number of aircraft given to Israel.

The accusation that the *training* of the IAF did not match the requirements of the modern battlefield is not adequate either. Exercises and training were intensive, updated, and adapted to meet the modern surface-to-air threats, even though lack of intelligence prevented shaping winning tactics for counter SAM-6 systems.

The *doctrine* of the IAF was changed significantly and it shifted the focus of the battle for air superiority from fighting against aircraft to the destruction of the SAM systems. The process of improving the IAF doctrine was based on the methodology of continuity and changes and the IAF adapted itself to the new environmental conditions. According to the tenets of that doctrine, the basic roles of the IAF included:

- Defence of the nation and its military forces against attacks of air forces;
- Destruction of the enemy SAM systems to achieve air superiority quickly and decisively;
- Massive destruction of ground forces in close support of the IDF units and independent interdiction;
- Destruction of Arab air forces was secondary on the roles list due to their weak offensive capabilities and strong defensive ones, mainly anti-aircraft defence and well-hardened shelters for aircraft. Thus, that role was to be completed by continuous operation in contradiction to the *Moked* (Focus) Operation, in which, three nations' air forces were destroyed in the IAF surprise attack at the beginning of the Six Day War.
- Destruction of strategic targets deep in the enemies' territories.

The small size of the IAF forced it to concentrate its efforts on a few different roles simultaneously, and accomplishment of each role was an essential conjuncture for shifting efforts to the next one.

These were the main roles of the IAF on the eve of the Yom Kippur War. It was created by the IAF, approved and adopted by the IDF and the civilian leadership as the Israel Air Doctrine. It should be admitted that the doctrine was not an ideal answer to the threats of the Egyptian and Syrian armies and doctrines, but it was sufficient to fulfil the IAF expectations if used properly.

THE IAF CRISIS OF 7 OCTOBER

The worst day in the Yom Kippur War, as stated, was 7 October. The situation in the northern front as well the southern front was quite close to a comprehensive defeat. Lines of defence were shattered to pieces, regular units were worn out and the organization and mobilization of the reserves had just begun. During this day, only a few and weak forces were deployed between the penetrating Arab armies and the heartland of Israel. Because of its high level of readiness and preparedness, the IAF alone could halt the Arab forces that crossed the borders. The IAF's operational plans, prepared for that day during the night, were compatible to its doctrine and emphasized the destruction of SAM systems before concentration on the ground forces. Since the situation of the Suez Canal front was considered more fragile than the northern front, the IAF was directed southward.

At the dawn of 7 October, the IAF began a well-organized attack against the Egyptian SAM systems along the Suez Canal. But just as the smile of success had begun to appear, the IAF was directed to shift its power to the Syrian front, where Defence Minister Moshe Dayan and Chief of Staff David Elazar feared the imminent collapse of the defence. Due to the constraints of time, space and the essential needs of the ground force, the anti-Syrian SAM array operation, known as *Dugman 5* (Model 5), was not executed as originally planned and hence it was a complete failure. It was the most important defeat in the history of the IAF, which influenced its operations during the war and many years thereafter. As a result the Syrian ground-to-air defences were not damaged, freedom of action was not achieved, and the IAF suffered significant losses in the crucial Close Air Support (CAS) mission in trying to halt the Syrian troops that threatened to conquer and capture the Golan Heights as they moved forward and crossed the June 1967 cease-fire lines.

The battle against the ground-to-air defence was not an isolated mission but was aimed at serving much more important missions; namely, to enable IAF freedom of action in the skies over the battlefield to destroy the Syrian armoured units, to save the Golan Heights, and to remove the threats to the civilians deep inside Israel. The IAF sacrificed many pilots in the efforts to halt ground forces without air superiority. More than ten per cent of the IAF aircraft were shot down in the first 34 hours of the war (from 2pm on 6 October to midnight of 7 October). More than 100 aircraft were destroyed during the war and more than half of that number were shot down during the first four days. These losses were so significant that the IAF Commander General Benjamin Peled was compelled to inform Chief of Staff Elazar that the IAF was quite close to its 'Red Line', and that future war plans should consider this scenario.[4]

It should be emphasized that during the critical phase of the war, the Minister of Defence and the Chief of Staff employed the IAF contrary to its principles of war, its tactics, training, the deployment of supporting assets such as electronic warfare and in the absence of information on the enemy, and lack of targets. That method reflected misunderstanding of the advantages and weaknesses of air power. Air power requires a certain time frame to fulfil its missions and to use its firepower for destruction of the enemies' armour units. Critical mass of force is also required to accomplish each mission. The partial operations against the Egyptian and Syrian SAM systems had underscored these basic requirements. Doctrine is not a sacred set of rules and sometimes it is not adequate to unique situation. But the justification for ignoring doctrinal recommendations is the outcome. The ignorance of the IAF counter-SAM doctrine led to high attrition rate, unsuccessful operations, and air inferiority over the battlefields. Later in the war, when the IAF began to fight according to its doctrine, it resulted in immediate successes.[5] The atmosphere of failure that spread out among the IAF pilots and commanders on the eve of 7 October was reasonable; but did the facts and events of that day justify it? The answer to that question is the central issue of the next part of the study.

THE EMPLOYMENT OF THE IAF ON 7 OCTOBER

Before analyzing the IAF operations, it is necessary to illustrate the situation along the fronts and the method and process by which the Minister of Defence and the Chief of Staff employed the IAF during that day. The situation along the fronts was quite dangerous. Dayan's description of the events impressively reminds the readers how critical the situation was on the Golan Heights.

> We landed at the Northern Command Post at 6am. According to the (Northern) Commander, Haka (Yitzhak Hofi), the southern part of the Golan Heights was entirely broken open. The Syrians have defeated the Barak brigade forces and advanced into the southern part of the Golan Heights, almost half way to the Jordan River. General Yiske Shadmi (adviser to the head of the Northern Command General Yitzhak Hofi) and (Division commander) General Dan Laner joined the Forward Command Post, supported the commander's pessimistic assessment. According to Yiske, the situation is 'extremely severe', and Dan Laner said quietly: 'The fighting in the southern part of the Golan Heights was finished, and we lost. We have no more forces to stop them. Additional armour forces, from the reserve, will not be ready to move against the Syrian before noon.[6]

Arieh Braun, a senior aide of Dayan added:

> During the meeting in the Forward Command Post of the Northern Command, General Hofi reported to Dayan: 'Eventually, we have

prepared, the bridges over the Jordan River for destruction [to prevent Syrian penetration westward].'[7]

General Shadmi delineated the pessimistic mood of that meeting:

> Time was running out. I said: 'Moshe [Dayan] ... the problem is what are the prospect of the Jordan Valley. There are no weapons in Dagania [a Kibbutz that Dayan defended in the War of Independence]. He was astonished and said: 'So, what should be done?' I answered: 'climbing down [from the Golan Heights] and organizing a second line.' Dayan was thinking for a while and ordered: 'Go there and organize the [defence of] the Jordan Valley.[8]

These illustrations reflect the assessment of the situation of the Northern Front. On the morning of 7 October, the Egyptian front seemed stable and under control. But developments of the battle changed it significantly and, due to the absence of a critical mass of forces, the Egyptians easily mobilized four or five divisions through the Suez Canal. By noon the picture of the battle had become critical. General Rehavam Zeevi (adviser to Chief of Staff Elazar), who escorted Dayan when the Defence Minister paid a visit to the Southern Command, recalled later that Dayan said to him: 'There is not a single tank between Tel Aviv to Abu-Ageila [in the Sinai Peninsula]. This is the ruin of the Third Temple.'[9] And in the words of Elazar: 'Yesterday, I instructed Gorodish [the head of the Southern Command Shmuel Gonen] to stabilize a new defence line on the Passes [some dozens kilometres behind the front-line].'[10]

Dayan himself summarized the dangerous situation of the state of Israel, using very pessimistic terms:

> The main danger now – is not just the loss of terrain, but mainly the attrition rate. We have a very limited number of tanks and aircraft, soldiers and pilots. If the IDF forces will continue to be worn out without a decisive victory in the war, Israel will be exposed to advance of Arab armies from Egypt, Syria, and maybe from Jordan... I don't remember ever such worries and fears...Now it is completely different: The danger to the State of Israel... Israel may expect fatal consequences, if it would not realize the new situation.[11]

His aide completed: 'The Minister said: "I am afraid deep in my heart that it will be impossible to defend the State of Israel"....'.[12] Prime Minister Golda Meir said in private discussions that if Dayan's expectations would come true, she would lose her will to live.[13]

These sources depict the influence of the surprise attack and its early results on the civilian as well as military leaderships. Some of the leaders feared the borders were broken and the security of the state was shattered. Their estimates included a serious apprehension that the Golan Heights and essential parts of the Sinai Peninsula would be captured. The civilian leadership in general, and the Prime Minister and the Minister of Defence in particular, were gravely undermined. Undoubtedly the Arab surprise attack succeeded in shaking the confidence of the Israeli leaders. At that dangerous situation Dayan said that only the IAF could save the state from an immediate existential threat.[14] Consequently, he and the Chief of Staff directed the IAF to attack the penetrating armoured forces even before achieving air superiority, in unfavourable conditions, heavy fog of war and lack of intelligence, knowledge, data and well-specified targets.

Such circumstances would prevent any air power from accomplishing desired outcomes. The contradiction between the requirements of the higher echelons and the limitations and weaknesses of the IAF inevitably led to poor results coupled with a high attrition rate. In comparison, one should remember that before the Six Day War began, there was a feeling of existential danger. The ground forces' commanders demanded to begin the attack at night, due to the risk of high attrition rate in a day attack. The IAF, on the contrary, insisted on daylight attack to achieve quick air superiority and thereafter, to concentrate on the destruction of the enemy ground forces in support of the IDF armoured forces. Despite the firm demands of the ground forces' commanders, the IAF succeeded in persuading the decision-makers to choose 7:45am as the H-hour. On 7 October, however, the decision-makers did not take the IAF's considerations into account and ignored cognitively the IAF weaknesses.[15]

THE INSTRUCTIONS GIVEN TO THE IAF ON 7 OCTOBER[16]

01.00 hr: Decision on the Missions on the Morning

- Defending the civilians and IDF forces
- First phase of the operation against the Egyptian SAM systems
- Offensive operation against the infrastructure of the Egyptian and Syrian air forces
- Close Air Support (CAS) to the ground forces, using the rest of the IAF aircraft

05.30 hr: Beginning of the Planned Operations:

06.00 hr: First Strategic Shift of the IAF Efforts

- Directive of the Minister of Defence to shift the IAF efforts to the Syrian Front
- Beginning of Massive CAS missions along the Syrian Front
- Cutting-off the operation against the Egyptian SAM systems
- Continuous defence of civilians and IDF forces

11.30 hr: Dugman 5 Operation
- Counter operations against Syrian SAM systems
- Continuity of defensive, CAS and other missions

12.45 hr: Second Strategic Shift of the IAF Efforts
- The direction of the Chief of Staff to shift the IAF efforts backward to the Suez Canal[17]

13.30 hr until Midnight of 7–8 October
- Massive CAS operations along the Suez Canal despite air inferiority
- Massive CAS operations along the Golan Heights despite air inferiority
- Continuous defence of the IDF forces
- Offensive operations against the infrastructure of the Egyptian and Syrian air forces

This timetable shows how the IAF shifted from one mission to another, from the southern front to the northern front and back. This was done even before it has had sufficient time to employ efficiently its power, and achieve significant results. This brief illustration of the IAF operations exposed the discrepancy between the doctrine and the manner in which the IAF was employed.

THE ACCOMPLISHMENTS

The main roles of the IAF included (1) defence of the state from enemy aircraft and missiles; (2) destruction of the enemies' SAM systems; (3) support of the ground forces; and (4) destruction of the Syrian and Egyptian air forces. What were the accomplishments of the IAF?

Defence of State from Enemy

The defence of the state, the borders and the reserve mobilization was accomplished successfully. The IAF fighters and its few HAWK SAM systems shot down about 25 per cent of the attacking Arab aircraft. As a result, the Arab air forces limited their missions only to the front lines. A Mirage pilot shot down the single KELT air-to-surface cruise missile that was launched toward Tel Aviv. Despite the Arab SAM systems, the IAF continued to defend the ground forces from air assaults. The results, almost unknown to analysts, were above any expectations: during the first 34 hours of the war, about 80 Arab aircraft were shot down and this was accomplished by less capable aircraft and when the missiles and C^3I network were facing a very difficult situation.

Destruction of Enemy Air Forces

In parallel to air defence the IAF tried to destroy the infrastructure of the enemy air forces by continuously attacking their airfields, C^3I assets and the like. The results of these attacks and the defensive and offensive air-to-air operations were astonishing. After 7 October those air forces shifted their missions to defending their infrastructure and ground forces. About 90 per cent of Egyptian and Syrian air sorties were directed to defensive missions and less than 10 per cent launched towards the IDF forces. Indeed, the enemy air forces did not play an offensive role after 7 October.

Defence of Golan Heights

The role of the IAF in defending the Golan Heights was indispensable. As discussed earlier, there were only a few and weak units in the southern flank. In the words of Dayan,

> I concluded that the single force, which is capable now to halt the Syrian forces, is the air force. We can't waste time, we must employ it immediately. If we fight according the doctrine [counter-SAM operation and then, Close Air Support] probably we will succeed in paralyzing the SAM batteries, but in the mean time – Syrian tanks will control the Jordan River. I called the air force commander and told him to employ his aircraft continuously and massively against the Syrian armour. Now, the air force is the last power that can do that. In the afternoon (of 7 October), we will have a fresh armour unit but by now, he is responsible. Otherwise we will lose the southern flank and who knows the fate of the Jordan Valley... It was the first time that I talked to the air force commander in such voice and such substance... it was much more than an instruction – and the response was instantaneous. Formations of aircraft have attacked continuously the concentrations of the Syrian forces despite the SAM batteries.[18]

During the next few hours, dozens of aircraft were scrambled to save the Golan Heights. This operation had a quick influence on the battle:

> At 08:20am the Minister of Defence flew back to Tel Aviv. He met the Commander of the air force and told him that our aircraft destroyed Syrian tanks despite the opinion of the Vice-Commander of the IDF (Yisrael Tal), who said that it is impossible. Dayan expressed again his appreciation to the air force during a meeting with the IDF commander, saying that: 'The air force activity is the defence of the State of Israel... This activity saved us.'...[19]

General Hod, the air force representative in the Northern Command summarized the IAF dominant role in the defence of the Golan Heights: 'We defended the whole southern flank of the Heights, only with aircraft. We didn't allow them to go down to Ein-Gev. In our sector, there was no single Israeli tank.'[20] Eventually, while the IAF achieved an edge of victory over the Egyptian SAM systems, following clear-cut ministerial and military instructions, it had to 'leave its shuffle' and without any preparations had to attack the Syrian SAMs in the north.

THE DEFENCE OF THE WESTERN FRONT

At about noon on 7 October, the situation on the northern front began to stabilize but by then the Suez front began to collapse and no fresh troops could arrive quickly to the scene. The IAF was needed to halt the deployment of the Egyptian armoured divisions east of the Canal. After the instruction of the commander of the Southern Command to withdraw the ground forces from the border on the Canal and to redeploy on the Mitla and Gidi Passes, the Chief of Staff instructed the IAF to enhance its activity in the Canal front and attack the bridges over the Suez and the crossing tanks.[21] General Peled, the air force Commander, related to one of the most perilous moments in the war in which he had to realize the determination of the IAF versus the feebleness of some generals:

> The Egyptians built 14 bridges over the Canal... The general Staff, headed by the Vice-Commander [General Yisrael Tal] began to plan a 40 km retreat from the Canal. I came out of the 'Depression Cellar' – the IDF Command Centre, slamming the door, threatening the bunch of senior generals: 'If you continue to plan a retreat, I personally, will be back and shoot you all'... I went back to the IAF Command Centre and instructed to attack the bridges. They were destroyed entirely... The cost was three Phantom attack aircrafts.[22]

The end of this story was told from other point of view:

> At 16:30 the Chief of Staff came back to the Command Centre and heard from General Peled that seven bridges out of fourteen, were destroyed in the first wave... and the rest will be destroyed by darkness or afterward... Today, the IAF fulfils its missions. Now it is believed that it is possible to stabilize the front.[23]

It is interesting to analyze the Egyptian point of view. General Shazly, the Egyptian Chief of Staff, reminded:

> During Sunday 7 October, the Enemy batteries were entirely disrupted. He was left with no armour at the tactical level... 18 hours after the beginning of our attack, there were no signs of the Israeli reserve forces arrival to the scene... Both sides have used this Sunday for a race of deploying forces toward the big battle... This Sunday passed in relative calmness on the main battlefield, but air strikes continued... Just now I have been informed that a huge number of parts of bridges, have been destroyed by the enemy's air strikes.[24]

An IDF analysis based on captured Egyptian documents came to the same conclusion:

Actually, in the region of the Third Army, there was no usable bridge, since 7 October 17:30, for at least 24 hours... That situation was a result of technical obstacles and the IAF activity, which succeeded in hitting and destroying the two bridges of Division 2 (and probably hit another bridge in the division 19 sector).[25]

Along the Suez Front, the soldiers fought bravely and consistently amidst superior numbers of forces, at the tactical level. But the IDF at the operational and strategic levels had gathered and mobilized its forces. Eventually, the IAF alone encountered the crossing divisions, and delayed their deployment on the eastern bank.

The intensive activity of the IAF coupled with air inferiority, due to the thick undamaged SAM systems, caused many losses in the first 34 hours when 28 aircraft were shot down. And during the war, about 103 aircraft – or more than twenty-five per cent of the IAF aircraft – were destroyed. More than half of them were downed during the first four days and that rate of loss is considered very high (Table 1).

TABLE 1
IAF LOSSES

Period	Aircraft losses (in percentage)	Casualties and Prisoners
First 34 hours	7.2	
First four days	13.8	87 (46 Casualties)
Total	26.3 (103 aircraft)	97 (53 Casualties)

Source: Ze'ev Schiff, 'The Israel Air Force', in Erez Ya'acov and Kfir Ilan, eds, *The Encyclopaedia of Military and Defence*, Tel Aviv: Revivim, 1985, pp.178–84 (Hebrew).

The preceding analysis of the air force roles on 7 October and its accomplishment leads to a conclusion that considering the arduous circumstances, the IAF proved its readiness, capabilities and agility, all of which were needed so badly during that day. The dominant influence of the IAF encompassed saving the southern flank of the Golan Heights, cutting off the Egyptian armour crossing of the Suez Canal, defence of the State of Israel and the IDF's mobilization of forces from aerial attacks, and neutralization of the enemies' air forces. Those accomplishments were achieved despite the shocking failure of *Dugman* 5 – the operation against the Syrian SAM systems and the air inferiority on the two fronts.

NEW LESSONS OF THE AIR WAR

Some of the lessons of the Yom Kippur War have been already analyzed and discussed. The air war proved again old and well-known principles, such as the crucial condition of air superiority and concentration of force, and this section will not deal with those lessons. It will reveal and emphasize a few hidden lessons, which may be appropriate for modern air forces.

A Coherent, Integrated Doctrine

The first days of the Yom Kippur War exposed a deep disharmony between the perception of the civilian leadership, the military commanders and the IAF. Both Dayan and Elazar operated on an unwritten assumption that the IAF was supposed to halt surprise attack until the reserves would be mobilized. On the contrary the IAF operations were based on the assumption that it would be given about 48 hours, devoted solely for gaining air superiority by decisive victory over SAM systems and the opposing air forces. Air superiority was considered as an essential condition for effective involvement in the ground battle.

The IAF doctrine in 1973 was derived from the lessons learned from the War of Attrition (1968–1970). The main threat to the IAF freedom of action was the relatively new weapon system – surface-to-air missiles. The Arab armies derived the same lesson and enhanced their SAM systems as a challenge to the IAF instead of their incapable pilots and C^3I systems. Consequently, the IAF defined the destruction of the SAM systems as its first mission in gaining quick air superiority. The dense and huge Syrian and Egyptian batteries enforced the IAF to devote about two days, using its full strength, to achieve victory. This concept of operation collapsed as the forward deployed ground forces failed to stop the Arab armies and the existential threats changed the strategic priorities.

Informal Mutual Understanding

On the morning of 7 October, the Defence Minister instructed the IAF commander to shift its forces to the north, ignoring the necessity of a decision-making process and without conferring with the Chief of Staff. He deliberately ignored the threat of the Syrian SAM systems even though he lacked any quantified analysis of the expected outcomes of such a decision. Moreover, he threw the responsibility of the Golan Heights upon the shoulders of the IAF Commander, thereby creating an almost impossible situation. A similar instruction was sent to the IAF Commander by the Chief of Staff, regarding the collapse of the Suez barrier. The emergency needs influenced those decisions. One can not, however, ignore the conclusion that the civilian and military leaders' instructions were based on ignorance and lacked detailed understanding of the advantages and weaknesses of air power and the IAF in particular. That conclusion may emphasize the requirement for continuous dialogue among the civilian leadership, the General Staff and the IAF commanders. The formal and informal dialogues should concentrate on generating coherent and integrated doctrine and concepts of operation. The IAF should build a mutual understanding of the unique definitions and principles to influence the operational environment on its capabilities and limitations. This conclusion is essential because the air force needs huge space, time and cyber dimensions for exploitation of its full potential, and hence it is sensitive to the constraints of its superior leadership.[26] It should develop such agility and flexibility that enables it to respond quickly and decisively to crucial requirements that would force it to fight in contradiction to its doctrine.[27]

Responsibilities of the Air Force Intelligence

The role of the intelligence in the Yom Kippur War should be analyzed thoroughly but this study is limited to dealing with its roles regarding the IAF needs, particularly for the counter-ground forces battle. The IAF was subordinate to the ground forces with which it was summoned to cooperate and support. The intelligence of the ground forces was responsible for providing the IAF with information on the battlefield and data on targets. Those parts of the doctrine have been proven a complete failure. It was caused because of wrong division of responsibility, authority and means. Air power requires precise data about many mobile targets, which are dispersed in wide area, in near-real time. These requirements are quite different from the intelligence requirements of ground forces, which concentrate firstly on the picture of the battle rather than on specific targets, well beyond visual range. In the words of Peled, 'The key for success is immediate and precise intelligence that is adequate to fulfil the requirements of the air force, about the whole area of operations and frequently'.[28]

The air force intelligence has the responsibility, authority and means needed to accomplish the IAF independent roles such as air superiority, interdiction and strategic attacks. On the other hand, it plays a secondary role when the IAF plays a subordinate function. A logical solution to the different requirements is building an independent air force intelligence organization. This, however, leads to a broader issue of the independence of the air force in the counter ground forces battle. Before dealing with this issue, some basic assumptions of the concept of operation of the IAF intelligence should be defined. It should encompass (1) a broad responsibility and authority; (2) a broad autonomy, independence, and various capabilities to satisfy the operational requirements of the IAF, in time, precisely, and in volume; and (3) temporary authority and systems that are essential to the IAF operations, since scarcity of resources may limit the capability of small nations to develop, produce and procure the required systems for the general intelligence and the IAF intelligence.[29] The comprehensive responsibility of the IAF intelligence is critical for the success of counter ground forces operations.

Independent Counter-Ground Forces' Role

The previous discussion of the role of intelligence was a prelude to a more important issue: the role of the air force in the ground battle. Modern air forces have become the dominant power in modern wars and they may decide the fate of the war once they are employed prudently. They proved their capabilities in the most basic roles, from air defence to strategic strikes. The only role in which they do not enjoy a dominant posture is the counter ground forces warfare and this limitation is connected to the differences between that role and the others. While all other basic roles are accomplished independently by air force operations, this role is executed under the command of the ground commander and this leads to friction between the two arms – air force and the army. Those chains of command and the unavoidable friction that is derived prevent the exploitation of the entire potential of the air force. An important lesson of the Yom Kippur War is the necessity to define an additional basic role for the IAF: an independent counter-ground forces role. The IAF should build the capabilities, organization and intelligence, develop the weapon systems, shape suitable doctrine and tactics, and receive the responsibility and authority that are needed to accomplish this role independently, according to the mission of the ground forces commander.[30]

Preservation of Power

The attrition of the IAF during the first days was too high despite the desperate situation and underscored one of the weaknesses of Israel: its limited capability to fight a prolonged war. One of the predicaments is: Did that weakness dominate the outcome of the war? The attrition rate forced Israel to appeal to the United States to urgently supply essential weapon systems, munitions and ammunitions. The Israeli Prime Minister expressed her willingness to fly to the US to accelerate the response of the US President. 'We badly need [US] support today. Tomorrow it would be probably too late... I am ready to fly to Washington incognito, to meet with [US President Richard] Nixon... I want to fly as soon as possible.'[31] Dayan was more candid:

> We couldn't and we didn't want to relinquish our demand for weapons... First priority has been given to ammunition and aircraft. We have repeatedly sent personal pleas and detailed and painful explanations that we have a crucial and immediate need for additional Phantoms [aircraft].[32]

The emergency American airlift was mobilized on 14 October and it satisfied the essential needs of the IDF and the IAF. It ensured the continuous supply of weapon systems and ammunition, which enabled Israel to change the course of the war and move from defensive to offensive operations – to cross the Suez Canal and encircle the Egyptian Third Army. But, the US – after compelling Israel to accept a cease-fire – did not allow Israel to capture the Third Army by siege. As Prime Minister Meir explained later:

> The supply of food to the Third Army was not permitted due to humanitarian gesture, but because we did not have an alternative.

The only nation that was ready to support us with weapon systems, was the United States... A person who suggests to manage the war, by disputing with the US, practically suggests that we will not win this war.[33]

Israel, which relied heavily on the support of the US during the war, and achieved the verge of decisive victory thanks to that support, was compelled to obey the American recommendations and to release its 'shuffle'. The rapid US response to Israel's requests accelerated Israel's response to the US demand and strengthened the US capability to enforce its will. The decisive Israeli victory was prevented not on the battlefield but behind the closed doors of the White House.

The main lesson to be learned is the importance of preservation of power. A nation that plans to manage its policy and the negotiation process after the war from a powerful position should manage the war according to the strategy that emphasizes preservation of power rather than victory that costs a high attrition rate. Preservation of the air force is essential to enable the policy makers the freedom of manoeuvre both to preserve the outcomes of war and during post-war negotiations. A strong IAF is needed to deter the enemies from renewing the war, and to win it if it breaks out, as happened after the Yom Kippur War. Small nations should keep in mind that the great powers exercise their military and political support as means to enforce policy. The limit of power is defined by its perseverance, rather than by victories. Pyrrhic victory alone is useless in the modern world.[34]

The IAF could not accomplish various roles at the same time as it was required to fulfil on 7 October. It has been strengthened since then. But on the other hand, some significant and power consuming missions have been added to its assignments such as 'second circle' nations, (that is, Iraq, Iran, etc.) and offensive and defensive anti-surface-to-surface-missiles warfare. The IDF doctrine emphasizes the need to strengthen the IAF and to close the gaps between the IAF basic roles and mission, and its capabilities to accomplish them swiftly, economically, and according the principle of preservation of power.

Readiness and Preparedness

On 7 October, the IAF succeeded in fulfilling its missions thanks to its readiness and preparedness, which shape one of its principles of air warfare. Realization of those principles is a resource consuming process. Pilots should be trained in various types of missions and that training is very expensive because of the cost of flight hours. A certain infrastructure such as communication, fuelling, maintenance, turnaround, and logistic should be built and C^3I network, early warning, and intelligence should be organized. As a result, readiness and preparedness have become central competitors to the IAF resources. The Yom Kippur War lessons justify the allocation of resources to realize this principle of air warfare.

CONCLUSION

The primary theme of this study is that the IAF had a dominant contribution in halting the invasion of the Arab armies, the defence of the civilians, the mobilization of the reserves to the fronts, offensive campaign against the Arab air force infrastructures and air-to-air warfare. The paradox is that despite its accomplishments, the IAF has a deep feeling of frustration because of its failure to achieve air superiority over the SAM systems. Instruction and orders of higher echelons that did not take into account the IAF doctrine caused this failure. The civilian and military leaders instructed the IAF to change its doctrine, its tactics and its concept of operations, and ordered it to destroy the invading armies before achieving air superiority and freedom of action. Despite this failure, the IAF played a decisive role during the long perilous day. It met the instruction successfully, but it suffered too many losses. The paradox of its performance on 7 October is that despite the heroic achievements, this day is considered by the warriors as the darkest day in the IAF history, due to the disappointing battle against the SAM systems. The IAF could not concentrate its forces on one or two missions. The IAF's doctrine consists of a modern version of the concentration of force principle and it is called allocation of critical mass. It means that due to the various requirements, the IAF can't concentrate its force on one mission. Thus, it allocates minimal forces to ensure the success of the mission. Too many missions on 7 October almost prevented the IAF from allocating 'critical mass'. That lesson should be learned, and that pitfall should be avoided.[35]

Indeed no detailed analysis has been initiated on the IAF roles, achievements and failures on 7 October. Since then the gap between requirements and capabilities has been widened. The lessons of wars are tools for military officers to improve the capability of their organizations to meet the next war successfully. This study suggests a coherent and integrated doctrine, an independent air force intelligence, an independent counter-ground forces' role, preservation of power and a continuous battle readiness and preparedness.

NOTES

1. Chaim Herzog, *The War of Atonement*, Tel Aviv: Yedi'ot Aharonot, 1994, p.230 (Hebrew).
2. Ezer Weizman with Dov Goldstine, *You Have Gotten the Sky, You Have Gotten the Land*, Tel Aviv: Sifriat Ma'ariv, 1975, p.329 (Hebrew).
3. Herzog, *The War of Atonement*, pp.240–7; and Eli Zeira, *The October 73 War: Myth and Reality*, Tel Aviv: Yedi'ot Aharonot, 1993, pp.225–34.
4. Hanoch Bartov, *Dado: 48 Years and 20 Days*, Tel Aviv: Ma'ariv, 1978, p.139 (Hebrew).
5. Shmuel Gordon, *The Last Order of Knights: Modern Air Strategy*, Tel Aviv, Ramot, 1998, pp.37–8.
6. Moshe Dayan, *Story of My Life*, Tel Aviv: Dvir, 1976, p.576 (Hebrew).
7. Arieh Braun, *Moshe Dayan and the Yom Kippur War*, Tel Aviv: Edanim, 1992, p.94 (Hebrew).

8. Bartov, *Dado*, p.51.
9. Michael Shashar, *Discussions with Rehavam (Gandhi) Ze'evi*, Tel Aviv: Yedi'ot Aharonot, 1992, p.169 (Hebrew).
10. Bartov, *Dado*, p.65.
11. Dayan, *Story of My Life*, p.598.
12. Braun, *Moshe Dayan and the Yom Kippur War*, p.98.
13. Bartov, *Dado*, p.67.
14. Dayan, *Story of My Life*, p.596.
15. Ibid, pp.594–6.
16. Dayan, *Story of My Life*, pp.594–601; and Bartov, *Dado*, Vol.2, pp.50–71.
17. Braun, *Moshe Dayan and the Yom Kippur War*, p.96.
18. Dayan, *Story of My Life*, pp.596–7.
19. Braun, *Moshe Dayan and the Yom Kippur War*, p.94.
20. Bartov, *Dado*, p.51.
21. Braun, *Moshe Dayan and the Yom Kippur War*, p.96.
22. Benjamin Peled, 'If you continue planning to retreat, I threatened, I will come back and shoot you all', *Biteon Heil Ha'avir* [The Air Force Magazine] 118 (December 1997 – January 1998), p.69.
23. Bartov, *Dado*, p.78.
24. Saad el-Shazly, *The Crossing of the Suez*, Tel Aviv: Ma'archot, 1987, pp.168–9, 173–4 (Hebrew).
25. Yona Bendman, 'The Third Army Crosses the Suez Canal, 6–8 October 1973' *Ma'archot* 296 (December 1984), pp.26–30.
26. Shmuel Gordon, 'Air Superiority – Necessity or Luxury', *Ma'archot* 348 (June 1996), pp.6–7.
27. *Conduct of the Persian Gulf War: Final Report to the Congress*, Washington, DC: Department of Defence, April 1992, Vol.2, pp.131–3.
28. Benjamin Peled, 'A Letter', *Writings of Commanders*, Tel Aviv: Israel Air Force, n.d., p.55 (Hebrew).
29. Gordon, *The Last Order of Knights*, p.365.
30. Ibid., pp.60–2.
31. Golda Meir, *My Life*, Tel Aviv: Ma'ariv, 1975, p.312 (Hebrew).
32. Dayan, *Story of My Life*, p.627.
33. Meir, *My Life*, p.320.
34. Shmuel L. Gordon, *The Bow of Paris: The Interrelation of Technology, Doctrine and National Security*, Tel Aviv: Sifriat Poalim, 1997, pp.286–93 (Hebrew).
35. Gordon, *The Last Order of Knights*, p.149.

Abstracts

Revisiting the Yom Kippur War: Introduction
P.R. KUMARASWAMY

Even a quarter of a century later the Yom Kippur War remains the most traumatic phase in Israel's history. Despite its military successes and subsequent peace dividends, the war does not evoke pride and satisfaction. The coordinated Arab effort in initiating the hostilities and breaching the 1967 cease-fire line still haunts many. It is remembered and debated primarily for the initial Israeli 'unpreparedness' and far less for the subsequent military successes. The death and destruction was physical as well as psychological and for many the war extracted a heavy personal price.

Israel's 1973 Intelligence Failure
URI BAR-JOSEPH

Despite the immense number of warnings prior to the outbreak of hostilities, Israel's Military Intelligence (AMAN) failed to provide sufficient warning. Because of its inability to properly interpret the wealth of intelligence information, Israel was taken by surprise on 6 October 1973. By creating an artificial consensus within AMAN, its head Eli Zeira presented a biased 'research opinion' to policy makers. By deciding against disseminating certain critical information to appropriate parties, he prevented the military leadership from the early mobilization of the reserve forces.

The 1973 Arab War Coalition: Aims, Coherence, and Gain-Distribution
AVRAHAM SELA

The 1973 war witnessed an unprecedented rallying of Arab states in active support of Egypt and Syria. Contributions by the Arab states included expeditionary forces and arms, financial aid and the use of oil as a political weapon against Israel's western allies. This was mostly motivated by the emotional rallying force of war against Israel rather than by early efforts of President Sadat, the leader and architect of the war, to forge a formal inter-Arab war coalition. Despite its initial success, the Arab war coalition was rapidly weakened by differences of interests and constraints, mutual suspicion and Israel's maneuvers. Sadat effectively maintained his autonomous decision-making and, while fully employing his advantage as a pivotal Arab actor toward the Superpowers to reap the lion's share of the war spoils for the sake of Egypt, left his Arab partners no choice but to follow him.

Operational Limitations of Reserve Forces: The Lessons of the 1973 War
STUART A. COHEN

The range of faulty 'conceptions' associated with the war was extended to incorrect estimate of the ease with which the IDF's existing force structure could cope with whatever military challenges it might be called upon to face. In many respects, the success of the IDF in recovering from the shock of the outbreak of the war and the initial run of defeats was achieved despite the reserve system and not by virtue of its application. The outcome of the war reflected far more credit on the reservists as individuals than on the framework of which they formed a part.

The Yom Kippur War: Diplomacy of War and Peace
SIMCHA DINITZ

His apprehensions over possible impeachment and removal from office did not inhibit President Nixon from taking decisive actions in support of Israel and ordering the largest airlift of military supplies. These supplies, initially delayed due to Defense Secretary James Schlesinger, played a critical role in the outcome of the war and in the ensuing peace with Egypt. At the political level, the airlift acted as a deterrent to the Soviets against contemplating intervention in the war, signaling that the US was able and willing to carry out massive movement of equipment even amidst domestic difficulties.

The Soviet Union and the Yom Kippur War
GALIA GOLAN

Throughout the war Soviet policy underscored the two contradictory natures of its objectives, namely to maintain détente and prevent confrontation with the US; and to maintain and if possible improve its traditional relations with the Arabs. Its unwillingness to arm Egypt with offensive capability partly contributed to the hostilities, and its efforts to achieve an early cease-fire in the interest of preventing escalation or need to intervene further angered Arab leaders. While it made significant efforts to remain a player in the region, its relations and standing with the Arabs declined as the US became increasingly dominant after the war.

From Crisis to Change: The Israeli Political Elites and the 1973 War
GABRIEL SHEFFER

If the June 1967 war constituted a critical turning point in the social, economic and political development of Israel, the 1973 war caused a major shift in the nature of the Israeli polity, including its political, bureaucratic and military elites. The Mapai/Labour dominated political and military elite which shaped and governed Israel since 1948 bore the brunt of the war. The old regime gradually gave way to the emerging neo-corporatist arrangement that was based on and nurtured by a new breed of political, economic and military leaders.

The Domestic Fallouts of the Yom Kippur War
SUSAN HATTIS ROLEF

Except for the immediate psychological effects and longer term economic effects, the war was much more of a catalyst for various domestic developments which would have occurred even if it had not taken place, than perpetrator of these changes. It speeded up the arrival of certain social and political changes in Israel. If the Six Day War of 1967 placed Israel in a certain optimistic day dream, the Yom Kippur War constituted an unavoidable awakening from that dream.

Perception, Image Formation and Coping in the Pre-Crisis Stage of the Yom Kippur War
GABRIELLA HEICHAL

The pre-crisis stage of the war was underscored by the misperception of the military that an alarm of at least 48 hours would precede any Arab attack. This did not materialize because of earlier false alarms, and the credibility of the warning depreciated in direct correlation with the number of alarms which had proved to be false. With hindsight it is apparent that the intelligence community did not distinguish 'signals' from 'noise'. Above all, as the only center for the evaluation of intelligence, AMAN enjoyed a complete monopoly over the flow of information and assessments.

The Air Force and the Yom Kippur War: New Lessons
SHMUEL L. GORDON

The IAF made a dominant contribution to halting the invasion of the Arab armies, defending the civilians, mobilizing the reserves to the front lines, launching an offensive campaign against the Arab Air Forces' infrastructure, and engaging in air-to-air warfare. The paradox is that, despite its accomplishments, the IAF has a deep feeling of frustration because of its failure to achieve air superiority over the SAM systems. This failure was caused by instructions of higher echelons which did not take IAF doctrine into account.

Index

Other Books in the Israeli History, Politics and Society Series

Between War and Peace
Dilemmas of Israeli Security

Efraim Karsh, *King's College London* (Ed)

> 'The 14 chapters, all admirably short and succinct, form a well-documented rebuttal to the arguments of an influential school of revisionist historians and social scientists who have dominated Israeli intellectual life of late. This book deepens and amplifies the concept of national security and will prove a welcome addition to any reading list for students of international relations.'
>
> *International Affairs*

Distinguished strategists assess the balance of opportunities confronting Israel at this critical juncture in its history and offers possible solutions to its pressing dilemmas. The contributors address such issues as the economic consequences of peace for Israeli security, the implications of the new world order for Israel's strategic interests, Israel's nuclear weapons and the operational and strategic challenges posed by the future Middle Eastern battlefield.

304 pages 1996
0 7146 4711 X cloth
0 7146 4256 8 paper

US–Israeli Relations at the Crossroads

Gabriel Sheffer, *The Hebrew University of Jerusalem* (Ed)

The dramatic global, regional and domestic changes that occurred after the unpredicted collapse of the Soviet Union created a need to examine a host of theoretical and practical issues, particularly in regard to security and foreign relations. The U.S.-Israeli 'special relationship' was no exception.

The essays by distinguished American and Israeli scholars deal with, among other things, the general global setting and its implications for this relationship; with 'hard' strategic factors; and with less tangible aspects, such as American images of Israel, the attitudes of other American religious denominations, and the situation of the American Jewish community and the influence of public opinion and the media on American policy towards Israel.

248 pages 1997
0 7146 4747 0 cloth
0 7146 4305 X paper

FRANK CASS PUBLISHERS
Newbury House, 900 Eastern Avenue, Ilford, Essex, IG2 7HH
Tel: +44 (0)20 8599 8866 Fax: +44 (0)20 8599 0984 E-mail: info@frankcass.com
NORTH AMERICA
5804 NE Hassalo Street, Portland, OR 97213 3644, USA
Tel: 800 944 6190 Fax: 503 280 8832 E-mail: cass@isbs.com
Website: www.frankcass.com

From Rabin to Netanyahu
Israel's Troubled Agenda

Efraim Karsh, King's College London (Ed)

'This book goes a long way to explaining at least the choices and room for manoeuvre Netanyahu has for the foreseeable future ... so it presents a comprehensive account of the profound changes which Israel has undergone in the 1990s not only in attitudes and policies towards the peace process but in domestic policies as well ... vital addition to the literature.'

Israeli Perspectives

The May 1996 election of Benjamin Netanyahu, the 46-year-old leader of the right-wing Likud Party, as Israel's youngest ever prime minister provides further proof of the volatility of Israeli politics. This volume discusses the sources of Netanyahu's victory and its domestic and external implications.

328 pages   1997
0 7146 4831 0   cloth
0 7146 4383 1   paper

Israel at the Polls, 1996

Daniel J Elazar and **Shmuel Sandler**, *both at Bar-Ilan University* (Eds)

'... well put together, lucid and provides a detailed account of one of the most important Israeli election campaigns in recent times.'

Israeli Perspectives

The 1996 Israeli elections were the first elections by direct vote for the position of prime minister in which a newcomer – Binyamin Netanyahu – defeated the most veteran Israeli politician, Shimon Peres. The result indicated not only a transition of power from the left-centre to the right-centre, but also the decline of the major parties and the ascendance of the smaller parties. *Israel at the Polls, 1996* looks at the parties, election campaigns and the processes that determined this outcome.

288 pages   1998
0 7146 4864 7   cloth
0 7146 4421 8   paper

FRANK CASS PUBLISHERS
Newbury House, 900 Eastern Avenue, Ilford, Essex, IG2 7HH
Tel: +44 (0)20 8599 8866 Fax: +44 (0)20 8599 0984 E-mail: info@frankcass.com
NORTH AMERICA
5804 NE Hassalo Street, Portland, OR 97213 3644, USA
Tel: 800 944 6190 Fax: 503 280 8832 E-mail: cass@isbs.com
Website: www.frankcass.com

In Search of Identity
Jewish Aspects in Israeli Culture
Dan Urian, *Tel Aviv University* and
Efraim Karsh, *King's College London* (Eds)

After 50 years of Israeli statehood, Israeli society faces a deepening crisis of identity. This is particularly evident in Israeli culture which, for quite some time, has been effectively disintegrating into several simultaneous sub-cultures. This process has gained momentum during the 1990s, due to the relaxation of national cohesiveness following the Arab–Israeli peace negotiations on the one hand, and to the growing post-modern influences on Israeli culture on the other. This in turn has brought to the fore a whole range of questions which have hitherto been ignored, not least the interrelationship between the Hebrew and Jewish aspects of Israeli culture. This problematic continuum between past and present, between Israeliness and Jewishness, lies at the core of this volume.

Contributors: *Eliezer Schweid, Charles S Liebman, Baruch Kimmerling, Gershon Shaked, Dan Miron, Avraham Shapira, Gad Ufaz, David Zisenwine, Eli Rozik-Rosen, Nurit Gertz, Mordechai Omer, Shimon Levy, Dan Urian and Dalia Manor.*

296 pages 1999
0 7146 4889 2 cloth
0 7146 4440 4 paper

Israel: The Dynamics of Change and Continuity
David Levi-Faur, *University of Haifa,*
Gabriel Sheffer, *The Hebrew University of Jerusalem* and
David Vogel, *University of California, Berkeley* (Eds)

The essays in this volume attempt to move beyond the question of Israel's 'uniqueness' to examine the pace and direction of change of Israel's political, social and economic institutions. Using the tools of comparative analysis, scholars from Israel, the United States and Europe describe the ways in which Israeli society is becoming more like other democratic industrialized societies and in what dimensions Israeli culture and institutions are slowing or resisting such convergence.

The contributions to this volume suggest that Israel is changing, even converging with the global community in some dimensions, but that the pace and direction of change is uneven. In some areas, change is evolutionary, in others glacial, slowed by tradition and entrenched institutions.

The topics explored include the Israeli judicial system, changes in political leadership style, the effects of economic globalization on Israel's political economy, the changing structure of interest group politics, the relationship between the business sector and the government, the evolution and future of Israel's ethnic divisions – both within the Jewish community and between the Jewish and Arab communities – and an analysis of the attempt to Americanize Israeli abortion politics and Israeli environmental policy.

1999 312 pages
0 7146 5012 9 cloth
0 7146 8062 1 paper

FRANK CASS PUBLISHERS
Newbury House, 900 Eastern Avenue, Ilford, Essex, IG2 7HH
Tel: +44 (0)20 8599 8866 Fax: +44 (0)20 8599 0984 E-mail: info@frankcass.com
NORTH AMERICA
5804 NE Hassalo Street, Portland, OR 97213 3644, USA
Tel: 800 944 6190 Fax: 503 280 8832 E-mail: cass@isbs.com
Website: www.frankcass.com

Israel's Transition from Community to State

Series Editor: **Efraim Karsh**, *King's College London (Ed)*

The birth of the Zionist Movement, coming in the wake of Jewish emancipation in
Western Europe and at a time of intensified persecution of Jewry in Eastern Europe,
meant that for the first time since Jewish dispersion, the possibility of the Jews discarding
their minority status in the lands they inhabited and creating their own vibrant home in
their ancestral homeland became a reality, however incomprehensible it may have
appeared in these early years. The next half-a-century saw great strides in the economic,
social and political life of the Yishuv that culminated in the creation of the State of Israel.
By way of doing so, Zionism altered the relationship between Jews in Mandatory
Palestine and the Jewish communities of the Diaspora, between Jews and their
Palestinian-Arab contemporaries and ultimately between Jewry and the British mandatory
power. With contributions from some of the leading scholars of Zionism and Israeli
history, this volume addresses many of the intellectual, social and political ramifications
of Jewish settlement in Eretz Israel before the creation of the State of Israel.

288 pages 2000
0 7146 4963 5 cloth
0 7146 8024 9 paper
Israel: The First Hundred Years, Vol. 1

Israel: From War to Peace?

The end of the British mandate in Palestine heralded the birth of the new State of Israel. It
also marked the end of one of the most tumultuous and momentous chapters in Jewish
history. But the new state, born into a hostile environment and struggling with the
manifold demands of sovereignty would have to face many post-Independence challenges
to its existence, not least in the form of armed conflict and confrontation with its Arab
neighbours. This volume examines the conflicts that from the 1948 until the 1967 Six Day
War came to define the Israeli struggle for existence. In doing so contributors analyze the
various military challenges to Israel from both the military and strategic perspective and
in terms of the demands that these conflicts placed on Israeli society and political life. The
final section addresses the recent peace process from the time of the Oslo Accords, while
focusing on some of the key issues in any future settlement, most notably Jerusalem's
future status.

288 pages 2000
0 7146 4962 7 cloth
0 7146 8023 0 paper
Israel: The First Hundred Years, Vol. 2

FRANK CASS PUBLISHERS
Newbury House, 900 Eastern Avenue, Ilford, Essex, IG2 7HH
Tel: +44 (0)20 8599 8866 Fax: +44 (0)20 8599 0984 E-mail: info@frankcass.com
NORTH AMERICA
5804 NE Hassalo Street, Portland, OR 97213 3644, USA
Tel: 800 944 6190 Fax: 503 280 8832 E-mail: cass@isbs.com
Website: www.frankcass.com